Tradition and Modernization

Tradition and Modernization

A Challenge for Law among the Dinka of the Sudan

by Francis Mading Deng

Foreword by Harold D. Lasswell

New Haven and London, Yale University Press, 1971

'Published with assistance from the foundation
established in memory of James Wesley Cooper
of the Class of 1865, Yale College.

Library of Congress catalog card number: 78-140526
International standard book number: 0-300-01407-4

Designed by Marvin Howard Simmons
and set in Baskerville type.
Printed in the United States of America by
Vail-Ballou Press, Binghamton, N.Y.

Distributed in Great Britain, Europe, and Africa by
Yale University Press, Ltd., London; in Canada by
McGill-Queen's University Press, Montreal; in Mexico
by Centro Interamericano de Libros Académicos,
Mexico City; in Central and South America by Kaiman &
Polon, Inc., New York City; in Australasia by Australia
and New Zealand Book Co., Pty., Ltd., Artarmon, New
South Wales; in India by UBS Publishers' Distributors
Pvt., Ltd., Delhi; in Japan by John Weatherhill, Inc.,
Tokyo.

To my parents

and

To Jane Glassman

Contents

Foreword by Harold D. Lasswell

Contemporary students of man and society have begun to realize that the culture-shaping role of law has been greatly underemphasized in recent times. Dr. Deng's perception of the creative potential of legal process is an important step in correcting a one-sided emphasis on the passive conception of law as a "mirror" or "register" of social forces. He has provided a remarkable case study of the past and possible future of law in Dinka society and in the larger context of which it is part.

Dr. Deng has brought to the task of examining his own culture an impressive objectivity of outlook that testifies to his success in acquiring the essential characteristic of a scientific frame of reference. The magnitude of this achievement is brought home to us when we consider the fact that the basic norms of a society are rather fully incorporated into the emerging personality system at an early age, and that they are subsequently defended by internal mechanisms and external sanctions. The internal mechanisms levy a punitive toll on the individual at the first flutter of a norm-defying image or feeling. The automatic toll is in the form of acute discomfort (anxiety) or a negative self-sentiment, such as guilt, shame, ineptness, incomprehension, powerlessness, impoverishment, or neglect. The inner policeman continues to operate after the individual has moved from his original social setting and is exposed to novel norms and sanctions.

The slow evolution of the scientific study of law and society in Western civilization—when compared with the physical sciences—provides a rough measure of the intensity of the predispositions that it was necessary to override. As the norms of science have been partially incorporated into the norm system of more peoples in the world community, it is easier for individuals to pass from early attachment to relatively nonscientific prescriptions to the acceptance and the application of a more scientific outlook. It would, however, distort the significance of this achievement in a particular instance if we were to imply that the path is free of inner and outer tension and conflict. That Dr. Deng participates productively in the culture of scientific explanation, and that he is able to treat the prescriptions of Dinka society, and of other societies, in a designative manner, is no trivial feat.

xi

In examining the role of law in society, Dr. Deng has been fully cognizant of the advantages of proceeding in the framework of a social process model that utilizes a fixed set of "value" categories and a flexible list of "institutional" terms. The advantage of the fixed list is not that it forces every pattern of interaction to be classified once and for all, but rather that it insists upon classifying every detail in reference to the shaping and sharing of every value. Hence it is a means of achieving whatever degree of observational intensity is appropriate to the amount of time and of other assets at the disposal of observers or decision-makers. When Dr. Deng examines the rich efflorescense of Dinka songs, he is able to consider the manifest content of the texts by the use of an analytic frame of reference that remains stable and hence provides comparable results when other data, such as the legal prescriptions of Dinka society or of any other society, are examined. This coding of value themes is a step toward exploring "who" with what "perspectives" in what "situations" utilizes which assets ("base values"), by employing what "strategy" (song message and mode of delivery) influences which "outcomes" and "effects." Dr. Deng has completed the groundwork for detailed investigations of singing (an "institutional" pattern) as it interacts with every other pattern in Dinka society.* As he demonstrates, it is convenient for some analytical purposes to consider learning, composing, delivering, and listening to a song as expressions of "skill," and to discover the "respect," "affection," "rectitude," "power" (or other values) affected by singing.

The songs provide a remarkable means of enlarging the outsider's empathy with the Dinka people. To empathize is to enter into the experience of another person. It is achieved by becoming acquainted with what comes to the focus of his attention and with how these exposures are reworked as images and moods. We gain understanding of the images and sentiments that in various circumstances cluster around the identifying symbols of the primary ego ("I," "me") and of the other egos who belong to the "self" and "other" than self. It is possible to glimpse the superficiality or the intensity of the value demands that are made upon the self (or other), and to see the map of past, present, or future events in the perspective of Dinka history. We begin to sense how the legal component of the power process permeates the experience of a human being who has been socialized in Dinka society, and to sense the opportunities and constraints that affect an "agent" of deliberate change.

Dr. Deng indicates how the "symbolic" realm is interconnected with the "behavioral" and "resource" (or environmental) realms. The behav-

* The song excerpts that appear in the present volume are part of a larger collection that has been prepared for publication by Oxford University Press in the Oxford Library of African Literature series, edited by E. E. Evans-Pritchard, W. H. Whiteley, and Godfrey Lienhardt.

ioral realm includes the channels of primary and secondary "communication" and of "collaborative" acts, such as producing, exchanging, con-
suming, or investing wealth. The "resource" realm includes the "raw
materials" (organic or inorganic) and the processed artifacts ("culture
materials") in the environment. The enormous role of cattle in Dinka
society cannot be grasped by the outsider who is blind to the symbolic
realm (which is partly reflected by the songs and formal prescriptions of
Dinka public and civic order) or the behavioral realm (partly indicated
by the time spent talking about or interacting with the herds).

Within the limits of the facilities at his disposal, Dr. Deng has brought
out the "more or less" rather than the "either-or" character of the "public order-civic order" components of Dinka culture. Conceptions of "law"
guide the observer's attention to the discovery of "public order" prescriptions, which are defined as those that are expected to be, and in fact are,
usually sanctioned (if necessary) by extreme value deprivations. Such a
definition is not employed in arguments about a hypothetical "cutoff"
point of universal validity in comparative legal studies. The intention,
rather, is to disclose the complexity of the context of values and institutions in which any "prescription" occurs. Some prescriptions are articulated in formal documents; however, when these "formulated" prescriptions are put in context, it is obvious that they may not qualify as "laws."
Research may show that they are not part of the expectations of enough
people to be included. Perhaps they are alleged to apply, though investigation demonstrates that they are usually ignored or, when breached, are
only mildly sanctioned. Furthermore, some formal prescriptions are not
expected to be, nor in fact are, enforced by "police" or by any other
specialized officials. However, the songs that informally mobilize ridicule
(and related forms of negative respect) may spring to the lips of enough
children, young people, and adults in enough situations to impose a
devastating deprivation on a norm violator.

It would be inaccurate to think of Dr. Deng's book primarily as an
exercise in classification. The aim is to use knowledge of the past as a
guide to estimating the intensity of the present predispositions that relate
to values and institutions, and especially to possible changes. The "dyna-
mizing" instrument employed by the author is the maximization postulate, which affirms that living forms tend to act in ways that maximize
net value outcomes (individually, collectively). The postulate leads to
the statement of many hypotheses, some of which are validated within
rough limits. For instance, the "cattle complex" in Dinka culture is an
intricate pattern of situational relationships in which the demand for
cattle is "indulged" by enough participants in enough situations to overcome any tendency to "opt out" of the complex. Inquiry reveals that the
traditional flow of value indulgences (and deprivations) that kept the

"cattle complex" alive are weakening. Sometimes this has come about because new situations provide alternative paths for relatively advantageous individual or group action. Sometimes the cattle-related situations result in higher costs and lower benefits. The phenomenon of "fading out" is affecting the "cattle complex"; hence structural changes in Dinka society are in many particulars farther advanced than might appear to the cursory observer. The focus of aggregate (and subaggregate) attention has been modified, perhaps in response to a new situation (a new radio or travel exposure, for example); and, in turn, altered demands, expectations, and identities modify the behavior and the resources that provide new situations (or modify established ones).

Given his sensitivity to the entire social context of Dinka society (internal and external), Dr. Deng is able to locate accumulating "reservoirs" of discontent and to consider the threats and challenges present as the Dinka people step into the future. These "reservoirs" of latent change provide potential allies in the coalitions whose cooperation is essential to the restructuring of Dinka society, if Dinka culture is to be enriched rather than impoverished by its response to an altering world environment. In evaluating future objectives and strategies, the author continues to make perceptive use of the distinction between values and institutions. He understands the importance of recognizing the basic unity of human beings. So far as we know, the bearers of any culture are all concerned with parallel basic outcomes, despite the fact that specific institutional perspectives and operations are inexhaustibly diverse. If we take the position that value directions are shared by all, it follows that value changes occur only in terms of "priority," "level of shaping," and "equality-inequality" of sharing. For instance, the processes of "modernization" usually include short- or long-range shifts in the priority of the value outcomes sought in traditional societies. Such "welfare" values as "wealth," "well-being," "enlightenment," or "skill" may rise relative to most "deference" values (such as "affection," "respect," or "rectitude"). It seems that "power" often retains its position. However, it may increasingly serve as a base of welfare rather than of other deference outcomes.

Less subtle than shifting value priorities are changes in the level of value "shaping" (often dramatized by the rising production of wealth for consumption or investment) or of value "sharing" (increases or decreases in the degree of general participation in the new wealth, or in well-being, educational skill, public enlightenment, and so on).

Since institutional changes are much less subtle than value shifts, competent observers are on more readily verifiable ground than when they study the initiation, diffusion, or restriction of specific institutional patterns. For instance, it can be demonstrated to what extent power institutions are increasingly secularized (as when the sources of transempirical authority proclaimed in the traditional myth are weakened in the name of "atheistic communism" or of some rival system of theology or metaphysics). Power institutions (including legal components) may be demonstrably changed when power allocations are abruptly or gradually altered.

By this time in our commentary it must be evident that, although Dr. Deng has relied heavily on the objectivity and the procedures of science, he has not permitted himself to become altogether absorbed by the scientific component of his total task. He is oriented toward all five tasks in a problem-oriented approach. In addition to the effort to explain interdependencies, he considers past trends and future projections; and he clarifies value goals and policy alternatives.

Thus, Dr. Deng's consideration of the legal component of the social process is remarkable for the fact that he avoids the trap of "scientism," or the demand to value only the making (and validation) of descriptive and explanatory statements. Enough is known about the role of the decision process in any society to recognize that, in times of change, the perspectives entertained by a comparatively few influential participants in the process exercise a relatively heavy impact on what happens. Since knowledge has consequences, it has responsibilities; and responsibilities include informed participation in the prescriptive process of the communities where one has a participatory role.

The principal intellectual obstacle to the acceptance of a dynamic view of law as an instrument of social change is the profound bias built up during the years when the physical sciences were attempting to establish themselves and to justify what eventually became a "postulational" approach toward all assertions, whether normative or descriptive. Not postulation but affirmation is the intellectual style of dogmatic societies, not excluding their legal philosophers.

Many of the findings that helped to achieve a measure of toleration for science were "universal" generalizations about phenomena that seemed to be well beyond the reach of deliberate human purpose. The prototype was furnished by astronomers and physicists. It is not astonishing to find that thoughtful students of law and society, struck by the seeming immutability of the natural order, began to search for propositions of comparable universality. Were there not cycles in the social process as "untouchable" as the procession of the sun, moon, and stars? Or routines as invariant as the laws of mechanics?

It was usually admitted that deliberate innovations could produce "seeming" changes. But the most rigorous theoreticians of the scientific subculture sought to demonstrate the cyclical or invariant patterns that presumably lay behind "appearances."

In passing, it may be commented that even in situations where the impact of an innovating few is "ephemeral," the impact is not necessarily irrelevant to human values. An elite that was installed or supported by an imperialistic power may, for instance, introduce institutional changes at the instigation of the outside power. Perhaps shrines are set up to the supergod of the superpower. Temples are built to foster the worship of the new divinity; priests inaugurate schools for the training of local youth to succeed them, and to extend the faith. Legal arrangements are introduced to provide for the support of novel installations by means of taxation, and the properties of some established cults are expropriated and turned over to the new elite. Every significant kinship or regional group is required to turn over a levy of children for the priesthood, as well as for the armies and administrative agencies of the new establishment. Thousands of human beings, loyal to the creeds and rites of local faiths, may rise in occasional revolt or rebellion. And eventually, perhaps, a rebellion provides the tidal wave of support for a successful revival of ancient faiths and for the restoration of early rites. The prescriptive codes of the conqueror are terminated and preconquest practices revive. Temples are destroyed or converted to the needs of local gods and priests, expropriated property claims are reinstated, and central arrangements for taxation, education, and observance are superseded. It is tempting to say that deliberate social innovation has totally failed, since the predispositions organized around the earlier set of culture patterns have reasserted their ascendancy. A cycle has run its course, and the value priorities and institutional practices of an earlier time are reinstated.

This, however, is a rigid and unempathic way to write the history of law and society. Why should anyone feel justified in ignoring the human cost of disruption, protest, rebellion, and revival? Or the possible value gains accruing—for generations, perhaps—in the traditionally oppressed position of women, serfs, or children, who may have enjoyed a wider freedom than in the original social situation? Whether short or long, the significance of relatively deliberate change is not to be dismissed by obstinate devotion to a tacit idealization of an initial state of "stability." Such an attitude dodges the goal-clarifying and trend-appraising components of a problem-oriented concern for man in society.

The scholar-participant who sought to restrict himself to the explanatory task, and who imagined that everything about him was absent from the situation save a staring cyclopean eye, has typically failed to consider his impact on what is happening. It may be that he, and his fellow jurists, do not notice that their effect on the study and practice of law is "reactionary" when deliberate innovation is stigmatized in blanket fashion as predestined to "failure." We suggest the possibility that the "low" points in many past cycles may have been high points of approximation to human dignity (perhaps by frustrating a centralized empire run for the benefit of a small elite of emperors, warriors, and officials). What cluster of conditioning factors failed to overcome the latent or active strength of restorative predispositions? What new factors, if present, might have changed the result? The inference is that an explanatory approach that allows itself to identify significant research questions as a result of goal-directed challenges may be enriched by the procedure.

Such a challenge stimulates systematic search for past circumstances in which relatively deliberate innovations at any phase of the authoritative and controlling flow of decision have survived (at least for long periods). Conspicuous instances are not difficult to find, particularly in cases where a new technique of resource management is conjoined with a novel ideological map. The expansion of the modern pattern of science-based technology exemplifies these possibilities. In the society with which Dr. Deng is most intimately acquainted, several layers of partially incorporated innovation have complicated the ideological perspectives and operational techniques of an earlier structure. The Arab, French, and British streams of influence have contained a progressively enriched technoscientific component, until today it is clear that a very considerable further increase is imminent. Hence a new subelite of the educated is rising to power regardless of internalized mechanisms or defensive maneuvers. Barring near-universal catastrophe, the transformation of Dinka society will continue; and it will accelerate.

In these circumstances, it is clear what an informed and responsible scholar-participant will bear in mind. Since what he says and does will have consequences if he thinks responsibly, he will consider these consequences in advance and seek to set up a procedure for the future that will provide a continuing, comprehensive, realistic, and value-oriented cognitive map of the context. Such a formidable task is precisely the one to which Dr. Deng has set himself.

It is perhaps worth underlining a feature of Dr. Deng's approach that may be obscured by the emphasis that has been put on his transcendence of the "explanatory" (scientific) task. In harmony with the policy sciences approach, Dr. Deng is preoccupied with the interplay between better policy and better science. So far as the social sciences are concerned, one implication is that better science depends in part on better policies in regard to the collective process of decision. The distinctive policy problem of the individual scientist, or scientific group, is the advancement of knowledge. The most specialized scientist is concerned with enlightenment, with improving cognitive maps of nature, life, and culture. Increasingly, it is clear that a strategic program of map improvement includes adequate preparation for studying the future. By mobilizing in advance for data gathering it is possible to obtain particular and aggregate data in terms of which the entire systematic structure of the behavioral and social sciences are reappraised; and the strategy of feed-back can be perpetuated.

Why is Dr. Deng enlisted among the ranks of those who are committed to the "impossible"? The reply, I think, is that he is sufficiently in command of himself as a person to resist "perfectionism." He is under no illusion about the distance between the local and the universal, the immediate and the ultimate, the ideal (the "maximum") and the feasible (the "optimum"), the predicted and the actual, the prescribed and the implied, the intended and the unanticipated, the conscious and the unconscious, the contemplative and the manipulative. He is under no illusion that we know enough to know in advance what we can or cannot do.

As the policy sciences develop they will continue to exhibit characteristic tensions between those who "think" and those who "do." No doubt many careers will be highly specialized to one or another role of scholarship, teaching, and direct participation in official and unofficial agencies. In all probability it will be increasingly common for career lines to gain in diversity so that at different career stages there will be role-taking at various phases of public and civic policy. In "transforming" societies, such variegated career patterns are relatively frequent. Perhaps in the future of Dinka society it will be unnecessary to go through a stage of exaggerated specializations before diversity can be restored.

Dr. Deng understands the unity of man's value orientations, and is himself committed to the inclusive goal of human dignity. And this is no empty verbalism. For Dr. Deng is among those who perceive that his own society is one where the realization of such a commitment is much less "utopian" than it is for many others. The statesmanlike question is whether the challenges of this era of accelerating transformation can be utilized to enhance the "quality of life" with the least sacrifice of life and of life-related values.

Law is perceived as among the strategic intruments for the fulfillment of overriding purposes; and law is a complex institution whose most important role is in consolidating decision structures and functions that conform to, and contribute to, the goal. Such authoritative and controlling power structures are details of the "constitutive process." The strategies of a constitutive process are successful to the extent that they mobilize the support required to consolidate institutional arrangements whose characteristics and consequences are compatible with the dignity, not the indignity, of man.

The place of law in communities of Dinka culture remains highly problematic for the future. As Dr. Deng shows, the Dinka are included in a larger political unit whose continuation is uncertain, partly because the decision-makers at the inclusive center have not been loath to employ the instruments of violent coercion against noncooperative elements in Dinka localities. The authority of the Center is not wholly accepted by the leaders (or presumably the rank and file) of the tribes. The situation is widely perceived as an attempt to apply naked power, and the outside observer, not the author, may infer that acute civil conflict is perhaps the travail that is required to consolidate more stable arrangements. As yet the central leadership has found it impossible to proclaim a set of prescriptive arrangements and particular policies that mobilize support, either by splitting the Dinka from one another, or by winning over an effective coalition. Similarly, the Dinka have not been successful in modifying central policy by proclaiming objectives that obtain support elsewhere in the present state. Where the channels of communication are thin, the institutions specialized to communication cannot perform their institution-building function in the larger area. They cannot build the myriad of new subsituations that change the focus of attention of significant persons and groups, and thereby modify the realm of the symbolic, and eventually the behavioral and resource realms.

Can the Dinka operate within the internal and external constraints described by Dr. Deng and still move ahead? Whatever the eventual answer, a preliminary contextual map is now at hand. A son of Dinka culture has articulated the humanizing core of his own tradition. Such an achievement should inspire members of the whole nation of man, whatever their subnation, to do the same for themselves and their fellows, and especially to seize upon the creative potential of law as an instrumentality of common purpose.

Acknowledgments

This book is a revised version of a thesis which was prepared and submitted in partial fulfillment of the requirements for the degree of Doctor of Laws at Yale University. It was completed in December 1967 and submitted in January 1968. My special gratitude goes to Yale Law School, where I received a generous fellowship and found the encouragement and the tools to undertake the thesis. I am particularly grateful to my supervisor, Professor Harold D. Lasswell, in whom I found inspiration, enlightenment, and kindness. Professor Quinton Johnstone's interest, guidance, and support were unfailing. I am also indebted to Professor Myres McDougal and to Professor Robert Stevens for their continued counsel and encouragement. Professor Mary Alan Caldwell helped to shape the work during its initial but more difficult stages. While visiting professor at Yale Law School, Professor Max Gluckman read earlier parts of the manuscript and made valuable and encouraging comments. Professor Arthur A. Schiller read the completed manuscript and also made valuable comments. I also benefited from the editorial assistance of Mr. Daniel Dean. The efforts of Miss Ann Lepkowski in typing and proofreading helped when time was a crucial factor.

To crown the immediate list, I am deeply grateful to the family of James Glassman who, as my host family and by unusual kindness and hospitality, gave me a home in the United States. Jane Glassman in particular assisted me on the book from its beginning to its end, sharing its frustrations and its pleasures and giving unfailing support and encouragement. In appreciation, I am dedicating this book to her jointly with my parents.

My interest in Dinka law could hardly have developed without the initial motivation and encouragement of the late Dr. Charles D'Oliver Farran, Professor (now Dean) Cliff Thompson, and Professor (now Dean) William Twining, then on the Faculty of Law, University of Khartoum. Professor Twining later gave me the benefit of his advice and supervision during the short period he spent at Yale Law School in 1965 as visiting professor. To my teacher, Professor Antony Allott, I am grateful for my first encounter with customary law as a subject of formal education.

It will be evident from my frequent reference to Dr. Godfrey Lien-hardt's works that I have benefited a great deal from them, but as a friend in addition to being the leading authority on the Dinka, God-frey Lienhardt has helped me in many more ways than by his writings only.

Last, but evidently not least, I am deeply indebted to Dinka infor-mants, composers, singers, and others, without whose materials this work would obviously have been meager, if not impossible.

To end the list is to do injustice to many, but to mention more is to enter an endless road. I therefore hope it will suffice to repeat my grati-tude to all who have helped in differing ways and degrees. While I em-phasize their contribution, I remain solely responsible for the faults and shortcomings of this work.

F. M. D.

New York
15 May 1970

Abbreviations

Farran	Charles D'Oliver Farran, *Matrimonial Laws of the Sudan* (1963).
Howell, "Ngok Dinka"	P. P. Howell, "The Ngok Dinka," 32 *Sudan Notes and Records* (1951).
Howell, *Nuer Law*	P. P. Howell, *A Manual of Nuer Law* (1954).
Lienhardt, *Divinity*	Godfrey Lienhardt, *Divinity and Experience: Religion of the Dinka* (1961).
Lienhardt, "Western Dinka"	Godfrey Lienhardt, "The Western Dinka," in *Tribes without Rulers,* ed. Middleton and Tait (1959).
Titherington	G. W. Titherington, "The Raik Dinka," 10 *Sudan Notes and Records* (1927).

Introduction

The Dinka are a Nilotic people in the Republic of the Sudan. According to the population census of 1956, they number about two million in a country of only 14 million inhabitants and 572 tribes. More surprising is their dispersed settlement. They occupy a vast territory stretching from twelve to six degrees north latitude, interrupted only by a relatively small enclave occupied by the Nuer tribe. Most of this area falls into two of the three Southern provinces, Bahr-el-Ghazal and Upper Nile, but one Dinka tribe, the Ngok, is now administered as part of Kordofan Province, one of the six Northern provinces. The Dinka are both pastoral and agricultural, but cattle dominate their lives. While resembling the other Nilotes of the Sudan and Uganda, their closest physical and cultural affinities are with the Nuer and the Shilluk tribes. This study applies to the Dinka as a whole, if only because of their strikingly high degree of cultural uniformity, but the focus is on the Ngok, who number about sixty thousand and occupy the area between longitudes 27°50″ and 29° east, approximately, extending from south of the River Kir (otherwise called Bahr-el-Arab) northward along the main watercourses of which Nyamora is the largest.

Like many traditional people throughout the world, the Dinka are on the verge of modernization. Lying ahead is a hazardous road with many stumbling blocks and dangerous corners. Change was far too slow during the colonial era, but postcolonial change has been much greater than the amount of care it has received. In addition, the change is unbalanced: small factions of society are more modernized than the masses; modernization has not affected all aspects of culture equally; introduced practices have been taken out of their source context; and changes have not been integrated into the receiving culture. As a result, modernization is disruptive. The violence, the unrest, and the revolutionary trends in the African scene today are matters of common knowledge.

The Dinka and their fellow Southern Sudanese have had a great share in this process. Its most conspicuous aspect is what has become known as the "Southern Problem," whose roots lie in the South-North dichotomy. Although there are so many tribes in the Sudan that tribalism still threatens broader loyalties, ethnic multiplicity is overshadowed by the North-South division. The South is Negroid and the North is Arab. Isolated from each other until a century ago when decades of mutual hostility arising out of slave raiding of the Southerners by the Arabs marked their initial contacts, and administered separately until the Sudan gained its independence in 1956, the two see little in common. The dominant North looks toward the Arab Middle East, and, because of its dominance, the Sudan is an active member of the Arab League; the South aspires toward its cultural kindred in Negroid Africa. Those Sudanese who do not see such broader horizons, and they are numerically greater, consider Southerners and Northerners different and mutually opposed.

The British left the country with this problem not only unsolved but intensified. Their successors, desiring to foster national unity, adopted Islamization and Arabization as strategies for cultural uniformity.[1] The Southerners, disadvantaged in numbers and in development, oriented toward their native cultures combined with received Western cultural elements,[2] saw subjugation in this form of unity. They remain opposed to it and regard the Northerners as colonialists.[3] The present political upheavals were first generated in 1955, a year before independence, when a battalion of the Southern Corps mutinied. This ignited a revolt in the South during which several hundred Northern Sudanese and an equal number of Southerners lost their lives.[4] The insurgence continues and the government has been engaged with the Southern rebel army, the Anyanya, in a fruitless attempt to quell the rebellion ever since independence.[5] Many innocent people fall victims to the "security forces" which have virtually been running the South since the war began. Thou-

---

1. The British had recognized and encouraged Arab-Islamic civilization in the North and discouraged it in the South.

2. Because the British feared that the introduction of Western culture might provoke the Arabs, the North was less exposed to it than the South. For instance, English and Christianity, while viewed as essentially alien by the North, soon became characteristic of the modern South.

3. K. D. D. Henderson, after thirty years' colonial service in the Sudan as governor and educationalist, wrote that "The whole picture is very similar to that in other parts of Africa, with the northerner unable to realize that he was regarded as just as much a coloniser as the British or Belgian D.C. over the border with whom he was compared." Henderson, *The Sudan* 178 (1965). The special committee appointed to investigate the 1955 revolt against the North wrote, "The Northern administration in the Southern Sudan is not colonial, but the great majority of Southerners unhappily regard it as such." Sudan Government, *Southern Sudan Disturbances* 7 (1956).

4. For a detailed account of the disturbances and their causes, see the report cited supra.

5. The Sudan became formally independent on January 1, 1956.

sands of refugees have fled into the neighboring countries of the Congo, Uganda, Kenya, Ethiopia, and the Central African Republic.[6]

This war was a factor in the downfall of parliamentary democracy in 1958 and its restoration in 1964. Having failed to solve the problem and facing defeat on account of that failure, the then ruling party handed over power to the army which also failed and was forced to resign by a popular uprising. With the return of democracy, elections were held in the North, but the war conditions precluded the possibility of elections in the South.[7] In the face of the political crises, Sudan has remained without a permanent constitution.[8] Whether it should be an Islamic state, as the name of the dominant political party, Umma, indicates, is a subject of controversy. But one thing all Sudanese are aware of is that the Southern Problem shakes the Sudan, even the interparty relations of the North.

The Southern Problem epitomizes the problem of unguided or ill-guided change. Even within the tribe there is turmoil involving traditionals and their modernized fellowmen. Some of these are traditional problems which have remained uncorrected, others are new, and many are a complex of both. Of course, modernization is inevitable. It is both a fact and a goal. Its acceleration is commendable because it shortens the time of suffering from ignorance, poverty, and disease which have repeatedly been identified as "our real enemies."

Among the Dinka, there has been little attempt at guiding social change. Different governments have implemented policies to promote docility among their subjects, but these have often been unoriented to the realities of the situation and have repeatedly defeated their own cause. This work is an attempt to pave the way in what is so far a tangled jungle.

The premise is modernization, which emphasizes the use of science and

6. Although these countries assist refugees, they maintain a neutral attitude. On the invitation of the Sudan government, some of these and other African countries were represented at the 1965 Round Table Conference as observers. On this occasion Southerners and Northerners sat together and discussed their differences. They came close to reaching an agreement, but the government, which had taken the initiative, was short-lived and conditions returned to what they had been. The new government and the South accused each other of causing this failure to achieve a lasting solution.

7. Later elections were boycotted by the dominant party in the South which alleged that they were rigged to favor the coalition Northern parties, the Umma and the NUP, which won nearly all the Southern seats in Parliament.

8. Since independence, the country has been run by a transitional constitution which was suspended by military regime in 1958 and readopted in 1964 when democracy was restored.

technology in the promotion of interactive values and institutions.[9] The fact that modernization aims at enhancing values—and we hypothesize that it normally achieves this objective [10]—does not necessarily mean that it has no disadvantages. As David Apter puts it: "Individuals may feel the loss of their moral personalities. Familiar communities are twisted out of shape. The future appears as a sea of adventures, not all of them pleasant." [11] Nor is the proportion of its advantages and disadvantages necessarily constant. We presume that it can be altered. The objective is to correlate modernization to the overriding goal of human dignity.[12] This concept requires the establishment of a social order with a social process entailing the broadest shaping and sharing of values and with emphasis on persuasion rather than on coercion. Social process means people seeking values through institutions by using resources. Values refer to the broad categories of events which gratify desires; hence, preferred events. For convenience in determining such preferences, eight value-categories [13] are used. These are power, affection, respect, rectitude, wealth, well-being, skill, and enlightenment.

Power is a voice in decision-making and executing, and its institutions include government and law at various levels, together with the parties and pressure groups which influence community decisions. The family and the clique of intimate friends are among the institutions of affection, as are also the expressions of loyalty to larger units. Respect is a value whose distinctive institutions include those which provide positive recognition of common merit as a human being and special merit as an individual. Rectitude is a value whose vehicles specialize in the formulation

9. See Lasswell and Holmberg, "Toward a General Theory of Directed Value Accumulation and Institutional Development," *Comparative Theories of Social Change* 12 (1966).

10. Although one must distinguish between the subjective satisfaction which may lead to continuation of modernizing selection and the objective evaluation of outcomes and effects, it is reasonable to presume that people will continue to make certain choices because, both subjectively and objectively, they maximize their values with reference to the particular choices which may not necessarily be advantageous in terms of a comprehensive evaluation of outcomes and effects.

11. Apter, *The Politics of Modernization* xi (1965).

12. As expounded by Professors Lasswell and McDougal in their comprehensive theory of "law, science, and policy." For examples of many of their writings on this, see McDougal and Lasswell *Law, Science, and Policy* (mimeographed materials) (1964); Lasswell and McDougal, "Legal Education and Public Policy," 52 *Yale Law Journal* 203 (1943); McDougal, "The Comparative Study of Law for Policy Purposes: Professional Training in the Public Interest: Value Clarification as an Instrument of Democratic World Order," 61 *Yale Law Journal* 915 (1952); Lasswell, "The Emerging Policy Sciences of Development," 8 *American Behavioral Scientist* 28 (1965); Lasswell, "The Policy Sciences of Development," 17 *World Politics,* 286 (1965).

13. For these categories and the definitions that follow, see McDougal and Lasswell, *Law, Science, and Policy.* See also the citations supra note 12.

of standards of responsibility and the justification and celebration of these norms. Among the institutions devoted to wealth are business corporations and partnerships, farm and professional units, trade union and consumers' cooperative associations. Well-being refers to physical and psychological integrity. Its institutions include facilities for medical care and prevention of disease. Among the institutions for skill as a value are vocational and professional organizations concerned with maintaining and improving the standards of performance and of taste. Finally, enlightenment is a value whose distinctive institutions comprise the media of public information and the agencies of civic training.

Of course, the content and the expression of these values and their institutions are to be seen contextually, and in such undifferentiated traditional communities as that of the Dinka, institutions are multifunctional and hardly specialized. In line with the above conception of the social process we identify the dynamic roles under the traditional and the transitional systems, explore their indulgences and deprivations, correlate the positive and the negative aspects of the systems to these indulgences and deprivations, and, finally, suggest ways of pacifying the situation, promoting justice, and mobilizing vital human resources for harmonious development. To appreciate the intricacies of the problem, a comprehensive picture of the society is necessary. The starting point is to see the Dinka as family-oriented. The family conditions participants at all levels, and it projects to broader circles the principles which govern familial relationships.[14] The fundamental determinant of value distribution is the myth of permanent identity and influence which aims at immortalizing a man through his lineage. Since this concept is closely associated with childbearing and its social implications, "permanent identity and influence" is used interchangeably with "procreation."

To perpetuate a person's name through the collective efforts of his family calls for the cooperation of the members; hence, the emphasis on unity and harmony as fundamental values. Since this emphasis minimizes dissent within the lineage, a sense of pride in one's lineage and in oneself as a dependent of that lineage becomes necessary. The Dinka are a very proud people, singularly and plurally. Such pride is a consequence of the honor and dignity required for maintaining a good name.

Participation after death depends largely on life remaining as similar as possible to that which the dead man left, so the myth of permanent identity and influence is conducive to cultural continuity.[15] Participation

14. Writing of segmentary lineage systems in general, Middleton and Tait say, "Relations between local groups can be conceived in terms of the kin relationships between the apical ancestors of the lineages by which the local groups define their membership. Lineage organization thus reflects the territorial organization of local groups." Middleton and Tait, eds., *Tribes Without Rulers* 5 (1959).

15. See Lienhardt, *Divinity* 20.

ranges from the supreme world of divinities and the dead [16] to the realm of the living which is stratified according to descent, sex, age, and culture. The dominant participants are the mythicals as opposed to the living, the chiefly clans as opposed to the commoners, men as opposed to women, elders as opposed to youth, traditionals as opposed to the "moderns," and the Arab North as opposed to the Negroid South. The use of the term "opposed" must be taken figuratively, for the process of confrontation and conflict is not as constant as the above formulas may imply. For example, conflict between the chiefs and the educated class is more intense than that between the chiefs and the commoners. The youth warrior groups are more overtly competitive with corresponding warrior groups of other sections than with their elders. Similarly, women are more opposed to each other than they are to men. And so on. I do not mean to imply that there are no points of agreement between opposing parties. On the contrary, conflict in alliance is characteristic of these relationships.

Conformity to and violation of community policies correspond to stratification and competitiveness. The mythicals, that is, God, lesser divinities, ancestors, and other dead, though sometimes criticized, are considered more virtuous than the living. They are the supernatural protectors of continuity, unity and harmony,[17] and persuasion, the overriding policies of Dinka society. In the value processes, they also ensure deferential treatment, which is an important corollary of the overriding goals. A person who violates these norms is threatened with divine curse and misfortune. Thus, divine coercion as a means of combating evil is preferred over worldly, and especially physical, coercion. A fundamental illustration of the moral weakness of man in comparison to the mythicals is the myth of God's separation from man as a result of man's wrong. God withdrew and willed that man be immersed in suffering and ultimately death.[18]

16. The ancestors are the most important but all the dead participate and are superior to the living. Through the customs of levirate and ghost marriage, every dead man should have issue begotten for him by his living relatives; thus all are at least potential ancestors. The importance of the dead among the living is true throughout Africa. Africans conceive of the family "as consisting of a large number of people, many of whom are dead, a few of whom are living and countless number of whom are yet to be born." Busia, The Challenge of Africa 33 (1962).

17. This is obvious in invocation and prayer. Dr. Lienhardt writes: "The notion that united action, by all the agents which can strengthen men, is necessary in an effective invocation is parallel . . . to the cooperation and unity of the members of the lineage and of the community taking part in the ceremony. Quarrelling and divisions weaken men's effectiveness in sacramental speech and action, and it is for this reason that past quarrels are denied [in prayer]." Lienhardt, Divinity 240.

18. For the various versions of this myth among some Dinka tribes, see id. at 28–55.

A similar correlation between receiving certain indulgences and demonstrating certain attributes is evident in the distinction between chiefly lineages and commoners. It has been said of some Dinkas that the dichotomy between chiefs and commoners is one of division of functions.[19] The chiefly lineages are men of peace who promote unity and harmony.[20] They must emphasize persuasion to reconcile conflicting parties. On the other hand, the function of the commoners is to defend the community by warring. The fact that this negates the ideal of harmony, though out of necessity, implies that they are morally inferior to the chiefly lineages who are deemed too virtuous to fight.

The observation that the lower the indulgences, the higher the negative attributes, though obvious in the relationship of the mythicals with the living and the chiefs with the commoners, requires more elaboration in the role of women. Because immortality is primarily aimed at continuing the male line, the society is patriarchal. Corresponding to the subordination of women is their reputation as being more destructive to social ideals than men are. Polygyny, while accepted and sometimes encouraged by women, is a source of jealousies among them, and although the influence of women is discouraged, these jealousies often generate conflicts among men. The myth is that it was a woman who caused the original split into clans,[21] and to this day women are believed to break kinship ties.[22] It was a woman who committed the original sin which prompted God's withdrawal from man.[23] Since women have little or no legitimate religious power, when evil befalls a person who wrongs a woman it is often interpreted as witchcraft, which the Dinka loathe. Denying women consent to marry results in elopement or other strategies which are sometimes condoned but are essentially condemned.[24] Since, normally, women do not own cattle,[25] they gratify themselves with the aesthetic values of cattle. In doing so, they identify themselves with their husbands or boyfriends in order to identify with their cattle. Thus, a

19. "Since these clans [the commoners] are also described as 'people of the war' *koc tong*, in relation to the spear-masters who are 'people of the fishing spear,' *koc bith*, and are distinguished from the latter by political function rather than by rank, I call them 'warrior clans.'" Lienhardt, "Western Dinka" 104–05.

20. Lienhardt, *Divinity* 139, 249. See also Howell, "Ngok Dinka" 239, 272.

21. For an example of myths to that effect see Nebel, *Dinka Grammar* 127 (1948).

22. For example, Father Nebel records a story of how a woman caused conflict between her husband and her son. Id. at 134.

23. But for the Dinka ambivalence toward women see Lienhardt, *Divinity*. 198–206.

24. See, for example, *Deng Ajith v. Maguith*, Abyei, Ngok Dinka Appeal Court (1960); *Akot Ral v. Lal Ayom*, Abyei, Ngok Dinka Court (1954); *Ajing Nyok v. Akol Kur*, Abyei, Ngok Dinka Court (1960). Cf. *Dau v. Kwol Kon*, Abyei, Ngok Dinka Court (1960).

25. See O'Sullivan, "Dinka Law," 40 *Journal of the Royal Anthropological Institute* 171, 178 (1910).

woman singing about her husband's ox refers to her husband as "I" and
therefore identifies herself with the ownership. Preoccupation with the
aesthetics of cattle, though primarily expressed by women and young
men, is an outstanding feature of Dinka society which impedes a more
economic way of utilizing cattle, which are one of the greatest resources
of the Sudan. So preoccupied with cattle are the Dinka that agriculture
and other methods of wealth accumulation suffer severely.[26]

The role of youth warrior groups also illustrates the pattern of indulgences, deprivation, and negative behavior. Although the myth of permanence favors all generations, the older a person, the greater his need
for immortalization. This principle applies in all value processes to give
priority to age; thus the elders are more privileged than the youth. Age
classification applies to both sexes, but because of the dominance of
males and the identification of women with their corresponding male
sets, male age grading is more significant.[27] As a consequence of their
subordination, male youth are even more preoccupied with cattle than
women are, with the same harmful effects on the economy.[28] Their lack
of lawful influence over their own marriages tends to increase sexual
offenses among young people. Such wrongs as seduction, impregnation,
elopement, and abduction are often used to induce a marriage otherwise
difficult to arrange. Most important is the fighting role of youth and their
exaggeration of physical courage.[29] This highlights their participation
and gives them an important range of alternatives. So preoccupied with
violence are they that while social ideals emphasize harmony, they engage

26. For their intense interest in cattle see Lienhardt, *Divinity,* 10–27; Titherington,
159, 175–77. In this article Titherington, remarking on the Dinka attitude to cattle,
writes, "The cattle are the focus of the [Rek Dinka] life; he lives for their service,
and is at times willing to die for them." P. 175. For the effect of social value of cattle
on economic development see Sudan Government, *The Ten Year Plan of Economic
and Social Development* 31 (1962). P. P. Howell states that "the Ngork are not enthusiastic agriculturists. This is partially due to their intense preoccupation with
cattle like other Nilotics." But he argues that the climatic conditions mainly account
for their interest in cattle more than their interest in cattle accounts for the neglect
of agriculture. Howell, "Ngok Dinka" 245.

27. While the age set of females is continually reinforced by new members covering
a long range of time, that of males is created every several years. The ceremony of
initiation differs from tribe to tribe and in some tribes from sex to sex. In most
tribes it involves marking scars on the forehead—a bloody requirement from which
some tribes exempt the women. For discussion of the age set system among the Ngok
see Howell, "Ngok Dinka" 258–61.

28. This is part of the males' superior claims over cattle. An obvious example of
how preoccupation with cattle impedes other occupations is the custom of *toc* whereby
young men are exempted from agriculture and allowed to go with cattle to far-off
grazings mainly to relax, fatten themselves, and compose songs about matters of interest to them.

29. Their physical courage is epitomized by the bloodiness of their initiation.

primarily in provoking wars which must then be fought by their territorial groups at large. To them, the wars are in self-defense, for neither of the warring age sets quite admits that its ferocity is a factor in the initiation of wars. Although the present chief has minimized intratribal wars, they are frequently threatened and several have occurred in the last decade.

The violent manifestations of these age sets are not limited to wars, but cover a wide range of activities, such as undertaking difficult far-off herding in the wilds even when it is not necessary, protecting the community from ferocious beasts, and even hunting them unnecessarily to show courage. In the administration of justice, the youth are the executors of self-help, sometimes in open disrespect for their elders.[30] In a case of seduction, for instance, while the father of the seduced girl is more likely to seek justice through the chief, her young relatives are more likely to grab their spears, attack the family of the culprit, seize as many of their cattle as they please, and, if intercepted, fight. It is primarily the fighting of youth which gave the Dinka their warlike reputation, prompting the colonial administration to reinforce the chief with state coercion.[31] In recent years, their vitality has been utilized in such activities as seasonal road repairs, the building of the chief's homes or public buildings, cultivation of public fields, and the like. It is significant to note that the warrior age groups are most important in those strategies which are regarded as a necessary evil, their main wrong being that they exaggerate them. The warring age groups also enjoy the expectation of future indulgences as patriarchal heads of their own families.[32] Thus, they are the future defenders of Dinka ideals, so that their nonconformity is not an opposition to the basic structure of their society.

A more fundamental opposition is encountered in the role of the edu-

30. Lienhardt, "The Dinka of the Nile Basin," 69 *The Listener* 828 (1963).

31. Titherington exaggerates somewhat when he says of the Rek Dinka that the system collapsed under the shock of the slavers' attacks "and its successor was pure communism; no one owned any property save what was in reach of his club and spear, no one acknowledged any authority or gave obedience to anyone, save so far as he could be scared into it by fear of magic or violence." P. 165. As we shall see later (Chapter 1) the Ngok were an exception in degree, since they have always been united under one chief. Nonetheless, the quotation applies to them insofar as ineffectiveness caused by the truculence of warrior sets coexisted with the recognition of the chief's authority by the senior factions of society.

32. As a Dinka puts it in a song,

They say that Mangar is not an ox for a younger man
He is for an older man.
I will not leave him
Am I not the older man? . . .
Was not an older man once a younger man?
And will not a younger man be an older man?

cated. Because of unbalanced modernization, there is an unbridged dichotomy between the old and the new forces which has given rise to mutual suspicions.[33] The confrontation is crystallized between the chiefs, who are generally illiterate, and the educated class.[34] While there are no candid statements on the matter, the traditionalism of the chiefs seems to be in accord with conscious policies of national authorities. Chiefs are seen by these authorities as a useful tool of control, while the educated class, by claiming devolution of power, are seen as separatists and even "imperialist" agents.[35] This keep-the-chief-traditional attitude, a British colonial strategy which the Northerners condemned at one time,[36] is not confined to the head chief. Indeed, his traditionalism implies the traditionalism of his tribal hierarchy which has become more centralized and equipped with the coercive powers of the modern state. The more threatened his position, the greater his resort to these coercive powers.

The Ngok chief, who had occupied an unquestionably superior but nonautocratic position prior to modern state influence, is now one of the most powerful and autocratic individuals in Sudanese tribal life.[37] Yet, though acculturated along Arab lines [38] and less traditional than most of his subjects, he is basically still traditional and not sufficiently disposed to modernization. While he provides a medium for the maintenance of unifying control by the central government, his motive in this cooperation is to guarantee his autonomy and that of his tribe free from the in-

33. K. D. D. Henderson makes the same observation with respect to the whole country. Henderson, op. cit. supra note 3, at 75, 122–23.

34. Id. at 69–73.

35. Sudan Government, *Basic Facts about the Southern Provinces of the Sudan* 43–47 (1964); *The Expulsion of the Missionaries* 14 (1964). See also the speech of Sayed Ahmed el Mahdi, minister of interior, reported in *The Vigilant*, July 2, 1965.

36. For the colonial arguments in favor of "indirect rule" through traditional authorities see Henderson, op. cit. supra note 3, at 75.

37. Dr. Howell, once district commissioner in the area, commented on the modern powers of the Ngok chief that "Administrative policy has tended to build up an effective autocracy in an essentially democratic society." Howell, "Ngok Dinka" 264.

38. Chief Kwol Arob, father of the present chief, is referred to in government records as the "Arabized Chief Kwol." Howell extends the idea to Chief Kwol's successor: "His son Deng Majok has carried the evolution a step further and has a burning ambition to pattern himself on the Ali Gulla Nazirate of the Homr (Baggara) with all the pomp of state visits to Khartoum, tribal gatherings, and in addition the Dinka ideal of wealth, a company of wives." Ibid. It would not be accurate to consider Kwol Arob and his son Deng Majok apers of Arab culture. They have assimilated much of the neighboring Arab political and cultural patterns, but this has been a selective process. Their emphasis on their political and cultural identity as Dinkas at least partially explains why the Ngok have not been assimilated though they have been in contact with the Arabs for centuries as a minority. Howell observes that "99 percent of the Ngok, despite generations of contact with the Arabs, are quite unaffected by any form of Islamic traits and are as completely Dinka as their Dinka neighbours to the South." Id. at 248.

cursions of the overwhelming Arab majority in the Missiriya Rural Council, the local government organ of the area. By virtue of his exclusive
identification and the limitations of his horizons, the overall national issues, such as the South-North conflict, though similar to those confronting him in Dinka-Arab relations, seem remote.

By traditional standards, the educated class does not qualify for leadership. Since education came late to the Dinka, the educated are generally
young. This identifies them as one age group and in their songs they
often refer to themselves as one. Culturally, their education is alien. But
they are better equipped for modernization. They hold the highest positions in such strategic values as modern skills and enlightenment. It
is they who have broadened their loyalties. They are the most appreciative of modern medicine and have greatest access to it. By virtue of their
inclusive religious adherence, their notions of rectitude are more extended than those of their tribal kindred. While their raciocultural background tends to lower their social standing in comparison to that of
Northerners,[39] they have, by virtue of their education, more respect in
modern society than has the average Southerner. Though they do not
possess accumulated wealth, it is they who comprehend something of the
processes of the modern market and it is they who hold "well-paying"
jobs.

Although these innovations affect the status quo in modern terms and
undermine traditional leadership, the traditional disqualifications, now
fortified by governmental support, still deny the educated the strategic
control they need to modernize the tribe. Because they are deprived in
traditional society they migrate to the modern sector of the country.[40]
But even there they have no access to power. The few among them who
join the civil service occupy positions insignificant for the purposes of
modernizing their areas. In addition, they are almost invariably posted
to the North where they are subordinate to Northerners in other values.

This deprivation of the educated class by the traditionals aggravates
the South-North problem, but the unchanging and even violent opposition of the educated Southerners to the government is not explained
only in these terms. Even within the North, descent and age are factors
in receiving indulgences.[41] The result is that youth throughout the country engage in opposition to the government and favor revolutionary

39. A popular way by which Northerners express disrespect for Southerners is to
say "Times have changed!" recalling the days of slave raiding.

40. Sudan government, *Survey Report of Employment of Southerners* 4–5 (1964).

41. Governor Henderson described Northern Sudanese society as "A society in
which young men are seen and not heard, in which a grey-haired son did not take
a seat in the presence of his father, and abstained from lighting a cigarette when
travelling in company with his elder brother." Henderson, op. cit. supra note 3, 75.

means of changing what they see as a static situation.[42] In the North, communism and Muslim Brotherhood, mutually opposed but equally radical, command the allegiance of the overwhelming majority of youth —an allegiance which is usually abandoned soon after one joins the establishment. The position of the educated Southern youth is complicated by raciocultural factors. The strategies of Islamization and Arabization are directly in conflict with their predominantly Christian and other Western influences. Many Southerners feel and are treated as uneducated because they do not know Arabic.[43] They believe that the system must be changed, and many would advocate doing so by force if necessary. Although both educated and uneducated Southerners are involved in the war with the North, the movement was begun and is still led by the educated.

The various value structures of traditional society which have generated traditional law are still being perpetuated. The modern legal system, while providing formal means of adaptation and modification of traditional law to modern exigencies,[44] favors the administration of tribal law by the chiefs and elders.[45] The seeds of modernity were first sown by the colonial powers, but legal process has not kept pace with modernizing changes, let alone paved the way for change. No clear policies are articulated; customary law is unknown to the national authorities; the modern class, poised between traditional and modern law, occupies an uncertain legal status; the tripartite system functions on an ad hoc basis and impedes the dynamics of legal development.[46]

The interplay of all the value processes, and particularly the failure of the legal process to resolve issues, has produced paradoxes in the relationship of the participants. For example, the mythicals represent the

42. With apparent exaggeration, Edward Atiya, one time headmaster in the Northern Sudan, wrote that educated Northern Sudanese youth were "Rebels against everything, not rebels of principle, but rebels in principle. Nothing but hot air in the Union and strikes in the lecture room. No respect for anybody or anything. . . . Every boy a hooligan and ever girl a tart. Juvenile delinquency and teenage rioting." Atiya, *An Arab Tells His Story* 138 (1946).

43. The committee appointed to investigate the 1955 revolt in the South found that "some Northern Sudanese, including high officials in the Administration, refer to the Southern intelligentsia as half-educated. Sudan Government, op. cit. supra note 40, at 7. See also Deng and Oduho, *The Problem of the Southern Sudan* 47 (1962).

44. Apart from appeals, reviews, and revisions of tribal decisions, national courts can influence customary law according to Sections 5 and 9 of the Civil Justice Ordinance of 1900, which was reenacted in 1929.

45. Chiefs and elders now apply customary law in accordance with the Chiefs' Courts Ordinance of 1931 and their decisions are rarely interfered with by national authorities.

46. See Thompson, "Sources of Law in the New Nations of Africa: A Case Study from the Republic of the Sudan," *Wisconsin Law Review* 1146 (Fall 1966).

ideals of society, but the uneducated Southerners, in ignorance of cause and effect, attribute much suffering to their coercive power. Where their exercise of coercion cannot be rationalized, they are considered whimsical.[47] The chiefly lineages are still considered by the commoners to be the spiritual fathers of the tribe, yet as they abandon their divine power and depend on what the Dinka consider imposed power of state, they lose spiritual reverence and become open to opposition.[48] Because of the pivotal role women play in the bearing and rearing of children, their influence is strong.[49] But the role of women must be depreciated. Even children must demonstrate independence from them, or male identity will be endangered. As a result, women are often forced to resort to unauthorized means, which reinforce the negative qualities attributed to them. The chiefs and elders have a cooperative relationship with youth warrior age sets; but, in addition to various civil disobediences, the young men often demonstrate violence unacceptable to the chiefs' and elders' sense of civil responsibility. The chiefs and the government are on amicable terms as a result of mutual needs to serve essentially different and sometimes conflicting objectives. The chiefs and the educated are basically united against Arab domination.[50] This is notwithstanding the fact that expediency might compel maltreatment of the educated class within the tribes in order to preserve the strategic bond with the government, without which the chiefs fear that much of their power and their limited autonomy would be lost. The educated class and the warrior age groups of traditional society are united by their age proximity and their somewhat parallel positions. Yet their conditions differ and a gulf exists despite their otherwise inclusive identification as one "age set." [51] The educated group is on the whole overtly opposed to the government in ways ranging from the guerrilla warfare of the South-North civil war to political opposition in Khartoum. Yet many of the educated who are not professionally involved in politics must work with the gov-

47. Lienhardt, *Divinity* 44–45.

48. Their traditional power is occasionally criticized as capricious.

49. The fact that maternal relatives are believed to be more spiritually powerful than the agnatic kin suggests that the female line is highly regarded, sometimes even more so than the male line.

50. In fact the chiefs are in the most precarious position since they are friends and enemies of both the rebels and the government. Some Southern chiefs fall victims to both the rebels and the security forces. Dismissal by the government is not uncommon. For alleged mass dismissals in 1965, see *The Vigilant,* February 10, 1966.

51. A young man of the Pajok lineage sings:
Our Pajok is manifold
There are the black Pajok
And the Pajok in foreign clothes.
The Pajok in foreign clothes
Have spoiled our land.

ernment in modest civil service since they still consider private enterprise a last resort.

The foregoing analysis indicates that the traditional emphasis on the goal of permanent identity and influence now reinforced by the superimposed national system as the fundamental basis for allocating values has generated many negatives. Vital human resources remain unutilized —indeed, are frequently destroyed. More than stagnation, the result is disintegration. There are, of course, positive elements in tradition: examples are the goals of unity and harmony and the stress the chiefs and elders lay on persuasion and on good human relations expressed in deference. The inequitable foundation of these positives undermines them and will continue to do so with increasing gravity. The revolutionary trends which have begun and which we predict will intensify throughout the country are sufficient signals. It is therefore imperative to reevaluate policies and to select alternatives conducive to the postulated goals.

Any solution which would approximate the goal of human dignity must balance the positive aspects of both tradition and modernity and must balance the interests of all dynamic groups. We posit the strategy of transitional integration in which law must play a pivotal role both because it is an instrument for effective enforcement of community policies and because power, a value specialized to law, is the most contested value. This is not to underestimate the importance of the other values as bases for power or as contested values themselves. The ideal is to see all values as interdependent aspects of a complex whole. The task of the law is to attain justice by indulging the presently deprived, giving special attention to groups and areas which would best promote modernization. It is with this quest for modernizing justice in mind that this study has described and analyzed the dynamics of participation and their present expression of substantive law in terms of indulgences and deprivations and also in terms of how they contribute to or detract from this goal. Furthermore, by tracing specific negatives to specific deprivations as sanctioned by law, a foundation can be laid for correcting them through law.

It is immaterial whether the participants are aware of their deprivations or of their potentialities. As Professors Lasswell and McDougal say, "We are not in favor of slaves or subjects, even when, on the conscious level, they love their chains." [52] Our analysis shows that potentialities for modernization are not limited to the educated, although it is they who are most aware of them and of existing injustices. In addition to having initiated some changes, traditional youth possesses character-

52. McDougal and Lasswell, *Law, Science, and Policy* (mimeographed materials) Pt. 3 at 3 (1964).

istics of physical man-power and competitiveness that can be used for constructive purposes. The inclination of women toward trade is influencing the economic life of the tribe. Among the Ngok, the role of the chiefly lineages has generally been to pioneer social change, although in terms of tradition. It is only when change has outpaced individual chiefs that they have intensified their resistance to it. But change is still led by members of their lineages. It should be borne in mind that tradition and modernity do not necessarily conflict. Nor is the issue merely one of the use of tradition to reinforce modernity.[53] One may reverse the above examples and find grounds for aiding tradition by modernity. If the warrior groups are used for modernization, the enhancement of their value position would mean their reinforcement. The same may be said for the recognition of the dichotomy between the roles of women and men and of building on the institution of chieftainship. Should tradition and modernity be in conflict, the strategy of transitional integration aims at achieving a balance of their interests which would render modernization as peaceful and nondisruptive as possible.

In advocating legal intervention in the guidance of change we are using law in its widest sense. The traditional theory of law as a follower of clearly established sentiments of society still has its advocates, but its innovative role has increasingly become recognized.[54] In Africa, this has especially been the case in "lawyers' laws," which "deal with the legal relationships arising from the complexities of modern commercial and industrial society," as opposed to "people's laws," which are "primarily concerned with the personal laws" in which traditions are most

53. "The capacity of old and new cultures to exist without conflict and even with mutual adaptations is a frequent phenomenon of social change; the old is not necessarily *replaced* by the new. The acceptance of a new product, a new religion, or a new mode of decision-making does not necessarily lead to the disappearance of the older form. New forms may only increase the range of alternatives." Gusfield, "Tradition and Modernity," 72 *American Journal of Sociology* 351, 354 (1967).

54. The principal advocates are Savigny and Ehrlich. See Savigny, *Systems of Modern Roman Law* (translated) (1867) and Ehrlich, *Principles of the Sociology of Law* (translated) (1936). The positivists' conception of law as expressing the command of the sovereign stands in conflict with Savigny's theory. The role of law as an instrument of policy is at the core of Professors Lasswell and McDougal's "law, science, and policy" system. See, for example, their "Legal Education and Public Policy," supra note 12, at 52. In Professor Eugene Rostow's words, "The principal function of law is to serve as one of the educational and formative influences of the culture, not merely in bringing the law in action up to the standard of the existing goal of law, but in perfecting the goal of the law." Rostow, *The Sovereign Prerogative* 141 (1962). See also Nyhart, "The Role of Law in Economic Development," *Sudan Law Journal and Reports* 401 (1962). For a general discussion of the interaction of legal and social change, see Friedmann, *Law in a Changing Society* (1969).

deeply rooted.[55] The fear is often expressed by academic lawyers that treading on such delicate grounds is dangerous. In the Sudan, leaving the field of law untouched is consistent with the general neglect of the traditional sector of the country. For various reasons, this area needs more attention than it has received and in this study considerable weight is given to family law. As traditional society is family oriented, what begins in the home affects the whole. There are many cases in which conflicts between chiefs and their sons or relatives ended with dramatic impact on the tribal and even on the national level. Educated men who lost in such conflicts because the government aligned with the chiefs left their homes and joined the guerrilla forces in the bush. Some have even raided to victimize the kinsmen with whom they had quarreled. Though extreme, this is an example of how consequences of what seems personal can affect the community. It will be shown that most of the problems on higher levels are indirectly if not directly traceable to familial modes of value shaping and sharing. Impediments to modernization are no exception. By tracing roles of participation from this personal level to the collectivization of family members into various tribal groups and ultimately into national groups, whether organized or unorganized, we demonstrate the public significance of the principles governing family relationships. It is therefore necessary to enter family premises if one is to use law as an instrument of justice and a means of distributing the bases of modernization. The fact that it is in personal law that traditions and feelings are most deeply rooted is itself a strong argument in favor of harmonizing this law with modernization. Failure to do so can cause serious strains not only on those enslaved by it, but also on those who struggle to maintain it.

It is nonetheless useful to take warning from the history of reluctance to change family law. Transitional integration seeks to avoid any radicalism which might be disruptive. The revolutionary method followed by Kemal Ataturk in Turkey is today at best controversial.[56] It has been argued that "events in Turkey have shown how undesirable, and indeed

55. Thompson, supra note 46, at 1148. See generally Twining, "Some Aspects of Reception," *Sudan Law Journal and Reports* 229, 232–33 (1957). For the distinction of lawyers' law and politicians' law and its significance to change see Friedmann, op cit. supra note 54. There have, however, been changes in family law in various areas. For modernization in Islamic law, for example, see Anderson, "Law Reform in the Middle East," 32 *International Affairs* 43 (1956), and Anderson, "The Modernization of Islamic Law in the Sudan," *Sudan Law Journal and Reports* 292 (1960). Friedmann says of Arab countries, "The effect of this transformation and the closer contacts with other systems has increasingly affected family law and, in particular the 'miserable lot of Muslim wives.'" Friedmann, op. cit. supra note 54, at 12.

56. For an appraisal of Ataturk's strategies, see *Revue de la faculté de droit D'Istanbul* 6 (1956); IX *International Social Science Bulletin* 1 (1957); Twining, supra note 55 at 242–44.

largely unsuccessful, has been the attempt to impose a European-style family law on a people with non-European social tradition." [57] In the words of Professor Allott, to "try to do as Ataturk did, and introduce a novel law having no previous connection with the country, would be an exercise doomed to failure in the modern African context." [58]

The significance of constantly keeping a panoramic view of the whole social situation is fundamental. Although we stress the role of law, it is important to realize that balanced change can only be affected by the interplay of all values, institutions, and disciplines. Since law permeates all of these, the point may seem too obvious, but it is by seeing the final indulgences and deprivations of any legal action in terms of all values that one can make a rational and advantageous commitment to policies. It is hard to say whether one can stratify the importance of these values, but insofar as past trends might have stressed or neglected some of them out of balance with the rest, corrective emphasis or de-emphasis may be necessary. However, the need for their widest distribution remains constant.

Implicit in the envisaging of the total situation is the importance of all levels of society. We shall discuss primarily the family and the tribal levels, but shall touch on the national level. In each of these, the balance of interests can be both voluntary and mandatory. In the latter case, most of the decision-makers on the family level will be tribal; on the tribal level, national; and on the national level, international with organizations or individual nation-states as mediators.[59] While the obligation of self-induced balance of interests falls on all participants, it is greatest on the more indulged, especially those in power. The more indulged the participants in modern values, the greater their demands will be. The *negative* implications of deprivation, rather than being eliminated, will continually assume higher and wider dimensions, and perhaps different forms. Rather than refuting the hypothesis that conflicts and other negatives resulting from deprivation can be eliminated by corrective indulgences, this merely shows the importance of seeing the problem in its widest possible dimensions.

The Dinka, like most peoples, are confronted with modernization which, while it benefits society, can also be disruptive and strenuous. It

57. Farran 29.

58. Allott, "The Codification of the Law of Civil Wrongs in Common-Law African Countries," (paper delivered at the Conference on Integration of Customary and Modern Legal Systems, Ibadan, Nigeria, August 1964) p. 6.

59. The point was first made in 1947 by the British colonial regime. Referring to the Southern Problem, the government predicted that "The whole subject might some day form a proper subject for consideration by an international commission." *The Sudan: A Record of Progress* (1947). See Document No. 2 in Henderson, op. cit. supra note 3, at 196.

needs to be accelerated, but it also needs to be controlled and guided toward the higher goal of human dignity. If the present trends continue, revolutionary and disintegrating developments incompatible with the overriding goal of human dignity must also continue. Transitional integration is a legal method of indulging the deprived without unduly depriving the indulged and of mobilizing the unutilized forces of modernization without unduly threatening the forces of tradition. This strategy is a contextual approach by which policies are constantly related to the objectives of all those whose support is vital for the success of a harmonious and balanced modernization.[60]

SOURCES OF INFORMATION

Because of present official disinterest, and in fact discouragement, there has been very little written on Sudanese traditional cultures. Professor Evans-Pritchard's works make the Nuer an exception.[61] The Azande, too, drew his attention, though mainly from the religious point of view.[62] Dr. Lienhardt's *Divinity and Experience* is the only thorough anthropological work on the Dinka, although it excludes the Ngok and, as the title shows, focuses on religion.[63]

There also exist a few articles and notes by anthropologists and colonial administrators,[64] but they are often too brief to be of much help and are not oriented to the basic problems. Change in general, and the role of law in particular, is most neglected. The only book on traditional law is Dr. Howell's *Manual of Nuer Law*, which is a statement of substantive law in initial transition. This book is thus an original document in many respects. I collected some of the material on two field studies among the Ngok sponsored by the Faculty of Law, University of Khartoum. This field work, though generally successful, had some failures. I experienced many instances of the official discouragement of traditional studies. Authorities refused me access to documents which they had never even looked at. Sometimes, documents were withdrawn after officials had allowed me access to them. The tribal chiefs, too, suspected the motives of research. My Southern colleagues who attempted a similar study in their own tribes were stopped and in some cases even arrested for alleged subversion. My position as son of the chief helped in this

---

60. For the importance of a contextual approach for developmental purposes see Lasswell, "The Policy Sciences of Development," 17 *World Politics* 286, 298 (1965).

61. Among his numerous works on the Nuer are *The Nuer* (1940), *Kinship and Marriage among the Nuer* (1951), and *Nuer Religion* (1956).

62. See his *Witchcraft, Oracles and Magic among the Azande of the Sudan* (1938).

63. *Divinity and Experience: Religion of the Dinka* (1961).

64. Mostly in *Sudan Notes and Records*.

regard. I investigated cases with chiefs [65] and elders, attended trials, and collected records of other cases, including those of my grandfather, Chief Kwol Arob! [66]

Other sources are my personal knowledge by virtue of membership in the tribe and lifelong experience with its administration of justice.[67] A more unusual source is a collection of several hundred tape-recorded songs. Although a few of the translations will be quoted here, I have prepared a separate volume of the songs for The Oxford Library of African Literature. The significance of these songs as a source of information is explained in that volume in terms of the role that songs play in Dinka life.

As the book was completed in 1967, its material should be seen in that context.

PRESENTATION

My aim in this book has been to be both comprehensive and specific. A total picture is necessary for policies of change to be adequately based; and an adequate foundation for transitional integration is laid by being specific enough to avoid presenting the Dinka as a collective whole and to probe behind the curtain of uniformity to uncover interactive forces and discrepancies. All Dinkas share common objectives of common ideals, but their ordinary pursuit of values involves competition, conflict, and failure in varying degrees.

These processes and variations are part of a total system with an inner logic and a hierarchy of values and norms which provides the yardstick for measuring and evaluating behavior. It is the search for the totality of the system and its inner logic which made me venture beyond the discipline of law. Indeed, the book might well have been prepared and published in two parts: sociological and legal. However, despite the fact that I recognized my limitations in integrating these disciplines, I was motivated and encouraged by the fact that Dinka life is itself integrated and it would have been a superimposition of discipline to present it otherwise.

The book is divided into four parts. Part I, "Participants and Postu-

65. Mainly other than my father to avoid suspicion. In fact, when I was once in the court of my uncle, who is also a chief, he said to me, "Be careful not to record what your father tells you and call it Dinka law." This reaction revealed both the opposition between the two (see Chapter 3) and the fact that the head chief is more innovating than his brother.

66. Unfortunately, many of the records were far too brief to be informative.

67. The house of the chief used to be the court, but even now, when there is an official court, litigation begins in the chief's house in the early morning and continues there in the evening after the official hours.

lates," contains the first two chapters. Chapter 1, "Organization of Participants," deals with the structure of Dinka society and identifies participants in three main categories: collective, individual, and mythical. Collective participants include territorial, descent, class, sex, age, and culture groups. Individual participation is emphasized to stress the role of the individual contrary to the commonly held view that it is the group which constitutes the legal unit in tribal society. By mythicals is meant the dead and the deities who play an active part in the life of the Dinka. The special significance of the family to the structure of Dinka society is also examined to show the family orientation of the society.

In order to trace Dinka social process systematically, Chapter 2 explores some of the fundamental goals toward which the system is geared. These are continuity in posterity (which I call the myth of permanent identity and influence) and unity and harmony. The list of overriding goals is of course not meant to be complete, just as the list of values discussed in the book is purely illustrative and not exhaustive. Even the placement in terms of hierarchy is not dogmatic. For instance, the values of pride and dignity, as the Dinka see them, are high-ranking, but they have been discussed here under other values with special reference to respect and not separately as overriding goals, which would also have been consistent with the whole structure of presentation. In any case, the interdependencies of all values foreclose any rigidity in classification.

Parts II and III discuss eight Dinka value processes, one chapter per value process, to elaborate the theme of who gets what and how from the system and what repercussions flow from these stratifications. Part 2 covers deference values (power, affection, respect, and rectitude) while Part 3 covers welfare values (wealth, well-being, skill, and enlightenment). The two main sections of each chapter consist of a general sociological presentation of the value process and its legal expression. Thus, under "Power," the two sections are "The Process of Power" and "Power and the Law," and under "Affection," "The Process of Affection" and "Affection and the Law." The sociological presentation discusses the various roles of the participants and traces them from the family level to the tribal level. On the family level, the relative value position of the husband-father, the wife-mother, the children, and extended relationships are examined. These roles are then projected to the tribal level along similar principles to cover chiefs, elders, youth age-sets and the educated class. The implications of these roles and their value positions are then traced to the national level. The classification of the section concerning the legal expression is based on familiar legal concepts which have particular relevance to the value category in question. Among the subheadings under "Power and the Law" for instance are "The Nature of Dinka Law" and "Appointment and Dismissal of Decision-Makers";

and under "Affection and the Law" are "Marriage," "Legitimacy," and "Vicarious Liability."

Parts I to III are purely descriptive and explanatory. Only in Part IV does evaluation come into the picture; hence the title "Policy Considerations." Apart from a short conclusion, Part IV consists of only one chapter which begins with a brief appraisal of the traditional system and of the trends adopted by colonial and national governments. The appraisal attributes certain negative aspects of the system to its injustices and predicts revolutionary trends on the part of those who now get the least or deserve more than the system permits. The theory and application of the suggested strategy of transitional integration is then expounded in the second part of the chapter. The last part of the chapter examines the future of customary law in the Sudan legal system.

Part I

Participants and Postulates

1. Participants and Structure

Dinka society can generally be divided into collective, individual, and mythical participants. These categories are both divergent and convergent, so that to speak of one is to imply the others. For instance, speaking of an individual implies his membership in one sort of group or another, and speaking of mythical participants implies, among other possibilities, a descent group, a mythical individual, and a one-time "natural" participant. The network of participation begins and ends with the family, whose role is thus both individual and social, private and public.

COLLECTIVE PARTICIPANTS

Collective groups are primarily territorial and descent, with age, sex, and culture groups interfused. The identification of participants and their situations will be traced from the most inclusive Dinka community to the family, and then to age, sex, and culture groups.

Territorial Groups

While there are variations in internal organizations, Dinka territorial groups are divided into three: tribes, subtribes, and sections. The degree of cohesion and effectiveness decreases directly with the degree of inclusiveness. The importance of the territorial groups as institutions for value shaping and sharing thus increases as we go from the tribes to the family.

TRIBES Dinkaland comprises some twenty-five tribes, or *bai* (singular *baai*), a term which also means "village," "home," "family," or "people," depending on the context.[1] Among the distinctive characteristics of each

1. Writing on the Western Dinka of Bahr-el-Ghazal Province, Godfrey Lienhardt calls what I call tribes "tribal groups." He considers tribes to be components of a tribal group. Lienhardt, "Western Dinka" 97, 102. Owing to the differences between the Ngok political system and that of the Dinka groups on which Dr. Lienhardt based

tribe are a common territory, a common name, and a common culture, for although all the Dinka are culturally homogeneous, there are variations in matters of detail. Though contiguous, they tend to be separated by natural boundaries like rivers, swamps, and forests. The population of each group varies from under 3,000 people to over 150,000.

While the Dinkas are spoken of as a totality, most Dinkas do not know their whole people. The more traveled or educated a Dinka is, the more of Dinkaland he knows, but rarely does he know all the tribal groups.[2]

The tribe is divided into subtribes.[3] Except among the Ngok Dinka, the subtribe is the largest body politic with recognized decision-making authority.[4] Among the Ngok the whole society constitutes a body politic. There is a tribal group with the same name in Upper Nile Province, living on the River Sobat, but since there has been no link for many generations, it cannot be considered a component of the Ngok tribe.

SUBTRIBES The Ngok are divided into nine subtribes. Each, though owing allegiance to the head chief, was traditionally autonomous. They now fall under a more centralized though still segmented tribal administration.[5] Dr. P. P. Howell lists the following as characteristic of a Ngok subtribe, that is, Howell's "section":

a. A common name.
b. A distinct and effective sentiment of a common purpose both for offence and defence. This was a reality for sections often combined against each other, and there is still an active attitude of political rivalry.

---

his terminology, this nomenclature is not applied to the Ngok but is cited here for comparative purposes.

2. Id. at 107.

3. Referred to as "tribe" in the terminology of Dr. Lienhardt. Id. at 102. P. P. Howell, who divides Ngok society into "main divisions," "divisions," "sections," and "subsections," considers our "subtribe" as a "section." Howell, "Ngok Dinka" 239, 249–55. Since his "main divisions" and "divisions" have hardly any contemporary significance, they are not given consideration here. His terminology is only used when convenient or necessary. Both Dr. Lienhardt and Dr. Howell find Professor Evans-Pritchard's classification of the Nuer tribe into primary, secondary, and tertiary sections inapplicable to the Dinka. Howell says, "The use of these terms which so accurately describes the Nuer system, only leads to confusion if applied to the Ngok Dinka." Id. at 251.

4. "The tribe is thus a political unit for defence in the dry season pastures, and is so regarded by the Dinka. It . . . also . . . marks the limits of the possible recognition of any convention that disputes should be settled peacefully." "Western Dinka" 117.

5. These subtribes are Abyor, of the Pajok lineage which rules the tribe; Mannyuar, the subtribe of the Dhiendior lineage, second to Pajok in leadership; Anyiel, Acueng, Alei, Acak, Bongo, Diil, and Mareng.

c. A common area of permanent habitation, though, nowadays, the boundaries are far from distinct.

d. A common grazing area which includes rights in fishing and hunting. A section would combine to protect their rights to this area and would fight if necessary.

e. A common system of nomenclature in age-sets, e.g. age-set names run through the section and not beyond.[6]

Above the subtribe, the Ngok consider themselves as one political entity. They have always recognized their unity under Pajok lineage, whose "history is essentially bound up with that of the Ngok tribe." [7]

It may be argued that the Ngok emphasis on centralization is the result of outside influence. Their early contact with the Arabs seems to have resulted in an influence which, though generally superficial, is considerable in their political process. Early reports describe the Ngok head chief in Arabic terms as *Nazir, Sultan,* or *Mek.*[8]

SECTIONS Subtribes of the Ngok are divided into twenty-three sections, which Howell calls "subsections," with the same characteristics as subtribes. Within the subsections, classification is based on descent and not on territorial bases.

VARIABILITY OF TERRITORIAL GROUPS As a pastoral people in search of better pastures, the Dinka spread over a vast territory. Linked with this is the natural increase in population and the fact that most of Dinkaland is often flooded during the wet season. The higher lands become scarce, necessitating partition in search of dry spots. Another cause of segmentation was adventurous or politically dissatisfied brothers or sons of chiefs who broke away and founded new tribes. Significant also is the constant slave raiding by Arabs.

Through this process of segmentation and fragmentation not only is the society disunited, but disunity is perpetuated. Each of these segments acts as a unit in opposition to a more distant outsider. Otherwise, it is characterized by internal conflict which impedes valued unity.

Descent Groups

The social order of the Dinka is one of interplay between descent and other identifications. There is a distinction between descent which transcends political boundaries and that which determines the structure

6. Howell, "Ngok Dinka" 255.
7. Id. at 265.
8. Id. at 264.

of a political unit. While both have significant consequences, the latter is more important. Descent groups are classified, according to their degree of inclusiveness, into kin groups, clans, subclans or lineages, families, and, within families, individuals.

KIN GROUPS *Alaraan,* which may be translated as "kinfolk," comprises people who are related by traceable or assumed descent. This would include patrilineal kin, *waar,* and matrilineal kin, *naar.* The intensity of kinship relationship is relative. Thus, members of the same clan from different sections or even different tribes would regard themselves as related, but with much less significant consequence than lineage relationship. While the English words "descent" and "kin" imply blood ties only, *alaraan* mainly implies blood ties, but also includes affinities by marriage, and even friendship.

CLANS The largest component of kinship is the clan, *dhien* or *gol,* literally "cattle hearth," an agnatic group composed of people descended from a common ancestor. The exact genealogical link may not be traceable. The intermediate ancestors may be confused or forgotten, and a jump of several degrees may be made to reach the alleged founder.[9] Although the male line is more important, the female line is highly regarded. The totemic and exogamous requirements of clans are observed with respect to both the father's and the mother's clans. The significance of dual descent is revealed in the following lines. The person in the song had failed to fulfill a kinship obligation due to the singer.

> O Ajith,
> Are you not Ajinh de Tong?
> Is not part of you my grandmother?
> And you being also the son of my sister?
> Is not our relationship complex as the stomach of a hippo?
> Are you not Ajith for whom I used to run to the court-tree of Abyei?
> How can you slip the mouth of your maternal uncle
> Like a tortoise dropping from the mouth of a seizing bird
> So that I spend my nights without sleep.

Most clans are widespread so that people of the same clan may even acquire a new clan name. A woman of Pajok clan boasts of how widespread their clan is.

9. "The agnatic genealogical structure of his whole clan . . . is not known to a Dinka; he knows that there are likely to be many sub-clans of his clan, all descended from wives or sons of the clan-founder whose name and existence have been forgotten long ago by members of his own sub-clan." Lienhardt, "Western Dinka" 105–06. See also Howell, "Ngok Dinka" 256.

Our clan Pajok is dispersed over the land
It is called Padhieu in the land of the Rek.

SUBCLANS OR LINEAGES   The subclan, also called *dhien* or *gol,* is the fragment of the clan within which descent is accurately traced. The subclan may be fragmented into "main lineages" and "sublineages." [10] We shall refer to the subclan and the lineal groups of varied depth as "lineages." All the descendants of a man constitute a lineage, and the number of lineages in any genealogy will be equivalent to the number of its male ascendants. The length of the lineage differs according to its importance. Ordinary lineage is traced to approximately ten generations, whereas it would be about fifteen in the genealogies of chiefs.

All the levels of lineal grouping within which there is a corporate identity of unilineal descent are significant for our present purposes. The broadest is where a clan head, *nom gol,* is recognized. In collaboration with the elders and the heads of component lineages, he constitutes the decision-making machinery.

THE FAMILY   Within the lineage is the family, *baai,* in effect a degree of lineage. The Dinka family may be polygynous, with its size largely depending on the wealth and the social esteem of the family head. Whereas *kic,* a commoner, or *abur,* a poor man, usually has only one wife, a rich man, *raan bany,* will have several, and a chief may have over a hundred.[11] When there art two or three wives, each *ghot thok,* literally "the doorway of the house," consists of a wife and her children. When there are many wives, each *ghot thok* includes a senior wife, her children, junior wives, and their children. There may be two or three of these in a family. The senior wife is the head of the senior house, and the second wife of the next house, and so on according to order of marriage. In the largest families each "house" may be redivided into smaller units with delegation

10. Lienhardt, "Western Dinka" 105. This book (i.e. *Tribes Without Rulers*) elaborates on societies with "segmentary lineage systems"—"acephalous" societies, one of the three types of African societies distinguished by Professors Fortes and Evans-Pritchard, editors of *African Political Systems* (1940). For general discussion of segmentary lineage systems in *Tribes Without Rulers,* see Introduction, pp. 1–30.

11. According to the 1955–56 census for the whole Sudan there were just over 2,000 people with five wives, a few hundred with six wives, and only 405 with ten or more wives. A census authority writes, "We may, therefore, conclude that the sensational stories about households with dozens and dozens of wives can be put among traveller's tales." Krotki, *21 Facts about the Sudanese* 39 (1958). Polygyny must not be conceived of only in terms of the immediate family. Even if such a family is monogamous, kinship ties bring wives of brothers, cousins, or the like into a kind of relationship akin to polygynous relationship. The term for any agnatic kinsman of the same degree is "son of my father." Since one's full brother is not referred to as "son of my father," half-brotherhood, which among the Dinka implies polygyny, is envisaged.

of authority by the head wives, especially if hamlets are far apart. This manner of grouping has important consequences which are discussed in various places of the book.

VARIABILITY OF DESCENT GROUPS   Just as territorial arenas are varied through the secession of some groups or individuals, so are descent groups. That some clans have lineages in all Dinka tribes is proof of their division. They may break through the process of migration already discussed. In addition, some clan or family members may be so discontented with the group's treatment of them, they may seek new associations. Even in such circumstances, blood ties are respected, rules of exogamy are observed, and reverence to common clan divinities continues. In extreme conflicts, blood relationships may be ritually severed. In such an event, rules of exogamy are still observed. Apart from these disruptive processes, a son becomes relatively independent on marriage, while a daughter transfers her dependence from her family and kin group to that of her husband.

Class Groups

Although the Dinka are an egalitarian society among whom equality forecloses "caste system" or class distinction in the conventional sense, they recognize class differentiations. The value pyramids are predicated on descent, with the family as the smallest but most significant unit. A few families form the elite, their clans midelite, and the bulk of the community the rank and file. Generally speaking, this structure pertains to all values.

The main cleavage is between *bany* and *kic*. *Bany* applies to all those members of the noble clans from whom chiefs, also called *bany,* are descended, though some individuals outside these groups may win access to power today. Among the Ngok they are Pajok and the Dhiendior. *Kic* denotes members of the nonchiefly clans.

The distinction between *kic* and *bany* seems to be uniform among the Nilotics and is found among the Nuer and the Shilluk,[12] but there are no barriers to social relations. As Evans-Pritchard says about the Nuer: "We

12. *Diel* among the Nuer, and *dyil* among the Shilluk, represent the first occupiers of the land. They are also the political leaders of the tribes. Professor Evans-Pritchard calls them "aristocrats." The *kic* are called *rul* by the Nuer and *wedh* by the Shilluk. Professor Evans-Pritchard describes a *dil* (singular) as follows:

If you are a *dil* of the tribe in which you live you are more than a simple tribesman. You are one of the owners of the country, its village sites, its pastures, its fishing pools and wells. Other people live there in virtue of marriage into your clan, adoption into your lineage, or of some other social tie. You are a leader of the tribe and the spearname of your clan is invoked when the tribe goes to

have called them [the *dil*] aristocrats, but do not wish to imply that Nuer regard them as of superior rank for, as we have emphatically declared, the idea of a man lording it over others is repugnant to them." [13] These words, though perhaps too strong, demonstrate the unique quality of class distinction in a fundamentally egalitarian society. To achieve influence through power or wealth, for instance, the society expects one to be socially conscious, kind, and hospitable. The Dinka word for "chief" or "rich" may also be translated as "kind," "generous," "gentle" or, in a word, "virtuous"—words which emphasize the relations of a person with other people and determine his potential for winning prestige among them.

Sex Groups

The distinction between males and females is very important in the shaping and sharing of values in Dinka society. While the woman is not a slave, she is considered inferior. But women occupy a very important role in Dinka society. Among other things, they are vital in building the child's character, and as we have said, maternal kin may in some instances be far more significant than the paternal group.

The attitude of domination-with-respect shown to women by the Dinka has sometimes led to extreme views. Imputed slavery is one.[14] The other is exemplified by those who allege that "The position held by the [Dinka] woman is a high one, and she is considered man's equal." [15] This, like the allegation of slavery, is inaccurate. Women provide the means to the more male-oriented goal of permanent identity and influence. Their destiny is almost universally marriage. The Dinka say that the woman is a stranger who will leave her lineage to serve the ends of another lineage.

Age Groups

Age sets, *riec* (sing. *ric*) among the Ngok play a very important role, which is much more emphasized than among the other Nilotes. Initiation takes a person out of social infancy which carries certain duties and incapacities and from which every Dinka longs to get away. When initiated,

---

war. Whenever there is a *dil* in a village, the village clusters around him as a herd of cattle clusters around his bull.

Evans-Pritchard, "The Nuer," *African Political Systems,* 215 (1940).

13. Ibid.

14. The Dinka themselves say that the woman is a slave (*tik k' alony*), though this is more figurative than real.

15. Titherington 153, 159.

one becomes *adheng,* a word which also means "gentleman," "handsome man," or "elegant man," as well as "rich," "kind," "generous," "gentle," or "virtuous." While initiation confers important privileges, adult indulgences are acquired piecemeal.

Dinka age sets are essentially subtribal. The aggregate of corresponding sets may be a functional entity in intertribal arenas, but even they would function through their subtribal divisions. Age sets are divided into male and female groups. While the age set of females is added to for ten or more years, a new group of men is created every several years. The ceremony of initiation differs from tribe to tribe. In most tribes, it is done by an operation known as *gar,* which involves scarring the forehead—a requirement from which some tribes, including the Ngok, exempt women.

Initiation, one of the Ngoks' most dramatic institutions, begins with a designation of a "father" and a name for the emerging age set a few years before their initiation. This "father" is usually an elder member of one of the chiefly lineages. The to-be-initiated then request their father and the chief to permit their initiation. Their request granted, a period of festivities precedes the cutting of some seven to ten deep, well-ordered marks known as *goor* across the forehead. The relatives of the initiates display great pleasure at their courage, for initiation signifies maturity and ability to endure pain. The initiation period (which goes on for several months) is the most colorful in the life of a Dinka. The initiates reside collectively by lineages in somewhat restricted villages. They have few responsibilities and many privileges. Their special dress, their initiation songs of bravery, and their dances are a great attraction to men and women, especially to girls. Initiation is usually performed early in December so that the north wind may help the wounds to cicatrize, leaving their foreheads clearly marked.

Termination of their status as initiates, *luny,* that is, "release," is marked by all-night dancing and singing. At dawn, unarmed, they are playfully (but painfully) beaten by the older age set into a river across which they must swim, and from which they emerge as adults. More mock fights, *biok,* with the older age set usually follow as further military training. They also demonstrate age-class conflict. Once fully acknowledged as an adult, an initiate changes dramatically. Correlative to his newly acquired privileges is a high standard of individual dignity and responsibility which distinguishes the initiated from "infants."

Culture Groups

Although the participants of Ngok society are culturally homogeneous, there are cross cultural relations involving non-Ngok and even non-Dinkas. While, according to Dr. Lienhardt, "The Dinka word for the large regional groupings of their people, the tribal groups, is *thai*," [16] a Ngok refers to all non-Ngok Dinka tribes as *thai* in addition to their names. Apart from the Nuer, whom the Dinka merely designate as Nuer, all other kinds of people are referred to as *jur,* a word which has been translated as "foreigners." [17] Among the Ngok, the word *jur* is usually used in reference to the Arabs, since their outside contacts are mainly with them. The Ngok refer to the Europeans as *turuk,*[18] and less often as *jur amer, "pink jur."* The Dinka also refer to the government as *jur,* thus identifying it as alien.

Another significant group is the educated class. In most Dinka societies, education was acquired through missionary schools, for it was not until 1944 that government education began, and even then missionary education continued to predominate. Consequently, these tribes call the educated class "children of the missionaries" *mith k'Abun.* Among the Ngok, where education was not in the hands of the missionaries, the educated are known as "those who write" *agat wal.* But neither the fact of having been to a missionary school nor that of writing and reading alone classifies a person. Education was largely oriented to non-Dinka cultures, so that culture alienation is implied. Implicit in "children of the missionaries" is the new culture to which education introduced them and the fact that the Dinka consider them culturally changed. It is rather significant that the educated are sometimes called *"Juur,"* that is, foreigners. Some boys and girls drift back into tradition. Others occupy levels of educational strata which distinguish them from their tradition-oriented tribesmen. This distinction has repercussions in all value processes. In some values they are more indulged; in others, more deprived.

Education among the Ngok, unlike that in some Dinka societies,[19] was pioneered by the chiefs and related families. Their initiative was probably provoked by the fact that one or two members of the *kic* had acquired some education with which they threatened the chief's power. Since then, most educated Ngok have been from chiefly backgrounds, and the higher their education, the more exclusively from chiefly families they are. In addition to appreciating education, the chiefs can afford it more than the *kic.*

Despite the diversity of their family backgrounds, the educated feel a sentiment of unity and a common purpose. Generally speaking, whether

16. Lienhardt, "Western Dinka" 108.

17. Ibid.

18. The word *turuk* generated from the Turkish period and has been used throughout the Sudan in reference to the British, without the negative connotations of the Turkish period.

19. Since the children who were sent to school were considered "lost," chiefs in these societies recruited the children of the commoners for the schools and "protected" their own children.

they are sons of chiefs or not, their exclusion from power is the same, although sons of chiefs may have more influence. In many ways, the educated class play the role of the age sets in traditional society, and it is noteworthy that they are referred to, and they refer to themselves, as *ric*, the word applied to age set. In this regard, they represent the younger generations, since among the Ngok no educated have yet become elders.[20]

INDIVIDUAL PARTICIPANTS

It is often alleged that the individual has little importance in traditional African societies.[21] This is based on a misconception of the intricate balance between the individual and the community in traditional society. It is particularly inapplicable to the Dinka. For one thing, it ignores intragroup relations and focuses on the broader intergroup relations.[22] Since interpersonal bonds are vital in traditional life, the whole community ultimately rests on the sum total of the cooperation of its individuals. Today, owing to the allocation of great powers to individual decision-makers, the individual's influence or lack of influence has become more marked.[23]

Within the tribe, the highest authority is the paramount chief, *Banydit*, sometimes referred to as head chief, who is always of the Pajok lineage.[24] He is assisted by two deputies; one is always of the Dhiendior lineage,

20. However, they seem to consider themselves members of one age set even when there is age discrepancy between them. There is reason to believe that this will continue as long as they remain a minority.

21. See Elias, *Nature of African Customary Law* 82 (1956).

22. Dr. Elias made the same point when he wrote: "The trouble is that the myth of kinship communism, while making such great play of the pervading group-sentiment, if not group-instinct, does not pierce the veil of clan corporateness in order to discover the tensions, the personal jealousies and rivalries, as well as the individual self-assertions that go on within the group itself. Anyone who cares to look into the actual social relations between the individuals who make up the group—whether this is family, clan or tribe—will realize soon enough that disputes do take place in all manner of situation." Ibid.

23. While their structure of authority has been reinforced by alien administration, the Ngok, unlike most Dinkas, have always recognized a similar structure. Howell reports that "such political power as is backed by the Government in the present system of administration was naturally accorded to the Chief of the spear by the Ngok themselves, and not only to the principal Pajok Family, but also to the minor leaders who are all Chiefs of the spear, either of the Pajok clan or the Dhiendior." Howell, "Ngok Dinka" 264.

24. After tracing the history of Pajok leadership, Howell cites an instance in which the successor was not the eldest son: "We have seen that one *Aiwel de Jok*, together with his father, is said to have led the Ngok to their present country and that his nephew was subsequently called over from the east to act as leader of the tribe after the death of Aiwel. The position has been held in this line ever since and according to strict promogeniture, the office descending to the eldest son of the eldest wife in each case." Ibid.

the other position is presently held by his half-brother. Each of the nine subtribes has its own chief, who is responsible to the paramount chief and his deputies.[25] Each of the subtribes has a number of *Masheikh* (derived from the Arabic *Sheikh*), "junior chiefs," depending on the number of sections in it. Apart from these are the court members, *makam*, a term derived from the Arabic word *mahkama*, "court." While these are specially appointed, all the decision-makers act as judges in the warranted courts and informally in their own jurisdictions.

The authority of traditional Dinka chiefs is interlinked with the religious beliefs of the people. It is apt at this stage to discuss the different religious functionaries, and how their political and religious authorities overlap. The priests and medicine men are purely ritual experts in divination and cure; they have no political or legal significance except in giving advice to remedy a wrong. Where, for instance, a person has committed secret homicide, and it is revealed by their diagnosis as the cause of deaths in his family, he is advised to admit his guilt and carry out the appropriate rites and legal measures regarding the payment of bloodwealth. Then there are those members of clans who trace their origin to the founders of the Dinka, the earliest leaders remembered. They are all referred to as chiefs. Since chiefs are believed to have divine origin, all the members of their clans are said to inherit this religious importance. All the smaller branches of the main lineages have their own divine chiefs. The members of these lineages have the power to bless or curse a person. Disregarding their word is believed to carry evil consequences. Their power is more than ritual; it is traceable to the origin of the tribe, and is inherent. This is why the Ngok call them Chiefs of the Flesh. They can arbitrate between conflicting parties, but apart from those among them who have governmental positions over defined territories or identified groups of people, their arbitration or mediation is based on the prestige of being men from lineages with a heritage of social esteem.

Bany de wut, chief of the cattle camp, is a man of influence who maintains order in the cattle camps. Young men and women usually move about with most of the herds in pursuit of better pastures, and may be far away from the established control machineries. The *bany de wut* is the representative of the political and legal authorities, as well as a decision-maker in affairs concerning cattle. For instance, execution of a judgment against the cattle of a person in the camp is usually affected through him; it is he who decides where and when the camp should move; in case of a conflict between camp members, it is he who arbitrates or mediates.

25. When the *Omda* of the Acueng died in the early 1940s, leaving no grownup son, Acueng decided to be administered by the chief of Abyor sub-tribe, the right-hand man of the paramount chief.

Another significant participant is *wun ric,* an elderly person who is the spiritual father of an age set. He selects the name for the age set and is responsible for instructing them about their role in society. He trains them in war tactics, and regulates their conduct. Violation of his judgment is believed to endanger the well-being of the culprit, and the age set may also impose punitive sanctions on the violator.

On the descent level, the highest authority is the clan head, *nom gol.* The clan heads, *niim ke gal,* are now appointed by the chief and their primary function has been narrowed to assisting in poll-tax collection, which has divested them of the respect traditionally afforded the position.

Within a nuclear family, the "man of the house" or "the father of the children" is the head. In a polygynous family, there is classification of wives and their children according to seniority of marriage. On the inclusive family level, *wendit,* or the eldest son, is usually the eldest son of the first wife. In the "house" of each woman, *wendit* is her eldest son. In other words, if the second wife has a son older than the son of the first wife (e.g. where the first born of the first wife is a girl) the son of the second wife is not the *wendit* of the family, although he would be the *wendit* of his mother's group. The youngest son, *kun,* although not as important as the oldest son, has a special significance. In addition to receiving more affection from both the father and the mother he is entitled to certain property rights which make him more indulged than the middle children.

MYTHICAL PARTICIPANTS

Certain conceptual entities are of such great concern to the Dinka that to exclude them from the structure of participation would be to overlook a vital aspect. They are here referred to as mythical participants and include divinities and the dead.

The Dinka believe in a supreme being, *Nhialic,* which is best translated as "God." Dinka belief in a complex system of spirits, *Yieth,* tends to blur their monotheistic conception of God.[26] To the Dinka there is only one *Nhialic,* but in their practical life they are more concerned with ancestral spirits and what Dr. Lienhardt calls "clan-divinities" and "free divinities" [27] than with the one *Nhialic.* Divinities usually have particular characteristics which manifest themselves through human ex-

26. As Dr. Lienhardt puts it, the Dinka "assert with a uniformity which makes the assertion almost a dogma that 'Divinity is one.' They cannot conceive of Divinity as a plurality and, did they know what it meant, would deeply resent being described as polytheistic." Lienhardt, *Divinity* 156.

27. See id. at Chapters II and III.

perience. Some of them are known to inflict specific types of pain or illness. Some are known to have certain likes and dislikes. When they "fall upon" a man and possess him, they can be identified by the peculiar aberrational behavior they induce in him. The relationship between a clan and clan divinity may be traced to a mythicized incident in the history of the clan. In this sense, divinities represent specific aspects of human experience.

Dr. Lienhardt explains the importance of experience in Dinka religion. Briefly stated, the memory of an experience is projected from the mind or interior of the remembering person to form an image which acts upon him, as he sees it externally.[28] Divine power is attributed to this externalized image, which is understood by the remembering person to be capable of making demands or of conferring benefits on him. Although the image takes an exterior appearance, the fact that it originates within the experiencing person and exerts influence on him shows a unity between him as the object and the image as the subject.[29] Thus, not only is there unity between self and image, but there is a unification of diverse experience within the self.

The following story illustrates the creation of a Pajok clan divinity. On their way westward under the leadership of Jok, the founder of Pajok, the Ngok were confronted with waters they could not cross. "Jok, with admirable self-sacrifice, pushed his daughter [Acai] into the river where she was carried off by the Spirit of the Water and in return the latter caused the waters to part and the people to march across dryshod." [30] The clan celebrates the memory of Acai annually, and offerings are made to her in the waters. She is believed to protect them from evil; in turn she makes demands which must be satisfied.

This story illustrates the origin of a clan divinity, but the same notion is applicable to the individual and the family. For example, a man who has suffered a serious disease may become recognized after the disease has passed as possessing a spiritual power to cure similar diseases. This is especially true where a man has suffered a disability or a deformation as a result of the disease. Once established, the power becomes hereditary. Not everyone of similar experience achieves the same results; it

28. Id. at 149.

29. Dr. Taylor expresses this unity of experiences with respect to African tradional religions in general: "Not only is there less separation between subject and object, between self and non-self, but fundamentally all things share the same nature and the same interaction, one upon another—rocks and forest trees, beasts and serpents, the power of wind and waves upon a ship, the power of a drum over a dancer's body, the dead and the first ancestors, from the stone to the divinities a hierarchy of power but not of being, for all are one, all are here, all are now." Taylor, *The Primal Vision* 72 (1963).

30. Howell, "Ngok Dinka" 242.

depends upon the degree of the impact made upon the person and his community by the memory of his experience. In all cases the memory must be honored by appropriate rites, sacrifices, or dedications of animals or objects. Failure to do so may result in harm inflicted by the neglected power.

The key concept in characterizing Dinka religion in its entirety is, therefore, experience. Divinity is not limited to any particular feature of human experience, but embraces all aspects of life. God is, therefore, a unification of infinite diversities. This concept of unity in diversity is characteristic of Dinka thought even in other fields. In Dinka political theory, for instance, segmentation is a necessary implement of social order and political unity. The family foundation of religion is evident in "the attribution of a universal fatherhood" to Divinity.[31]

Mankind as a totality is subject to God. The relationship between God and individuals is sometimes expressed in personal terms. A man may say "God of my father," *Nhialic e wa,* or "God of my forefather," *Nhialic e kukuar,* or even "God, my father," *Nhialic wa.* God as a unity is conceived of as too great and far removed from individuals, hence the need for implementing Him through lesser divinities.[32]

Associated with divinities are the dead. The relationship between them and their living kin is not merely a sentiment. Indeed, the demands of the dead have priority over the demands of the living. This, as we shall see in more detail, is the immortality that gives meaning to Dinka religion.

Mythical participants—God, lesser divinities, ancestral spirits, and the dead—can only be understood as a projection of Dinka realities into the unknown, whether in life or in death. The outcome of this conceptual unification of the known with the unknown, and the living with the dead, is the perpetuation of tradition.

THE FAMILY AS THE MICROCOSM OF DINKA SOCIAL STRUCTURE

The Family and Territorial Groups

While the organization of the Ngok has been traced from territorial groups to the family, the pivotal role of the family can be traced to territorial groups.

---

31. Lienhardt, *Divinity* 158.

32. Dr. Lienhardt, summarizes this conception of God as both a multiplicity and a unity: "Divinity is manifold as human experience is manifold and of manifold world. Divinity is one as the self's manifold experience is united and brought into relationship in the experiencing self. . . . Divinity, then, corresponds to experience common to all men, and to the Dinkas' recognition that a single human nature and condition embraces all. . . . The different name by which different people know it are matters only of different languages." Id. at 156.

r the *ghot thok* or *mac*
tter the "cooking-fire-
ans "cattle hearth," is
sects away and sit to
ected to continue the
d eventually the clan,
ot be seen only in the
e, the term also covers
indicated by the con-
r the names of their
ame is preceded with
"family," "home," or
ld read *paan de Deng.*
f *paan* and a combina-
he ancestor. A clan by
"home of Jok," or the
he prefix *dhien* means
y to start his own line-
nds to spread far and
ssible. The name then

s bound together by a
f a dominant lineage,
ogether, have common
n. Because of the unity
on of lineages is called
gether. But the theory
notion of people thus
ns, with similar bases,
subtribe is a dominant

kens. It may be that in
for defense. Usually,
ght by the subtribe in-
tensive and communica-
ies lasted longer, giving

the two dominant line-
nforce affinities by mar-
the other the paternal.
however, among the
ches more than six de-
rules of exogamy.[33]

Chapter 4, p. 150.

18

Because of the conceptualiza t

term, *baai,* is applied to both. **I**

tive term. The growth of the **f**

and fragmentation. It multiplies

On territorial bases, it creates

forced not only by the associati **o**

tion of familial relationship an **c**

and could be extended over the

primogeniture to its logical con **c**

least in theory) to the founder **o** f

of Dinka chiefs should be rela **t**

festation of the Dinkas' deman **d**

unity of their tribes and of the **i** r

valuing the autonomy of their **c** c

tive familial proximities.[35]

To emphasize the role of des **c**

that descent ties are more impo

trary, territorial divisions have

extend beyond the territorial **e** n

to one another. Yet, despite this

tification, not only is descent th

fication, but in fact it generat **e** s

ritorial arenas represent an op **p**

though they are reinforced by th

territorial identifications is there **f**

constantly influences and reinfor **c**

The Family and Descent Groups

The family is a descent grou **p**,

are extensions of the nuclear fam

of its founding ancestor, and th **e**

being an intertwining of agnat **i**

interfamily network.

The Family and Class Groups

In view of the significance of t **h**

role of the descent groups in str **u**

and commoners, the role of the **fa**

34. In tracing the history of Pajok, **H**

had four sons and a daughter: Aiwel, **B**

became leader of the Twij, Dhion of th

Howell, "Ngok Dinka" 242.

35. Lienhardt, "Western Dinka" 117.

The Family and Sex Groups

According to the principle of permanent identity and influence, every man must marry and create a family with him as the male head. Since polygyny is practiced, women are very much in demand and every woman in Dinka society gets married. Thus, for both men and women, until married they are affiliated into their family of birth in which sex is a factor in the shaping or sharing of values; if married, they are members of a new family in which sex continues to be a differentiating and stratifying factor.

The Family and Age Groups

Since the age-set system emphasizes territorial identification, the interaction of territorial and descent identifications is applicable to it. In initiation, a group of families unites its unreleased initiates into a *ghot thok,* which competes with other groups in songs, dances, and fights. In intersectional situations, they unite as members of a section, and in subtribal situations as members of the subtribe, the largest unit in which the age set is recognized. Thus, while we may begin with the more inclusive circles and end with the family, we may also trace the age set from the family to the more inclusive circles. Just as territorial entities are reinforced, even to the point of being controlled, by descent, so are the age sets. The age-set system is meant as a modification of the kinship system, although it is determined by it, and kinship loyalties are modified by loyalties to age mates. Indeed, it is sometimes said by the Ngok that territorial entities evolved out of age sets breaking away from the control of the older groups and founding their own settlements.[36]

It is unlikely that such dramatic breaks ever occurred, for, among other things, the newly initiated groups often do not own separate herds except for personality oxen.[37] Since a more indulged status is acquired on marriage, partition probably took the form of younger generations moving away with their families to new settlements without any dramatic severance of all relations. This does not negate opposition. Indeed,

36. Howell shows the interlinkage between the age-set system and the territorial structure: "Territorial sections (*Wut*) are explained by the Ngok in terms of kinship. The names of territorial divisions or sections—ALEI, MANUAR, ANYEL etc.—are said to be those of former age-sets and, in explaining the system, the Ngok seem to visualize a series of definite age-divisions. They . . . refer to a phenomenon of special significance which they call *biork* . . . an institutional battle between a younger age-set and a senior one. . . . The Ngok say that after a fight of this sort, the younger age-set, representing a younger generation, would break away to form a camp (*wut*) of their own and this would develop into a more permanent division of the tribe." Howell, "Ngok Dinka" 252.

37. See Chapter 7, pp. 245–50.

it is a more serious expression of opposition than *biork*—institutionalized warfare between age sets—because it is a separation, however gradual or peaceful. Since the age sets represent different families, descent affinities among them are too loosely shared to affect their social identifications, and the bond of age-mateship becomes the uniting factor. This could be why among "the Ngok the age-set system seems far more developed than among the Nuer, and perhaps Dinka tribes elsewhere, and of a greater functional significance." [38] Apart from the fact that the age sets constitute new family aggregates, the contradictions of Dinka social process soon begin to work to perpetuate old descent groups. The lineage system is so entrenched that while "each man wants to found his own descent group, a formal segment of the sub-clan which will for long be remembered by his name," [39] each Dinka is astonishingly proud of his descent, which is now for him to prolong, and in a new situation, old genealogies, old clans, old descent hierarchies, and old ways begin to root and even assume a controlling significance. The opposition is short-lived, and a new one begins to grow, only to fall again into conformity.

The Family and Culture Groups

The conditions of today provide opportunities for individuals to adopt new ways at a rate which may by far excel the rate at which their families adapt. Yet, cultural distinction among the Dinka is ethnic or racial in that descent plays an important role. A person is a Dinka not only because he conforms to the standard Dinka behavior, but also because he was born and bred a Dinka. Thus born and bred, he is a Dinka whatever his new cultural acquisitions. Cultural adaptation narrows but cannot entirely bridge the gap. This fact underlies the mutual ethnocentrism which often characterizes crosscultural interactions.

The Family and the Individual

In Dinka society, an individual is always a member of one family or another. So important is family affiliation that illegitimacy is unknown in Dinka law. A child is always the legal progeny of a family, whether that identification is also biological or merely social. Of course, there are social stigmata attached to the status of an adoptee and particularly to birth outside wedlock, but these never amount to legal incapacity.

38. Ibid.
39. Lienhardt, "Western Dinka" 117.

The Family and the Mythical Participants

Mythical participants are conceived of as individuals even when such conceptual individualization may mean multiplicity in unity. As individuals, they have familial affiliations similar to those of real persons. Indeed, on the whole, it is through the family institution that divinities and ancestral spirits lead their worldly life, and it is toward this end that procreation is pivoted. Even in the case of inclusive deities, the Dinka refer to them in such familial terms as "God of my father" or "God, my father." [40]

The Family and Unity in Diversity

Unity in disunity, so characteristic of the Dinka organization of participants, is the outcome of the emphasis placed on the family as a social unit. In essence, this emphasis is individualistic in that it is generated by the individual-oriented importance of enhancing and immortalizing the individual's shaping and sharing of values. As such, sentiment and united action are concentrated in the immediate circles. Since anyone not a member of this immediate group is an outsider, inclusive identifications are increasingly reduced by the multiplicity of intermediate identifications. As we pass the border lines of descent, solidarities begin to give way and there is cooperative unity only at times of great need, such as warring against more distant outsiders. Otherwise, internal disunity is strengthened. These problems are aggravated by the dispersed residence of the Dinka. Each person and his family want enough land around their homestead to cultivate their crops and graze their herds. These scattered residences show a sense of individualism characteristic of the Dinka, yet paradoxically combined with solidarities and a strong sense of communalism. So far apart are the homesteads of individual families that when a large-scale need arises, such as in wars, each household can only receive the message through runners, war drums, or war cries. In some cases, a group may fight a war to the end before allies know of it.

40. See Lienhardt, *Divinity* 122.

2. Overriding Goals

The Myth of Permanent Identity and Influence

The myth of permanent identity and influence is essentially a myth of immortality which augments and guarantees continued participation even after death. Procreation gives the myth its biological emphasis. "Dinka fear to die without issue, in whom the survival of their names—the only kind of immortality they know—will be assured." [1] Even when dead, a man demands the expansion and the continuation of his lineage. This is the idea behind such institutions as levirate and ghost marriage.

The myth, however, demands more than childbearing and child rearing. *Kooc e nom,* "standing the head," which the Dinka use to designate the significance of this myth, is more than *dhieth,* birth. As we shall see, a man may complain about his son by saying that he, the father, has not given birth, *akic dhieth,* implying that he is not proud of his son as a prolongation of himself. In this sense, *dhieth* is synonmous with *kooc e nom,* but the biological and social dimension of the myth of permanent identity and influence is more evident in *kooc e nom,* which can be achieved by adoption or by representative procreation. Standing the head becomes symbolic of a much deeper and more pervasive representational continuity. For the dead, it is in essence a transmission of this world into the hereafter or of the hereafter to this world through the memory of the dead and his experience. The vitality of this memory lies in the maintenance of conditions as the dead left them, otherwise they cease to reflect him. Since the degree to which one is remembered is relative to the significance of one's experience, the memory of the ancestors who have lived longer and done more is greater than that of the ordinary dead. Furthermore, the intensity of lifetime relations is an

1. Lienhardt, *Divinity* 26. Marquet observes the same attitude to children among the Tutsi: "When a Tutsi informant was asked what the people of his group wished for above all, the answer came immediately: 'children and cows.'" Marquet, *The Premise of Inequality in Ruanda* 82 (1961). Emphasizing the importance of procreation to Africans in general Radcliffe-Brown wrote, "An African marries because he wants children . . . the most important part of the 'value' of a woman is her childbearing capacity." Radcliffe-Brown, "Introduction to the Analysis of Kinship System," Bell and Vogel, eds., *A Modern Introduction to the Family* 13 (1960).

important determinant. Hence, the smallest social unit, the family, is the primary means to social as well as biological immortality.

The close association of the mythical participants with the principle of permanence gives particular significance to the use of the term "myth," but the combined biological and social significance of this myth gives it a form of reality which makes the usual conception of the word "myth" inapplicable. The word is already well established in the social sciences to mean frequently occurring or recurring ideas and operations, in other words involving practices, but it has historically and popularly gained currency as a means of designating certain aspects of folklore, and it continues to connote unreality. While its subjective connotation is important for our present purposes, the word is not intended to express or imply judgment of approval or disapproval, or degree of realism or unrealism. Instead it is used as defined by Professors McDougal and Lasswell:

> A synoptic word for perspectives, i.e., symbol patterns regularly occurring in practice, or reoccurring ideas and sentiments. The total body of the pattern of all perspectives of a value in a social contest. A community myth is comprised of identifications, demands and expectations.[2]

To emphasize the continuance of one's identity and influence in this world even after one's death is not to be understood as implying that the Dinka do not believe in any form of existence in the unknown world of the dead. Admittedly, their belief on this matter is complex and unclear. They categorically discard the Muslim and Christian concepts of life hereafter as introduced to their converts and insist that once a person is dead he cannot live again and be judged in his second life. On the other hand, apart from calling upon the dead in prayers, which implies a recognition of some form of existence, Dinkas sometimes speak of joining their dead and of reporting to them matters of interest or significance among their living. The existence in the next world and the continued participation of the dead with the living are not in conflict; they are interdependent. People die and disappear. The reality of their one-time existence remains but they also become part of the unknown which largely depends on belief. Continued participation is a physically and socially explainable immortality. These two themes become divested of much of their meaning if not seen as interactive and interdependent.

By emphasizing the survival of every individual through a lineage, the Dinka myth of permanent identity and influence gives importance to both individual and group identities. This is significantly illustrated

2. McDougal and Lasswell, *Law, Science, and Policy* (mimeographed materials) (1964), Glossary at 17.

by the system of naming. The Dinka do not apply one family name to successive generations. Instead, each man bears his own name, which is equivalent to the first or Christian name in the Western system. His father's first name is then added to his own name for further identification. This addition of the names of ascendants continues according to the requirements of the particular circumstances. Allor de Biong de Kwol d'Arob involves Allor son of Biong, son of Kwol, son of Arob, with "de" or "d'" standing for "son of." Some tribes use "e" to denote "son of," and some use no connective, though the combination of names implies it. Every child is taught from a very early age to recite and be proud of his father's genealogy to the most distant ancestor remembered. Each ancestor's biography is related to the present status of his lineage. The identity of the lineage and its influence are thus explained in terms of the achievements of its founder.

The communal aspect of the myth is also evident in the fact that continuity creates a chain of ancestors and their descendants seen as a lineage or lineages. In the system of naming, people trace their genealogy through individuals; but the clan, the lineage, or the family, as the case may be, is collectively called by the name of its founding father, that is, by adding a prefix to the name of the founder, such as "Pa-jok" for the clan founded by Jok, or by an explicit identification of the descent group as that of so-and-so. This segmental significance of permanent identity and influence elucidates the nature of the mutual, the competitive, and even the conflicting interests of individuals and groups at the various levels of Dinka society.

UNITY AND HARMONY

The fundamental goal of traditional Dinka society is social order envisaging ideal human relations in unity and harmony and therefore preserving the stratification of the myth of permanent identity and influence. This conformity tends to promote cultural continuity. Over this goal the overwhelming majority of the community see no controversy. But modern trends, both indulgent and depriving, have qualified its expression, and among the educated elite have almost replaced it with the goal of modernization and "freedom" from what is viewed as the yoke of Arab North colonialism. While these goals are not apparently in conflict, tradition produces roles in the decision process which are depriving to the young modern elite, thereby foreclosing freedom as a prerequisite to progress.

The characteristics of the traditional goal can best be described by examining a concept called *cieng,* which occupies a pivotal position in the Dinka community process. Dr. Lienhardt writes that "The Dinka . . .

have notions . . . of what their society ought, ideally, to be like. They have a word, *cieng* or *cieng baai,* which used as a verb has the sense of 'to look after' or 'to order,' and in its noun form means 'the custom' or 'the rule.' " [3] Father Nebel translates "morals" as "good *cieng*" and "benefactor" as a man who knows and acts in accordance with *cieng.* He also translates *cieng* to mean "behavior," "habit," or "nature of" or "custom." [4] But *cieng* is far more complex: as a transitive verb, it also means "to inhabit," "to live together," "to treat" (a person), "to dominate," or "to wear" (clothes or ornaments), and as an intransitive verb it also means "to last long." As a noun it means "conduct," "human relations," "way of life," or "culture." Wherever the word "law" would apply, the Dinka use *cieng.* This is in addition to the noun form of the verbs above. These usages represent a multiplicity and a unity which may be either descriptive or normative. In the latter case, an appropriate adjective is sometimes added. "To *cieng* badly" and "bad *cieng*" are standard negative evaluations, while "to *cieng* well" and "good *cieng*" are positive. Without an adjective, *cieng* usually implies the positive. This is the case in such common expressions as "This is *cieng*" and "This man does not know *cieng.*" Each value process has its own *cieng,* which is an inseparable component of the overall Dinka *cieng.*

While united in their basic goals, the identifiable components of *cieng* differ in meaning according to the context of usage. In these different contexts a Dinka knows precisely which meaning of *cieng* is in use so that there is no question of confusing the meanings. No question could arise, for instance, as to whether a particular usage of *cieng* refers to individual conduct or to the conduct of a group. Nor can there be confusion as to whether it refers to a single custom or to the totality of Dinka customs and ways of life. This does not mean that there can be no disagreement where opinion is required. For instance, whether a conduct of a member is in accordance with *cieng* or not may be a matter of opinion. Whether a particular set of facts invokes a particular rule of Dinka *cieng* may also be debatable. However, such disagreements would not be about the descriptive usage of *cieng* or its goal value, but rather about the questions raised by that particular usage.

In its various meanings, *cieng* emphasizes human relations. Even when referring to abstract rules, *cieng* is a "cultural process" in which the human factor is dominant. Emphasis is laid upon idealized human relations as an end rather than as a means of self-serving individualistic values, even though such values would ultimately facilitate Dinka approximation of the ideal in human relations. For this reason, deference values like power, respect, rectitude, and affection are the focus of *cieng,*

3. Lienhardt, "Western Dinka" 106–07.
4. Nebel, *Dinka Dictionary* 315 (1954).

while welfare values like well-being, wealth, skill, and enlightenment are seen in terms of the deference values. For example, Dinka education, rather than emphasizing knowledge for its own sake, puts emphasis on what constitutes good relations. *Cieng* is not so much concerned with wealth accumulation as it is with providing for the needy. In agricultural economy, for instance, *cieng* would tend to stress sharing the produce rather than increasing production. Sharing labor is indeed stressed, but only to help the owner of the field produce his normal yield.

Dinka perspectives about good human relations are expressed in the demand for unity and harmony among men and the attuning of individual interests to the interests of others.[5] This goal is more than avoidance of conflict and violation of other people's rights; it imposes a positive obligation to foster a solidarity in which people cooperate in the shaping and sharing of values. Coercion is contrary to *cieng,* for solidarity, harmony, and mutual indulgence are more meaningful if achieved voluntarily or by persuasion.

It is important to note the descriptive-normative combination in *cieng* as a goal. The objective is not only the improvement of human relations, but also the continued adherence to the norms inherited from the ancestors. It is in this context that "to last long," one of the meanings of *cieng,* is especially relevant. The "was" and the "is" are thus vital determinants for the "ought." The participation of the mythical entities is rooted in this conception of *cieng* without which the leadership of mythical entities would be restricted. There are, therefore, two levels to the goal of *cieng.* On its highest level of abstraction, *cieng* is a guiding force above Dinka community process. It aims at an ideal social order in which people are united in full harmony with no quarrels or frictions and with mutual indulgences. On the lowest level, it requires and generally achieves conformity with the sum total of community expectations, which are in fact segments of the ideal. Failure to conform

5. The importance of unity and harmony has been observed about many traditional African societies. For example, Professor Gluckman writes, "Many writers have discussed the process of law in tribal societies in such phrases as restoring the social balance or equilibrium, securing the agreement of both parties to a compromise judgment and, above all, reconciling the parties. This is the main aim of Barotse judges in all cases that arise between kin, for it is a dominant value of the society that villages should not break up and that kin should remain united." Gluckman, *The Ideas in Barotse Jurisprudence* 9 (1965). See also Bohannan, *Justice and Judgement among the Tiv* 64 (1957); and Howell, *Nuer Law* 21, 28–34. Dr. Elias draws a distinction between Western and African traditional law. He argues that the traditional method aims at adjusting disturbances of the social equilibrium and restoring peace and good will while the European method tends to widen the gulf between the parties by concerning itself with facts and application of legal principles, granting all rights to one of them and excluding the other without consideration of the social implications. Elias, *Nature of African Customary Law* 269 (1956).

is considered "not *cieng*" (in the normative sense of the word) or *"cieng"* (in its descriptive sense), which is bad. At this level, it is recognized that solidarity, harmony, and indulgence are not always attained because individual dispositions may be such as to disrupt these goals. *Cieng* provides for this contingency by measures ranging from mediation to authorization of violence. It is in this context that "domination," that is, coercive strategy, can itself be evaluated as *cieng* if it is aimed at pacification of disruptive dispositions.

Cieng begins at home with the family and follows the fictional concept of the tribes as a family. This is evident from such expressions as *cieng baai*, denoting people living together in the family, home, tribe, or nation. In fact, the starting point of the various meanings of *cieng* is "living together," which puts emphasis on the intensity of social interaction implicit in *cieng*.

Although everyone is a beneficiary of *cieng*, the position of the elders, particularly the father and the ancestors, is highest. If the shaping and sharing of values is to be augmented and continued in their name, conflict with them must be minimized and their indulgence maximized. In this hierarchy, God stands out as the All-Embracing Father, followed by lesser divinities. This gives *cieng* the attribute of sanctity, welding the events of the past to those of the present and the future and mingling them with the manifestations of God, lesser divinities, and ancestors so that the realm of the human and the divine are inseparably bound together. The practices of the ancestors are seen as the prototype of cultural heritage which is thereby elevated to a superior standing, bestowing a divine essence on human experience.[6]

In the light of the warlike realities of Dinka society, it seems perplexing that the Dinka claim to live up to *cieng* at any significant level. The fact is that opposites coexist: fragmentations and solidarities, stratifications and egalitarianism, harmony and violent conflict.

We have demonstrated Dinka fragmentation and disunity.[7] It must, however, be emphasized that together with this disunity there is a very strong sense of unity. This paradox may be explained by the emphasis on permanent identity and influence in descent.[8] Members of a kin

6. As an educated Dinka articulated it, *"Cieng* becomes that which God would approve of. And God's approval would not come in the form of sending a man to hell or heaven. It will mean physical health and prosperity here on earth." Skeptically, he added that this will of God "can be very oppressive."

7. See Chapter 1, supra.

8. The delicate balance between the exclusive and the inclusive interests in procreation are observed by Dr. Lienhardt: "The Dinka positively value the unity of their tribes, and of their descent groups, while also valuing that autonomy of their component segments which can lead to fragmentations. The bsais of this occasional contradiction of values lies in each Dinka's ambitions . . . A man . . . wishes to be-

group recognize brotherhood by reason of being the progeny of a common ancestor. "They help one another against outsiders, and . . . act together with little or no submission to any external control . . . And the freedom from domination which every Nilote expects as his birthright is largely assured by such bonds of common descent." [9] Yet, even within the nuclear polygynous family, the identity of the individual "house," [10] including junior wives with their children, is always expressed through jealousies against other houses which, while deplored by the Dinka, are nonetheless striking.[11] As we proceed away from decent as a unifying force, allegiances to the common cause are diminished to the point of mere fiction at best, except for age sets and the educated class, which present strong alternative solidarities.

Social stratification coexists with a strong sense of independence which creates a sense of equality, at least traditionally. It is repugnant to the autonomous spirit of Dinka society to permit any person or faction to lord it over others. While stratification existed, the more indulged were to identify themselves with the deprived and be indulgent to the more deprived. *Cieng* emphasizes social consciousness rather than equality; but social consciousness overshadows inequality.

Harmony and conflict are seen as sometimes complementary by the Dinka. In order to enhance the former, the Dinka believe that a man should reveal his grievance and if necessary fight for his cause, verbally or physically. Physical combat among children is encouraged more by older children and young men than by the elders, but it is not seriously disapproved of even by the latter if well supervised. Between adults, "fighting" with words (sometimes in insult songs) is the appropriate strategy, and warring is reserved for extreme exigencies. However, being predisposed to the concept of physical violence as a masculine quality,

---

long to a large descent group, because the greater the numbers of his agnatic kin who have still not formally segmented into separate agnatic groups, the wider the range of people from whom he can hope for help . . . in quarrels either within the tribe or outside it. On the other hand, each man wants to found his own descent group, a formal segment of the sub-clan which will for long be remembered by his name, and wants to withdraw from his more distant agnatic kin in order not to be required to help them . . . These values of personal autonomy and of cooperation, of the inclusiveness and unity of any wider political or genealogical segment and the exclusiveness and autonomy of its several sub-segments are from time to time in conflict." Lienhardt, "Western Dinka" 117–18.

9. Lienhardt, "The Dinka of the Nile Basin," 69 *The Listener* 828 (1963).

10. See Chapter 1, p. 7. A similar terminology exists in some other African traditional societies. See, for example, Schapera, *Tswana Law and Custom* 15 (2nd ed. 1955).

11. Since the concept of polygyny is interfused into the descent system, cowives' jealousies are equally pervasive.

young men continue to fight individually,[12] in interage-set conflicts, or as warring units of territorial entities.

The manifestation of conflict widens with the inclusiveness of arenas. In descent circles, there are methods of opposition sanctioned by the society and cloaked with harmony. Dependents can state their grievances to their superiors in a polite manner. On important issues, this may be done through a song addressed to the superior. In the case of women, there are certain religious rituals [13] which the Dinka do not consider rebellious, but which essentially are. Generally, therefore, violence is minimal in intimate circles. *Cieng* comes into grave jeopardy in the more inclusive situations. Violence among adults begins with the use of clubs for fighting on the sectional level, and ends with spears from the subtribal level onward. Thus, the effectiveness of *cieng* as a goal is in accord with the segmentation and fragmentation of Dinka society in which the family and the cattle camp rank high. The fictional conception of the whole tribe as a family extends familial *cieng*, but only with reduced effectiveness. Above the tribe, but within the Dinka world, only a measure of *cieng* is maintained; beyond this, *cieng* is too minimal to be of significance.

In the modern sector, a remodeling of the social context is taking place. The traditional familial bases which delimited the goals of unity and harmony are broadened, and yet are jealously and even violently circumscribed. While unity is now extended by the educated class, sometimes to the extent of overlooking tribal demands, a clear-cut limit excludes the North from the circle. The traditional theory and practice of broadening loyalties in opposition to a larger adversary is utilized. Tribal segmentation is recognized as a threat to the fundamental goals of the educated, but is overshadowed by the South-North identification.

Harmony, too, is widened to include circles far beyond descent or the tribe, yet civil and military conflict marks its limits. Though resembling the traditional age group, the young educated class no longer pursue warfare as their official function, as do their traditional counterparts. This is partly because they are "tamed" by education and partly because they regard warfare as the responsibility of the nation state. In any case, the national army executes the governmental military policies against the Southern separatist activities with which the educated are directly or indirectly aligned. Some of them do engage in guerrilla warfare, but the predominant majority organize political opposition to the national

12. In such a case they use clubs and spears. Adult males usually do not wrestle or fight with bare hands; women and children often do.

13. One of these rituals is to become possessed and make demands which are attributed to divinities or ancestoral spirits. See Chapter 3, p. 35.

government, and a small minority, though opposed to the government, are apolitical. In short, unlike their counterparts in traditional society, whose activities are sometimes in excess of, but not opposition to, the social order, the educated class play an oppositional role in modern society. In this regard, we have already seen how their relationships with the chiefs are affected.

The total picture with respect to unity and harmony is therefore one of paradoxes. Traditionally, unity and harmony are strong, but disunity and conflict nonetheless exist and increase directly with the distance from the family circle. In the modern sector of the Dinka, unity and harmony are extended along tribal lines and throughout the South by the educated, but the line is marked by disunity and violence between the Negroid South and the Arab North.

Part II

Deference Values

3. Power

The attainment and maintenance of the goals of unity and harmony call for authority and control to be vested in a person whose decisions pacify people. These goals are less effectively realized the further removed one is from the family level. Consequently, territorial situations call for more pacification. In order to understand the dynamics of power at more inclusive levels, we must first examine the power process in the nuclear family.

The decision-making process in the Dinka family must not be understood as one in which the paterfamilias is decisive only in family decisions; his role is best understood if it is borne in mind that the family is an all-pervasive unit. While in most modern states the capacity to partake in the decision process is based on age, the Dinka subordintae age to marriage and the founding of a new lineage. Even then, full independence takes place by a piecemeal process in which the power of the head of the extended family, even over his married sons, and his claims in the various value processes decrease with time. The authority of husband-father of the immediate family or the extended family takes many forms. In Dinka law, which fuses liability with responsibility and crime with civil wrong, it is the father who sues and is sued on behalf of the family, and it is he who pays or is paid in cases involving fine or compensation. This is consistent with his control over the conduct of his family. Thus, within a group, he is competent to exercise all functions. Should the case go higher for lack of a satisfactory settlement, his decision provides a starting point in the courts.

The power hierarchy of the family is headed by Divinity in all its manifold forms—the Overall Father, ancestral spirits closest to Him, the head of the lineage seen as the closest living link with the ancestors—and proceeds downward according to one's age and the marriage status of one's mother in a polygynous family. Women are in perpetual tutelage: marriage only transfers this tutelage from the father to the hus-

33

band. The more senior a wife, however, the more sacred cows [1] included in her bride wealth, and, hence, the more fully she and her offspring are linked with supernatural powers to reinforce the continuity of the family in posterity. In this, the role of the mother approximates that of the father, but is seen through his.[2]

Marital relations are characterized by the wife's submissiveness to her husband's will. This may be out of deference or in expectation of deprivation in the event of default. Deprivations may entail such measures as beating, or reducing the number of cattle allotted to her. A sanction which the Dinka consider even more serious is when the husband abstains from eating the wife's food, usually implying abstinence from her bed. Since this would deprive her of procreation, it is a serious punishment, and the husband is usually paid cattle of appeasement by the wife's kin, with little or no regard to the merits of the case. Another strategy is the threat of religious sanctions which endanger the wife's health and may cause death. Fear of divorce, despite its rarity among the Dinka, is also significant.

These deprivations must be seen in the light of the elder's emphasis on persuasion, which is accurately described by the Dinka word for court, *luk*. *Luk* entails an attempt to explore the roots of a problem and reach a harmonious solution. Resort to coercion is only justified when the wrongs involved are evident but cannot be corrected otherwise. This is presumably why a diviner is able to link illness or misfortune with the prior conduct of a wife. The paradox here is that religious sanctions apply even in the absence of the wronged husband's prior knowledge of his wife's misconduct. Hence, the infliction of harm takes place without the intermediate stage of persuasion, and this threat haunts the wife. Persuasion is also modified by the fact that the Dinka consider it undignified for the husband to make it a habit to discuss rights or wrongs with his wife. Habitual beating is similarly viewed.

The wife is not entirely denied power; there are areas where she has separate, though subordinate powers. The degree to which a wife participates in decisions depends partly on her own personality; it is also of great significance whether or not she has children, particularly sons, and

1. Although the Dinka honor all cattle as sacred, special cattle which are dedicated to God and spirits are even more so.

2. The Divinity-father-mother-child interplay in procreation as the basis of power is described by Dr. Lienhardt in this passage: "In Dinka there are important interconnexions between notions of creation and of fatherhood. *Dhieth* means both "to beget" and "to give birth to," so that verbally, the activities of men and women are not distinguished from each other. When a man was asked what happened in coitus, he described the physical act, and added . . . "That is called begetting (*dhieth*), and Divinity will then slowly create (*cak*) the child in the mother's belly." Lienhardt, *Divinity* 39.

their ages; other factors, such as her social background, or the character of her husband, may be relevant. If the husband has been unreasonable in the exercise of his power, she may complain to the family elders or even sue him in court, directly or through her kin group who continue to guard her interests. These are limited protections, for in general the Dinka call the wife a slave, *alony,* though the usage is more metaphoric than real.

There seems to be a correlation between the deprivation of women and a practice of ritual rebellion among women which, though infrequent, is significant. By this practice, a woman allegedly becomes possessed by a mythical power or powers.[3] While she is in a state of hysteria, elders of the family beseech the powers to reveal themselves and state their claims. The woman usually makes demands in the form of righting a wrong by a member of the family, particularly the head, or she may relay complaints from the ancestors for having been forsaken in one way or another. The outcome is nearly always the propitiation of the powers by dedication or sacrifice of beasts.[4] In most cases, the possessed are either junior wives or women otherwise known to suffer some deprivation. A woman who is too frequently possessed, however, may get the reputation of being frivolous and may be ignored.

In father-child relationships, the father wields familial authority by threatening severe deprivations. In the case of younger children, corporal punishment is employed. Where children are older, other punitive measures, divine or secular, are imposed. The Dinka link the father's power with his permanent identity and influence, particularly in his capacity as the procreator. A wronged father or a senior relative will pat his belly with the words "child of my belly" to justify his claim to authority. The Dinka believe that such conduct is dangerous to the child. Even without words or gestures, an "ache in the father's belly" represents the grievance the father feels in his child's attitude and threatens evil. This power is termed *kec,* "bitterness," a term well suited by the English translation since the power is rooted in indignation. Being the controller of all the family base values, he threatens with deprivations in all the values. In extreme cases, severance of descent affiliations may result. Since values largely accrue through descent, the severity

3. Interestingly enough, Dinka girls seem to train themselves for this practice from childhood games. In these games, children's game songs of a religious quality are collectively sung, movements which tend to prompt hysteria are made by some, and, in many cases, even when they do not mean to get into such a state, little girls become actually "possessed."

4. Another method by which women exert influence is through dreams about demands of mythical participants. The effect of these dreams is quite similar to that of possession by powers, and they similarly often end with propitiation or sacrifice. This medium is rare but effective.

of such measures cannot be overestimated. As Lienhardt states, "A serious breach with his father is one of the worst things that can happen to a man of any age." [5]

The father-child relationship is also one of interplay between persuasion and coercion, marked by the same paradoxes as in the husband-wife relationship. Conflict resolution emphasizes persuasion, especially with adult children, but the stress on religious sanctions, which are effective on the mere fact of wrongdoing by the child or indignation by the father, has coercive implications.

Rules of avoidance between the sons, particularly the eldest son, and the father have an underlying purpose of minimizing conflicts. Since the eldest son is normally the heir and the first to achieve independence, the rivalry for power is greater in his case. But the rituals of avoidance usually include the most senior sons, even though they may not be the principal heirs.[6] Since daughters stay in the female section of the family and leave the family on marriage, ritual avoidance is unnecessary.

Should harmony be irreconcilably disrupted between the father and a child, the loser is nearly always the child. A case is reported in which a father permitted his son to be imprisoned instead of consenting to his marriage to a girl the son had seduced and whose father would have been appeased by marriage. When an observer expressed to the son an opinion critical of the father, the son replied, "Why, is not your father like Divinity? Does he not bring you up and look after you? And if he injures you or helps you, is it not his affair? How should you be angry about it?" [7]

The relationship of the father and the child is not merely one of unqualified authority on the father's side and obedience and submissiveness on the child's side, for despite the filial piety demanded by the Dinka, there is a peculiar assertion of individual rights if they are suppressed by the father. As is evident in many "cathartic" songs,[8] conflicts between son

5. Lienhardt, *Divinity* 44.

6. Avoidance includes not eating with the father, not sitting on each other's beds, preferably keeping separate company. It is interesting to observe the serious, almost antagonistic attitude displayed even in the most affectionate father-senior-son relations. Such measures, far from being hostile, are calculated to maintain harmony in the home.

7. Lienhardt, *Divinity* 42. Of course the father's power is not all that unlimited.

8. *Waak,* literally washing songs, form another category. They are composed during a sort of retreat and they play a "cleansing" role. Hence, the term "cathartic" songs. There are periods when young men and occasionally a few older men isolate themselves in far-off camps. During these periods, they drink as much milk as possible, supplemented with meat. As its name, *toc,* literally "to lie," suggests, they lie down, fatten themselves, and move as little as possible. They compose songs about matters of special interest to them. Usually, these are pressing problems so that singing about them has a cleansing effect.

and father are particularly acute when the son wants to marry and start his own lineage, and the father refuses his consent or grants it reluctantly.

> Because of Awut,[9] I have become lean like a child [10]
> I say to my father
> I have become lean because of Awut.
> I am a man with a confounded mind
> I do not know who to give the seat of my father [11]
> To go and sit on the bed,[12]
> I do not know who to give the bed of my father.
> Our words have ended with the times he would send me for water
> And the times he would say, "Go and bring a mat from the byre"
> I would bring them to my father
> Is that not the value of a person's son?
> People have confused us
> I am like the son of a stranger
> My father has tapped his chest in refusal
> O clan of my father, shall I be only a tribesman?

Such criticisms are encouraged; the son's character as a man is appraised according to the degree of both his respect for his father and his readiness to demonstrate opposition whenever his filial rights are violated, or whenever he sees his father in any wrong. In exercising this right, the child must approach his father in a reverent mannor. This song, in which the young man whose father is dead complains to an elder against his guardian uncle (whom he refers to as "father"), shows the delicate balance of criticism and politeness.

> My great father, Majak,[13]
> You are our eldest,
> We the orphans of the clan.
> If you see me guilty
> Put me in jail
> If my uncle is in the wrong
> Tell him gently.

9. Awut is the name of the singer's girlfriend.

10. It is a commonly held view among the Dinka that the demands of marriage often make the bridegroom become lean, especially if he is not adequately assisted by his kinsmen.

11. The singer signifies the status of the bridegroom's father as the principal negotiator on his behalf.

12. Dinka men, unlike Dinka women who usually use mats, often use beds for seats.

13. The singer's grandfather's cousin. In Dinka usage, he is referred to as his "grandfather."

The words of an elder should not be rebuked
Keep it soft.

Such complaints are usually addressed to the person meant to be influenced, and in most cases he takes an amending action either out of
conviction that the dependent has established his claim, or out of affection. His corrective indulgence may even be the gratification of being
recognized, especially through the public medium of a song and a dance,
as the authoritative decision-maker. If the son fails to win the sympathy
of his father, he may complain to the lineage elders or even the chief's
court. Some sons seize their parents' herds and take them to the chief's
home to facilitate settlement. Where the conflict is too grave for settlement (a rare situation), the son may be authorized to disaffiliate himself
from the father and a ritual of severance may then be carried out by
the chief in court.

Although a daughter is also expected to state her claims to the father,
a militant attitude is less approved of in her than in a son. Nonetheless,
some daughters can be as militant and effective as sons about their rights.
Serious conflicts are usually over her marriage. She may desire marriage
to a man not approved of by her father and resent the man he approves
of. If a father is determined to have his way, the daughter is expected to
abide by his word. Through elopement or pregnancy she can, however,
inconvenience him.

The mother-child relationship differs markedly from that between
father and child. The mother is subordinated to the son. A son who is
influenced by his mother is considered "the son of a woman" and is
ostracized and ridiculed by his age mates and adults and not favored by
his father. A male child is encouraged to take pride in and identify himself with the father and the family at large more than with the mother;
this is partly because mothers are reputed to display jealousies detrimental to family solidarity. In the interest of the polygynous or extended
family the mother's power must be discouraged.[14]

The Dinka recognize that their antimother attitude is a concealment
of a strong mother-child relationship in polygynous families. Both the
child and the mother have little contact with the father when the mother

14. A song is quoted later (Chapter 6, p. 229) in which women are alleged to break
the agnatic ties of clans. Even the parochialism of clan loyalty at the expense of
wider unity is attributed to women. For the story of how women caused the original
break into clans see Nebel, *Dinka Grammer* 127 (1948).

In another story a mother influenced her son to lie that it was her father's sacred
spear with which he had killed a lion, thus making her father win the contest
of spiritual superiority. The father, suspicious of the fact, cursed his son to die
if he had lied. The son died. The father's comment was: "Let him be gone, he was
persuaded by his mother and consented to her deceit." Id. at 134. Such conflicts between paternal and maternal loyalties are not infrequent in Dinka society.

is nursing. There is a taboo against sexual relations during this period. When the child is weaned after two or three years, he is sent to the maternal kin, who call him by his mother's name.[15] This, if done by the paternal kin, is considered insulting to the dignity of the child, who should be identified with the father.[16] During this very significant period in a child's growth, the child is intensely associated with the mother. It is this which makes him vulnerable to the mother's influence—the very reason why the Dinka place such enormous emphasis on its discouragement.

Dinka mothers, realizing that their sons' rejection of their authority does not imply disloyalty, and being most concerned about their sons' image, condone this deprivation. The son's resistance to his mother's domination is a factor in his own position in the family, and an important factor in the status of the mother as well. In fact, a Dinka mother is said to forbear ritually the divine power to inflict harm on her child however wronged and aggravated she may be.[17] Should she ever lose her temper and curse the child, the Dinka deem the curse ineffective.[18]

The mother's influence over the daughter, though also detested, is more recognized and appreciated. Daughters being closer to mothers, unlike sons who after weaning are encouraged to keep away from the company of women, cannot equally resist motherly influence. Besides, their future tasks are those of wives and mothers, and they must receive appropriate training and instruction from their own mothers.

While the mother does not, or should not, directly exercise much power over her children, her power is expressed through male supremacy by way of her agnatic kin. The spiritual power of the maternal grandfather and, through him, of the eldest maternal uncle is considered very great. The Dinka regard him in certain cases as more "bitter," *akec*,[19] than the paternal seniors, even though he himself may be far younger than his sister's child. His demands on a son must receive special attention, and his share of the bride wealth of his sister's daughter must be paid promptly; if deferred, evil is likely to ensue. Thus, he is given priority over the father and the paternal uncles. It would seem that the

15. Thus, in the example given earlier (Chapter 2, p. 24), if Allor's mother's name was Nyankiir, he would be called Allor *de* Nyankiir by his maternal relatives.

16. The paternal kin do not object to the maternal kin calling the child by her mother's name. This is, however, a case of the institutionalization of competition.

17. The mother's power is not discouraged where it entails proper upbringing in the eyes of society. Only that aspect which impedes the objectives of society is discouraged, but because the line is often blurred, the total picture works against women.

18. At the child's birth, the mother, touching the child with the tip of her tongue, utters the words "May my tongue be ineffective against this, my child." In some Dinka societies the mother is not allowed to lash a son of any age.

19. Contrast the cursing power of the father.

repression of the tremendous affection for the mother necessitates its expression elsewhere. The mother's agnatic kin, being the closest by descent, are the beneficiaries.

The source of this power can also be more directly traced to male supremacy rather than to an expression of a mother's power through male supremacy. The patriarchal power of the daughter's father follows her and her offspring into her marital lineage. Reference is often to "maternal uncle" rather than to maternal grandfather. This, we assume, is because in most cases by the time the latter's grandchildren would be able to confer benefits, the grandfather would have died, leaving his eldest son, the maternal uncle, in his shoes.

Most potentially injurious to harmony in familial relations is the relationship between wives. In polygynous families, each wife is subordinated to a senior wife according to the order of their marriages. In especially large families, a set of pyramids, each headed by a senior wife, exists. Where hamlets are separate, the head wives are represented by wives junior to them but senior to the other resident cowives. The overall family power structure is in the form of a pyramid in which the most senior wife is the most powerful, the second the next, and so on. Decisions are made at these various levels through the representative head, although there is no bar to resorting to the male head. The arena is active, with each wife or group of wives trying to exert more influence directly on the husband. This is the root of *tiel*,[20] jealousy, which is thoroughly detested. Cowives often accuse each other of witchcraft; such accusations are sometimes expressed in indirect terms, such as in naming of pets.[21] The frictions between cowives, though detested by the husband, tend to contribute to the effectiveness of his control over the family, for each wife or faction of wives becomes submissive to the husband's will to win favor.

While the power of the mother is minimal, the position of the children depends on the mother's position. The eldest son of the most senior wife is the principal heir and in the position of father to his brothers and sisters, especially in the event of the father's death. If the son is an infant, a paternal uncle steps into the shoes of the father until the senior brother is old enough to take charge. There are cases, however, when the son of a junior wife may show such ability that he turns out to be the effective "senior" while the son of a senior wife may, if anything, remain a nominal head.

20. Although the word *tiel* is independent of polygyny, in most cases it calls to mind cowife relations and therefore polygyny.

21. There are some cases in which cowives named dogs "Snoring stranger," "A witch knows no ties," and "That is the way they behave" as indirect insults to other cowives. Where a husband's maintenance for a wife and her children was unequal to that of her cowives, a woman named a dog "One who is badly maintained."

Although children should defer to each other according to seniority, conflicts among them are not infrequent. In the case of half-brothers and -sisters, they are correlative to cowife competitions. They are more frequent among girls. In the case of full brothers and sisters, conflicts are far less serious and less discouraged. The Dinka consider conflicts between immediate siblings normal. Children are encouraged to reveal their grievances rather than nurse them against their brothers or sisters, provided that they do not reflect cowives' jealousies. In the case of little children, even physical fighting may be condoned. In the case of senior children and adults, persuasive strategies are used. When the father is alive, his decision, in conjunction with other lineage elders, usually settles the matter, although it may go to court failing settlement. Where the father is dead and a senior brother, full or half, is the guardian, most conflicts result over marriages. The guardian brother may delay the marriage of his younger brother to prolong his tutelage, protect cattle from bride wealth, or for any other reasons. The younger brother may, as in the father-son relationship, plead his grievance in direct talks or through a song ceremonially sung to the older brother in his home by the younger age set. The social impact of this institution is so great that, as in the case of the father, it often bears fruit.[22]

If the younger brother does not succeed, he may take the case to the elders or the chief, who would by then have heard of it. Since the younger brother feels more equal to his older brother than to his father, such conflicts are likely to be marked with a stronger self-assertion by the younger brother than is the case in father-son relationship. This may be expressed in self-help (e.g. by the seizure of cattle to facilitate settlement) or by more violent action.[23] Despite the emphasis the Dinka place

22. In the following song, for instance, a man sings against his clan and particularly his guardian brother.

> I asked for Nyibol when she was a baby carried in her sling;
> I asked for Nyibol when she was a child before she grew.
> The marriage is kept on the ground by clan Paguiny;
> The marriage is kept on the ground like a sacrificed bull.
> People, do not keep the marriage on the ground.
> Malual Gitjok, Malual de Kat [see gloss],
> Your brother is confusing the marriage
> When our herds are not finished.
> He tells me "Look for a girl."
> And then says, "I do not like this girl for your wife."

Gloss: Malual is the singer's brother, Gitjok his ox name, and Kat his father.

23. In one case among a tribe of the Bahr-el-Ghazal Rek Dinka, a guardian brother was unwilling to authorize and pay for his brother's marriage. His reasons were upheld by the chief's court. One night, the younger brother left the cattle camp a short while before his older brother. Hiding on the way, he waited, attacked him with spears, and killed him. Then he ran to his brother's house and killed his wife and child, and ended by killing the chief and himself.

on unity and familial harmony, it is therefore important to note these self-assertions and internal conflicts.

In their various power situations, whether it be vis-à-vis the father, the older brother, or other senior men, the male children occupy an important role in the family. They represent the continuum of their father's power and that of the original clan founder. They are the patriarchal heads of tomorrow. Important also is their warring skill. A Dinka male child is brought up continuously fighting. This fighting is much more than a physical expression of grievance against another child. It is partially a game and partially a method of segregating children's age sets. When herding or playing, fights are provoked in many ways.[24] They entail wrestling, hitting with bare hands, or flogging with whips or branches of trees. Sometimes they are more inclusive and serious, such as a mock war between two sections of a cattle camp in which sharpened shafts or stalks of durra are used as spears. The child's adventurous character is also developed by games and sports. He grows into adulthood measuring virility by physical courage and strength.

While the elders use persuasive strategies and resort to the coercion of divine power when necessary, the youth resort to physical coercion even when the elders' methods have not failed. Any wrong, such as homicide, sexual violation on a woman, defamation of an elder, theft, and the like are met with violence even when the law upheld by the elders prescribes civil settlement. In essence, then, the youth negate the collective ideals of the Dinka. Nonetheless, a father is greatly gratified by the aggressiveness of a son as long as this does not endanger the harmony of the family. Apart from the need to broaden influence and ensure continuity, their protection of the home is a factor in a father's desire for a large number of children. This was an acute need when there was no police force in the modern sense and punitive action against a culprit by the community at large was nonexistent except in a few cases like theft and witchcraft. Even then the youth were resorted to for the execution of physical sanctions.

With the advent of modernity the hierarchy described above is in a state of flux. The Dinka youth are beginning to see that the bases of power no longer need be only inherited; wealth can now be acquired by personal labor instead of by a father's gift *inter vivos*, a bequest, or a sister's bride wealth; well-being is less and less believed to be vulnerable

24. When it is a child's turn to direct the cattle in case they stray, he is told on his return that so-and-so had insulted him in his absence. He will ask the person imputed to have insulted him whether he did truly do so. The answer is almost invariably yes, lest one be mocked as a coward. Thus begins a fight. Adults may misrepresent to a child that his family honor has been injured by another boy, or any such provocative stories, and the result is always a fight between the children involved.

to ancestral or paternal spells; modern enlightenment does not accrue with age (indeed the reverse is true; while elders' indulgence lies largely in outmoded skills, the younger generations have been introduced to modern ones); new respect notions are generated; affection circles are changing and the intimacy and reliance on the family is becoming so disrupted that from complete family involvement, the younger generations, through education and travel, are becoming isolated from the family; sources and institutions for rectitude are altering; indeed, power concepts in the modern situation are in a process of rapid change. All these changes, it must be emphasized, have visible impact and yet have not entirely altered the situation. They are in collision with what is still a predominantly patriarchal setup.

While those indulged in the new values may range from uneducated laborers to people of varying educational levels, they are united by some notions of age. Most influential of these is the educated class, which in turn falls into different strata. In schools this class was educated toward the assumption of power from the elders while showing them due reverence. These lines from an elementary school children's song composed in the 1940s illustrate this early conditioning.

> I am a small boy.
> But I am the man of the future.
> I am the goodness of my land
> And I will do my best.
> Teach me that my mind
> May accept the word of learning.
> Learning is power,
> Learning is the best.

Because of the inclusive significance of this predisposition, it will be pursued under tribal power. Here, it is enough to remark that whether the cause be education, travel outside Dinkaland, acquisition of wealth in towns, or any such reversal of the old ways, the result is an increase in the demands of the youth. In this, a youth is likely to conflict with the patriarchal head, now rendered vulnerable by the increasing belief in the impotence of the old sanctions. More and more, cases come into the chiefs' courts in which fathers or older brothers seek the enforcement of authority or obligations on a defaulting member of the family: such questions as whether the father has authority to prevent a younger man with self-acquired wealth from marrying before his unmarried older brother, or whether a son should marry the girl designated by his father when in the course of his travels outside the tribe he has chosen a different girl, are increasingly presented.

The system still being fundamentally traditional, the loser, whether in familial mediation or before a higher authority, is often the younger person. On the tribal level, the patriarchal authority is upheld by the chief. Apart from the obvious attraction of urban centers as sources of modern values, the choice between submission to tradition and urban migration works in favor of migration. But a power-minded youth finds his impact on the national power process even smaller than on the local level. The more self-assured among them focus their oppositional efforts against the national government, which is deemed responsible for their deprivation.

Intergenerational conflicts in the family are not always so consistent. In fact, the types of conflicts which have been traced from the family to the national level are far less frequent than the conflicts which begin on the tribal level, with the family as a cooperative unit. The older traditional members recognize the merits of the modernizing members and although they view them with the courtesy and the respect due to "strangers," they also confer upon them a part in the decision process. The modernizing members, in turn, show reverence to the traditional seniors and their voice is channeled in conjunction with, if not through, these seniors. In other words, the forms usually remain traditional. The traditionals see in the modernizing members a source of elevation for the family, and look to them for wider influence in intergroup arenas, especially in the tribal situations in which the chief is the most outstanding character. The chief, with his circle of subordinate chiefs, views this remolding of the family power process as a threat to the traditional values and institutions. This is particularly so because the modernizing youth see the position of the chief as undemocratic. They may be commissioned by their descent groups precisely because they believe that in the tribal arenas, and especially vis-à-vis the chiefs, they are able to see things the traditionals cannot see, and therefore protect the family rights better. The modernizing groups are thus a threat to the chiefs. The course of this conflict, and its paradoxes, will be traced later.

Just as the tribe is family dominated, the power process on the tribal level is dominated by the family process. There is a segmentation of power such that each family is to some degree an autonomous unit in much the same ways as each unit of the social structure is autonomous. Certain families provide the specialized decision-makers at each level of the social structure as a matter of right dating from time immemorial and perpetuated through primogeniture. The restrictions of both descent and age create paradoxes in this process, although the conditions of modern Sudan are exerting an impact on the situation. The forces of tradition and innovation are, in fact, so strongly interactive that at the present time it is impossible clearly to separate what has recently been abolished from what is still in effect. The process is further complicated by the fact that various governments, while injecting significant changes into tradition, have sought to cloak their innovations with tradition. The result is both new practices in old forms and old practices in new forms.

In its manifold forms, power process on the tribal level centers around the paramount chief, his subordinate chiefs, and other elders. From them the decision-making bodies are constituted. Before the impact of the modern state, this power structure was pyramidal in a series of generally identical though stratified levels, but today there is a hierarchy in which subjection to superior authority and ultimately to the paramount chief has reduced the autonomy of the subordinate units to a striking degree. The tribal institutions still exist on the lower levels but their ultimate effectiveness is tied up with the authority of the chief-in-council with junior chiefs and elders. A discussion of the tribal power process therefore must focus on the chief, although it is also important to envisage him in a council of elders: even though such a council tends to follow the chief unquestioningly, it is significant to the Dinka that the chief does not act alone.[25]

The most powerful lineages, Pajok and Dhiendior, trace the origin of their divine authority by religious legends which are continually told to reinforce the contemporary power structures.[26] To an outsider the emphasis put on legends, especially in songs, is bewildering, and often the religious beliefs embodied in them appear archaic. But to the Dinka, such legends explain why things are the way they are. They give the social system stability and promote its continuity.[27]

The stories of authority also show the significance of primogeniture and the attributes of the chief as the father uniting not only the living members of his community, but also the community and its mythical leaders. The first wife is the first expected to perpetuate the role of her husband by producing the heir, and her bride wealth must consist of many cattle dedicated to ancestors.[28] Since a chief's senior wife has the additional importance of being the prospective parent of the next chief,

25. Howell, "Ngok Dinka" 262–63. See the Barotse system as described by Max Gluckman. Gluckman, *The Ideas in Barotse Jurisprudence* 30–32 (1963).

26. For example, see the story of Acai, Chapter 1, p. 15.

27. Dr. Lienhardt explains the significance of mythology to Dinka political theory and practice: "The preeminence of the claims of spear-masters, their hereditary priesthood, is established by myths which the Dinka recount in some detail, and with much interest. They represent the beginning of a systematic correspondence between religious conceptions and traditional political experience." Lienhardt, *Divinity* 171.

In reiterating the stories of the origin of power and its historical development to the present day, the Dinka do not merely attach pride to history. Their motive is to show the consistency of the present in the light of past trends to explain continuity.

28. Although the bride wealth of every wife should include such cattle and every wife may be referred to as "wife of the divinities," the first wife is more fully so than the others.

the community contributes to her bride wealth. Her marriage is often characterized by larger communal ceremonies and religious rites than those of other wives, and her success as a wife and mother is a matter of general concern and prayer. She is referred to as "the wife of the tribe" or "the mother of the tribe" and thus becomes a uniting factor, as her male offspring is expected to unite the tribe and link its leadership with the ruling ancestors.

Her first son receives special instructions, informal but intense, as the prospective chief; he is continually reminded of the responsibilities of his role as the unifying force of his own descent groups and the tribe. To demonstrate the group sentiment behind him, he is installed as chief with elaborate ceremony of festivities and rituals. Amid hymn singing and invocation, decorated with sacred ornaments and holding the sacred spears, the insignia of office, he is ceremonially lifted to the sky [29] to demonstrate to God and other mythical participants the community's allegiance. This must be done by members of the commoners' clans to demonstrate the concensus of all classes behind him. Once installed, the chief holds his office for life. Since the colonial administration introduced the idea of deposing chiefs, a deposed chief continues to coexist with the new chief. The question of who would be the more powerful, the government's "puppet" [30] or the people's chief, is not always easily answered. The one might have the power of the state to implement his authority; the other, the allegiance of the community as its traditional symbol of unity. Generally, state power tends to build traditional status while its withdrawal tends to diminish it.

The chief's status as the head of the tribal family is reinforced by marriages with the various factions of his tribe and other Dinka tribes with whom he has diplomatic relations—he is always the man with the most wives. The present Ngok chief has carried the strategy much further, partly because of the additional problems confronting his administration as a result of today's waning belief in religious symbols: he now has approximately two hundred wives. Since the rules of exogamy are very strict among the Dinka, these marriages link him with families unrelated to him by blood or close marriage affinity, thus augmenting his status and increasing his bases of power.

The principal task of the chief and his elders is to adjust human relations. Owing to the family orientation of the system, most problems of social relations are either familial or interfamilial. Within the family they concern individuals; outside the family they often concern groups, although such groups are usually represented by individuals. When

29. Hence the terms *jot nhial*, "raising up," and *dom*, "holding," used to designate the ceremony.

30. See Henderson, *The Sudan* 163 (1965).

there is a disaster such as crop failure or epidemic, his task is seen as one of mediating between the empirical and the mythical participants to correct the loss of harmony and unity believed to have caused the problem. Even in these cases, however, the ancestors or divinities are invoked as members of one family group or another. In inclusive situations the mythical members of the chiefly descent groups are invoked as protectors of the whole tribe. This is revealed in a song, now sung on the inauguration of every Ngok paramount chief, which was first sung on the installation of Kwoldit,[31] an ancestor of the present paramount chief, by Kiec, his age set.

> Dongbek [32] has honored us with Kwol
> "Kiec," he said, "this is a ray to lighten your way
> May Kwol give you the life of my father, Bulabek."
> On our way through the land of Bulabek,
> We had no chief to guide our way
> No chief to arrange our words
> Kiec, this is the light to brighten our path
> The light to show us the words of truth.[33]

The functions of the chief-in-council are manifold. He is the community policy-maker. He regulates the markets, traditional and modern, within his jurisdiction. He collects taxes, which in the past were composed of gifts of grain and livestock to the chief but today are paid to the government in cash. He supervises health facilities. He is also associated with education within the tribe and presides over the committee for admissions to the elementary schools. In short, his role includes all fields of governmental control. In the traditional aspects of these fields as well as those in which he has been specifically given authority, he legislates, adjudicates, administers, and executes.[34]

The role of the chief goes even further than these functions may indicate. He is expected to indulge his community, both as a collectivity and as individuals. The continuous theme of self-sacrifice in the stories of chiefly families is a testimony to the responsibility his position bestows upon him. A needy person, whatever his need, looks to the chief for personal remedy. In order to meet these responsibilities, the chief must be endowed with all the values essential for his duty, and hence he should be the tribe's most indulged and most indulging person, with no favoritism to his immediate descent groups or to any who may wish to

31. *Dit* means "great" or "senior."

32. Kwol's father.

33. For the religious significance of illumination and enlightenment which confer divine wisdom see Chapter 10, p. 316.

34. But while his authority is thus pervasive, his powers are limited.

unduly influence him.[35] Logically, then, the chief should be most receptive to new practices which will maximize his values and therefore increase his indulgence to the community, and the Ngok chief has in fact been the leader of Ngok social change. This has consistently been a selective innovation, weaving the new with the old while preserving the chief's distinctively Dinka character. This is part of Ngok Dinka expectation, as reflected in these lines from a song in praise of the late chief Kwol Arob:

> O Kwol, keep the people of your father
> And lead them to the people of the world.

This by no means contradicts Ngok Dinka conservatism. Innovation is so restrained and selective that it reinforces rather than threatens tradition. It is this linkage of the old and the new which gives the chief the experience essential to his unique position, thus equipping him to continue the heritage. When a stranger comes into the tribe, it is the chief's function to meet him first. What follows from an extraordinary meeting may be a matter of exaggeration and fantasy. Small incidents may become miracles to be recounted as manifestations of the divine powers which have descended through the divine ancestry of the chief. When, for instance, the Northern nationalist leader Mohammed Ahmed, the Mahdi, overthrew the Turko-Egyptian administration with very rudimentary weapons, the Dinka were enraptured by the fall of a government which had more or less institutionalized slavery, and the name of the Mahdi as the Guided One was echoed among the Dinka. Arob Biong, an ancestor of the present chief, went to see him, as did many of the Kordofan chiefs. He was impressed by the holiness of the Mahdi and even named one of his sons begotten during this visit Mahdi. The Mahdi became accepted in the lineage as a divinity. When it became apparent that the change was not to their advantage and that slavery, rather than eradicated, was even more overt, the Dinka successfully resisted the Mahdist regime, but continued to assimilate the concept of the Guided One into their religious thought. Mahdi became a divinity linked with Deng, the divinity most common to chiefly families. They even prayed to this new divinity to help them during the disruptions of the Mahdi's

---

35. This song shows such expectation.

> Deng does not know his father
> Deng does not know his mother
> Deng "the Decorated One"
> The Chief does not know bias
> The Chief is never bribed
> Deng, go ahead in the lead,
> Go ahead.

own revolution. The following hymn recorded and translated by Dr. Lienhardt,[36] illustrates the point.

It is Mahdi [37] the son of Deng [38]
To whom we ants [39] pray on earth, our Deng
We invoke the clan-divinity along with Deng
The ant-men have been miserable for eight years,[40]
What hurt us in the past [41]
What the creator [prophet] [42] from above spoke of.
It is to Mahdi son of Deng we ants pray below, Our Deng
We invoke the clan-divinity and Longar.[43]

When, during British rule, Chief Kwol [44] traveled by airplane, his flight became linked with the powers of divinity. It is only when change takes the form of revolution that the guidance of the chief becomes undermined, since he himself lags behind. But even here, the competition is largely internal, for we find that the most educated of the Ngok Dinka are from the families of chiefs, and especially the paramount chief's household. This value position, though not occupied by the chief himself, is associated by the Dinka with chieftains and gives the sons of chiefs a special responsibility in the eyes of the community. Their expected role of pioneering leadership, though interpreted in terms of tradition, has always kept the Ngok chief above his society and faciliated his functions.[45]

In carrying out his duties, and in accordance with the overriding goals of the Dinka community, the chief-in-council is supposed to emphasize persuasion rather than coercion. Indeed, when one recalls that *luk*, "to

36. Lienhardt, *Divinity* 164–65.

37. As the Dinka have no letter *h*, "Mahdi" is pronounced "Maadi."

38. An important divinity of Pajok lineage. About divinity Deng in general, see Lienhardt, *Divinity* 90–103.

39. The Dinka symbolize man as an ant in relation to God.

40. It is not clear which period is referred to, but it might be the period of the wars of slavery or of resistance to colonialism.

41. Again the period meant is not clear.

42. This probably refers to Deng. As we saw earlier (Chapter 1, pp. 14–15) the Dinka conceive of divine power as a unity in multiplicity, so that any mythical participant, such as the one referred to here as prophet, is also seen as creator.

43. The singer is a descendant of Ayuel Longar, a cultural hero.

44. Chief Kwol succeeded his father, Arob, the first Ngok chief to come into contact with the Anglo-Egyptian government. See Henderson, "Note on the Migration of the Missiriya Tribe into South West Kardofan," 22 *Sudan Notes and Records* 61–72 (1938). See also Henderson, "Sudan Reminiscences" 14 (1962; unpublished).

45. As Dr. Lienhardt observes of Dinka prophets and chiefs of the spear in general, "they correspond to the balance of change and permanence of their life which the Dinka encounter in experiences of foreign influence and control." Lienhardt, *Divinity* 170.

persuade," also means "court" or "trial," [46] it can be understood that litigation among the Dinka is not a fight in court. The chief and elders are mediators whose aim is to reconcile the adversaries. Unless they succeed in this, the conflict is not adequately resolved. Every detail is examined, every chief and elder who wishes to be heard is heard, and a general dialogue of persuasion continues until the alleged wrong is revealed to the party at fault and the parties concur.[47] In serious cases, when a final settlement is reached, a ceremony of reconciliation usually follows either in front of the chief or privately. Only then is the case fully resolved and harmony restored.

The chief is endowed with the divine power of life and death, and other forms of indulgence and deprivation. This can indeed be very awesome, since his subjects may not be sure of what amounts to an offense deserving a curse. However coercive this may be, the Dinka know that the chief should not err and invoke the divine power unjustifiably or it will be ineffective. Consequently, the fear of the chief's religious sanction is not as awesome as it might seem. Persuasion is still his primary tool.[48]

46. See also id. at 248.

47. Dr. Lienhardt made the following observation about Nilotic procedure of settling disputes: "I suppose anyone would agree that one of the most decisive marks of a society we should call in a spiritual sense 'civilized' is a highly-developed sense and practice of justice, and here the Nilotics, with their intense respect for the personal independence and dignity of themselves and others, may be superior to societies more civilized in the material sense. . . . The Dinka and the Nuer are a warlike people; and have never been slow to assert their rights as they see them by physical force. Yet, if one sees Dinka trying to resolve a dispute, according to their own customary law, there is often a reasonableness and a gentleness in their demeanour, a courtesy and a quietness in the speech of those elder men superior in status and wisdom, an attempt to get at the whole truth of the situation before them. . . ." Lienhardt, "The Dinka of the Nile Basin," 69 *The Listener* 828 (1963).

For the importance of concurrence and persuasion in other African traditional societies, see for example, Bohannon, *Justice and Judgement among the Tiv* 64 (1957): "Tiv litigants would seem to believe that the proper and correct solution to a dispute 'exists.' It 'is.' The task of the judges is to find it. . . . When a right decision has been reached both litigants will concur on it, even though the particular judgement may not be wholly in favor of either."

48. Dr. Howell has explained the persuasive role of the Ngok Dinka chief: "The *bany de ring* . . . cannot impose his authority without the consent of the people. In this sense, he represents the "voice of the people" and articulates their wishes. He is invited to arbitrate and by patient persuasion leads the disputants to reach a compromise. This attitude is still apparent in the work of any Dinka Court just as it is among the Nuer. The *bany de ring* has, of course, ritual powers which strengthen and emphasize his function in society as a peace-maker. He articulates moral values inherent in the social system. He has the power to curse but is not expected to use his powers to his own ends and certainly does not impose his authority by threat of

The chief's office is particularly alien to physical coercion as a means of implementing policies. He should not back physical force as a sanction. He should not even see blood. In the case of aggression on his tribe, when force is deemed necessary to stop force, the chief should pray for victory far away from the battlefield. In a war between his own subtribes, the chief, being the uniting element, should not take sides, and his prayers for victory take a preventive form. He may draw a symbolic line, place his sacred spear on it, and pray that heavy casualties be inflicted on any group crossing the line in disobedience of his orders against fighting. This might even be his own group.

While the tribe unites behind the chief, and the chief, with his council of elders, strives for harmony, there are paradoxes of disunity and conflict over power which in the past were narrowed by the recognition of only a few lineages as the wielders of tribal power. The fact that, generally speaking, identical powers were wielded on the descent level and on the tribal level minimized the motivation for power among the commoners, although in rare cases dissatisfied commoners might disaffiliate themselves and join the jurisdiction of another chief. Nowadays, individuals may still disaffiliate themselves by changing residence, but a collective action of that sort would most probably be disallowed.

More serious are the conflicts between and within the Pajok and Dhiendior lineages.[49] The subordination of the one to the other was traditionally expressed in a form of division of powers which tended to minimize tension between them. Since settlement of feuds was the most important function of the chief, the division of power was over jurisdiction in homicides and other bodily injuries. The Dhiendior had jurisdiction where these were inflicted by clubs, and the Pajok assumed power where spears were used. This is significant because clubs are used on the sectional level and spears on the subtribal level. Howell states, "The distinction of functions indicates that the Dhiendior only arbitrate in localized incidents, while the Pajok can, theoretically, be called in

---

curse, unless, in so doing, he is in fact representing the opinion of the more level-headed elements." Howell, "Ngok Dinka" 262–63.

Dr. Elias has also observed about African rulers in general that "it is not the possession of sheer force that secures obedience to a King's or Chief's order. The African ruler is regarded as endowed with all the attributes of worldly power so that he can promote the well-being of his people in the ways and to the extent acceptable to them. His is not the role of a masterful overlord who can by arbitrary exercise of power impose his will upon the masses. And this is so even though he is clothed with the aura of mystical majesty." Elias, *Nature of African Customary Law* 22 (1956).

49. For the rivalry between Dinka spear chiefs in general, see Lienhardt, *Divinity* 212–18.

when the dispute reaches the tribal level." [50] Political opposition is further reduced by continuous intermarriage between the Pajok and the Dhiendior so that the chief and his deputy are always related by blood or by marriage. Nonetheless, conflicts do occur.[51] In the past, such conflicts might lead to disaffiliation, with the deputy chief terminating his allegiance to the paramount chief and setting up a new group, though the whole of his own lineage would not necessarily follow him since, among themselves, the struggle for power and jealousies would also exist.

The struggle for power within ruling families is essentially not different from the family frictions discussed earlier, but more intensified by the importance of the disputed positions. Conflicts may be between father and son, between brothers, or between other members of the extended family. The areas of conflict are innumerable, but one can single out competition over succession as an outstanding point of confrontation.

It is perhaps worth emphasizing that competition for power between and within the chiefly clans did not normally place in question the fundamental acceptance of the chief as the uniting leader. Rarely did people break away from his authority, though frictions and jealousies did create opposition groups both within and without his descent. This opposition was often subtle, so that half-brothers or chiefs known to be in opposition might nonetheless appear united and in agreement.

Understanding the intricate balance of these oppositional practices will explain the tremendous allegiance and reverence the Ngok have had for their chiefs for centuries. It has been facilitated by the fact that the paramount chief as an individual and as a member of a descent group consistently occupied or was believed to occupy an elite position in respect to all values. Nonetheless, it is significant that his position has always been competitive, so that the questionableness of individual attributes has always been combined with the unquestioned acceptance of the institution.

50. Howell, "Ngok Dinka" 263.

51. In the stories of chiefly families it is said that Longar, as ancestor of the Dhiendior clan, contested Jok of the Pajok clan over chieftainship by claiming greater spiritual power. Longar challenged Jok that each should invoke his sacred bull and let them fight. The result was to determine who was the more divinely inspired leader. After much provocation, Jok accepted the challenge. Jok's bull won decisively. The question of Pajok-Dhiendior struggle over power is not a matter of ancient history. It occurred again between the late chiefs Kwol Arob of Pajok and Jipur Allor of Dhiendior, the respective father and cousin of the present chiefs Deng Majok and Deng Akonon. More recently, a conflict occurred between Deng Majok and Col Jipur, the son of the late chief Jipur Allor. With the intervention of state administration, the matter was resolved with Col Jipur being deposed. His uncle, Deng Akonon, who had unsuccessfully contested Col Jipur by claiming that the authority was in fact his father's, took over from Col Jipur.

More paradoxical than the competition for power among chiefly families is the role of warrior generations. Here, intergenerational competition for power, disobedience and criticism of authority, and the excessive use of violence all interact simultaneously. The younger generations do not participate in authoritative decision-making, and even when a relatively young man is favored by rules of primogeniture to be chief, his office demands of him the attributes of an elder. Thus, the respective roles of the elders and the younger generations are diametrically opposed in a way which shows a correlation between deprivation in civil power and resorting to unauthorized strategies.

While the chief is an all-embracing father to young warriors, a challenge to his authority is a gesture of manly courage. A debtor who is unwilling to surrender a cow in execution of his debt may consider it manly wit to avoid litigation, even if it means disobeying an order to appear in court.[52] The following lines, though extreme, illustrate something of the administrative problems posed by the independent character of warriors and the overemphasis on the family as a unit of social order.

> My grandfather was a warrior and knew no master,
> And knew no master of the fishing spear
> And sought a club and struck and killed the master of fishing spear
> And called upon the clan divinity of his own father.[53]

A young man who has gone to far-off grazing areas in violation of the chief's orders may take pride in such a challenge to authority. A young man accused of having seduced a girl or committed adultery will insist on denying it to confound the court.[54] The chief and his court are likely

---

52. Such is the pride shown by this song.

> I have avoided the chief;
> When he went that way,
> I came this way;
> And when he came this way,
> I went that way.
> I dodged the chief like a spear,
> And then I followed his steps.
> I confuse the matter like the war cries of a liar,
> Then I abandon it all,
> No one will ask me.

53. Collected and translated by Godfrey Lienhardt. See Lienhardt, *Divinity* 18–19.

54. An incident is reported in which a man denied having made a girl pregnant. After a lengthy attempt to convince him to admit the truth, the court decided to put him on oath. This was quite unusual, for normally the woman is ultimately made to take the oath and compensation is imposed, but here the girl was rather confused about the dates and could not establish a prima facie case to shift the burden of proof

to be attacked in songs appraising their administration. Among the Ngok, the paramount chief and his senior chiefs, unlike the rest, are usually not attacked. If criticized, the criticism is communicated in a polite or disguised way. However, in the majority of Dinka tribes, even the most senior chiefs are open to insults through songs.

The paradoxes created by the spirit of warriors go far beyond disobedience and critical appraisal in songs. They are the instruments of self-help by physical coercion. It is the collectivization of the fighting roles of youth, moreover, that forms the role of the warrior age sets. Ideally, this quality is developed to protect the tribe in quite the same way as male youths are encouraged to fight for the family when necessary.[55] After the initiates are "released," they retire with their "father" who must be an elder from the chiefly clans and a warrior, and he instructs them on both warring skills and war ethics. They must only fight a just war, and they receive the blessing of members of the chiefly clans that God and ancestors may be on their side to ensure victory. Such is the spirit of this ancient war song.

> I remain, I do not vex myself
> I remain, I do not provoke other tribes
> I remain, I am a sacred bull.
> Those who point their spears at me
> Beware of the Flesh of my Father,
> Those who wish to seize my herds,
> Beware of the Flesh of my Father.

In the following song, the tribe acknowledges the power of their divinity to side with them should their own force be undermined. It is made clear that they were attacked and that they are defending themselves under the direction of their chief, Deng.

> If the word of war subdues me
> My father Majok [56] will sharpen his spears
> And he will give them to me.
> We have been ambushed in the camp.
> The spear shafts have turned red with blood.
> Deng asks, "Do I really have a tribe?"

---

onto the man. The older brother of the defendant pressed him hard not to invite evil by swearing falsely. The younger brother surrendered and admitted his wrong, whereupon his brother remarked, "Son of a woman; in my youth I would never have surrendered so soon."

55. In Dinka war, relatives fight side by side so that the notion of family protection reinforces tribal protection.

56. It is not clear whether a divinity or a human being is intended by this name.

"Yes."
"Are you really men who can defend the herds?"
"Yes."
Malek, Malek, who will conquer hundreds.

Usually, however, the warrior age sets provoke and fight wars even in opposition to the chiefs and elders. Where, for instance, members of an age set compose songs defamatory of other subtribes, or where they violate territorial boundaries in grazing, there are civil means of remedying the wrong. However, the age sets would consider it unmanly to wait for any peaceful settlement.[57] The wars they provoke are not fought by them alone. All, young or old, must then join, for to fear to fight in such a war is one of the most shameful things a Dinka can do, and such a person may never enjoy the company of his fellowmen.

The role of female age sets in violence is identical since they, like wives, identify themselves with the corresponding male age sets, who are in theory their future spouses. In war, they follow the men to assist the injured, collect spears for those who are fighting, and encourage them. In their war songs they say "I" when they in fact mean the corresponding male age set, just as Dinka wives do when praising their husbands in song. Even the aggressiveness and the disobedience of the male age sets are expressed by women as theirs and they take pride in them. Indeed, it is in the relationship of the sexes that such values as honor, pride, and dignity are most conspicuously expressed, and aggression and violence are common facts of such expression.

The violence of the warrior age sets is not confined to *biok* fights and wars. They take physical measures against a member who has disgraced the group by committing an offense or who has otherwise let down the group. Usually, such wrongs have a moral nature—theft, one of the offenses against which moral sentiment is highest, adultery, rape, or refusal to participate in collective labor of the age set, or any other act which the group would consider injurious to the honor, dignity, or integrity of the member and therefore of the age set. Usually, the members of the age set seize the wrongdoer's personality ox and ceremonially skewer it

57. An incident is reported in which a senior member of the Pajok lineage was in council with Cuor age set who were about to attack a Rek tribe. While this elder was counseling against the idea, the *awil*, a man who leads songs in war or in a dance, began to lead a war *dor*, a special type of song used to arouse emotions in peace or in war demonstrations. The *awil* got full charge of the age set and off they ran into war, singing war songs. The *awil* was a relative-in-law of the elder and, according to Dinka customs, their relationship should be marked by highest respect for each other. The elder shouted very angry insults at his relative-in-law, as the group was led in violation of his instructions. This story shows the importance of the age set and how it may overwhelm the specialized decision-makers to whom it is supposedly subjected.

with spears, killing it in a disgraceful manner to symbolize their attitude toward its master.[58]

All these manifestations of excessive violence could be construed as compensation for being deprived of the established persuasive strategies. It is the age set's only form of participation in power. We noted that if a young warrior happens to participate in the decision process as a chief or any such authority, he suddenly becomes opposed to violence. It is significant to remember that such a youth would not be really a representative of his group, since his new position turns him into an "elder." His group do not therefore consider themselves participating through him, as would probably be the case if he were chosen by them to represent them and channel their voice.

It would, however, be a mistake to overemphasize the competitiveness of the younger generations, as individuals or warrior groups. Essentially, even in their disobedience they are very obedient. Their opposition does not amount to questioning the basic structure of power, including intergenerational stratification. They are the elders of tomorrow and the vigilant youth of today whose role, though resented by the elders, is also admired and encouraged. This admiration and encouragement goes beyond necessary violence. A young man who herds far away in disobedience to the chief's orders is attacked, but his courage may also be admired even by the chief, and the chief's anger with him might soon turn into a smile. Important also is the fact that a man does not fight merely for the sake of fighting. Usually he has a cause, or thinks he has a cause. His fault may lie only in taking offense too readily or in taking matters into his own hands.[59] This characteristic of violence as an instrument

---

58. This method of punishing wrongdoers is also practiced by young female age sets, although in their case the ox of the wrongdoer's brother is seized.

59. Titherington during the early period of British rule observed Dinka preoccupation with violence among the Rek: "Hardly a man but bears the marks of severe club and spear wounds, and fighting is still the most important part of a boy's education. Having regained control of himself, he readily admits that his resort to the *argumentum ad baculum* has done more harm than good, and that he regrets it: he admits willingness to pay compensation for the injuries he inflicted. If he was the first to take up club or spear, he urges that insulting words, hand-blows, or the sight of his brother thrown on the ground provoked him beyond control. Serious fights resulting in several deaths have been known to flare up immediately from such trivial beginnings as a slapping match between two girls who both wanted to draw water from a well; or a small boy accidentally drowned in a water-hole where some others were swimming. . . .

"Mean revenge and treachery do not enter into their scheme of things. It is almost unknown for killings to occur except in fair fight, which either side could have avoided had they the strength of mind to do so; but, as things are, such a course would be taken for mere cowardice. The Raik life is still inclined to violence, but the meaner crimes which elsewhere smirch the records of police courts are notably absent." Titherington 169.

of justice gives it legitimacy in the eyes of the Dinka, and yet a legitimacy opposed to the overriding goals of unity and harmony.[60] It is these ambivalences which made the violent role of the age set a sort of institutionalized practice which coexists with the persuasion of the older generations.

The colonial regime aimed at reversing traditional trends without radically changing traditional values and institutions. It replaced segmental autonomy with power concentrated in the chief who continues to perform all governmental functions. The subtribal chiefs, the sectional chiefs, and the descent authorities were left responsible only for the administrative functions and were stripped of the judicial and executive functions now vested in the paramount chief, his deputies, and the *makam,* who in various groupings constitute the Ngok Dinka chiefs' courts. These innovations have resulted in a complex process in which traditional practices still apply, but with minimum effectiveness. All traditional authorities continue to exercise a semblance of powers, and most matters which reach the higher authorities will have passed through the traditional decision process, which is merely time-consuming, for in most cases the opinion of the paramount chief is sought.

Since he combines all governmental functions, the Ngok chief has become one of the most burdened of all governmental agents in the country. In judicial matters, at least, the result is an accumulation of cases; and even when settled, execution is problematic. The present attitude of the Dinka, being less a matter of *cieng* than of compelled obedience, is to refrain from paying the judgment creditor until the court seizes the judgment debtor's property (such as an ox or a cow). This may take a very long time, even where the unpaid debt is for taxes. But in all cases, the order must be given by the paramount chief or his deputies. In judicial matters, when cases reach the chief's court, those stripped of their judicial authority continue to participate and do, in fact, influence the outcome significantly. When they have been the decision-makers on the lower level, they act as informants to the superior court, and their previous decisions often form an important part of the new proceedings.[61]

Apart from the changes in the power structure, the chief-in-council has been reinforced with modern means to remedy the ineffectiveness of the traditional authority. In order to countervail the negative forces

60. Lienhardt, *Divinity* 210.

61. Only the *nom gol,* the clan head, whose function has become more specialized to tax collection, is rarely a participant in the all-embracing decisions of the chief-in-court, except where taxation is concerned. For other purposes, the clans are represented by elders who, while not given the specialized name of clan head, are important participants.

of tradition, the modern state authorities are negativing its positive aspects as well. The coercive strategies of the modern state, including fine, flogging, and imprisonment, were made available to the persuasively-oriented chief, and although he himself has no power to try murder cases and inflict the death sentence, he can sit as a member of a major court empowered to try such cases.

The initial importance of chieftainship among the Ngok, the reception of Arab political practices with their emphasis on social stratification, and the introduction of further emphasis on the chiefly status by various regimes all combine to make Ngok power structure even more hierarchical than that of other Dinka tribes and, indeed, of the other Nilotes.[62] The effect of a traditional and yet innovating leadership has made the Ngok political system effective under the new conditions. The Ngok have abandoned "living by the force of the arm" even more than the other Dinka tribes. However, the chieftainship is losing its religious sanctity and the reverence due the chief as a secular spiritual leader is now being replaced by fear of secular punishment. The chief and elders continue to practice persuasion, but to a comparatively lesser degree than they did in traditional society. The authority of the chief is therefore increasingly seen as naked force, and as open to criticism as it is feared. This is even more striking where, as among some Dinka tribes, a chief is appointed whose ancestry has no tradition of leadership, although a degree of divine authority usually evolves in consequence of such a governmental appointment.

It is significant that the Dinka refer to the government, even that represented by the chief, as *jur,* "foreigner." Thus, the sanctity of divine leadership, though not altogether supplanted, wanes. The traditional conflicts between and within Pajok and Dhiendior begin to intensify. Because of restrictions on mass political disaffiliations (which have been unsuccessfully attempted), these conflicts manifest themselves in political opposition. By discrediting the chief, his opponents hope to take over. Ambitious commoners who come into conflict with the chief in one way or another begin to agitate, though often with the backing of some members of the chiefly family whose expectation of taking over is usually greater. Complaints have been raised to national authorities which were calculated to discredit the chief in one way or another, although they have invariably failed to do so. Disobedience of the types discussed earlier also continues, and although fear of "naked force" predominates,

---

62. It is this point which Dr. Howell made with apprehension: "There is no serious danger in this except that former administrative policy has tended to build up an effective autocracy in an essentially democratic society; a system which might ultimately prove a stumbling block to the introduction of a democratic system of Local Government." Howell, *Nuer Law* 264.

some younger generations still view disobedience as a demonstration of manly courage.

In court, the chief and elders, though retaining a great deal of persuasion, are often tempted to consider themselves umpires applying the law and may quickly resort to coercion. The Dinka reaction to the police, flogging, and imprisonment is one of indignation, and to have undergone these indignities is considered a cause for complaint. Until recently, a policeman sent to seize a man's cow was likely to get hit on the head with a club.[63] Today, governmental punishment has become accepted as one against which there is no retaliation. It is something to be feared and yet to be faced with courage and without shame, unless the wrong was such as would be shameful by traditional criteria. Singing about prison experiences is common.

> Is there any man like me with Ajuong of my father?
> There are people with malice under the court tree,
> I hate the behavior of the people of Abyei.
> We quivered from the effect of whipping
> I slept with the remaining food on my side
> Like a lion sleeping with its victim ram
> I slept with a lump of meat
> I turned into a beast
> I am the man who eats the food of fever.
> O Tharjak of the father of Dau,
> Why have you abandoned me?

The picture is more complex than this, for the chief is still the persuasive traditional father in addition to being a modern coercive figure. In his traditional role, he is a highly revered and feared person whose word bears extraordinary weight, so that once he gives an opinion it is almost always the point of consensus even among those whose opinion has differed. But the threats and challenges to his authority prompted by change certainly have significance in that they have added to the intensification of the chief's newly acquired autocracy. In order to predominate, he now combines tremendously persuasive strategies in normal situations with ruthless coercion over those who dare challenge his administration. The result is an extraordinarily powerful but very controversial chief who combines the ideals of a Dinka chief with the tools of the modern state in intensified form.

63. A man proudly sings:

> There are no policemen here
> To be sent to seize my cow
> The only policeman here
> Has considered the words of the past.

With respect to tribal warfare, the effectiveness of the modern administration, especially during the rule of the present chief, has been
positive and fights between various subtribes have been reduced. In their
place, road construction and other public works were introduced by the
British rule and labor at these tasks eventually came to be accepted as a
demonstration of manhood. This was discouraged after independence
as a form of forced labor incompatible with "freedom," a change which
has left age-set spirits without a constructive outlet. To the same effect
has been the present chief's opposition to initiation. No alternative has
so far been suggested, and though the period between one initiation
and the next is continually lengthening, age sets have still been pressing
for initiation. They still threaten tribal administration by their coercion,
and nearly every year they attempt tribal war, which results in the state
police and sometimes military force being brought in to pacify them.
Since the warrior groups consider it bravery to challenge the government
with disobedience, the task is formidable. While subsequent punitive
measures may discourage expectation of another war, the effect of
punishment as a deterrent is minimal. To have served a period of imprisonment for the crime of warring is a heroic deed, celebrated by the
convict's age set with dancing and the slaughtering of beasts. Even
where the Sudan penal code has been interpreted as imposing the death
sentence on killers in tribal wars, deterrence has not been successfully
accomplished.[64]

Corresponding to the suppression of initiation, warring, and other age
set activities is the infiltration of youth into towns in search of new opportunities. In the past, such an act would have been regarded as dis-
honorable and a topic for an interage-set insult song. Now it is more and
more viewed as a manly adventure. To the economists of Khartoum, this
is certainly a positive trend. To many who see the social conditions of
these laborers in towns, it is social disintegration: they become exposed
to indignities far worse than those of the traditional and the modern
sectors. From an economic point of view, it means enriching the already
relatively developed sector at the expense of the traditional sector. It
also poses the administrative problem of tax collection and necessitates

64. A recent incident illustrates how contrary the result can be. In a war between
the Ngok and the Rek, two brothers were accused of having killed one of the deceased. The younger brother declared himself the sole killer. He was tried by a
major court and sentenced to death. When the death sentence was announced and
interpreted to him from Arabic, he suddenly burst into a war song in the courtroom.
The Arab judge, bewildered by this conduct, turned to the interpreter, asking what
that meant. Told that the convict was singing in pride and courage, the bewildered
judge asked, "Does he understand that he is sentenced to death?" whereupon the
convict himself intervened with the little Arabic he knew, "Your honor, I do." On
revision the sentence was commuted to seven years' imprisonment.

the imposition of vicarious taxation on the remaining relatives.[65] The
economic considerations of this youth migration will be examined later.
At present it is sufficient to note its link with the participation or non-
participation of the warrior age sets in the tribal power process and its
links with the national situation. There, traditional youth become more
involved in the Arab-Negro, or North-South, problem. In encountering
other Southerners, they not only begin to see things in common, but are
in fact encouraged to identify themselves as a group by the attitude of
the Northerners. In addition, they begin to see themselves occupying a
low status in comparison with that of the Northerners. The political
issues around the South-North dichotomy begin to be meaningful to
them and may easily be expressed in the traditional warrior spirit.[66]
When they return from the North to their tribes, it is among these people
that the traditional antipathies against the Arabs begin to take definite
political form as a South-North feud. This feud may take the form of a
civic political movement or military action.

To return to the interrelations within the tribe, while turmoil over
power exists in the relations between the chief and his traditional subjects, it has an additional dimension in his relations with the modern
elite. Indeed, the intensification of the opposition shown by his traditional competitors originates at this point of confrontation. It would,
however, be wrong to assume that the form of education from which the
modern elite has evolved was consciously aimed at creating a group
hostile to traditional authority. While children were taught to revere
the chiefs, education was essentially aimed at modernization, and its
implications were bound to create conflicts with them. Background information about educational strategies will elucidate the point.

Before the Arabization of the educational system and the substitution
of Northern Arab teachers for the indigenous staff, Dinka elementary
education was much more tied up with tribal life than is the case today.
Adult education was being introduced and children were encouraged to
influence their age mates and elders to accept education, then still unpopular. Thus, unlike their traditional counterparts whose education
consisted of fighting, schoolchildren were not only being changed by
education, but were being predisposed to engineer change in society.
They were also taught to revere their elders and tribal leaders: if the
chief passed even fifty yards away, schoolchildren were to stand up in

65. The Ngok chief sought to pass an order to stop this migration and force the
return of those who had already left. Being contrary to the Constitution, this request
was not granted.

66. It is significant that the recent clashes in Khartoum between the Southerners
and the Northerners in which several hundred people died were said to have been
provoked by the violent agitation of the Southern laborers.

respect. Social occasions were held in which parents and tribal leaders gathered to see children demonstrate their social responsibility and reverence to them.[67]

While schoolchildren were thus encouraged to revere their chiefs, the very modernization which they called upon the chief to accelerate was presented to them in a way which undermined tradition and the bases of the chief's power. Since most of the early education was through missionary schools, the divine prerogative of the chief was instantaneously invalidated by education. Far more than impotent, his divine power was part of a religious system which was presented as "evil." Tribal divinities and ancestral spirits, the backbone of traditional authority, became reputed as "evil spirits," *jak rac*. The outcome of this duality was reverence for the chief combined with repudiation of the underlying principles on which rested his traditional authority, for, although the divine prerogative of the chief is distinguished from "black magic," the attack was against Dinka religion as such. In the songs the children were taught to sing, praise for the chief was combined with the condemnation of traditional religion. This combination of submissiveness to authority and modernizing revolution which children implemented in various little but significant actions is reflected in these lines from Ngok schoolchildren's songs.

> We are an age set which respects orders
> We respect orders.
> Our young age set in white assembles in Abyei [68]
> The school is convened.
> The age set in white knows the words [69]
> I shall change the land
> I shall turn the land upside down.
> I am small, but I am a man
> I sit in the place where words flow
> Master, Wor [70] of the Brown [71]
> Our mothers all cry,
> "All our children have gone astray,
> The land has remained without a child"
> Mother, I do not blame you,
> There is nothing you know.
> The word of wisdom of the earth is creeping on
> It comes crossing the lands beyond

67. Among the methods used here were songs.
68. Ngok administrative headquarters where the school is.
69. Of knowledge and wisdom.
70. The name of the headmaster.
71. Wor's father's ox color-pattern.

In Khartoum, a child is born, and he goes [72]
Nothing subdues our determined group.
I called our group
And we laid the foundation
I am building my home
The home of the children of learning.
The home where words flow even at night.
Age set in white,[73] who write, mouthpiece of the chief,[74]
Write the message
The message which I shall write
The bearer cannot read
It will be seen by him who reads
Never by a pagan priest
Your priests, I do not honor them.
The age set in white knows the words
Brother who is still behind
I will leave a message for you.
When you come, do not be late.
Our age set in white is going ahead
Turn and see, turn your back and see
You are late—turn and see
The role of the age set of Wor
Is displayed with guns over the plains
The sounds of the drill are heard
It is the display of the camp of gentlemen.

The natural consequence is that the chief is divested of attributes essential to leadership. In all the value processes, the rate of change having become accelerated both by this formal education and by intense contact with other modernizing agencies, the chief suddenly lags behind the modern elite far more than ever before in Dinka history. Thus surpassed, his authority becomes exposed to more opposition. Because of their enlightenment in the modern aspects of the chief's power, they pursue the demands of their groups against the chief or his agents. Among these may be a complaint against communal responsibility in tax collection; or over the prior right of their group member to marry a girl the chief is interested in marrying; or over the legality of a chief's marriage opposed by some relatives of the girl on the grounds of alleged violation of the rules of exogamy; or over what they consider the unfairness of a special court decision, and the like. Such individual matters quickly arouse

72. To school.

73. Going to school is here identified with wearing clothes, which men traditionally did not do. The color white is identified with clothes generally.

74. As chiefs do not write, they must depend on the educated in this respect.

collective action on the side of the elite members concerned, backed by members of their descent groups and other tribal supporters. This means that the action of the modern elite reinforces the oppositional attitude growing among the traditionals. Nor is the attitude limited to those unrelated to the chief. Members of Pajok opposed to the chief may exaggerate others' grievances or their own to instigate action; agitation follows which may well reach provincial or Khartoum authorities. Although personal interest induces one to take such a step against the chief, complaints concern matters of public interest. The supporters of the initially indignant person may have had no interest in the cause of his grievance. Yet. it must be emphasized that the origin of the complaint always characterizes the issue as personal. Besides, as was noted earlier, most educated Ngok fall into one or another of the chiefly families in competition over tribal power. What might be a complaint in the public interest is often made in collaboration with these traditional competitors, thus overshadowing its public nature. In consequence, the educated class, despite agreement over the social interests involved, split according to the grouping of their traditional elders. Very rarely do they take joint action unbiased by these traditional alliances.[75]

In all cases, whatever the grievance against the chief, it is futile to complain to the chief's court, even though there are statutory courts presided over by his deputy chiefs. The result of such litigation is invariably in favor of the chief. Any serious grievance against a chief is taken to higher national authorities. The primary interests of these authorities lie in maintaining the paramountcy of the chief. His accusers are therefore always the losers. Those who have attempted to oppose him by arousing hatred against him or by raising cases to the national authorities have ended in jail.[76] In nearly all cases, however, they return, appease the chief, and are reconciled with him. Sometimes, a strong alliance follows.

Although such areas of conflict may prompt collective action by both moderns and traditionals, a more inclusive area of conflict between the chief and the modern elite is over the political problems of modernization. The moderns see the chief lacking in bases of modernizing leadership and also supporting the Arab North government, whose policies they consider both colonial and impeding to the development of the Dinka. These national issues are reflected in incidents involving conflict

75. The educated members of the chief's family, unless they be themselves in conflict with the chief (and even then in a less hostile manner), are sometimes described together with their senior as autocratic.

76. Such was the fate of one of the deputy chiefs and vice presidents. Under the guidance of the educated members of the family, he sought to discredit the chief. He was jailed and deposed.

among the Northern government officials, the chief, and the modern elite.

In the various forms of conflict between the chief and the modern elite he is fully supported by his council of chiefs and elders. The few who may dissent do not do so in the council itself but in conspiracy. Otherwise, the educated class gets the reputation of being "without hearts," *acen pioth,* and in Dinka usage the heart includes the mind. The respect of the traditional leaders for education itself suffers markedly, and since the chief and elders extend procreational conceptions to the tribal level and conceive of those in the educated class as their "children," despair is often expressed in such words as "We have not given birth."

Overshadowed and overwhelmed by the power of the traditional elite and unable to realize their aspirations for the development of their society, the modern elite migrate into towns northward or southward. There they follow various occupations but unite with the Southern youth in their opposition to the government. Their demand for a share in the power on the national level is overshadowed by the same factors which disqualify them on the tribal level. Political leadership in the country is explained in terms of descent and cultural continuity, a fact which gives party leadership to certain preeminent descent groups committed to Arabism. Seniority and experience, which are often generational factors, also take precedence over other qualifications. The importance of generational considerations in the national power process is exemplified not only by the position of the educated Southern youth, but also by that of the Northern youth. While the deprivation of the Southern youth gives rise to his opposition to the Northern government, that of the educated Northerner induces opposition to governmental policies and encourages membership in the Communist party and Muslim Brotherhood, both of which are radical in their own differing ways and popular at school and college levels. This membership, rather than essential alignment with the ideologies of the respective groups, is a form of participation in power. Most Muslim Brothers and Communists tend to abandon their membership when they join government service, for then they identify with their seniors to climb the ladder. That these form the bulk of the Sudanese intelligentsia was shown by the overwhelming majority with which the Communists won the graduates' constituency in the postmilitary rule elections in the Northern Sudan. Outlawing the Communist party without an adequate resolution of the factors involved only has the effect of exacerbating strikes, demonstrations, and similar measures characteristic of youth and somehow seen as indicative of masculinity, as is violence in traditional Southern society.

While we do not purport to explain the migration into the urban centers only in these terms, we mean to underline the importance of this factor among the educated Dinka. It is no exaggeration to say that their commitment to their traditional society is almost messianic and that it would oblige them to serve even under the crude conditions of the traditional sector. In any case, their objective is to change the depriving aspects of these conditions. Conflict with the traditional elite is therefore an important aspect of the problem. Nearly all the educated Ngok who had started with modernizing occupations within the tribe left one by one as a result either of personal or collective confrontation with the traditional power elite or of increasing Arab incursion into the leadership of their occupations. Examples of such trends are many. The first was the migration of all the Ngok teachers when Abyei Elementary School was Arabized. With this change, not only was the gap between the classroom and the home widened, but in addition the social activities conducted by the school to demonstrate the merits of education and induce change ceased. Consequently, the impact of the school on the society has been reduced. Local government within the tribe, once in the hands of a Dinka executive officer and his Dinka staff centered at Abyei, now consists of occasional visits by a Northern officer who is several hundred miles away and cut off for half the year because of inadequate communications. Other examples of educated elite migration prompted by personal or collective conflicts between the traditional elite and the modern elite could be cited.[77]

It would be wrong to align the chief unconditionally with the outside adversaries of Ngok society. The Ngok, traditionals and moderns alike, admire in him the strong character that has maintained the tribe's identity amid the Arab majority and Arab ambitions in Dar Missiriya District and Rural Council. Ironically enough, his support for the Arab government is partly prompted by the support of the government for the autonomy of the Ngok vis-à-vis the Baggara Arabs. Given his lack of education as well as the limitations on his powers by the centralization of national administration, his achievement is remarkable and is a source of great discomfort for his Arab neighbors whose majority votes in the council have proved impotent if opposed by the chief as detrimental to Ngok interests. The decision of the council in such cases is likely to be vetoed by the province authorities. Thus, while the initial decision in favor of remaining in the North instead of joining the South was largely

77. An agricultural expert who not only influenced people by intimate village-to-village contacts but also because he was a Dinka left and there has been no substitute. The local government accountant, a Dinka, resigned and left the tribe and has been replaced by an Arab. A Dinka who was supposed to begin a cooperative movement with the Dinka executive officer abandoned the scheme. Medical services, once administered by a Dinka medical staff, are now in the hands of Arabs with whom most patients cannot communicate.

his, the essence of his present support for the Arab government is opposition to Arab domination. The disagreement between those who are anti-North and the chief is therefore one of levels rather than of kinds. The chief views the problem in intertribal terms, while modern educated Dinkas see it in its national dimension: they want to join the South in opposition to the North, while the chief sees the immediate issue as the Ngok-Baggara dichotomy. Indeed, except for the extremists among those opposed to national unity, there are common grounds for agreement in that both the moderns and the chief call for diversity in unity. The local autonomy or federation demanded by the Southern elite parallels the separate identity demanded by the chief, although, of course, the former has wider implications. Despite their differences, therefore, there is essential agreement between the modern and the traditional power elites, of which both sides are aware. Here, the inconsistencies and paradoxes of changing Dinka society interplay. Although the traditional and modern elites are mutually antagonistic, they are also mutually allied. In quite the same way as the father of the present chief used to ask for his son's assistance in intertribal and governmental affairs, so the present chief looks to the educated class for advice vis-à-vis Arab tribes and the government, although the final decision remains with him and his council.

In the case of Southern youth, the problem is complicated by raciocultural factors. Not only are there discrepancies between the North and the South owing to the latter's lag in modern terms, but in addition, the criteria for qualification are along Arab cultural lines.

The conflicts in their widest dimension have negatively affected the positions of the dynamic participants in the various arenas of Dinka society and the Sudan. It is obvious that the government's goal of national unity, far from being approximated, is continuously jeopardized. The longer the struggle, the wider the rift between the North and the South. If in 1953 and even in 1955 the South had been offered the regional government proposed in 1965, the problem might have been mitigated, but by 1965 it was too late. The government has failed in maintaining public order, and the more it attempts to achieve it by coercive strategies, the more intensified are mutual coercion and the breakdown of order. The attempt to control the rebels without concessions is proving to be like chasing an unruly horse without grain. Just as such a horse does not care for the master's grain in store, the Southerners do not trust concessions by what would then be a victorious power. Of course, there was fear of losing face in negotiating with rebels at the Round Table Conference in 1965, but it is also true that negotiations following the downfall of the military regime would have been taken as part of the return to democracy rather than as a loss of face. As it is, what the government considers the prerequisite to order is only perpetuating disorder.[78] The fact that eight years after the change of Southern policy "tragic disturbances" broke out in the South, and continuously are intensified, is sufficient to warrant a reevaluation of the new policy.

The modern elite are also failing in their objectives of power and modernization of the South. The chiefs, as examples have shown, are poised between the mutual opposition of the government and the modern Southern elite. Consequently, they may win the confidence of both sides or suffer the loss of confidence on both sides, sometimes with harsh consequences. The maltreatment of some chiefs by the Southern rebels and their dismissal and sometimes even imprisonment by the government are cases in point. The bulk of the tribal community in the South are faced with a war and weapons even further beyond their comprehension than were the ancient wars against slavers. In this way, many of the tribesmen hitherto isolated in the tribal system with its limited but autonomous power are being enlightened the hard way. They begin to see the power that matters as a monopoly of the North, and become more articulate about their anti-North attitude, thus widening and intensifying South-North animosities. In short, then, the overriding goals of unity and harmony together with the objectives of the various participants have crumbled and are crashing down under the violent conditions of South-North struggle.

POWER AND THE LAW

The Nature of Dinka Law

The importance of power to law is made apparent by the concept of law as a form of power process. In the Dinka context, as in the African context, the interpretation of this concept has raised a controversy over the nature of law. Here a contextual reexamination of Dinka law is

78. Commenting on the turn of Southern policies and all the steps taken to implement them, a government publication stated: "All these measures were intended to promote a common outlook and a common feeling of citizenship. An era where the whole machinery of Government aided by an auxiliary of powerful command over the minds and hearts of the people: the Christian [mission] . . . directed towards inculcating the hatred of the Northern Sudanese into the minds of their southern compatriots was apparently brought to a close. Time and patience, however, are needed to uproot all the misconceptions and distortions instilled in the credulous minds by conscious indoctrination over many years. A change of heart, judging by the tragic disturbances in the South 8 years after this revision of policy, cannot be achieved overnight. Mutual confidence has to be cultivated patiently and consciously before the clouds of distrust and induced animosity are dispelled." Sudan Government, *Basic Facts about the Southern Provinces of the Sudan* 17 (1964).

attempted; the examination of the idea of law as a form of power process must therefore take place in the light of the shaping and sharing of Dinka power as discussed, and must include a consideration of the rapidly changing Dinka society.

Dr. Howell has argued that Dinka law was merely custom before the introduction of "organized force" by the modern state.

> By "Customary law" is meant the body of "Native Law and Custom" nowadays administered in the Court under the Chiefs' Courts Ordinance of 1931. Such expressions are themselves something of an anomaly if any strict definition of the term "Law" is applied, but they are sufficient to indicate generally those customary rules governing human relationships which in the past were subject to sanctions too indeterminate to be called legal, but which are now applied in the courts with the consistency and organized force sufficient to turn them into "law" in a more exact sense.[79]

He has expressed a similar opinion about the Nuer, whose culture is so similar to that of the Dinka that for the present purposes observations about one are generally applicable to the other.[80] According to Professor Evans-Pritchard, "in a strict sense, Nuer have no law. There are conventional compensations for damage, adultery, loss of limb and so forth, but there is no authority with power to adjudicate on such matters or to enforce a verdict." [81] When he later found himself using the term "law" in relation to the Nuer, Evans-Pritchard qualified it as "a moral obligation to settle disputes by conventional means." [82] Accordingly, he conceived of Nuer society as an "ordered anarchy." [83]

Without detracting in any manner from the appreciation the writer has for the works of these scholars, and before drawing a distinction between the traditional and the received Western conceptions of law, it is pertinent here to appraise these statements with the hope of dispelling the notion that the Dinka and the Nuer had no law. Such appraisal is important not only for purposes of accuracy in description, but also to facilitate policy recommendations. Being normatively ambiguous, the word "law" is associated with a state of social order that human beings desire by virtue of need for order. Although Evans-Pritchard and some of his followers, like Howell, conceived and admired Nilotic societies (e.g. the Nuer and the Dinka) as lawless but ordered, most people would consider

79. Howell, "Ngok Dinka" 272.
80. The fact that these studies have been largely done by the same persons or close associates makes the point even more striking.
81. Evans-Pritchard, *The Nuer* 162 (1940).
82. Id. at 168.
83. Id. at 296.

law indispensable to order, and their logical conclusion about lawlessness would be a demand for the introduction of a legal order with little or no guidance from the preexisting system. It is to maximize the advantages derivable from the traditional order that a proper perspective of Dinka traditional law is called for. It may be argued that since customs have now become recognized as "law" with the introduction of "organized force," the issue does not arise. This argument, however, cannot be sustained. The process of adoption and adaptation from traditional law is continuous. By operation of Section 9 of the Civil Justice Ordinance of 1900 (as reenacted in 1929) and Section 7 of the Chiefs' Courts Ordinance of 1931, traditional law may be accepted or rejected on the grounds of "justice, equity, and good conscience" and "justice, morality, and order" respectively. While these provisions acknowledge customary law as "law" in practice, denying it any legal status could have prejudicial repercussions in the administration of justice and minimize the assets of traditional law.

Howell's main argument is that in traditional society there was no organized force behind customary rules. "The primary sanction," he says, "and one which is most affected by the establishment of public security and ordered administration today, is the sanction of self-help; retaliation if a wrong is committed or the use of force to claim right." [84] Here, we see an indication of some of the paradoxes of traditional society which were discussed earlier. Following the argument that law enforcement was unorganized, Howell continues:

> Further sanctions are social reprobation, unpopularity, loss of the privileges which the individual possesses as a member of a community and which the community possess as part of a larger social group. Such privileges are both social and political. They are also economic, because so many economic activities must be carried out collectively . . . There is also a religious sanction.[85]

Strictly speaking, these measures should only be exacted with the approval of the decision-makers, which will depend on whether they are justified. In any case, they constitute one side of the coin from which a conclusion of lawlessness is not justifiable. Assuming that traditional power relations are unorganized, one may argue, as do Professors Lasswell and McDougal, that "law can be either organized or unorganized," and that "whether a general pattern is to be considered 'law' depends upon the severity of the deprivations which are involved." [86] No one can

84. Howell, *Nuer Law* 23.
85. Ibid.
86. Lasswell and McDougal, *Law, Science, and Policy* (mimeographed materials) Pt. 3 at 44 (1964).

deny the severity of the deprivations underlying traditional power, although legitimate deprivations normally follow a long attempt at persuasion and may take a religious or a secular form. Even if organization were
a necessary condition for law, what constitutes organization is relative.
The preceding discussion of Dinka society shows that the position of the
chiefs and elders in the power process is part of a broader Dinka social
organization. Naturally, as a result of the paradoxes indicated in the previous section, their effectiveness was minimized. Yet they exercised a
degree of organized force, and had a degree of effectiveness. Howell himself observes that "social aberrations and disputes were settled by the
intervention of the elders and in more serious cases by the mediation of
the *bany de ring.*" When he added that "this does not, however, mean
that there were anything in the nature of organized tribunals," he was
unfortunately assuming a form to which any law-enforcement institution
must adhere in order to deserve the term "court" or "tribunal." Again,
when he said that the intervention of specialized decision-makers did
not mean that "all disputes were settled amicably," he was only stating
the contradictions of Dinka society which have been pointed out.[87]

Indeed, organization and effectiveness in traditional society are easily
inferred from Howell's account. Writing about the Nuer, he says that
traditional legal methods centered around the leopard-skin chief as the
authority for the settlement of disputes. The leopard-skin chief had
great influence in the society, and was backed by the community sentiment. "His actions were dictated by political conditions prevailing
within a restricted community. The Chief was the focus of political desires and vested in him were the forces of public opinion." [88] Of the
Ngok, he writes, "The *bany de ring* have certain recognized functions to
perform for their people. The principal one is that of arbitration between hostile parties within the groups, the composition of homicide
cases and the settling of disputes which are too bitter to be composed by
the elders concerned." [89] On the part of the litigants among both the
Nuer and the Dinka, it was essential, Howell claims, that they desire
to settle their dispute, and would therefore enter into full and free discussion to facilitate agreement. They believed that giving way to the
chief and the elders did not necessarily mean "loss of face," because of
the sanctity of the chief and elders and their role as mediators. " 'Saving
face' is a primary consideration . . . in the settlement of disputes." [90]
Agreeing with Professor Evans-Pritchard, Howell asserts that "only if
both parties want the affair settled can the Chief intervene success-

87. Howell, "Ngok Dinka" 273.
88. Howell, *Nuer Law* 28.
89. Howell, "Ngok Dinka" 262.
90. Howell, *Nuer Law* 26.

fully." [91] The use of the adverb "successfully" implies that he could intervene anyway, though allegedly without success. Indeed, Howell admits that "it was . . . expected that he would make the attempt to intervene." [92] Once it is established that he could intervene without the consent of the parties, we embark on a complex set of circumstances and would not be justified in assuming that the chief would not succeed. It is said that his actions were dictated by the political conditions prevailing at a given time, on a given issue. This means that he would only act if the public sense of justice so demanded or at least expected. According to Howell, "If a man chose to ignore a ruling given by the Chief, he could do so with impunity, but if public opinion was behind the Chief's decision, he might lose the privileges which membership of his group gave him." [93] This was most likely to be a strong deterrent to the losing party and might make him recognize the justice of the case on the other side.

Of course, in any society, settlement of disputes by specialized decision-makers presupposes a desire for adjudication, though this desire may be held only by the complainant. The society may be represented as a party by specialized persons in a conflict initially private, as is often the case in criminal law; but without the complaint of the wronged person, the court may be expressly barred from adjudication. In certain compoundable criminal offenses such as simple and grievous hurt, criminal assault, and adultery, no magistrate or court can take cognizance of the offense except upon a complaint by the victim or someone else on his behalf.[94] On the other hand, in cases of homicide, a Dinka chief would intervene independently of the immediately aggrieved parties in much the same way as the state would initiate criminal proceedings. In essence, therefore, Dinka society was never peculiar in regard to the desire of the parties to litigate, nor can we confirm the thesis that the chief was only a mediator whose pronouncements rested on the whim or the generous will of the litigating parties. With all the forces of the community behind him, he was expected to be an objective judge, independent, yet considerate of the parties immediately involved.

It is misleading to argue that the Dinka and the Nuer were societies "lacking legislature, judicial and executive organs" [95] and to conclude that they had no law. As Dr. Elias points out, "it is highly doubtful whether one can say, as does Professor Evans-Pritchard about the Nuer,

91. Id. at 28.

92. Id. at 27.

93. Id. at 29.

94. See Sudan Code of Criminal Procedure, 1925.

95. Evans-Pritchard, "The Nuer," in Fortes and Evans-Pritchard, eds., *African Political Systems* 296 (1940).

that an African society can be so small in its scale of social organization that it may be said to have no system of law. . . . Since certain fundamental conditions must subsist for human life to be possible in any part of the world, the task of African law, as of English law, cannot differ very much however widely their modes of operation may differ." [96] Even now that the Dinka have courts set up by state legislation, the traditional Dinka terms referring to "court" (*luk*), "chief" (*bany*), and "judgment" (*long*) have remained the same. The need has never arisen to construct a new terminology to suit these allegedly alien concepts.

Although we appraise critically Dr. Howell's and Professor Evans-Pritchard's interpretation of Dinka and Nuer traditional societies, it is important to see the distinctive characteristics of the society which led them to their conclusions. In both its organization and its content, Dinka law is profoundly affected by the implications of the principle of permanent identity and influence underlying Dinka power process. Since this is rooted in the family, which is pervasive, authority and control, though stratified, are similarly pervasive, and in any situation calling for their exercise, the process of decision begins on the family level; only failing settlement here does the case proceed to the specialized community-wide decision-makers. How high in the hierarchy of power structure a case goes depends on the success or failure of the more immediate relatives of the conflicting parties.[97] The discussion of Dinka legal process must thus begin on the family level, continuing to the territorial level as a fictional extension of the family. This diffusion in the organization of power is a factor which has led some to deny any coherence to Dinka power process.

Another factor in the conception of Dinka law as custom is a lack of visible force behind the origins of law. The mythical participants, all regarded as ancestors, are central to the power process. Dinka law is therefore a perpetuation of ancestral authority and control in the heritage of Dinka experience.[98] The attribution of the origins of power to mythical participants has the result of highlighting the religious form of power. This is only a starting point, for Dinka society is undifferentiated

96. Elias, op. cit. supra note 48, at 31.

97. O'Sullivan, writing about the Southern Dinka, said, "Sections may mean families, divisions of a village, or even divisions of a tribe. Each head of a family keeps his family and property intact, generally in a village of itself; but where families have had to combine . . . they still have a definite section for each family. It is the old people of such sections who form the court." O'Sullivan, "Dinka Law," 40 *Journal of the Royal Anthropological Institute* 177, note 1 (1910).

98. "The origin of Dinka laws," observed O'Sullivan, "appears to have been experience as applied to suit the tribal mode of life, and this experience and resultant customs are of such antiquity that it is almost hopeless, from lack of written records, to trace them back to a known stem." Id. at 175.

in that its component units are multifunctional. The power position of the chief is consistent with his position in all the values, and the deprivations that support his authority and control are equally pervasive. There are thus as many forms of power as there are values, though the roots remain religious. The expectation of spiritual contamination or blessing behind any authoritative decision-maker may be manifested in deprivation or indulgence of psychic or even physical well-being, as well as of wealth, skill, enlightenment, or deference values. With the primacy of religion, all values are thus brought to bear on power as the value specialized to law. The attribution of divine origin to power must not overshadow its secular aspect.

The close association between the divine and the secular in Dinka law has the result that ideals, though far from being achieved, are intensely associated with practice. The goals of unity and harmony, with their attendant persuasion, which find their optimal expression in religion, are emphasized despite the disunity and conflict so characteristic of Dinka society. This coexistence of the positive and the negative cannot simply be conceived of as a gulf between mystic idealism and reality. In law, as in Dinka society as a whole, they are the offshoots of the family orientation of the society.

Because of the importance of every person for the objectives of perpetuity, together with the resultant personal familial sentiments permeating the social web, the structure encourages the significance of the individual's relation to his group as well as the relation of the group to him. The society ultimately rests on the sum total of the cooperation of its individuals, with the role of each seen only within a composite whole. On this foundation there has evolved a sense of justice which gives regard to the individual sense of justice, though as part of a group. Severe deprivations are resorted to only when the individual disregards the sense of the community after a lengthy attempt at persuasion, thus alienating its regard for him.

Similarly conducive to legal persuasion are kinship loyalties behind individual disputants. Members of a kin group "act together with little or no submission to any external control . . . and the freedom from domination which every Nilote expects as his birthright is largely ensured by the strength of such bonds of common descent." [99] Above, we were concerned with community regard for the indivdual sense of right and wrong; here, persuasion is based on the fact that to impose a judgment without mobilizing the public sentiment, including that of the wrongdoer's group, would provoke not only the individual concerned but also all those who owe him loyalty. Instead of settling the case, it may intensify the conflict between the respective groups. Indeed, cases

99. Lienhardt, "The Dinka of the Nile Basin," 69 *The Listener* 828 (1963).

usually take the form of groups versus groups, although this does not mean that individuals do not litigate. Emphasis has therefore been placed upon reconciliation to bring about the harmony necessary for the maintenance of minimum tranquillity and order.

Another pragmatic foundation for persuasion is that problems for litigation usually concern very personal matters, particularly those resulting from a complex network of marriage affinities. These issues, being of a domestic nature, involve people who often must return to the same "doorway," *ghot thok,* or "fireplace," *mac thok,* words which are patently definitive of family bonds.

Collateral to this is the need to foster a sense of unity and joint action, a need which is prompted by the expectation of violence ingrained in the practices of youth for whom it is the main status symbol, by external aggression from other tribes, and by the natural insecurities of life implicit in the circumstances of the people. The Dinka say, "A bundle of few sticks is easily broken, but a bundle of many is not." The need for joint action and harmony being strong, regard had to be shown to people at all levels if social unity was to be maintained.

It was to stress the importance of persuasion in Nilotic society, and its divine and secular bases, that such scholars as Professor Evans-Pritchard, Dr. Howell, and Dr. Lienhardt concluded not without admiration that it functioned although it lacked the ingredient of organized coercion necessary for law. As Dr. Lienhardt has stressed, the divine wisdom of the chiefs is the principal factor in the effectiveness of justice without secular force.

> The centrally important gift which masters of the fishing-spear are thought to have had transmitted to them by their ancestors is the gift of insight into truth, and of speaking "the true word," that is, of representing a situation as it really and absolutely is . . . [I]n ordinary secular disputes points of difference between the disputants, and many other matters, are represented at length before any gathering which will attend them.
>   . . . The traditional purpose of *luk* was the presentation of the whole of a situation to the disputants and to the community, so that its rights and wrongs . . . were apparent in such a way as to transcend the individual views of truth held by those in conflict [and to be seen as such by them]. [100]

These various aspects of Dinka law have now been profoundly modified by the adoption and adaptation of Western power traits. With these innovations, everyone concedes that as it is applied in Dinka courts today, Dinka law is "law." However, the approach of identifying tradi-

100. Lienhardt, *Divinity* 242–48.

tional Dinka law as "law" but differentiating it internally in terms of social organization, value-institutional interplay, and policy contradictions and inconsistencies underlying generational roles is taken here because it enables us to examine the facts and construct alternative policies on the basis of these facts. In this way, we can implement the maximization postulate by increasing the rationality of selection and rejection from the traditional context. Furthermore, it cannot be argued that the modification of Dinka legal processes by the introduction of secular legal coercion has eradicated the negative aspects of tradition, for they still exist.

The relevance of the traditional paradoxes in terms of intergenerational delimitations goes further than this. The patterns of the traditional system are finding a parallel expression in the modern Sudan in a more inclusive and therefore more serious situation. The cleavage between culture groups, descent groups, and generations is producing similar contradictions between aspiration for unity, publc order, and progress on the one hand and the realities of disunity, violent breakdown of law and order, and attendant retardation of progress on the other. Thus, traditional legal process gives us a theoretical basis on which to approach the policy questions of Dinka society within the context of the modern Sudan.

Appointment and Dismissal of Decision-Makers

Within the family, the specialized decision-makers acquire their position solely by virtue of their status. It is in the more inclusive descent arenas like lineage and clan that appointment has been introduced. Clan heads, whose function has become specialized to tax collection, are appointed by the paramount chief in consultation with the junior chiefs and the elders immediately concerned. While in the past the position was hereditary, its specialization has both reduced its status and necessitated the selection of people most able to discharge the new function. In all these positions, a person who is not designated for them may acquire such influence as to be pivotal behind the formal appearance of the designated official.

Where positions are hereditary, there is no dismissal. This means that on the descent level only clan heads who are appointed by the chief may be dismissed. But even in cases where there is no dismissal, a person unworthy of his position may be rendered a mere figurehead by social pressures and a more worthy person may assume the effective role.

The appointment of the decision-makers on the territorial level is now vested in the national authorities or delegated by the paramount chief, who is himself appointed by the head of state with the advice of provincial authorities. Although primogeniture is followed in such appointments, the facts on which to apply the rules are sometimes uncertain and the internal conflict of rules is an additional problem. This is quite apart from other disqualifications due to ill-health or physical defect. Furthermore, the impact of governmental policies has led to the manipulation of traditional rules of succession. The result of all these considerations is that it is not always the eldest son of the most senior wife who inherits the position.[101] The view of the tribe is often considered through a system of representational group-voting. In the case of sectional, subtribal, and tribal chiefs, subtribes vote as groups, while in less important situations, the matter is left to the group immediately concerned.

The leading case in recent history which brings to light all the complexities of primogeniture as well as the family conflicts over power, the extension of the family process into the tribal level, and the expectations about the role of the Dinka chief in traditional terms and in the light of national policies is the case of succession to the late chief Kwol Arob. Kwol sought to marry Nyanaghar as his first wife. She was betrothed to him, and his father gave some cattle, including sacred cows dedicated to God and ancestors, as betrothal wealth. Later, it appeared that she could not be persuaded to consent to the proposed marriage, and her family, not wanting to coerce her, decided to break the betrothal; but Kwol's father refused to accept the return of his betrothal cattle. This point is important, for it was later alleged that the betrothal had not in fact been broken.

After being refused, Kwol married Abiong. In the meantime, Nyanaghar became ill with an unknown disease. This was divined to be the result of refusing a chief in marriage, which could be fatal. Her family apologized to the chief, carried out a ceremony of appeasement with him, and offered him their daughter. Kwol's father added more cattle to complete the bride wealth and Nyanaghar was brought home as Kwol's wife. For ritual and other purposes, Abiong was treated as the first wife. But the situation was confused by other incidents. For instance, to facilitate the procreational potentials, tribal elders gathered in prayer and sacrifice so that the ancestors and God might bless the women. They handed Nyanaghar a fishing spear which, when held by a woman who

101. For instance, Jok, the founder of Pajok clan, could not have been the eldest son of his mother since his mother is referred to as "the mother of Anau" (see Lienhardt, *Divinity* 176) and according to Dinka custom, a person is called with reference to his or her oldest child. Anau did not predecease Jok nor was he disqualified on some obvious ground. Jok merely broke away and led part of the tribe with him, later overwhelming his older brother (see id. at 177). We also know that Jok's great-grandson Kwoldit was not the eldest son, for the tribe specifically asked his father, Dongbek, to give them Kwoldit instead of Kon, Dongbek's elder son.

has given birth, shows that she has borne a baby boy, and they prayed that her firstborn be a boy, implying that they wanted her to bear Kwol's successor. To Abiong, they gave a fighting spear, which symbolizes a baby girl. There was no attempt to reconcile this with the prior treatment of Abiong as the first wife. The two women gave birth according to the elders' prayer: Nyanaghar bore a son, Deng Majok, while Abiong first bore a girl and then a son, Deng Abot. The two half-brothers grew up as friends and when they got married they had their homes next to one another, some ten miles from their father's home. Later, their father made them both his assistants and for all purposes they seemed to have equal authority. But Kwol Arob seemed to favor Deng Abot over Deng Majok, although he thought Deng Majok more progressive and thus more effective in modern situations than Deng Abot. He would ask Deng Majok to assist him in his dealings with Arab chiefs and with government officials.[102]

Deng Majok quickly won the admiration of many British officials as a progressive and competent administrator,[103] while Kwol's popularity with the government began to wane.[104] In 1942, there was a tribal fight in which Deng Majok further demonstrated his administrative competence. While Kwol Arob remained at home as a traditional Dinka chief should, Deng Majok went to the battlefield and played an important role in ending the fight. This was misinterpreted by alien administrators as Kwol's condonation of the fight or at least his administrative shortcoming. As a result, the government decided to make him retire, and Deng Majok was given the paramount administrative and judicial powers of the tribe, assisted by Deng Abot and the leader of Dhiendior, Jipur Allor.

As chief, Deng Majok continued to innovate. He strengthened tribal administration into a more coordinated hierarchy. He levied taxes in

102. Kwol had himself been referred to by administrative records as "the Arabicised Chief," but of Deng Majok more has been said: Beaton wrote in 1947 that "[he] models himself after the Missiria [Arab] *Nazir Umumi* . . . dresses as a Missiria and hopes to tread the Arab way to greatness." "District Handbook," Nahud District Headquarters, Kordofan Province.

103. The degree to which Deng Majok assimilated alien ideas was nonetheless commented upon rather unfavorably by some anthropologists who were then administrators in the area. These facts are cited because Deng Majok's adaptability was a major factor in his succession. In various ways, he distinguished himself from his father and brother in this regard. Howell, "Ngok Dinka" 266.

104. Although his image among the Ngok and the earlier British administrators would classify him among their ideal chiefs, later records argue that his long period of power had turned him into "a tyrannous" ruler (see id. at 265). Howell remarked that "The authority acquired by Kwol Arob from his association with the Government had enabled him to impose his will on the Ngok, especially through the agency of an established tribal court, in a way which would not have been tolerated in the past." Ibid.

cash, and provided the cash to buy the cattle from the people in order to encourage cash economy. He built his house of bricks and corrugated iron. He sent all his children to school to provide the first pupils for the newly opened elementary school at a time when education was abhorred. He made the Ngok join in the annual Arab intertribal competition in tribal dances, horse display, sports, and the like. Whether in the family or in the tribe, he demonstrated the modern significance of the chief as an innovator. Kwol Arob, however, remained influential: having conceived what a British district commissioner calls "an entirely unreasonable dislike" [105] for Deng Majok, he clearly hoped to establish the succession of Deng Abot despite government policy.

On his deathbed, Kwol willed that Deng Abot should inherit the sacred spears and maintain the traditional role of the Dinka chief, while Deng Majok should continue as the government chief and the leader in intertribal affairs. This anomalous division of roles had been unknown to the Ngok and was unacceptable to Deng Majok. The spears were in fact given to Deng Abot by the old members of the chiefly clan, but they were finally prevailed upon by other elders after the intervention of the district commissioner to hand them over to Deng Majok.[106] Deng Abot continued to agitate and the threat of violence increased. He was arrested and banished for a while, but on his promise to cooperate, he was allowed to return and ritual peace settlement was made. Later, he was made deputy chief and vice-president of the court.

Some of the reasons for the controversy are set forth by Dr. Howell.

> The action taken over this matter has been criticized in other Dinka areas on the grounds that it is not essential that a Government "Chief" should also hold the sacred spears [107] . . . But the controversy among the Ngork themselves is not so much whether the President of their Court, itself clearly an alien institution, cannot carry out his duties as leader of the tribe without the sacred spears, but which of the two sons of Kwol Arob is the true successor to their father's ritual status. . . . No one is quite certain which of the two, Majok or Deng Abot, is the son of the senior wife, though it is known that Deng Majok was born first." [108]

Some maintained that since Abiong came home first, she was the first wife, and she was considered as such in everyday life. Others maintained that the betrothal of Nyanaghar, particularly when sacred cows

105. Ibid.

106. For more details, see the account of the other district commissioner quoted by Howell, id. at 266–69.

107. While this is not disputed with respect to these other tribes, the two had long been combined among the Ngok.

108. Howell, "Ngok Dinka" 269.

were included, amounted to a marriage. This is in accordance with the
Dinka conception of betrothal as a stage of marriage which forms part
of it, determining certain rights and duties. However, the betrothal here
had been broken except for the fact that the cattle were not returned.
The argument goes that in Dinka marriage, and therefore in betrothal,
unless the bride wealth is wholly returned or there is an express agreement to the contrary, the marriage stands. This justified the attitude of
the elders in praying that Nyanaghar should conceive a son.[109]

The wounds caused by this conflict have not healed and the brothers
still combine mutual antipathy and opposition with familial unity and
piety. The clan itself is subtly divided between Deng Majok and Deng
Abot.

These events have been recounted at length because their importance
permeates Dinka power process and its significance in modernizing policies. Most obvious of the factors illustrated by the story is the dominant
role of the family on the tribal level. The relations between father and
son, half-brothers, co-wives, and all the various features of the family

109. A further line of controversy is provided by Howell. He writes that "Aruop
[Arob], father of Kwal, had two sons—the eldest of which was Koijanum." Howell
makes a technical error here in that *koojenom*, among the Dinka, literally "standing
the head," refers to begetting children in order to found and continue a man's line
of descent even if the man is dead. To speak of the wife of "Koijanum" therefore
means a wife married to "stand the head," in this case of a dead relative. It is
not itself a name. Howell continues: "This son died as a youth. Later, when Kwal
grew up, according to Dinka custom it was incumbent on him to marry a 'ghost wife'
to Koijanum with the cattle which would normally have been the latter's inheritance.
He therefore married a girl called Nyan Ghar Kir of the DIIL section, but she refused to live with him and his cattle were returned, all except one. Kwal then married Abiong Malek of the ALEI section, with these same cattle. Meanwhile Nyan
Ghar had been persuaded to change her mind and therefore Kwal remarried her,
using this time his own cattle. Because there remained one cow of Koijanum's in
Kwal's marriage to Nyan Ghar, the question as to whether she was Kwal's wife or
Koijanum's arose. A ritual test was performed in the presence of all, including Aruop
himself, and after slaughtering a white goat, it was agreed that Nyan Ghar was
Kwal's wife and the senior, while Abiong was Koijanum's. Both women conceived by
Kwal and before giving birth, the sacred fighting spear was placed against Abiong's
hut so that she might produce a girl child, while the fish-spear was leant against
Nyan Ghar's hut in order that she might produce a male child to be Kwal's successor. This came to pass and Abiong bore a girl while Nyan Ghar bore a boy
who is Deng Majok. Later Abiong bore Deng Abot and after him Nyok. It must
be understood that although Kwal was *genitor* and guardian of Deng Abot and would
in normal usage be referred to as his father, he is not the *Pater* or legal father
at all. Deng Abot is the legal son of Koijanum. The argument therefore becomes
very involved. Although Deng Majok's mother must be considered Kwal's eldest wife
(since Abiong was not his wife at all), it is quite possible for him to claim that
Koijanum was Kwal's eldest brother and therefore his heirs would claim to succeed
Kwal."

process earlier discussed become matters of tribal and national concern and are, consequently, intensified. The case also shows the interlinkage of primogeniture and the will of the people. The intricacies of the rules of succession, even in primogeniture, show the desire of the community to exercise its choice, though within a narrow circle. The fact that the case could have been approached from two or more angles, though posing the question of what the relevant facts were, demonstrates the point. Of course, governmental influence is quite apparent. However, it is striking that the people pressed their claim to choose their leader, and it is equally striking that they acted, or at least claimed to have acted, in accordance with tradition. This suggests that in Dinka practice the community's acceptance of its chief is a prerequisite to his authority. The fact that Kwol had been deposed and Deng Majok appointed by the government does not invalidate this suggestion, for we are told that "the tribe had accepted the leadership of Deng Majok," and that if the government handed over the sacred spears to Deng Abot, "the tribe would be hopelessly divided." [110] Even if we assume that the choice of its leader was implanted by the government, the enthusiasm with which it was appreciated and exercised would suggest a latent desire to have a say in the appointment of a leader.

This case created or encouraged what has become part of the expectations of the Dinka. In all cases which followed upon the death or dismissal of subtribal and sectional chiefs, the facts surrounding the case have permitted at least two people to compete and elections are held. Admittedly, these elections are very much influenced by both the government and the chief, and certain categories of people, like the modern elite, are discouraged as a matter of policy. But the fact is that the Dinka have come to regard elections as normal. The method of election is usually collective; that is, by families, clans, sections, or subtribes according to the importance of the position in question. More and more people who are not the eldest sons of the most senior wives or whose line once held the disputed chieftainship but lost it for one reason or another are now becoming entitled to compete. Yet, the importance of descent in the eyes of the Dinka remains intact. Authority based solely on personal attributes is still unknown. The force behind chieftainship is still the authority of the ancestors. Although Dinkas now say, "they [the competitors] are both children of the same father [or the same grandfather]," the group of those who wield effective power is kept small. It is the need of ancestral backing which made Deng Majok ask an elder [111] whether he

110. Id. at 267.

111. Bulabek Biong, a senior member of the Pajok clan. The elder was dying when Deng Majok sought his counsel. Present was Acuil Bulabek, the son of the dying elder, who first furnished this information to the writer.

could justifiably claim succession to his father's divine authority, and
the reason that he was told that "no evil would fall on you as the chief."

Another important factor in the story of Deng Majok's succession is
the relevance of generational factors in modernizing leadership. In the
family power process we spoke of the ambivalences which modern conditions have injected into the relations of the elders and the younger
generations; the former, usually not possessing the bases of modernization or not able to keep pace with it, look to the latter for assistance.
Yet, the threat posed by such admission of incapacity in the face of innovation nourishes the resentments of the younger generations. This
occurred between Kwol and his son Deng Majok when Deng became a
competitor for Kwol's authority. Such conflicts between father and son
or between brothers have had serious repercussions not only in the development of the Ngok but also in South-North situation.[112] In this
particular case, whatever the motives of the national decision-makers,
it is significant that the choice was in favor of a person predisposed to
change. Although this predisposition is minimal compared to the demands of today, at that time it was an outstanding factor. The principle
of this decision runs counter to the prevailing governmental policy of
keeping the chiefs as traditional as possible. Indeed, opinion among administrative officers of the time was divided. The innovating attitude
of Deng Majok was displeasing to some elements, who saw the virginity
of Dinka culture spoiled by Arab influence.

The motive of the present-day national administration might not be
the preservation of tradition but rather the ensuring of the chiefs' amenability to governmental policies and the minimizing of the tribes' demands on the national government for greater autonomy and modernization. This attitude becomes especially obvious among the government
officials who come into contact with tribal administration and to whom
the chief is subjected. The justification for subordinating the chief to
these officials is that they are superior to him in modern values, especially education. To have chiefs equally modern and educated would
eliminate the grounds for their subordination and encourage more autonomy, a development which would be contrary to the present form
of unity.

The choice of Deng Majok in preference to his father and to Deng
Abot has a quality of contravening tradition in order to uphold it. On
the one hand, the decision purported to depose Kwol, although Dinka
chiefs are traditionally rulers for life. Assuming that he had the right to
designate his son Deng Abot as his successor or that Deng Abot was en-

112. Sons and relatives of chiefs have been known to leave their tribes, join the
rebellious army of the South, and then return to attack and victimize their ruling
relatives whom they had originally opposed.

titled to the chieftainship by some principle, then the choice of Deng Majok was again a violation of tradition. On the other hand, we have seen the importance of the chief as the symbol of unity in traditional society. This importance throws light "on the whole question of the status and function of [Pajok lineage] in Ngok country," [113] and has been reinforced over the centuries by the fact that the chiefs have consistently occupied an all-pervasive elite position.

That the Ngok chiefs have always led change is evident from the fact that they have long adopted certain traits of Arab culture, though they have always assimilated them into their own culture in a manner which renders such descriptions as "Arabization" erroneous. Contact with the West through British rule articulated change more positively. In this, Kwol began to lag in his later years and was surpassed by Deng Majok. To maintain the traditional status of the chief as the most indulged and indulging according to the value conditions prevalent at the time, Deng Majok's choice was consistent with tradition. This was also a factor in the overwhelming support he received from the community. Those who dissented were only those factions of Abyor subtribe and Pajok lineage led by senior members to whom Kwol's deposition and the contravention of his dying will implied their own generational disqualifications.

The principles in the case of succession to Kwol Arob have been applied in several other cases of junior chiefs. In some cases, the implementation of national policies was less disguised. Thus, in the case of succession to *Wakil* (deputy paramount chief) Jipur Allor, the competitors were Jipur's son, Col, and his father's cousin, Deng Akonon. Deng's father had been the *Wakil,* but Deng had not succeeded because he was then an infant. The issue was put to tribal elections and Deng Akonon was the choice of all but an inconsiderable minority. The paramount chief and the national authorities, on the other hand, favored Col, who was appointed *Wakil* on the basis that since the government had been happy with Col's father, and the time of Deng Akonon's father was quite remote, Col should be allowed to assume his father's position. Several years later, Col agitated against the paramount chief; he was accused of arousing hatred against the chief, was tried under Section 8 of the Chiefs' Courts Ordinance, and was convicted and discharged from the chieftainship. This time Deng Akonon contested the position with Col Jipur's half-brother, and with an apparant preference for Deng Akonon, the paramount chief decided to leave the matter solely to the tribe. Deng Akonon was elected.

In another case involving the *Omda* (chief) of the Anyiel subtribe, similarly competitive claims were put to vote. Arob Madut, the son of the deceased chief, competed with Ajuong Tiel, an agnate whose grand-

113. Howell, "Ngok Dinka" 270.

father had been chief, but whose father had not succeeded because he was too young. Ajuong won the election and became the Omda. Arob mourned his father's position with a song.

> Where is the robe? [114]
> My ancestral robe has become the tail of the goat.[115]
> Where is the robe?
> My ancestral robe has become the tail of the giraffe.[116]
> Chiefs of the land
> Those who knew my father
> Please bring back my robe to me,
> Man who knows my father
> Please claim the robe for me.

These cases show that the traditional processes have been so modified that both the people and the national authorities can manipulate them to their advantage. Although the government and the chief have the final word, among the Ngok this has not overridden some degree of descent qualification. There are, however, cases in other Dinka tribes where claims to hereditary succession have been disregarded in the interest of ability.

Deng Majok's succession thus marked a new phase in Ngok Dinka power process, but the change has been more a matter of degree than of kind. The need for accelerating change increased and with it the demand for a chief who was more competent to direct the new conditions and thus maintain the traditional distinction of the chief on a modernizing level. This new phase of increased demand for innovating chieftainship now poses even greater challenges. The choice between the continuation of the chieftainship as a dynamic institution for modernization and its elimination now lies with the national government. The chief's position has both the potential of modernizing influence and the danger of autocracy which may well lead to its abolition.

These factors also apply to the dismissal of chiefs. While traditionally a person qualified by descent and generation could not be removed from a post, local authority now not only may be dismissed but may be punished for breach of duty, including not being amenable to governmental policies.[117] By and large, the chiefs cooperate with the government, but the government's bias against them naturally brings the chiefs closer to

---

114. Of chieftainship.

115. This reference is to a legend about how the goat lent its tail which was never returned.

116. A similar legend.

117. Recently, *The Vigilant* announced a mass dismissal of important Dinka chiefs in Bahr-el-Ghazal on the ground that they were cooperating with the rebels.

the rebellious or opposing educated class, and ultimately widens the gulf between the South and the North.

Jurisdiction and Powers

The essence of the pyramidal structure of Dinka society is that jurisdiction and powers are identical though stratified. While modern impact has steepened this pyramid in favor of the chiefs' power, the situation remains traditional. In intrafamily matters, the authoritative decision-makers have jurisdiction over all values and people within their units, subject to such division of functions as may be determined by sex and/or age. These diversified roles fall under the ultimate control of the pater-familias. Although he does not wield the power of life and death in the conventional sense, he is believed to be endowed with the power to curse a serious offender to death. Should he thus kill a member of his family, he proves the legitimacy of his measure, for the powers of the ancestors to whom he appeals are effective only for a rightful cause. In addition, his trial would involve the paradox of his judging and compensating himself since the loss of the person and the benefit of compensation are both his. The point is, however, far from being a procedural loophole, for his punitive measure is lawful per se, and the injury he causes is sufficient evidence in his favor. In one story, a father who had cursed his son is said to have remarked proudly, "Let him be gone; he was persuaded by his mother and consented to her deceit." [118] In rare cases, however, both the head of the family and the mythical participants may be adjudged capricious, or too impatient. The head of the family may be wronged, but as a head is expected to pardon minor offenders. If he does not pardon them, another member of the family may bring an action in front of higher descent or tribal elders or chiefs.

When matters proceed higher, the family head plays an important role, whether the case be against him or between his subjects. Where he has made a decision, it often provides a starting point; where he has not, his suggestions to higher authorities are invited, and when these authorities make a decision, his approval is often sought to assure the effectiveness of the decision. His role is equally important in cases of interfamily situations, for then the head represents his group.

Certain matters have now been taken outside the jurisdiction of the family head. For instance, in intrafamily murder cases, jurisdiction is with the state courts, although the tort aspect remains a family matter. The family is thus becoming a less autonomous unit. Matters which would have been settled internally in the past now go to higher tribal authorities. The problem of whether a traditional family head should

118. Nebel, *Dinka Grammer* 136 (1948).

still claim control over his educated members who not only have been modified culturally, but who are often away from the family, is a pertinent one in contemporary tribal society. This becomes particularly significant in such matters as a conflict over the marriage of a family member when a guardian, in exercise of his traditional authority, expects his ward's compliance. Despite this, the family remains a vital institution both because of the jurisdiction it retains and because the higher authorities often approach family cases as family matters.

The chief's court is at a higher level. Its jurisdiction and powers, which cover all values and people within the chief's administrative unit, are now being regulated by the Chiefs' Courts Ordinance,[119] and the Abyei Court Warrant.[120] The former prescribes for full jurisdiction in criminal and civil offenses under native law and custom over the territory and natives of the Southern Sudan. But in civil cases in which one or more of the parties is a government official or is a native not domiciled or ordinarily resident in the South, the court can only have jurisdiction with the consent of such a party or parties, and in criminal cases in which the accused is a government official, the court only has jurisdiction with the consent of the resident magistrate. In criminal cases in which the accused person is not domiciled or ordinarily resident in the South, he can apply through the court to the resident magistrate before his trial begins to have his case moved into another court of competent jurisdiction. In such an event, the chief's court shall stay the proceedings and refer the application to the resident magistrate for decision. The chief's court may make such orders as it thinks fit regarding the detention of the accused, or sending him in custody to the resident magistrate, or taking guarantees for his appearance before the chief's court or the resident magistrate. Section 6 also provides that a chief's court shall have no jurisdiction in criminal cases over a government official who is not a native of the Southern provinces.

The Ngok chief's court follows the provisions of Section 6 with some modification. With respect to subject matter, the warrant of the court adds some ordinances to the traditional categories of cases, civil and criminal, over which the court has jurisdiction.[121] While certain cases are excluded [122] where it is required under Section 6, the consent of the

119. Cf. 1931. Vol. 10. *Sudan Laws.*

120. Issued by the governor-general in 1945 under the Chiefs' Courts Ordinance.

121. Among these are the Local Government Ordinance, the Preservation of Wild Animals Ordinance, the Locust Destruction Ordinance, the Hashish and Opium Ordinance, Diseases of Animals Ordinance, and certain cases under the War (Prices Charges) Order.

122. They include murder, offenses against the state or relating to the military forces, offenses relating to slavery or to the harboring and the screening of offenders with respect to the above-mentioned offenses, and any offenses against government

resident magistrate or of the parties to the court's jurisdiction is assumed, and if the chief's jurisdiction is questioned by the parties, the consent of the resident magistrate is usually given. This flexibility in the application of the provisions is necessitated by the crosscultural intercourse following the abandonment of the policy of ethnic segregation pursued by the British.

For the same reason, however, territorial limitation has often greatly fettered tribal administration. With the infiltration of his people into towns, the chief has made it an annual practice to tour these towns. The Dinka, to whom separation of powers or jurisdictional limitations are inconceivable, expect full jurisdiction from the chief. Even cases which had gone to Arab chiefs' courts might be revived in the belief that a Dinka chief is the right authority to settle them. It was not until recently that the provisions of the Chiefs' Courts Ordinance were enforced to stop him from assuming jurisdiction in such cases. For such administrative purposes as tax collection, his jurisdiction extends over his subjects who are still domiciled in his tribe though resident in other tribal areas.

In crosstribal cases, the chief in whose area the litigants are resident may assume jurisdiction in consultation with the chiefs of the parties or the chief of the other party if one party belongs to his tribe. He may choose to stay the proceedings for a special court [123] which has jurisdiction "where the accused is subject to the jurisdiction of one chief and the complainant is subject to the jurisdiction of another chief." Where the accused is himself a chief, a special court may also be convened when in the opinion of the head of state the ends of justice will be served.[124] Similarly, where the alleged offense is so grave that the powers of the chief's court appear to be insufficient, Section 8(1)(c) provides for the constitution of a special court.

The powers of the Ngok chief's court are set out in Schedule 1 of the Court Warrant (see Table 1). In practice, the traditional composition of the court is followed and membership is open to elders, although only official court members stamp their seals on the court judgment.

An important factor in the limitation of jurisdiction is the law which the court must apply. A chief's court is mainly empowered and inclined to apply its *lex fori*,[125] though as we have seen, specific governmental ordinances may be included in its jurisdiction.[126] The court is often not

---

ordinance except where the provisions of any ordinance form part of native law and custom.

123. Which may be convened under Section 8(1) (a) of the Chiefs' Courts Ordinance.
124. See Section 8(1) (b).
125. In accordance with the provisions of Section 7 subsection (a).
126. By the operation of Section 7 subsection (b).

informed or is ill-informed about the *lex domicilii* of the parties if it is other than the law of the court. Since the Dinka are largely culturally homogeneous, the problem is less acute in the case of non-Ngok Dinkas than in the case of Northern Arab litigants. For that reason, an Arab representative sits in the Ngok court as an assessor to inform the court on Arab law, and in Arab areas of Kordofan a Dinka assessor informs Arab courts on Dinka law.

TABLE I

President or Vice-President	Composition	Jurisdictional Limits	To Whom Appeals Lie
Chief Deng Majok	President with 1 vice-president and 5 members	Sentence of 3 years' imprisonment; 100 head of cattle or money equivalent; 25 lashes; and may hear civil suits worth up to £S 100 or 50 cattle	Resident magistrate (formally district commissioner) Dar Missiriya— Kordofan Province
Chief Deng Majok	With 3 members	Sentence of 2 years' imprisonment; 25 head of cattle or £S 50 fine; 25 lashes and may try civil suits up to £S 50 or 25 head of cattle	Same
Subchief Deng Abot and Sub-chief Deng Akonon, each in his own court	Vice-president with 3 members	Sentence of 1 year's imprisonment; 15 head of cattle or £S 30 fine; 10 lashes; and may try civil suits up to £S 30 or 15 head of cattle	Court under the presidency of Chief Deng Majok

Regarding the law to apply, it may be asked whether educated Dinkas should be subjected to tribal courts. If so, should they be governed by tribal law? In view of the fact that the Sudanese legal system is largely based on religious adherence, and since the educated Dinka are nearly always Christians or Muslims, the issue is of contemporary significance. Nothing in the Chiefs' Courts Ordinance or in any other enactment restricts or expressly extends the jurisdiction of the chief's court over Christians and Muslims, nor is there any judicial pronouncement on the point. On specific issues such as monogamous and especially Christian marriages, there is a difference of opinion among some writers. Major Wyld, for example, writing on Zande law, argues for the jurisdiction of the chief's court over such marriages.[127] Dr. Farran, on the other hand, interprets applicable statutes and cases as denying such jurisdiction. His argument rests, *inter alia,* on the fact that the chiefs' courts, being composed of tribal leaders totally lacking in any civil-law training, are in practice singularly unfitted to adjudicate on Christian and monogamous marriages, which can only be dissolved for certain matrimonial offenses which must be proved by civil law—not customary law—standards of evidence, and that chiefs' courts have no authority to apply the civil law.[128]

With respect to Muslims, Section 38 of the Civil Justice Ordinance says that in personal matters "civil courts [among which chiefs' courts are included] shall not be competent to decide in a suit to which all parties are Mohammedans, except with the consent of all the parties." Instead, by Section 6 of the Mohammedan Law Courts Ordinance, they fall under the jurisdiction of Islamic courts, and are governed by Islamic law.

In practice, in the case of both Christian and Muslim converts, the chief's court assumes jurisdiction and gives regard to the Christian or Muslim rules applicable to the converts. In a recent case, for instance, a Dinka chief's court permitted a postmortem divorce in modification of customary law. A Christian Dinka woman, whose husband had died and who by tribal law would have lived with his pagan next of kin, applied for divorce from her dead husband. The court agreed, provided that the dead man's bride wealth was returned. This having been done, she was emancipated from the levirate union. In most cases, however, Dinka courts apply the Dinka law.

It needs to be stressed that religious conversion or acculturation does not ipso facto disentangle a person from the preconditioning factors of his cultural background, even though he may be substantially changed and may aim at changing important aspects of his native culture. The problem thus lies in the fact that the Sudanese legal system does not provide for intermediate stages. The issue is much deeper than merely one of jurisdiction over the educated class. To what extent are the presently constituted courts, both traditional and modern, and the laws they apply, equipped to handle the complex problems of acculturation now facing traditional but developing societies of the country? Provisions qualifying the application of customary law where it is contrary to justice, morality, or order, and those providing for the application of justice, equity, and good conscience in cases not provided for by the law,

127. See Farran 180.
128. Ibid.

could be so construed as to make for development in the law and cover novel situations. At present, however, such creativity hardly exists: the formally trained state judges are entirely ignorant of customary law and the chiefs know nothing of modern state law.

The pluralism of the Sudanese legal system and the problems it raises will be considered in later chapters. At this stage, it will suffice to say that for modernization purposes the chiefs' courts are unable to handle these conflicts because the chiefs usually lack any education, let alone legal training. This is undoubtedly a factor in the indignation often felt by the educated class when subjected to the chiefs' courts. The problem is particularly striking in criminal cases where the chiefs' motivation to retaliate against what they consider to be a general opposition to them by the educated class may lead to miscarriage of justice, often with no redress on the national level. This widens the gulf between traditional and modernized groups, and the circle reinforces itself.

The Functions of Decision

Because of the segmentary organization of traditional Dinka society and the emphasis placed on intimate groups, collective and private functions were largely undifferentiated and the punitive aspect of sanctions was intertwined with the restitutive or retaliatory aspect. This has led some people to conclude that the Dinka had no notion of punishment, and by implication, of crime. Stubbs sees the objective of Dinka law as the adjustment of social balances and not punishment.

> The Dinkas have no criminal law as understood by the European. Their customs aim at adjusting the balance of values upset by any act. If "A" causes the loss of "B's" cow, leg or life, he must compensate "B" or his clan to the value of the loss sustained. Except in a few specified cases, the reasons for the damage or the manner in which it was inflicted were immaterial.[129]

Howell writes, "Ngok Dinka law was essentially private law. . . . Penal sanctions are now applied to offences which in the past were in no sense criminal, for punishment is a concept entirely alien to the Ngok." He reasons that "in the past there was no conception of individual punishment inflicted upon the person of the killer [in case of homicide] because there was no organized authority with penal sanctions behind it in existence." [130] But Howell negates his own argument when he suggests

129. Stubbs, "Customary Law of the Aweil Dinkas," *Sudan Law Journal and Reports* 451–53 (1962).

130. Howell, "Ngok Dinka" 273, 275. Saying the same of Nuer Law, Howell suggests that "when speaking of Nuer systems of social control in the past we should not be

that "We can, instead, as recommended by Professor Radcliffe-Brown, distinguish between 'the law of public delicts and the law of private delicts.' " [131] The criteria of this distinction are the criteria often used to distinguish criminal wrong from civil wrong, the only difference being that crime does not necessarily, though it may, include private injury, while public delict necessarily has a criminal, that is, public, aspect. Since Howell denies the law of public delicts on the ground that "There is no evidence of a penal sanction applied by anything which resembles 'politically organized society,' nor anything which indicates that such procedure is enforced by the will of the community, that is, which extends beyond those segments which are actually at feud," [132] in the case of homicide, his insistence on the crime-tort private-public delict distinction seems inconsequential.

With respect to the requisite collective action of the community and the allegation that traditional society did not have organized force, it may be recalled that apart from the coercion behind community decision-makers, certain functional groups exercise force against certain wrong-doers. Howell himself admits that there were "cases where collective action was taken against certain anti-social persons, witches and the like." [133] Instances have been mentioned in which the age set of a culprit would act jointly against him. Furthermore, in cases of proposed incestuous marriages, people would forcefully seize the cattle paid as bride wealth. We have also demonstrated that the chief, representing the community, may initiate proceedings for the settlement of a blood feud.

---

justified in making a distinction between criminal and civil law, though we might, in some instance, be justified in doing so now." His reason is that "such a distinction is based on the conventions of legal principles inherent in our own culture, and . . . are not applicable." Howell, *Nuer Law* 219.

131. Howell, *Nuer Law* 219. Radcliffe-Brown explains the distinction thus: "In any society, a deed is a public delict if its occurrence normally leads to an organized and regular procedure by the whole community or by the constituted representatives of social authority which results in the fixing of responsibility upon some person within the community and the infliction, by the same or by its representatives, of some hurt or punishment upon the responsible person. This procedure, which may be called penal sanction, is in its basic form a reaction by the community against an action of one of its members which offends some strong and definite moral sentiment and thus produces a condition of social dysphoria. The immediate function of the reaction is to give expression to a collective feeling of moral indignation and so to restore the social euphoria. The ultimate function is to maintain the moral sentiment in question at the requisite degree of strength in the individuals who constitute the community." Radcliffe-Brown, *Structure and Function in Primitive Society* 212 (1965).

132. Howell, *Nuer Law* 223.

133. Ibid.

The relevance of the magnitude of blameworthiness in such collective action is also obvious in the fact that in offenses like homicide where community indignation is highest, the assessment of damages is affected by the actor's criminal intent. The greater the intent, the greater the damages assessed for the injured party. Howell recognizes this though he explains it in terms of his own theory by saying, "theoretically the question of intention does not enter into the assessment of compensation because the principal object of the payment is to restore the balance which has been disturbed, but Nuer do, in fact, take it into consideration." [134] It is hard to see how the theory can be sustained when facts are not only available but in conflict with the theory. Howell further explains the situation in two ways. First, "The Nuer often say that there really should not be any distinction at all.[135] Again one wonders whether what "ought" should disguise what "is." For his second ground, Howell argues that "in the cases of unintentional killing the indignation of the dead man's kin will be less than in cases of intentional homicide and a compromise more likely." [136] The fact that the motives increase the intensity of indignation itself indicates that this indignation has a punitive quality. Why else would the law impose more compensation to prevent retaliation? If it were conceived of merely from the point of view of the dead man's kin, the law would not be justified in predicting a desire on their part to be compensated rather than to retaliate. Compensation is a superimposition in the interest of the society in its multiple form. Among both the Dinka and the Nuer, it is never the aggrieved groups but the community-wide decision-makers who demonstrate desire for compensatory redress. The relatives of the deceased nearly always seek vengeance, and in fact the proceedings for the settlement of homicide suits include a mock refusal and attempted retaliation by the aggrieved relatives. Howell, writing on the Ngok, himself confirms this hierarchy of interests when he says, "There is clearly an inherent wish to come to terms, for feuds can only lead to social disintegration and in view of opposition from Arabs in the north and Nuer or other Dinka tribes in the south, a high degree of political coordination must always have been necessary." [137] It would be rather difficult to argue that this desire for settlement in the interest of the whole community is greater among the individual groups concerned than in the eyes of the whole society confronted with foreign aggression and endangered by disunity.

134. Id. at 41. The reader is reminded here that Howell's writings on the Nuer are of interest to the Dinka not only because their legal systems are quite similar but also because Howell has studied them both and has similar views on their jurisprudence.

135. Id. at 223.

136. Id. at 42.

137. Howell, "Ngok Dinka" 275.

Viewing the Ngok process as one of restitution rather than of both restitution and punishment, Howell argues that a close relationship between contending parties lessens the intensity of the indignation felt by the aggrieved, and a too distant relationship does not particularly necessitate a settlement.

> If the maintenance of the balance was not necessary, either because the two individuals were closely related and the disturbance was in consequence less acute, or because the groups concerned were too remotely connected, the likelihood of compensation was small.[138]

Rather than that a close relationship lessens indignation, it may be argued that "the closer the relationship, the greater the danger of antagonism and the stronger the control over destructive retaliation." [139] That is why in such cases the Dinka emphasize appeasement payment which is much more in value than ordinary compensation for the same injury inflicted against a nonrelative. As for a distant relationship, especially between members of feuding tribes, the wrong between them is not rendered less wrongful by virtue of distant relationship. The difficulty in the settlement of a conflict of this nature is comparable to the difficulty in the settlement of a case of a person under a foreign jurisdiction, that is, a criminal in exile in an unfriendly country.

To demonstrate further the existence of social interest and a punitive concept, we may mention that among the Ngok, if two or more persons inflict an injury on an organ of the body for which there is a fixed rate of compensation, each one of them must pay the full rate as if he alone had caused the injury. Compensation is therefore more than just restoring the value lost through the injury.

An understanding of Dinka society as a unity in multiplicity is crucial to the notion of community interests involved in wrongs. It is wrong to consider individuals and interest groups apart from the society. The familial foundation of the society means that the society is approached from localized groups to inclusive ones. The result is a community envisioned as a composition of individuals and groups. These individuals and groups are private participants who must be seen as fractions of the composite whole, identical in essence, though not in degree, to this composite whole. Society as such can only be injured through these identifiable persons and groups. If a son commits a wrong against his father or any other family member, the father's response is in his capacity as a political figure in society. One group is in conflict with another; the action of the wronged group is not merely that of a private

138. Howell, *Nuer Law* 223.
139. Kuper and Kuper, *African Law: Adaptation and Development* 11 (1965).

being, but also that of a political entity which can defend community policies. If the chief is wronged by an individual or a group, he litigates not as a private person but as a chief, and the consequences of the wrongdoer's action are graver for that reason.

Individual and group interests are therefore seen as aspects of social interests. The fact that certain individuals and groups, that is, family heads or chiefly clans, are the center of social interests in no way contradicts the fundamental identification of all individual and group interests with social interests. The discrimination, if we may so call it, is one of degree and not of kind. Since the contravention of unity and harmony more directly affects the wrongdoer and the wronged, emphasis was placed on compensation and reconciliation.

It may be argued that the notion of collective and vicarious liability which is characteristic of Dinka society negates the punitive aspect of compensation. This, in Dinka conception, is not the case, for the interdependence of the individual and his group causes punishment of the group to be conceived of as punishment of the individual, and vice versa. The group, through its head, is thought better able to shoulder the pecuniary burden. Since each component group is seen as a fragment of the society, in the ultimate result the community is assuming liability for the individual whom it has failed to control.

It is because of these intricacies of Dinka legal process that the dichotomy between crime and civil wrong, or public and private delicts, is not precisely applicable to traditional society. It is more expedient and accurate to speak of forms and degrees of involvement in the settlement of disputes, forms and degrees of wrongs, of deprivations imposed on the wrongdoer, and of indulgences conferred on the wronged. Similarly, social interests may be stratified and dichotomized according to the individuals or groups involved, but are seen as intertwined. It is because of this involvement of the public with the private that the society preserves the status quo on all levels of social organization.

Today, there has been an impact on the decision functions by the intervention of the modern state. This has led to the attempt to separate the powers of the chief. The police have been introduced as a separate entity with a separate role. This has also led to the distinction between crime and civil wrong. The police concern themselves more with the former, although the latter is also ultimately made effective through them. These changes have, however, not altered the situation substantially. As with most aspects of Dinka society, one may say that traditional decision functions have been modified rather than supplanted. The decision-makers remain multifunctional and the public and private outcomes of contravening the law remain intertwined.

Following the classification and definitions of Professors Lasswell and

McDougal,[140] we will discuss the decision functions of prescription, intelligence, recommendation, invocation, application, appraisal, and termination. Prescription is a phase of decision process in which general rules are crystallized. It is an articulation of the general requirements of conduct. Among the organs specialized to the making of authoritative and controlling general requirements are constitutional bodies and legislatures. Intelligence involves the obtaining, processing, and dissemination of information for the guidance of decision. It is usually prior in time to prescription or recommendation about past events and making estimates of the future, especially of the costs and gains of alternative policies. Recommendation is the promotion of action by proposals. It is usually prior in time to prescription in a given sequence. Invocation is the provisional characterization of conduct according to the requirements of prescriptions, including demand for application in concrete instances. It consists of making a preliminary appeal to a prescription in the hope of influencing results. Application is the phase of decision process in which prescriptions are definitely related to concrete cases; the administering of general policy in particular instances. Examples are court holding and administrative decision. Appraisal involves the examination of official acts according to the goals of the institution; it is the assessment of the success or failure of policy; the formulation of the relationship between official aims and levels of performance. Termination is the ending of prescriptions and of arrangements established under their authority. Examples are legislative repealing of laws and judicial reversing of court decisions. The expression of these functions has to be seen in the context of the community in question. Being multifunctional, components of Dinka society carry out the same functions, though at different levels and in different forms.

PRESCRIPTION   Although some articulate means of prescribing have now been introduced on the territorial level, prescription among the Dinka is largely customary. An essential part of ancestral participation is the perpetuation of their practices. This provides a basis for a set of norms identified as the "*cieng* of our ancestors." This normative aspect of Dinka experience and its ancestral origin create an expectation of severe deprivations in case of contravention. This sanction welds the religious with the secular in a way which renders its authority unquestionable, though there may be breach of the norms.

The ancestral origin of Dinka law extends the authoritative prescriptive role to descent and generational seniority among the living. Accord-

---

140. See McDougal and Lasswell, *Law, Science, and Policy* (mimeographed materials) 32–33 (1964). For the definitions in order of the functions, see their Glossary, at pp. 23, 14–15, 14, 15, 1, and 27 respectively.

ing to this principle, the worldly representatives of the ancestors are believed endowed with the authority to pronounce and interpret ancestral prescriptions, as well as to prescribe for novel situations in the light of the fundamental principles of the Dinka code.

On the family level, the patriarch is the representative of the mythical prescribers. Other family members may prescribe on a relatively lower level, and their prescriptive power differs according to sex and age. While that of the mother is generally discouraged where it leads to disunity and conflict in the group, it is necessary for the purposes of proper upbringing. This makes the mother's prescribing function a determining one, especially in polygynous families where there is a wide sharing of the father's attention. In view of cowives' jealousies, this function may, and often does, affect family unity and harmony. For instance, a mothers' pride and honor may require that she prevent her children from frequenting the huts of halfmothers since this might be negatively interpreted as a method of inviting gifts. In her desire not to overburden her children she may prevent them from herding the cattle, the sheep, or the goats of their halfmothers. Where she fears that the influence of half brothers and half sisters on her own children may be corruptive, she may discourage association with them. In practice, the motives are often entangled with prejudices rooted in jealousies.

Whatever the motive, the repercussions can be far-reaching, a fact which explains the discouragement of the mother's power. The situation may be made even more complex by the subjection of younger wives to the older ones, whether in the immediate polygynous family or in the extended family. Here, a senior wife has direct and indirect influence over the wives and children of her group. The children, according to sex and age, have also a prescriptive relationship.

When projected to the tribal level, the chiefs and elders, perpetuating the collectivity of ancestral prescribers under the banner of their own ancestors, are the community-wide prescribers. Ancestral experience having formulated the prescriptions, most of the contemporary prescription is merely upholding, interpreting, and extending this ancestral legacy. As new situations arise, the chiefs and elders are believed equipped to see the divine and the secular truth on which they base their prescriptions. Their new prescriptions are thus authoritative. They become so linked with the past ancestral practices that they are often not set apart from the prescriptions transmitted through posterity.

Today, the process is more articulate, and is carried out either administratively or judicially. Administratively, the range of matters with which the chiefs concern themselves by the delegation of the local governmental authority is wide though, at least formally, specific. The national statutes prescribe that customary law and specific national ordinances or regulations are to be applied by local courts. It is inherent in the application function that expectations for future action be created. Through the process of distinguishing, new cases pave new ways and therefore new expectations.

An example of this occurred when, in 1951, in the case of Nyananyuat,[141] Chief Deng Majok proposed marriage to Nyananyuat, a granddaughter of his grandfather's female "ex-slave." The relationship involved was as shown in Table 2.

TABLE 2

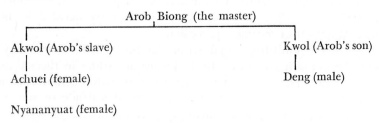

The girl was in favor of the marriage. She later expressed her love in a song.

> Deng Agaany [142]
> I do not care what people say
> I only know the words we said
> You and I alone.
> Wherever the case may go,
> If it is a place where people dance
> I will dance and sing
> "It is only Deng and I
> That is my man.
> Even if I be hanged
> That is my man."

But many relatives on both sides objected on the grounds of exogamy. According to Dinka law, bars to marriage cover all traceable degrees of blood relationship, although certain exceptions are made in the case of a sixth- or seventh-degree relationship through a principal female. The rules of exogamy apply fully to legal offspring who are not necessarily blood relatives, such as children of adulterous unions or children adopted through marriage to the mother. In Nyananyuat's case, the relatives who refused consent did so on the ground that the same principle applied to adoption by slavery, since in Dinka society one's slave was considered one's child. The argument of Deng Majok and those who consented to the proposed marriage was that adoption by slavery was

141. Abyei, Ngok Dinka Court (1951).
142. Praise name.

quite a different institution, which did not create an exogamous relationship similar to that of affinity by marriage. The Ngok court decided
in favor of Deng Majok, and the dissenting relatives appealed to the
district commissioner. By that time, the case had assumed a political
dimension which divided the kin group of Deng Majok. In view of the
magnitude of the case and suspicion that a court within Deng Majok's
jurisdiction might have been influenced by his status, the district commissioner referred the matter to a special court constituted under Section 8 of the Chiefs' Courts Ordinance. Although the chiefs who constituted the court differed in opinion, the majority decided in favor
of Deng Majok, thus setting a precedent.

Owing to the multifunctional nature of the system, courts may go
beyond distinguishing in order to do justice according to the merits of
individual cases. This aspect of prescriptive application is now enhanced
by both the modification of the tradition-bound attitude of the court
and the expectation of enforcement by governmental agencies. A few
cases will illustrate this prescriptive aspect of application.

Among the Dinka, impregnation is a wrong calling for compensatory
redress in the case of an unmarried woman, and requiring imprisonment
in addition to heavier compensation in the case of a married woman.
Prior to the case of Ayom Kwol [143] in 1953, all those who had sexual
intercourse with a woman during the same month of her impregnation
were irrefutably presumed responsible and therefore liable. Here Ayom
confessed (according to custom) three men as having had sexual intercourse with her the month she became pregnant. During the course of
litigation that followed, the defendants caused Ayom to become confused about the dates, and all of them claimed having had intercourse
with her a month after the month she had alleged. Ayom could not
prove her allegation, but the court felt sure that the young men were
simply cunning and avoiding the liability they deserved. Ayom was put
on oath to ensure that no other man had had intercourse with her who
might be responsible. The three men were then presumed responsible.
For future cases, the court prescribed that anyone having intercourse
with a woman within two months of her pregnancy would be liable for
such pregnancy. All the chiefs and the subchiefs were instructed to
promulgate the new rule.[144]

The second case of prescription by application involved the institution of *cuet* whereby the age set of a person suspected of certain offenses
publicly victimizes the personality ox of the wrongdoer or, in the case

143. Abyei, Ngok Dinka Court.
144. This new rule continued to apply until 1957 when the assembly of chiefs and
elders once more decided to revert to the old rule requiring one month. This change
does not negate the principle illustrated above.

of a girl, her brother's ox. The action is taken immediately on the publication of the defamatory matter. It is supposed to be both a punitive measure and an initiation proceeding to encourage the accused, if innocent, to clear his or her name, and therefore that of the group with whom he or she identifies.

In *Nyanluak's* case,[145] a girl of distinguished beauty and popularity for whom many cattle had already been paid as a betrothal fee was alleged to have stolen the butter gourd of another girl in the cattle camp. On hearing of the allegation, members of her age set gathered from all the surrounding cattle camps. Singing their group songs, they went to her camp with the intention of seizing her brother's personality ox. Considering the seriousness of the situation and the repercussions of this action on the girl, the senior men in the camp attempted to persuade the age set to postpone its action until the matter had been investigated. In the meantime, the men sent word to the chief. That same evening, her fiancé came and, singing ceremonially, untethered one of his personality oxen which was included in the betrothal cattle, and took it as a token of betrothal termination. Immediately upon being informed, the chief sent a number of tribal policemen to restrain further action by her age set and to summon the group into court. The court investigated the issue and decided that there was no ground for the accusation. The age set was instructed that any further action on the matter might lead to its own liability. Thus a precedent had been set against immediate action by the age set of an alleged wrongdoer.

An important prescribing aspect of application is embodied in Section 7 of the Chiefs' Courts Ordinance, which requires native law and custom to conform to "justice, morality, and order"; In the case of suits proceeding to the national level, Section 5 of the Civil Justice Ordinance conditions the application of custom according to "justice, equity, and good conscience." In *Matet Ayom v. Deng Majok* [146] the spirit of these two laws was put into operation.

Apart from the authoritative prescriptions of the specialized decision-makers, private practices of various forms establish expectations which become identified with Dinka law and custom. For instance, we have seen that the institution of self-help is largely the function of warrior groups. In view of its traditional dominance Dinkas generally recognized that when certain wrongs were allegedly committed, certain retaliatory measures followed. The implications are indicative of how any one func-

---

145. Abyei, Ngok Dinka Court (1952).

146. Abyei, Ngok Dinka Court (1955), a case involving the custom of gift withdrawal. On the authority of this case, the chief's court held in *Nyuong v. Wor Abyei*, Ngok Dinka Court 1959, that Nyuong could not claim the return of his friendship gifts from Wor.

tion such as invocation or application may have prescriptive or other functional consequences.

These various forms and degrees of prescription among the Dinka must now be seen within the national context where the supreme prescriptive function resides. While prescription is mainly a function of ancestral legacy, its roots in Dinka experience imply a subtle process of continuous adoption and adaptation which is becoming more articulate as social mobility becomes more apparent. As is the case with the whole Dinka system today, the end result is largely determined by the quality of those in charge of the social machinery.

INTELLIGENCE   The interactions between the traditional and the modern sectors have in large measure led to the articulation of the intelligence function, but the information available to the decision-makers on matters of cross-sectors is very inadequate. Consequently, from family to tribe, intelligence function is largely traditional.

Within the family, guidance on policy matters comes from the mythical participants, whose information is largely channeled through divinations or dreams. Although such mythical information may emphasize the interest of individual members or that of component units, it is often in the interest of the group as a whole. Among the living, information on policies is channeled through the family hierarchy. Such information may concern the general good of the group, but may also have the objective of influencing the family head in favor of the informer and in disfavor of other family members. In such a case, the process is often confidential and reflects what the Dinka consider "gossip," *lum,* or *lom,* reflecting intrafamily jealousies especially prevalent among cowives but also extending to their children. As it has a disharmonizing effect, such information is often viewed with abhorrence. Even if grievances are justified, the Dinka would rather bury them than voice them if they reflect cowives' rivalry. They believe that an ancestral curse may befall a member who offers information which leads to internal frictions. In fact, internal mishaps are often interpreted on this ground. This in itself is indicative of the frequency with which the ideals are negated in practice.

In interfamily situations, though the other members of the family may assist the family head in gathering information, such information is channeled outward through the family head. As is the case with the family, the territorial hierarchy is a self-informing body. In cases of disputes, apart from the evidence of the disputants and their witnesses, any chief or elder who has heard the case informs the superior chiefs or elders of the factual circumstances of the case together with his own opinion on its merits. Anyone may state facts or opinions in any assembly or court. In the case of opinion, special qualifications, especially on the ground of age, are respected as a matter of course.

Pivotal in the whole system is the chief, whose position as head of the tribal family is reinforced by his network of personal ties throughout the tribe. As a leader of his own family, he is believed to have the guidance of his ancestors, whose experience with the situation is transcendent. Through his multiple marriages, his family circles permeate the tribe, thus widening his familial sources of information. As a tribal leader, his home is a center of tribal gatherings and is therefore a meeting place of the greatest intelligence man-power of the tribe, both officials and private persons.

His sources are further broadened by the fact that those desirous of gaining the chief's attention and favor perform intelligence functions for him in both his public and private affairs. It is common to see a person kneeling beside the chief's chair murmuring information, or to see the chief in a circle of several elders sitting in seclusion from the public receiving some information of importance and confidence. It is often aimed at providing him with evidence of subversion against him. No matter where or for what reason a person conspires against the chief, it comes to his notice in a very short time, and immediate action is taken against the plot or the chief prepares himself for a confrontation with his enemies. The Dinka have a saying that the chief's ears and eyes are wide open and his arms are long, to show the ease with which he gathers information and the consequential facility with which he is able to handle his opponents. A person may attempt to avoid the chief's authority by leaving his jurisdiction, but since the tribal chiefs are often in diplomatic contact, their intelligence functions are reciprocally coordinated.

In addition to these traditional processes, there are new ones. For instance, the chief is now assisted in certain administrative and judicial matters by police intelligence. A court clerk keeps a record of any decided cases to inform the higher authority, that is, the chief or the national officers.[147] This record of cases is, however, of little assistance to the chief as an appellate authority, or to the national authorities, or to any interested party. Recently, there have been pressures from the national appellate authorities for the improvement of reports, but since court clerks are always men of little education, the chances of improvement are doubtful.

Another important source of the chief's information is the educated

147. According to Regulation 16 of the Warrant of Ngok chief's court, the record should contain the date and place of hearing, the names of the parties, the names of the witnesses examined, a short statement of the charge or claim, the defense and evidence of the judgment, and the name of the president of the court and the official members present at the hearing. The record of the case must be read in court in the presence of the accused in criminal cases or the defendant in civil cases as soon as it has been written and the judgment thereupon signed or sealed by the president and the official members of the court.

class. In fact, one of the main areas of cooperation between the chief and the educated class is the intelligence function in the modern context. The chief often confers with his educated relatives, whether or not the situation at hand involves a discord with the national authorities. While it is a point of cooperation, it is also a point of conflict. The educated members who bear grievances against the chief are seen by those in the traditional sector who oppose the chief as best equipped from the modern intelligence point of view to gather information on the people's grievances against the chief and address it to national authorities. In this, however, they encounter a stumbling block. Consistent with the self-informing quality of the power structure is the dependence of national authorities on the intelligence function of the chief. Since they are, as a rule, ignorant of traditional conditions, and since they do not want to act counter to the chief, the word of the chief is generally conclusive in intelligence—a factor which tends to augment his power.

Intelligence function, as part of the whole power process, is conditioned by the stratification of Dinka society in which there is a mystic dependence on supernatural powers and ancestors, and in which the living participants are structured according to family and age. The inequities implicit in this stratification result in tensions and the investment of intelligence in such tensions. Today, these crises are more apparent in the tribal and national intelligence function, but in essence they pervade the process from the family level.

RECOMMENDATION   Recommendation is often associated expressly or by implication with intelligence. When the divinities and the ancestors communicate with the living decision-makers, their revelation often involves a suggestion as to the appropriate measures to be taken. Again, if a wife informs the husband that she has overheard a cowife uttering a curse against the family head or admiring another man, the information calls for action on the side of the husband against the alleged wrongdoer. On the other hand, the recommendation may be more direct. The husband may seek counsel from his brothers, senior wives, or sons, either in intrafamily affairs or in external interactions.

On the territorial level, the intelligence channel of the decision structure often accommodates implied recommendation. Besides, the chief may seek advice from other chiefs and elders. As we have seen, he consults the educated class on certain matters, and is principally depended upon by the national authorities for recommendation.

INVOCATION   Invocation is a widely used function in Dinka society. The Dinka are a very litigious people, and a number of factors may account for this. The highly valued relationships of the Dinka largely depend on continual reciprocal obligations and executory contracts or quasi-contracts which make the people credit-oriented. There is always some duty to assist some kinsmen which when discharged gives rise to a reciprocal duty to assist the donor in the future; bride wealth and reversed payments are rarely completed promptly; it is in the essence of bartering livestock that only partial payment is promptly made; and these are only a few examples. The situation is aggravated by the fact that a Dinka is very reluctant to surrender his livestock, the material means of discharging debts. Even a clear case must be disputed in the attempt to protect the holy animal—the cow, the sheep, or the goat. Since traditional proceedings are not adversary in the Western sense, any dispute over these obligations may be taken to court. The Dinka word *kany,* which may be translated as "debt" or "claim," covers just about all obligations, contractual or reciprocal. Because litigation is persuasive and requires much talking, it is a popular means of demonstrating verbal skill.

The question of who invokes and how he invokes is a relative one, depending on the level of social organization and the characteristics of the participants involved in terms of the broad categories here adopted. Within the family, invocation may be used against family members by other family members in front of family decision-makers with competence differing according to the gravity of the case and the corresponding seniority of the decision-maker. The mythical participants are believed to invoke by inflicting deprivations of specific characteristics which are either easily identifiable by all or require the analysis of ritual experts. Often, the deprivations are physical and are an outward expression of inward social ills nursed or known by the sufferer or the diviner as the case may be. The deprivations inflicted initiate the revelation and therefore the treatment of these social ills. Once initiated, the invocation of the mythical participants against a family member is taken up by the wronged members and becomes part of the general function of invocation, be it within the family or in intergroup arenas. When an intrafamily invocation leads to no settlement, the case may be taken to higher authorities. Cases may also involve complaints by the family head against any member of his group. Generally, as part of the suppression of intrafamily claims, intrafamily invocation is discouraged. When it occurs, even in front of the territorial authorities, it is approached as a family matter. This is becoming especially significant as the tendency to dichotomize between family conflicts and other cases increases. What are first approached as family matters may assume a strictly legal form, although even the strictly legal invocation is largely an invitation of mediatory and conciliatory proceedings.

Except for intrafamily conflicts adjudicated by tribal authorities, tribal invocation is often done by groups, or individuals representing them. Such representatives are generally elders, although younger members of the family may invoke on their behalf. Women do not normally invoke unless there is no able male in the family or the invoking woman has acquired primacy over the available men, as women occasionally do.

In the case of such public figures as the chief, invocation on his behalf may be inflicted upon the wrongdoer by ancestral curse. When the source of such a curse is diagnosed, the supposed wrongdoer takes measures to appease the chief and be reconciled with him. The chief may also invoke personally, and the effect on his adversary is bound to be more serious than the effect of a private individual's invocation.

There are cases where the chief will initiate proceedings in the name of the community, even though he is not the victim of the offense. Such is the case in homicides and group fights. Today, the public side of invocation is also represented by the police. This has led to the classification of offenses into criminal and civil, with the police handling the former. Even in such cases, participants who are more immediately affected are adjoined on personal bases.

The procedures of invocation are relatively informal. Anywhere and at any time, a person may invoke in front of any authority.[148] The fact that in Dinka time-conception the past is welded to the present implies that there is little correspondence to the Western type laws of limitation. Among the Dinka, what matters the most is the act. When it occurred is of little significance, unless, as in the case of impregnation, time is an essential factor in the wrongfulness of the act, or unless such lapse of time implies compounding of the offense.[149] Founded on the same ground is the fact that invocation against a person may be effected through his heirs should he be dead. It will not matter that he has been long dead if the merits of the case are established and he had not compounded the offense expressly or by implication.

The procedure begins with the statement of the invocation to the adjudicating authority. If there is a prima facie case from the complainant's statement, the chief will give the complainant an order for summoning the defendant. If the defendant absconded, in the past there was no effective means of compelling his attendance, although the chief

148. Regulation 12 of the Court Warrant now requires the payment of five piastres (ten cents) as a fee to be paid by the complainant before hearing. No further fee is required in case of appeal. Usually, the sum is paid when the complainant has won his case and it is about to be recorded.

149. Dr. Lienhardt observes the initial response of the Dinka to the concept of time limitation in litigation: "In the early days of European-type court-procedure among the Dinka, it was found very difficult to persuade them to see that the period which had elapsed since an event was at all significant in the attempt to settle a dispute. Even now, a Dinka may think it unreasonable and unjust that a cattle-debt or an injury of many years' standing should be less serious as a subject of litigation than an event of the immediate past." Lienhardt, *Divinity* 150 note 1.

might inflict a curse in serious cases or authorize self-help. Today, the police may be sent to force the defendant's appearance either directly or indirectly by attaching his cattle or other livestock. Should he appear on the appointed date, the claim is heard by the chief either sitting formally in the officially constituted statutory court or informally wherever he happens to be. No person can state his case if he is not authorized by the court to do so. This authorization is usually effected through a court official known as *agamlong*. *Agamlong* is appointed on the spot by the court and is not a permanent official, though he is often experienced in that field. His role is to repeat in a loud voice any part of a statement made in court. A case is introduced if the *agamlong* responds or is ordered by the court to respond to the plaintiff's statement of his claim by repeating it. This practice of repetition, apart from encouraging the court to keep track of the statement, also helps to ensure order. This is equally true where a statement by a witness or an opinion by a court member is involved.

In the last half century or so there appears to have been an increase in litigation, although there are no available statistics to substantiate this observation. Indeed, it may be that the increase in the number of lawsuits is only apparent and not real because, as a result of concentration of power in the head chief, litigation concentrates around him. His home is regarded as synonymous with his court, and he continually hears complaints from the time he wakes up until he goes to bed. It must be noted, of course, that while there are three divisions and an appellate division to the Ngok chief's court, there is only one chief's court under the presidency of the paramount chief; or in the case of component divisions, under the presidency of his vice-presidents. Since the court of the paramount chief is supposed to be reserved for serious cases of first instance and appeals, this concentration of activity in the chief's home is paradoxical.[150]

While concentration on the chief's power may give the appearance of an increase in litigation, an actual increase would not be surprising and may be explained in a number of ways. In the first place, it is likely that the decrease in the institution of self-help has increased the number of cases which require resort to the chief's court. A slightly different aspect of this may be that, in the past, expectation of retaliation aided private

150. Recently, there have been attempts by the police to prevent litigation in the chief's home. People have often been beaten away from the chief's house in pursuance of this policy. In some cases, the chief himself orders the police to permit entrance; however, police restraint may reduce the crowd but hardly ever stops litigation. Even when the crowd inside is reduced, one sees people spread over the area outside the enclosure, waiting in twos or threes for the chief's appearance. When he appears, it is often time for the police to prevent too much encroachment on him and beating may be resorted to.

and immediate settlement of conflicts. The significance of retaliation as a factor both in the prevention of offenses and in the increase in litigation is implied by these lines in which a man praises his father's fighting spirit during the early days when it was more of a necessity than today.

> During the old days when words flowed like fish
> A man who had disputed a cow with my father
> Slept wondering how he would respond the next day.
> Mangar de Jang d'Aguer
> My father, Row, attacks with two horns.

In the past, settlement of disputes was woven into the entire social web and devolved along segmental lines. In most cases, resolution of the conflict took place in *locus in quo,* and often concerned the parties and close relatives only. Divorce proceedings and the consequences of divorce, such as the return of bride wealth, did not necessitate the chief's adjudication. Today, the establishment of an institution whose function, though overlapping other functions, is specialized to litigation, has created expectations favoring litigation. Correlative to this is the increasing tendency to conceive of litigation as adversary and the court as an umpire. The function is therefore less demanding for the court than it used to be when persuading the wrongdoer of his wrong rather than merely passing judgment was the primary consideration—a factor which now favors litigation even over trifles. Far from being avoided, litigation is seen as invited by the establishment of a special institution. It has thus become in the eyes of the Dinka a form of occupation and a source of wealth. During the season when people do not have much to do (e.g. when the harvest is completed and the fields cleared), a man explores his relations with others to find some ground for claims to pursue. The hardships of litigation, such as walking long distances to the chief's headquarters and sometimes going hungry in the course of these journeys, have assumed an adventurousness now taken as evidence of masculinity in Dinka youth.

Litigious circumstances are also created by a breakdown in the traditional order, either as a result of change per se or as a consequence of misguided or unguided change, and probably both. Titherington observes the negative moral implications of change among the Dinka.

> Some men who have been in the North show great moral deterioration, and chiefly concern themselves with making dishonest profit out of their less sophisticated brethren. This, however, is probably not so much innate depravity as the stage of transition through which all (including newly-made Christians) have to pass who throw off their old tribal prohibitions until they learn—sooner, later, or

never, according to character, teachers, and the example set them—
a new morality.[151]

And there is more to it than just moral deterioration. Today, kinship
obligations which hardly ever came to court are increasingly being adjudicated. For example, a man may acquire money by laboring in the
modern sector, buy cattle, and marry with no regard to age priority in
his kin group. This may prompt litigation. Many cases come to court
involving pecuniary assistance in bride wealth, payment of taxes, or
famine relief during years of bad crop. This is quite apart from offenses
introduced by the state or modern-traditional administration. Furthermore, because of the decrease in cattle among the Ngok Dinka, a judgment debtor may find himself unable to discharge the debt and the court
may encourage him to invoke against someone else in the hope of re-
covering the necessary amount. Usually, such litigation immediately follows the original one, and the court is often predisposed to favor the
judgment debtor if he has a prima facie case.

It must be noted that, despite change, there are still remnants of self-
help which are usually undesirable even from the indigenous legal point
of view but are sometimes justifiable according to the circumstances, and
are so much a part of Dinka practices as to be considered customary. For
instance, in order to coerce a person into settlement, the plaintiff seizes
his cow. Again, to hasten compensation in sexual violation of a woman's
rights, the relatives of the woman seize many of the best of the wrongdoer's cattle. After the settlement, they are given their due and the rest
of the cattle are returned. These practices represent the ineffectiveness
of the traditional system and have been most affected by the modern-
state impact.

Application

The function of application is the one most affected by innovation,
although it still welds tradition to incoming modernity in a striking way.
It is carried out by participants in ways similar to those already discussed. In the family, ultimate application is vested in the family mythical participants who inflict spiritual contamination resulting in physical
injury on the wrongdoer. Among the living, the patriarch, having a superior ancestral power, has the ultimate authority of application. Behind
him are divine and secular sanctions. Others also apply according to the
context and gravity of the subject matter of application.

The applying function today largely focuses on the tribal level as a
result of the influence of the modern state. Because of the emphasis put

151. Titherington 180.

on the chief, most cases now reach him before final settlement, a factor behind his overcrowded "docket." The control of his subordinates is thus becoming less effective.

While the chief is the focus of litigation, there are other court members appointed in accordance with statutory provisions. The guiding principle being mediation and reconciliation, evidence is admissible or inadmissible according to whether it is conducive to this end. The statements of the parties, their witnesses, and the court members are often lengthy and inclusive of much that would impress an outsider as irrelevant. Speakers often digress into stories, proverbs, and even jokes to substantiate their points. The whole situation is thus brought together and objective truth is sought to restore unity and harmony.

While the range of admissible evidence is wide, the same principle that widens it may restrict it. There is a general bias against any evidence which tends to aggravate the indignation of adverse litigants and thus impede settlement. Hearsay evidence generally connotes *lum*, "gossip." Direct evidence is preferred to circumstantial evidence. The latter is seen as a form of lying, because telling an untruth as the result of an error is considered not to be lying consciously but to be telling a lie nonetheless. In circumstantial evidence, the possibility of error is higher than in direct evidence, and "truth" in this wide sense is an important aspect of Dinka law of evidence. Again, interested evidence, but not evidence of an interested party, can only widen the gap between the interest groups involved. An interested person may speak, although he may decide not to. Should he speak, he is usually expected to emphasize the wrong of the side in which he is interested. This attitude is especially important among the judges and since the process of litigation involves the gathering and the evaluation of evidence simultaneously, it must be demonstrated throughout the proceedings. Of course, a person to whom the judges and especially the pivotal judges are known to be related, or in whom they are at least interested, has a higher expectation of winning the case. A tactful judge or elder can best favor his relative by condemning him. Unless the wrong is too apparent, such an attitude often encourages the court to find in favor of the relative. Even when the wrong is apparent, the indignation of both the wronged person and the court is mitigated by the alignment of the chief with them against his own relative. If a chief or any court member is an immediate party to the case, he may not act as a court member, for among the Dinka no one can be a judge in his own case.

There is no definite rule about where the onus of proof lies. The issue is whether the court can prove guilt or innocence from a neutral standpoint. Generally, the plaintiff is expected to establish at least a prima facie case. In certain cases, however, there is a strong tendency to pre-

sume guilt, sometimes almost irrebuttably. Such is the case in sex offenses, for the Dinka believe that women rarely lie in such matters, and
that men are often the aggressors and the liars.

The fact that all those involved in the administration of justice, other
than the immediate parties in conflict, are concerned with the legitimate
claims of both parties without bias means that there are no advocates in
the Western sense. Sometimes, those members of the court who have
seen the case at the lower level will argue for the side they had favored.
This, of course, may prejudice the case, and the likelihood of its doing
so depends on the creditability of the member.

Where a question of fact cannot be resolved, ultimate resort is had to
oath-taking. The oath may be administered to either party; in certain
cases, such as sex offenses, where there is a strong presumption in favor
of the plaintiff, he or she takes an oath on the ashes of the cows of the
chief. Once an oath is administered, punishment or compensation is
imposed on the defendant. However, the Dinka oath does not defer judgment to the life hereafter. The idea is to call upon the mythical participants to reveal the truth so that the situation may be rectified if the
court has erred. Therefore, should perjury result in evil, and it is revealed and admitted by the prejurer, the evil effect must be "washed
away" and the status quo ante restored.[152]

In some cases, this is more theory than practice, for the restoration of
the status quo may be inequitable in individual cases. Such was the situation in *Matet Ayom v. Col Monybaai*.[153] Matet Ayom was accused of
adultery with the wife of Col Monybaai, but denied the accusation. After
putting the woman on oath, the court ordered Matet to pay compensation in the form of cattle to Col on the understanding that should Col's
wife be found to have committed perjury, Matet's cattle would be returned. During the two years following the trial, two nephews of Col
and his son died of a disease diagnosed to be the effect of perjury. The
matter was reported to religious functionaries and the woman was ritually purified of the curse. When Matet requested the return of his cows,
however, the court of first instance held that he could not recover because the perjury had not been officially brought to the court's notice
by the injured husband. Without such an official notification, the court
still considered the wife's evidence as valid because of the rule that the
chief in whose court the oath had been administered was the only one
competent to remove the curse after the admission of perjury. However,
a practice has developed whereby any member of the chief's clan can
unofficially and effectively purify without the official knowledge of the
chief. As this was the case in Matet's case, the court refused to take

152. See Machrell, "Dinka Oath on Ashes," 25 *Sudan Notes and Records* 131–34.
153. Abyei, Ngok Dinka Court (1957).

cognizance of an unofficial purification. Matet appealed to the chief's court, which reversed the decision on principle, but the execution of the judgment was never effected.

In another case, *Col v. Ring Aguer*,[154] Col's sister was impregnated by Ring's father, Aguer. The girl was put on oath and Aguer was made to pay compensation of three cows to Col. One cow was payed promptly, but the payment of the other two was deferred until such time when Aguer, then without cattle, could afford to pay them. On paying the one cow, Aguer invoked his divinities to kill the cow if the girl had taken false oath. The cow died and some years later Aguer himself died. After Aguer's death, Col sued his son for the two cows of the judgment debt which had been deferred. Ring pleaded perjury, as the first cow had died in accordance with his father's prayer. The court rejected Ring's defense on the ground that his father's prayer and the incident of the cow's death did not constitute sufficient evidence of perjury. Besides, Ring was held estopped on the ground that his father had had sufficient time before his death to allege perjury. His failure to do so was seen as evidence of his conviction about the justice of the situation. His son could not be heard to deny such justice. The relevance of the time factor may be explained in terms of the peculiarity of the oath and its effect. Besides, Aguer's silence until death rendered time to be of the essence since it implied his recognition of the justice of the original decision or of his compounding of the claim on the basis of perjury.

In the process of gathering and evaluating evidence, any court member may speak without regard to priority. In practice, the more senior the court member, the less he says and the more important what he says. When the case has been exhausted, the evaluation of the evidence has led to a general identification of where the wrong lies, and the court has successfully or unsuccessfully persuaded the wrongdoer of his wrong, it may then proceed to give final judgment and fix the sentence or compensation. Here, order of seniority is followed with the junior members speaking first. The president of the court always speaks last and has the final word.

There are certain statutory restrictions on the court. By virtue of Regulation 8 of the Court Warrant, it may not try a criminal case unless the accused is present before the court, nor can it hear a civil suit unless the defendant either is present before the court or has been so summoned as to have a reasonable opportunity of being present. Regulation 9 of the Warrant restates the condition of Section 7 of the Chiefs' Courts Ordinance by requiring the judgment to conform to Ngok native law and custom, provided that they themselves conform to justice. According to Regulation 10, unless the president and all members present at the

154. Abyei, Ngok Dinka Court.

hearing of a case are unanimous, the judgment will not be valid until it is confirmed by the district commissioner (today resident magistrate). This requirement is similar to the customary practice of consensus among those involved in the settlement of a case, if conflict is to be considered truly resolved. However, whereas traditional consensus was an outcome of mediation, compromise, and reconciliation, the provisions of the court regulation have established a practice which has rendered the chief even more pivotal in the modern adversary litigation. Since consensus is a necessary condition to settlement, his judgment is always the point of consensus and there is practically never any dissension. Although he naturally considers the opinion of the rest of the court, he may not concur with the dominant view, and yet his word would be the judgment of the court.

The court may not pass a sentence of flogging in addition to one of imprisonment or of a fine. When imposing a fine, the court may order that in default of payment of the fine the offender be imprisoned, provided that the sentence should not exceed the maximum powers of imprisonment of the court as composed.

The whole case, including the judgment, must be recorded, read in court in the presence of the accused or the defendant, and signed or sealed by the court members. According to Regulation 11, this judgment, once declared, can no longer be altered in full or in part without reference to the district resident magistrate. This does not, of course, affect the right of the chief to hear appeals from the junior courts. It assumes his being a party to the judgment. Since national authorities tend to confirm the decisions of the chief with minimum interference, there is little likelihood of his decisions being invalidated.

The fact that a decision has been reached does not mean that application is completed. Responsibility for the execution of any court's decision lies with the person presiding over the court which passed the judgment. When a court passes a sentence of imprisonment, the prisoner is sent under escort to the nearest government prison with a committal order duly filled in and sealed or signed by the president of the court.[155] The presiding chief is also responsible for seeing that the fees are fully collected and paid to the proper authority. He must also see that compensations awarded to the injured are duly paid. During the early part of the British administration, fines went to the chief, who usually distributed them among his relatives and subordinate chiefs. Chief Kwol Arob is reported to have told the civil secretary that he would rather

155. Until the prison was built in the chief's headquarters, prisoners used to stay in the chief's home and labor for him. Now, they are put in prison but they still labor for the chief and other government officials in addition to doing any other public work that may be assigned to them.

give the fines to the government, since their distribution created too many problems.[156] Now, Regulation 15 of the Court Warrant absolutely forbids the president or any of the vice-presidents to pocket the fines or the fees in full or in part.

While execution of judgments in civil matters may be thought easier now than in the past because of the state machinery behind the court's decision, the practice is the reverse. Before the impact of colonialism, cases might drag on for quite a while, but, once judgment was given, execution quickly followed. The judgment debtor immediately identified the cow or cows that he would give the judgment creditor. From the court room the latter went to fetch his cows from the former. Today, various factors have rendered execution difficult. One of the reasons is the increasing lack of moral compulsion behind litigation, since it is increasingly viewed as a means of wealth acquisition which the losing party should impede as much as possible. The increasing emphasis on the adversary form of litigation is contributing to this. The spiritual power of curse which the court once wielded and the self-help which was often expected are now being replaced by police force, although there are insufficient policemen to seize every judgment debtor's property in execution of judgments. There is also the general decrease in cattle, which are often the subject matter of litigation. In short, final application, though backed by the forces of modern state, is following a paradoxical trend.

The function of application now provides an alternative to self-help, but it has interposed a hierarchy in which the chief has assumed much of the powers of the lower levels. While the processes of change are themselves prompting more litigation, this concentration of power has rendered application largely one man's function, with all the deficiencies which that implies. The worst part is in the execution of the sentences.

APPRAISAL   Although the conservatism of the Dinka implies a basic acceptance of the structures and the processes of authority and control, appraisal of decisions is a broadly shared function throughout the various levels of social organization. It may be performed by anyone. Naturally, appraisal may be authorized or unauthorized and has degrees of effectiveness.

Within the family, the mythical members are thought to be the supreme appraisers through dreams, divinations, or possessed people, usually women. Their conduct may be appraised by the living, usually in songs, hymns, or prayers. This appraisal generally takes the form of praise but it may be critical, though only with reverence. In a prayer for a sick man, a master of a fishing spear said, "Why is it, O Divinity, that

156. Henderson, *The Making of Modern Sudan* (1953).

when one son is left alive alone out of all the children his mother bore, you do not help him, that he may be in health? . . . And you Agany senior [the dead father of the sick man] why have you left your child in misery in his father's tribe?" [157] When the Seligmans wrote that the outlook of the Dinka may be summed up in the passage from the Psalms which says that "This is the Lord's doing; it is marvellous in our eyes," [158] they were correct only if they meant that the Dinka show great devotion to and respect for mythical participants even when they appraise them critically. It would not be accurate to say that they are never criticized.

Among the living, the father-husband assumes a position analogous to that of the mythical participants. As we saw earlier, his decisions and conduct in general may be and often are appraised, but this appraisal should not demonstrate disrespect or disobedience, except in extreme cases and with the approval of the community. Many are the songs in which a wife or a child appraises the family head with a tactful combination of criticism and praise, although the dominant theme may be critical.

There is relative freedom among the rest of the family to appraise one another. While this is also done in direct speech, songs provide the most dominant medium of appraisal.

The process on the tribal level is quite similar. We have already quoted a number of songs in which various tribal authorities have been praised or condemned. When a group such as the court is appraised, the role played by individual decision-makers is specified. The higher the authority, the less and the more tactful the criticism against him. Usually, the tendency is to praise the chief. In the case of opposed tribes, people of one tend to sing very insultingly of the senior personalities of the other. The following song, composed by a litigant of another tribe about the Ngok chief, shows a somewhat indirect but obvious criticism. The singer had eloped with a betrothed girl to another tribe and returned to Ngokland after they had begotten children, hoping that she would no longer be taken from him. The woman and her children were given to the original fiancé according to strict application of Dinka law. In mourning the death of Kwol Arob, the present chief's father, the singer alleges that he would not have decided the same way and thus criticizes the present chief by implication.

> What carries my children away
> O Bird of the tribe Awan
> What takes my children across the land?

157. Lienhardt, *Divinity* 223.
158. Seligman and Seligman, *Pagan Tribes of the Nilotic Sudan* 178 (1932).

> If only I could get hold of Kwol d'Arob
> To clear him off the mud in his grave
> He was the man who knew the world
> I would put him back into the seat
> And the family of Ring [the singer] would prosper.

In a song of a similar tone, the singer-immigrant appraises the chief critically by suggesting that outsiders had better leave the tribe since Chief Kwol Arob is dead.

> Let us bury the Great Dorjok (Kwol) de Yar (Arob)
> Those who want to return to their tribes
> Let them leave in haste.

While such appraisals may be addressed to specific decision-makers to rectify the situation, they are often after-the-event complaints which are not made in anticipation of adjustment. They have more of a therapeutic than a restitutive consequence for the singer. Generally, however, they act as a check to the decision-makers.

There are, of course, other more direct methods of appraisal addressed to decision-makers of competent jurisdiction in the hope that they will put a situation right. An obvious way is through appeals. While, as the preceding examples illustrate, a great deal of appraisal is initiated by individuals or groups most immediately affected, the higher authority may request a rehearing on his own initiative, or the case may be one for which confirmation by a higher authority is required. According to Regulation 13, the court of the president (chief), sitting with a vice-president and five members, may hear appeals from the court of the vice-president. In fact, the chief often reverses the decisions of the lower court.[159] From here appeals go to the resident magistrate, but, as we have seen, the chief's rulings are rarely reversed.

Among the Southern Dinkas there are courts of appeal above the paramount chiefs which are constituted of tribal leaders other than these chiefs. A similar situation exists among the Northern Arabs, where an appellate authority is appointed over a number of otherwise independent chiefs. The augmentation of the Ngok chief's autonomy as a result of the remoteness of central control is a factor in this difference between his court and those of his neighbors. Though more in touch with their Northern neighbors, Arab appellate chiefs would not qualify for the Ngok appeals because of cultural diversity.

The appraising function, while very popular from the family to the tribal level, is therefore of little significance beyond these stages. While

159. When rehearing a criminal appeal, the court may cancel, alter, or reverse the decision of the lower court.

appraisal against any authority other than the chief-in-council is sometimes effected, it is too insignificant to affect basic policies. The chief-in-
council, with his elders, the most pivotal authority on fundamentals, is
hardly affected by appraisal before higher authorities. This is a feature
of power concentration of which the repercussions are manifold and intertwined. It is basically a factor in the perpetuation of the present state
of affairs on the tribal level.

TERMINATION   Termination implies change, and as we have seen, continuity is a primary implication of the myth underlying Dinka power
process. This does not rule out change and termination, but it impedes
them. A suggestion for the abolition of a seemingly irrational custom is
usually answered, "It is the *cieng* of our forefathers of the distant past."
Of course, the degree of rigidity depends upon the importance of the
custom in question. Practices of minor significance may be terminated
without affecting the basic policies. It is the major practices which show
resistance to change and termination.

   Today's rate of change has enhanced termination. Since this impact is
more apparent on the tribal level, termination is also more evident on
that level. Qualifying provisions in the statues governing the functions
of the courts lay down conditions for termination of a customary law by
reason of its being contrary to "justice, morality, or order," or "justice,
equity, or good conscience." Such judicial actions as termination of the
custom of gift withdrawal and seizure of the personality ox of an alleged
offender are instances of the increasing tendency in favor of termination.
Collateral to the increasing power to terminate in general is the power
to terminate specific decisions on appeal. Since norms are deeply ingrained, there is an expectation on the part of the public that it will be
informed of any change. The maxim *ignorantia juris non excusat* has
very limited application in traditional law. For this reason, the critics
of the decision in *Matet Ayom v. Deng Majok* [160] argued that it was
wrong to apply a law before notifying the public of the change in advance. Normally, a change in the law is not presumed published merely
because it has been pronounced by a competent authority. Word is
spread through the hierarchy of chiefs, clan heads, and elders so that
most people will have heard of the change when it is applied to specific
fact-situations. Sometimes, however, the need to change the law is
prompted by the facts of the particular case under consideration. Such
was the position in *Ayom Kwol*, where the court felt that the boys were
fooling the girl to avoid an apparent responsibility. In such a case, application of the change is prompt, but, as was the case in *Ayom Kwol*,
the change is equally publicized before future application. Being ori-

160. See Chapter 7, pp. 268–69.

ented to the justice of the particular situation, such termination often lacks general justification.

Termination by the superior tribal authorities is more pronounced than that by national authorities because cases reaching the national level often involve the opinion of the tribal chiefs, whom central authorities do not want to discredit by supersession. In cases arising in the cities, where the chief's rulings are not directly in issue, and sometimes even cases challenging the ruling of the chief, the national authorities may go to the other extreme of applying the qualifying provisions without appreciating the traditional conditions they purport to serve. This is not only because of the judges' cultural preconditioning, but, more importantly, because of their ignorance of customary law. In such a case, change is haphazard and unoriented to the context.

In review, termination in Dinka society, though traditionally subtle and still slow, is increasingly utilized. But in view of the limitations of those who operate its machinery, it is often inarticulate and limited in perspective. Its problems are an integral part of the problems of the competitive participation in power which marks the present-day Dinka and Sudanese society.

4. Affection

Because of the pervasive role of the Dinka family, the exclusive and the inclusive aspects of affection are fused. The family provides the emotional dependence which marks family relationship in any society and in addition provides the bases for broadened loyalties. It broadens intimate circles by extending them beyond the spouses and their children, but weakens social identifications by subjecting them to the personalized circles in which blood or the fiction of blood is the foundation.

Within the family, continuation of the lineage necessitates emphasis on affection for mythical participants. Whenever a beast is sacrificed to them, which is one way of expressing loyalty to them, the sacrificial meat must be shared by the members of the family or the kinship. The meat is divided according to fixed principles to symbolize unity in the "Great Fathers," as mythical participants are often called. A Dinka chief explained to Dr. Lienhardt that "the people are put together, as a bull is put together."

> Since every bull or ox is destined for sacrifice, each one demonstrates, potentially, the ordered social relationships of the sacrificing group, the members of which are indeed "put together" in each piece as represented in their precise relationship to each other [and to their mythical participants] in the meat which it provides.[1]

The expression of affection for the ancestors takes other forms. Cattle are dedicated to them and kept in the herds, the bulls and oxen among them being eventually sacrificed. If a man dies before marrying, a wife or wives are married for him to perpetuate his line. Cattle dedicated to mythical participants are included in the bride wealth and the reverse payments of every marriage. In this way, the claims of the mythical participants to the affection of the woman and her offspring are justified. As soon as a woman is married she is expected to know all the names of her husband's clan divinities and their emblems, as well as the genealogy

1. Lienhardt, *Divinity* 23.

of the family. From the time her children start to speak they are made
to recite all the names of this genealogy in their proper order. This is
the first criterion for testing a child's intelligence. Just as the mythicals
participate in the payment of the bride wealth, they share in the bride
wealth of female offspring. Their portion must be provided first and
promptly.

Affection between mythical and real participants is reciprocal: mythical participants should also have affection for their living members, or
the living are justified in withholding their affection or the expression
of their affection.[2] If not shown affection, they too may withhold affection or its expression.[3] The retaliation of mythical participants to the
withholding of affection is expressed in their failing to help or in their
inflicting deprivations. Since the effect often precedes Dinka thought
about the cause, any deprivations are likely to be attributed to the withdrawal of mythical help. This calls for propitiation and appeasement. If
the mythical participants are the first to withhold affection or refuse to
be appeased, then, because of their primacy and despite justifiable retaliation on the side of the living, the most expedient thing to do is to
blame them in prayer but to propitiate them further and request pardon. When a man claims that he will give no more if he is forsaken, he
hopes to influence the mythical participants with threats of reprisal.
Since a person does not lose face by succumbing to a superior authority
and in particular the mythicals, such threats are not often carried out.

Based on the same grounds as the paramountcy of the mythical participants is the primacy of the paterfamilias in the affection process of
the living. Because of the concept of permanent identity and influence,
the affectional relationships of the various living and deceased members
are interdependent. Although mutual affection between a man and a
woman is not a condition precedent to marriage, the Dinka place much
emphasis on it. The man's affection for a proposed bride is often the
subject matter of the songs composed during the period of relaxation
known as *toc*. The singer declares his affection for the girl, his wish to
marry her, and his request for help from his kinsmen. Courtship, with

2. Such is the theme of these lines from a song collected by Fr. Nebel and quoted
in Lienhardt, *Divinity* 142: "I give to divinity, Flesh, my red bull / If I am forsaken,
I shall give no more."

3. This is the essence of these words attributed to Divinity:

> If a man loves me,
> I love him;
> And if a man hates me,
> I hate him;
> But not with all of my heart shall I hate,
> For am I not the prosperity and happiness of the ants!

its elaborate speech techniques rich in parables, metaphors, and the like is a universal institution aimed at achieving mutuality in affection. Because of the interplay between the individual and the group interest in marriage, such affection is a matter of concern to the age mates of both parties and to their kin folk. According to the custom of levirate, any of a man's agnates may well be a genitor someday. And according to the custom of female replacement, any of a woman's female relatives may one day be put in her shoes. But interest in the mutual affection of the spouses is more pervasive than that. It is the name of the man's group which is to be continued and will continuously be involved. The woman's group hope to prolong their line by using the cattle of her marriage to obtain wives for themselves.

The group interest in the affection of the spouses-to-be is shown in their participation in courtship. Relatives and friends, whether as individuals or groups, are expected to spend time with the girl and her female relatives or friends—even though the man is not with them. On their visits, conversation rotates around persuading her to *gam,* "accept," or *nhiar,* "like or love," him. Usually, whatever her real feelings, a girl puts on a show of refusal. But the involvement of relatives and friends aims at occupying her with courtship whether she loves their man or not. The Dinka say that this is to countervail anticipated competition. An unmarried Dinka girl is open to competition and it is the technique of competing individuals or groups to gossip against each other in the hope of alienating the girl from the competitor. This is often a subject of the songs of Dinka youth. These are lines from one.

> I am courting a young beauty in Abyor
> But gossipers whisper into her ears
> "Is Kwol Tiel Magak the man to marry you?"

This may cause a fight between courters, as these lines indicate.

> The courtship of Ajang de Deng
> Is in a boiling-pot
> There is a man who is hiding
> A man who speaks behind my back
> My ox, Mayom, I will blow him open
> The man who gossips to my bride
> I will blow him open.[4]

Such gossip may also be directed to the girl's relatives to influence them not to give their girl to the proposing man.

---

4. The dance to which this song is sung is a variation of war dance. However, despite the fighting attitude it reveals, the content is different from the ordinary war songs because the conflict is individual and not collective.

The sons of Kwol d'Arob have thrown me to the Ngok
They have thrown me to the Ngok of Arob
The Ngok gossip about me
Arab d'Allor is a man without a mother
Do not give him this only girl
He is a man who cannot hold a hoe.
Do not give him this only girl
Do not give him Alai.[5]

The final word in courtship is reached after the age set (usually relatives and friends) of the couple meet to discuss the question of her affection. Even in cases where her affection for him is known, the group
conference is essential. In theory, the pivotal decision is that of her
age set. Should they accept contrary to her will, they are expected to
persuade her to consent. In practice, a determined refusal may never be
shaken. If she is known to be in love and is not desirous of concealing
the fact, she will usually say that the decision lies with her age mates,
but in such a case the acceptance of the age set is a matter of course.
Their affirmative decision is usually phrased as "We have loved him,"
and this automatically binds her to follow suit, either immediately or
after a show of resistance followed by age set persuasion. An age set's
refusing consent when the prospective bride likes the prospective groom
is practically unknown. For one thing, the group are quite interested
in their girl's being married, because of the importance of the status and
the wealth it brings, among other things. Besides, in their preconference
relations, members of the age set have the opportunity to influence the
girl. Should they fail, the girl will of course refrain from convening
them to hear their judgment.

There are other methods by which a betrothed girl shows her affection
for her future groom. For instance, according to the custom of *mioc* she
visits his home with her age mates, carrying gifts of food or other materials. Several days of festivities and social intercourse between the respective age mates of the couple ensue.

Most of this premarital demonstration of affection should be viewed
as an interlinkage of anticipated conjugal affection and age-set affection
within and between corresponding sex groups. Consistent with this is
consideration of the subjectivities of those most immediately involved in
the forthcoming marriage, although their subjectivities are attuned to
the group interests. This is largely a practice of youth and to a lesser
extent of seniors marrying young girls, not a practice of the elders who
are the authoritative decision-makers on the marriage.

The elders are usually engaged in marriage negotiations without any

5. The bride.

regard to the "acceptance," the "liking," or "love" with which the immediate parties and their respective groups are concerned. Courtship
and mutual affection between the couple are seen by their elders as important, but only for convenience, and are not a requirement for the
essential validity of marriage. The couple is to marry in order to beget
children, maximize group values, and perpetuate group participation.
This being basic, their affection for each other is secondary. This subordination of the need for mutual affection among the parties often
leads to such customary but detested practices as elopement, impregnation of girls by unauthorized lovers, institutionalized rape (in which a
man's age mates may assist in enforcing consummation of a marriage on
a refusing bride), and "adultery" with betrothed but unwilling girls.

Once marriage is complete, the process of affection takes a turn in
which the husband becomes an even more central figure. Of course, he
is expected to show affection for his wife, and this may take many forms,
such as sexual relations, gifts, especially of livestock, help in the cultivation of her private field, and so on. Because of the transcendence of permanence through children, his affection for her children enhances his
affection for her. His affection for her also determines his feeling for
her children. One of the most serious punishments a man can impose
on his wife is to deprive her of children.

Paradoxically, mothers of initiated men or married daughters cease
to bear children. Even before their initiation or marriage, teen-age children whose mothers continue to bear children are usually, though jokingly, ridiculed by their age mates and even by senior people. The reason for this is not clear. It may, however, be explained in a number of
ways. To give one example, since men with wives of that age usually
marry young girls both in their own interest and in order to serve the
senior wives, the relationship of the senior and the junior wives, which
is usually symbolized as one of mother and daughter and is less marked
with the usual cowives' jealousies, would be strained by their competition over the husband's bed. Such a strain would seriously impinge on
the usual principles of deference between them and jeopardize the
unity and harmony of the family. The explanation the Dinkas give, and
one which is implied in the reason given above, is that to continue bearing children is contrary to the moral integrity and the dignity required
by the position of a senior woman. It is important to note that it is not
so much childbearing as it is sexual intercourse which is here detested.
In any case, the advantage is the husband's and the detriment the wife's.
Dinka women, being devoted to and dependent on their children, are
sufficiently gratified. They may not feel and certainly do not express
resentment.

The wife shows her affection in devotion to her husband and in the performance of her conjugal obligations. She must take good care of him, particularly in regard to nutrition.[6] Although a Dinka husband is not expected to express his affection for his wife in words, she is expected to verbalize her affection for him in songs which, though not expressing affection as such, praise the husband either directly or indirectly by praising his personality ox or his lineage. In these songs, she refers to him as "I" and thus identifies herself with him.[7]

Because of the interplay between affection and the myth of permanence, the longer the marriage, the deeper the family affection. What really matters is the children. A barren woman may be and usually is divorced if the husband is not rich enough to marry other wives to bear him children. A woman who mistreats the children, whether her own or her cowife's, finds her husband's affection for her significantly decreased. A woman whose children die may lose affection and be divorced. Such a wife is often suspected of being responsible for the children's death by concealing some wrongful conduct on her part, such as adultery. The wife's affection may be alienated on the same grounds, and the husband's impotence may lead to divorce.

The husband's supremacy in conjugal affection means that his sex interests over her are protected, while hers over him are not. Thus, polygyny is allowed, while polyandry is unknown. Female exclusiveness and male freedom in sex are shown by the fact that before the impact of the Arabs and the West, Dinka men went naked, while married women had to wear long leather skirts. Girls had to wear short skirts on formal occasions and might be nude when informal.

In these inequities are rooted some of the factors most damaging to family affection. They make married life one of inconsistencies in affection. In most cases, on marriage, even if there is no "romantic love," there is at least unity in expectation of children. When children are born, the father-mother relationship deepens, but the inequities of her position will have created tensions leading to the weakening of affection. Dinka women are well aware of these inequities. Although they may speak of them as the natural consequences of their status as women, mal-

---

6. The practice of *agoor*, whereby a woman leaves special food to offer her husband behind closed doors, is generally condemned as inhospitable, but it is universal and is expected of a loving wife, even if the man only tastes it and gives it away. A popular children's play song which the Ngok attribute to the Tuic goes:

Shall I ever grow
To marry a wife
To cook for me by day
And also by night.

7. In one song, for instance, the wife says, "I have never said a word to be carried on" when she means her husband has never said a word of gossip.

content often results which, though repressed, is nonetheless real and injurious to the overriding goals of unity and harmony. Given the expectation that almost all cases of unfaithfulness by wives will be confessed because of strong religious compulsion, the degree to which the wife's discontent is expressed is impressively low. Dinka women are very faithful. But unfaithfulness exists which at least in part may be attributed to the wife's inferiority.[8] The paradoxes of the wife's affection position are shown in this song of a woman whose analysis is unusually "liberal" by Dinka standards.

> Perish, O people;
> Perish, people of our land.
> With their eagerness to judge,
> They grab a person's case
> When they do not know its cause.
> Marriage of a woman is bad.
> When she is married,
> She is most admired.
> And when she lives
> And gives birth to a child
> To be a man among men,
> She is pushed aside.
> So she steps out of the hut,
> She is in search for another man.
> For her it is good
> But to the Dinka, it is evil,
> She is a woman who seeks men.

Disaffection may cause divorce, which can be initiated by the wife herself. However, because of his supremacy and the wife's greater dependence, the husband usually initiates it. Even when she is the initiator, it is normally through her male kin.

The principles governing the relations between the spouses also apply to the parent-child relationship. The affection of the parents for the children and of the chlidren for the parents is an important factor in the principle of perpetuation. The father being the main beneficiary of perpetuation, the society emphasizes father-child affection over mother-child affection. The father's affection is expressed in caring for the child's physical and spiritual well-being, providing him with food and livestock, instructing him—in short, indulging him in the values controlled by the father in his capacity as the family head. A child who falls out of his father's favor therefore faces a fundamental deprivation.

8. On the other hand, we may speculate that the greater the female equality, the more freely and frequently disapproval is expressed in unfaithfulness.

It is a common theme for young men to mourn their father's death in songs and attribute their difficulties in society to this loss.[9] By virtue of this dependence, a Dinka child incurs an obligation to his father. He is to assist him in life when able to do so,[10] and more: this filial affection is the father's insurance against mortality. The perpetuation of the father's role is best achieved in the child's affection. Consequently, a Dinka child, especially a son, grows up being made to discriminate in favor of the father. He is asked which of the parents he loves. To answer in favor of the mother and acquire the reputation of "a woman's child" is a lack of wisdom which even the mother would discourage. An overwhelming portion of Dinka song is devoted to pride in one's father and expressing affection and respect for him.

Nonetheless, a Dinka child is often more closely associated with the mother. When the mother is nursing, which may be for two to three years, sexual relations between the spouses is forbidden. The mother shares the bed or sleeping mat with her unweaned and sometimes with her weaned child. Her association with the husband is thus discouraged in favor of her association with her child. This intensifies the mother-child relationship. In addition, because of polygyny, the child is more often identified with her. It is this strong attachment between mother and child which the Dinka purport to discourage in order to maintain the paramountcy of the father. While a Dinka child calls his father "Father," he calls his mother by what in Western terms would be her first name. This gives primacy to paternal deference but also reveals the intimacy between mother and child. Ideally, a Dinka child is the focus of family affection, but because the family institution is primarily for the father's lineage, his father's position is manifestly superior even though real emotion favors the mother. These factors interplay in this song:

> My wife called me
> "Hold my child
> Things are getting wet in the rain.
> O son of my mother [11]

9. In other songs these lines appear:

In the Court of the Chiefs
I have seen the misery of an orphan
. . . .
When my father disappeared at Maker of Abyor
I was almost called "*Ber*, dog
Ber black dog without colors"

Ber is the Dinka word for calling dogs.

10. This is what is meant by the proverb "It is what you bear which redeems you."

11. An intimate way for wives to refer to their husbands and it is usually used either indirectly by any wife as in songs or directly by senior wives.

I am not disdaining you
Hold my child
Things are wet in the rain
I am not disdaining you."
In the evening
We sat around the fire to talk.
Between my wife and me
The Little One got up to walk
My wife cried in fear,
"O son of my father
Come to my side
The Little One will fall into the fire."

There are many bases of affection for a child, but cutting across them is pride in the child's physical courage. Titherington, observing that "the relations between children and parents are most affectionate," adds that "[I]ndependence [12] begins at an amusingly early age," and "any early sign of courage gives great delight to both mother and father, and the child is petted and even kissed for it." [13] This helps develop in a Dinka male child the warlike attributes of youth.

The close association between the affection of the husband and wife and that of the parents and children makes father-child affection susceptible to the negative aspects of husband-wife relationship. Because of her greater though disguised influence, she can interject through her children all the grievances and the bitterness of the inequities she suffers. This is why in most cases of father-son conflict there is an element of father-mother relationship. There are more grounds for conflict between father and son than the mother's influence. Although he is a protector, the father is also an impediment to the son's value position, which depends largely on the father. On his side, too, the father is threatened by the son, who is his successor. It is the son who will inherit the father's young wives and beget his half-brothers for the lineage. This is often a threat *inter vivos,* for as the father ages, his fear that young wives will be attracted to his sons increases. Adultery by sons, though a serious offense, does occur.

The areas in which the son poses a threat to the father are manifold. The hostility caused by these threats is behind the custom of avoidance between parents and children. While they are often thus avoided or resolved when they occur, conflicts between father and child, unlike those between mother and child, may lead to the severance of relations. This is carried out through a ritual which may be performed by the court and which disaffiliates the child from his father, although it does

12. From excessive parental control and protection.
13. Titherington 204.

not terminate his clan affiliation. The child may initiate proceedings for such severance, but it is unlikely that he would do so since he would be the more deprived.

The theme of combined affection and hostility between father and son sometimes appears in Dinka songs. In this song, for instance, a favored son boasts of his father's affection for him and interprets it as the result of his knowing the best way to manipulate his father to his own advantage. He also speaks of untoothing his father, which means that he does not expect conflict with him. He believes that he uses affection to win affection, but his symbols reveal ambivalence.

> Those of you begotten by the son of Yar,
> Who among you knows his fatal spot?
> Is it the senior Deng or the junior Deng?
> Is it Allor Maker, or is it Biong?
> I have discovered the fatal spot of my father.
> I hit it with ease on the surface.
> What will vex me
> When I untoothed my father last Winter?

While the parent-child affection is similar for both sons and daughters, there is less concern about the affections of the daughter. Maternal attachment is less discouraged. The daughter's main contribution to lineage permanence is that she provides the bride wealth to continue the agnatic line. She leaves her group and joins that of her husband. Although the current attitude is to understand the more pervasive social functions of bride wealth and therefore see it less as a "price," the Dinka themselves speak of girls, though somewhat ironically, as "slaves," *aloony,* who are "sold." Since they leave their own group, they are also spoken of as "strangers," *alei.* Their position must not, however, be seen as undermined by this sarcasm, for apart from the values they acquire by extending kinship ties, they remain attached to their own groups. In certain respects a girl remains more loyal to them than to her marital kin, a fact which justifies her dependence on them in the event of a crisis with her husband. It is they who will propitiate and conciliate the husband whenever he is indignant. Since she remains attached to her kin, she can and does influence the family affection process.

Family affection comes into grave jeopardy in cowives' relationships, which are marked with jealousies. These jealousies may involve group versus group or wife versus wife. The reputation of Dinka women as jealous despite the demands of the society is encountered at every level of Dinka life.[14]

14. For a story illustrating the myth that it was a woman who caused the original break into clans see Nebel, *Dinka Grammar* 127 (1948).

There are various customs which may be viewed as ways of minimizing tensions among wives. Where there are two wives, the junior wife is put under the senior and assumes the role of a daughter. In certain parts of Dinkaland, if the senior wife has adult sons, the junior wife calls them "uncles," *walen*. Thus, where there are only two or three wives, the whole family is reduced by fiction into a monogamous, or nuclear, family. Where there are many wives, the two principal wives stand in the position of senior and junior wives, each heading her own "house" of wives, thus reducing the two groups further into a nuclear family. This fiction is not complete because the two groups are kept separate, but the husband at least reduces the number of people to be controlled. He then deals mainly with the two (or three, as the case may be) who are the leaders of the groups.

Tiel, "jealousy," is controlled by the dominant character of the husband and the sons. Their success as men is partly dependent on how well they maintain harmony among their women. A son is encouraged to dispel his mother's jealousies and those of the internal group with which he is identified. His character is esteemed by the degree of his disapproval of *tiel*. Most mothers take pride in instilling this quality in their sons. A mother often encourages her son to show more consideration to her cowives than to herself. Boys must assemble the food prepared by their mothers and eat together. They are encouraged to fight in defense of each other. They must learn to look after each other's cattle as "our father's cattle" and therefore "our cattle," even if the cattle are allotted to individual wives.

Nonetheless, *tiel* exists even among the children. It is particularly striking among the daughters, over whom the mother's influence is more pronounced, although it also marks the relations of half-brothers.[15] The *tiel* of daughters is the subject of many bedtime stories. These stories show the common existence of *tiel* and demonstrate the community's disapproval, and their moral is nearly always that a jealous person suffers some major punishment. This appraisal is made without any feeling of contradiction, because most people allege that it is the opposing group and not they who are jealous.

15. In this song, a man addresses his half-brother with whom he aligns in a family disrupted by *tiel*:

It is our camp with Col of my father.
Kerbeek, Col, let us move away from here,
A place where people have become vile.
Talking like a dog that eats what he is not given is bad
Malou, people are bewitching me.
Since our father left us in this world
Tiel has given birth to a calf.

Under the conditions of change a new trait has entered the picture of family solidarities; the present influx into urban centers is extending affection beyond the family. Temporary search for jobs by some members of the family is a common phenomenon. The resulting separation is increased by lack of telephones, telegraphs, mail delivery, or other methods of communication. Because of this a Dinka proverb says that absence is like death. Absence is further disruptive because the absentee often acquires different perspectives. For the educated, new perspectives create a greater rift between them and the traditionals. Since all those who leave acquire values through their own endeavors, they tend to be less acquiescent to the traditional family obligations which expressed affection. This change, dramatized by the discrepancies in value acquisition, makes traditionals view modernizing changes with disfavor. This is a factor behind occasional reference to the educated class and people in similar situations as "heartless," *acien pioth*.

Affection based on blood and in-law relationship extends itself into broader descent groups with similar characteristics. Apart from the particular fictions of familial extension marking the status of the chief and similar public figures, there is a general fictional extension of kin identification permeating social relationships. Relational extension is facilitated by the rules of exogamy which compel marriage beyond present blood and (to a lesser extent) marital affinities.[16] As we follow the threads of family bonds into the territorial level, blood and marriage give way to other forms of social identifications. Prominent among these is the territorial identification behind chiefly lineages, generational identification with age sets, and modern national and educational identifications.

Territorial identification behind chiefs gives a new dimension to familial fiction in that the territorial unit itself is conceived as a type of family whose interrelationship is not personalized to itself in the same way that ordinary familial indentfications are. A person may refer to the chief as his father. However, the position of the chiefs as heads of the fictional families—the territorial units—is reinforced by their multiple marriages into the tribe and between their own families. From the point of view of the commoners also, marriage into the chiefly clans is an important advantage.[17] Of course, marriage into and from such families is

16. The extension of blood ties in reality and in fiction is evident in the extensive use of kin, step-kin, and in-law terms. For examples see Seligman, and Seligman *Pagan Tribes of the Nilotic Sudan* 151–53 (1932).

17. The Dinka think it good to marry into and from such clans. "In their idiom 'they climb up the roots of the masters.' To have a master of the fishing-spear as a brother-in-law, and as the maternal uncle of one's children, is to make specially available for them the benefits of the invocations (among other things) which he has the power effectively to make." Lienhardt, *Divinity* 200.

difficult, for although the Dinka have no caste system and anyone may marry within the limits of exogamy or other rules restricting marriage, it is easier for a rich, respected, or popular family, or one distinctly indulged in any other particular value, to marry from or into chiefly families than for a person who is relatively deprived. The singer, desiring to marry into the Pajok, whom he symbolizes as God, shows the difficulties of his objective:

> I follow after ivory [18] into the byre of God.
> I creep under the bosom of the Creator,
> I am trailing the clan Pajok;
> I pursue the clan Pajok
> Begging them to give me Ayan.
> But who will give me Ayan?
> Has not my father entered the earth?
> Ayan, daughter of Allor,
> If only my father had lifted the earth,
> My father would have brought her to me.

After he presented his song, Ayan was given to him. Another, wanting to marry the daughter of Chief Deng Majok, whom he refers to here by various praise names, tells of the magnitude of his undertaking, though confident of his social standing and his wealth:

> . . . I am coming into the byre of the Creator,
> O that my father Gitbek were alive
> I would not be in misery.
> Abul, daughter of Mangar wearing the robe
> I will strive for you.
> I know of no one higher than you . . .
> Abul, friend who is high
> Daughter of the tribe
> Though you are beyond reach
> I will not despair.
> Mangar, my age set
> Do not fear my father Deng Majok, the chief.
> I have chosen Abul like ivory in the clan of Arob.

Affection among the Dinka is also extended beyond blood and marriage by friendship. The Dinka realize that friendship can be stronger than blood relationship. In this sense, it provides an alternative to family affection. Apart from ordinary friendship, there is a contract of friendship by which the contracting parties undertake to assist each other whenever need arises. Failure to abide by this agreement may lead

---

18. The bride is symbolized as being valuable as ivory.

to the breaking of the friendship, *riak maath,* and the restoration of important things exchanged in the meantime. Judicial opinion is against this custom and it is now being erased from Dinka law. While friendship is an alternative to the family, it is also conditioned by the family. This is reflected in the rite of blood fusion in which friends prick themselves and fuse blood to symbolize blood relationship. The reciprocal gifts connected with friendship often take the form of assistance in the payment of the friend's bride wealth or the bride wealth of his kinsmen. Collaterally, a friend shares in the distribution of incoming bride wealth. In such cases, analogous exogamy may apply; or, if marriage is allowed, friendship is terminated.

One of the most important alternatives to the family in the process of affection is the age set. Age setting begins during childhood with mock initiations and collective activities. The child's scope of affection through age sets becomes broader and broader until it reaches the subtribal level on adult initiation. From that time, the age set becomes permanent: the dominant warrior group represents a recently initiated age set, while the ruling set represents an age set associated with the ruling chief and with authority in general. If a young man succeeds to authority, the ruling age sets are a complex of both his elder predecessor's and his own. These provide a further complement to the chief's affection circle. In addition, the "fathers" of the age sets are always chosen from the chiefly lineages.

Among the most important aspects of the solidarity of age sets is their close association with the marriage of every age mate and with other male-female social activities. Despite corresponding age grouping, earlier maturity of women results in males going below their age set for social relationships with girls. Since corresponding male and female age sets are in theory to associate because they are potential spouses, this incursion by older sets is often seen as interference with an exclusive right. This, coupled with the strategy of attracting affection by physical courage, results in interage-set fights.

The use of violence in connection with affection is not confined to this collective generational competition. Since there are often many impediments to marriage, such as young lovers, most sex offenses (which may also involve violence) are committed by frustrated young men, sometimes with the assistance of age mates. So prevalent are these that while the community generally disapproves of them they are institutionalized and used to justify those marriages which are otherwise difficult to arrange. For instance, elopement or pregnancy may force the elders to consent to a proposed marriage. Nonetheless, they are offenses which might prompt violence. Before the colonial influence, fights between families and even more inclusive groups were often caused by these provocations. They still occur, but the tendency is to fight in court.

The educated are somewhat similar to the warrior age sets in that they too represent an alternative to the family, and their circle is the most extended. Their education deemphasizes their differences and they find unity in it and in their common objectives. They reflect a fermenting situation in which generational and cultural factors are intensely interactive. In accordance with traditional expectations, their affection for elders is more emphasized than that of the elders for them. In their marriages, their elders must make the ultimate decision. In most cases, these educated men have older brothers whose marriages have priority. Even though they may have the wealth and other prerequisites for marriage, they are expected to assist the older ones before they themselves marry. Some manage to achieve compromises, but the general situation is one of conflict.

Another major deprivation is the lack of an educated female group. An educated man often finds no common base of affection for an uneducated girl. When modernization was still viewed as a vice and the educated as alienated and deprived, the problem was one of their being rejected. The singer in this song was a man in competition with an educated man during this early period.

> When I see a man who rides a bicycle
> I see him as though he were adopted.
> You are not the son of the "father" [missionary],
> The "father" is not your father.
> My woman, Ajok, forget him
> Do not put shame on yourself
> His proposal will end under *abyei* [19]
> And under *ngaab*.[20]
> The cheap marriages of schoolboys,
> They are easily shaken by the wind
> The marriages are waved by the wind.
> Forget the daughter of the chief
> You will never fulfill the marriage.
> For the daughter of Giir Mayuot,
> I shall compete with the people of bicycles.

Now the public has accepted the educated class as privileged in many ways, and the problem is one of the educated rejecting uneducated girls.

19. This does not refer to the administrative center of the Ngok but to a tree from which Abyei derives its name. Dinkas usually meet their dates under trees and much courtship takes place under trees. During the day time, trees provide shade and at night they help to conceal couples from the light of the moon and the stars.

20. Another tree.

Many are the cases in which fathers propose marriages for their sons to illiterate girls and the sons refuse, or accept only to be divorced.

On the national level to which their identifications extend, the educated encounter the difficulties of ethnic diversity. The failure of affection in this circle expresses itself in various forms. Intermarriage between Northerners and Southerners is minimal. This is because Islam does not permit the marriage of a Muslim woman to a non-Muslim. The obstacle is therefore greater for Southern men. Though the Southern coauthors, William Deng and Joseph Oduho, exaggerate the point, especially in relation to the upbringing of children, this observation rings true.

> Sudanese Arabs are in continuous relation with African women and girls who are taken as concubines with the object of creating a progeny which will call itself Arab. . . . On the other hand it is practically unthinkable for a Southerner (no matter how Islamicised he may be) to marry a Northern girl.[21]

L. A. Fabunni, a Nigerian observer wrote, "The writer is reliably informed by a Northern Sudanese friend that it is practically impossible for a Southerner to marry a Northern woman, but that a Northern male can easily marry a Southern beauty." [22] To be exact, it would be practically impossible for traditional Dinkas to accept marriage of a Dinka woman to an Arab. Northern men can only marry "loose," urbanized Dinka girls. On the other hand, intermarriage between Muslim and Arabized Dinkas and Northern women does occur, though this is a rarity. This means that rather than one-sided discrimination by Northerners, there is a more fundamental and mutual racio-cultural undertone, for intermarriage between these two sections is resented by the traditional elites of both the North and the South. Some of the educated youth of both sides profess indifference to this, but, because of the predominance of the traditional elites, their liberalism is of no significance. In intermarriage by either Northern or Dinka men, the women involved often represent an anomalous group with little, if any, social standing. The status their marriages create is also seen as inferior to both culture groups. That being the case, such intermarriage is of little consequence to the South-North affection process.

Another instance of the failure of South-North affection is that they have separate clubs as a result of a de facto segregation. In the University of Khartoum, association between Southerners and Northerners is limited. With only a few exceptions, they maintain separate tables in the dining hall, and occupy separate rooms in the hostels. Even the students'

21. Deng and Oduho, *The Problem of the Southern Sudan* 53–54 (1962).
22. Fabunni, *The Sudan in Anglo-Egyptian Relations* 356 (1960).

union, of which all students are automatically members, became segregated when the Southern students disaffiliated themselves in 1960. Inside the South, the problem is greatest. Anyone who mingles with both groups is susceptible to suspicion by both. Northerners in the South "object to an administrator who frequents a Southerner's club, or who through close personal contact attempts to gain their confidence." [23]

The failure of South-North affection is more than one of nonmarriage or nonassociation. The civil war is evidence of the total failure of affection and it is in turn reinforcing the failure. In its *Basic Facts about the Southern Provinces of the Sudan,* the government called the colonial period "An era where the whole machinery of Government aided by an auxiliary of powerful command over the minds and hearts of the people: The Christian mission . . . was vigorously directed towards inculcating the hatred of the Northern Sudanese into the minds of their Southern compatriots." [24] The government called for time and patience to alter the situation. Abundant evidence shows that the situation has altered, but for the worse. This deterioration affects all the dynamic participants, their objectives, and their value positions. It is evident that the government, far from evolving national consciousness, is facing disintegration. Even effective control over the South is reduced to the minimum and utilization of the Southern resources for maximizing values has become out of the question.

The greater the disaffection between the educated Southerners and the Northerners, including the government, the less their chances of participation in the power shaping and sharing. Intra-South factionalism increases with the differences in approach to the South-North problem, and affection among the Southerners, though enhanced by rising nationalism, is also endangered. With the social breakdown resulting from this disaffection, the goal of development dissipates.

Within the traditional context, disaffection on the national level becomes reflected and the vicious circle aggravates itself. The chiefs gain and lose the affection of both the government and the educated Dinkas, and indeed that of their traditional tribesmen. The traditional youth, resorting to their popular strategy, react to the South-North war by taking arms against Northerners. Then it is no longer the war of youth but of all. It is not easy to separate the aggressor from the self-defender, for the war is a cycle reflected narrowly between the traditional and the modern context, with both sides claiming retaliation. However, the suffering of the traditionals in this war and their decline in inclusive value terms by far surpass those of the moderns for whom the press and

23. Sudan Government, *Southern Sudan Disturbances* 125 (1956).

24. Sudan Government, *Basic Facts about the Southern Provinces of the Sudan* 17 (1964).

the more enlightened Northern participants occasionally act as watch-dogs of democracy and of human dignity. In the traditional sector, on the other hand, the security forces, largely unenlightened and undiplo-matic, are ruthless in their expression of disaffection for the far weaker tribesmen.

AFFECTION AND THE LAW

In view of the interdependence of values and their merger in the family institution, the legal issues involving affection permeate the social process. Here, we delimit the discussion of Dinka law concerning af-fection to a few categories. These are marriage, divorce, legitimacy and legitimation, and wrongs (including crime and tort). They will show how the relationships described in the preceding section are sanctioned by law.

Marriage

From what has been said about perpetuation as a fundamental goal modality of Dinka society, the importance of marriage must have be-come evident. To marry not only fulfills an individual objective, but also discharges a social duty. Dr. Farran quotes the following passage from a report by the present writer about the importance of marriage among the Dinka.

> There is not the least exaggeration in saying that the Dinka con-sider marriage as the first [thing] in the standard of importance. The duty to marry . . . is so strongly felt by all and believed in, that to have married is to have done the main duty in society. Thus any young Dinka will always think of the means to marry, whatever his social status may be. A person who, after having reached the age of maturity, has not the means to marry, is usually considered as *ayur,* i.e., low in the estimation of the members of society. Even if the only thing a young man can afford is marriage and nothing additional he would prefer to marry and *toom Nhialic nyin,* i.e. to gaze on God's face, by which is meant to remain without any-thing but his wife and God will again look upon him.[25]

Since continuity through procreation involves the whole lineage if not the clan, marriage is not simply a union of a man and a woman, but an alliance between two bodies of kin. This transforms the personal desire for marriage into a social duty.

In a society in which the family is the basic institution and in which

25. Quoted in Farran 68.

values are interrelated, marriage is a means to all values. It gives access to affection. In rectitude the guidance of the ancestors and other mythical participants is ensured through familial identifications. Apart from being a way of establishing a self-contained unit under the power of its primary benefactor, marriage may be used as a means of power. Domestic servants being rarely available, marriage provides a man with a woman's services. While it necessitates wealth disposition by way of bride wealth, it is also considered an investment for the anticipated marriages of female offspring. People assist in the payment of bride wealth with the expectation that the issue of the marriage will reimburse them with profit. When in this song a young man warns his elder relatives not to ask for the tusk of an elephant if he is left hunting alone, he is metaphorically warning them not to expect a share in the bride wealth of his daughters if the relatives do not help in paying his bride wealth.

> A son of man should not be left alone
> To struggle with people all alone
> Like a black bull of the buffalo.
> This marriage—the marriage of Alai—
> Has been dug out with words of feud
> The marriage has provoked a feud
> It has provoked a feud between me and my uncles.
> Do not think the matter simple.
> If it is because my father is gone,
> If it is the absence of my father, Allor, the son of Kwol
> And I am blind to the fact
> Then, please say it quick
> That I may know the truth . . .
> To stand and face the elephant
> To fight a lonely war with the elephant:
> But should he fall one day
> Please, forget his tusks,
> Do not ask for the tusks.

Social obligations and debts are sometimes discharged on a promise to pay out of the bride wealth of an unconceived child. In well-being, since the Dinka depend largely on magicoreligious prevention and cure, ancestral protection is secured through marriage. Another aspect of wellbeing rests in the warlike past of Dinka society which demanded a constant supply of fighting men. Marriage enhances one's status in society. It is only after marriage that one really becomes sui juris.

Cutting across this network of value interplay is the principle of perpetual identity and influence as expressed in procreation. When a woman's services are the incentive for marriage, they are sometimes con-

ceived of as a relief to the mother. Providing services becomes an indulgence by her progeny. In this song, a man who was unable to marry
for lack of cattle attempts to move his kinsmen to help him.

> I call upon the Creator
> Give me the vagina of a frog [26]
> So that I may redeem my mother from the mortar,
> So that I may redeem my mother from grinding
> When my guests come home . . .
> I wish I were born a girl in the clan Pajing
> So that I may redeem my mother from the mortar,
> So that I may redeem my mother from grinding.

In another song, a man protests that he is not married.

> Father, do not hide the truth from me;
> Let me know the truth.
> It is not that I am old
> It is the misery of Aluel Yak
> She struggles with the mortar and the pestle
> And drags herself stooping to fetch water from the river,
> Then she comes to cook
> When none of her age group still cook.

In most cases, on marriage a man separates his residence from that of
his parents so that it may seem groundless to use helping the mother
as the reason for marriage. But usually a young man wants to impress
his age mates with his family's hospitality, which calls for more effort
than elderly parents might make.

Affection between the spouses is sometimes directly expressed in terms
of procreation. In the following lines, the singer dreams of married life,
and associates his wife's affection and respect for him with his anticipated status as father of a child.

> O, the good times of marriage
> When adults chat over small things
> And then the woman holds the man
> And says, "Father of so and so."
> Then I answer, "Yes, yes."
> While I put my spears away
> I put the spears away after a journey
> Aker, I do so without words.

---

26. He asks to be turned into a female. His choosing the vagina of a frog does
not seem relevant except perhaps to make the thought less embarrassing.

In this song, although the affection for the future wife is not linked with the desired child, it is implied by the reference to the child's mother and her sister.

> Uncle, uncle, I want a little one who will hug me
> Uncle, uncle, I want a little one to whom lullabies will be sung
> One who will cry, "Ee-ee" while his mother cooks my food.
> Then I tell my sister-in-law,
> "Come and see what the little one is doing."
> Our age set, I would say to my sister-in-law,
> "The son of your sister is crying."
> Uncle, uncle, I want a little one who will hold me.

Viewing it from the standpoint of sanctions, the duty to marry is enforced by the threat of deprivations of the values that would otherwise accrue through marriage. The kin group of a person refusing marriage may withdraw its affection from him. Ancestral curse is deemed effective against a person who abandons the continuation of the lineage. A withdrawal of respect may also be expected.

FORMS OF MARRIAGE Conspicuous expressions of the role perpetuity plays in Dinka social and legal processes are found in marital unions some of which are quite unknown in Anglo-American culture. The various forms of marriage are simple legal marriage, the levirate, ghost marriage, and other types of marriage which, though they could be fitted into the category of simple legal marriage, are differentiated by their alien origin.

Simple legal marriage is the normal union between a man and a woman. In polygyny the man may be married to another woman, but the woman must be unmarried although she might be betrothed. In a simple marriage, the children are expected to be the husband's legal and biological issue, and trace their line through him. Apart from polygyny, therefore, simple or ordinary marriage does not differ markedly from marriage anywhere.

Simple marriage does not end on the death of the husband, although it may be terminated by divorce. A widow merely transfers her union to the levirate, by which she lives with her husband's nearest agnate. This may be his eldest son if the woman is not his own mother or judged too old for him. It may also be with the next brother, nephew, or cousin of the dead man. With the consent of the widow, the deceased husband's legal heir may delegate the right of cohabitation to another relative. The principal heir retains an overriding right over the widow so that in case of any interference with the marital rights of his dead relatives, he is the representative entitled to recover. Such was the case in *Deng v.*

Gwiny de Col [27] where Deng brought a suit against Gwiny for adultery with Deng's father's widow then living with another relative by agreement. Corresponding to his overriding right over her is the heir's duty to the widow, even though she might be living with his agent. Such an agent is limited in his authority and in most cases is not entitled to sue if there has been an infringement of conjugal rights.

Since the heir merely steps into the shoes of the deceased relative for the purpose of procreation, a marriage ceremony is neither necessary nor performed. It is therefore somewhat misleading to term this type of union "levirate marriage." The important thing is that the procreative potential of the widow must not be frustrated by her husband's death, nor should the man's name and participation end merely by reason of his death. The children of the levirate union are therefore considered his legal children. He is the pater and his living agnate is merely the genitor. Even in common usage, the genitor is never referred to as the father of the children. The children themselves will refer to him as half-brother or uncle, according to his relationship to their dead pater. His role is well described by the Dinka term for the levirate, *la ghot,* "entering the hut" of the dead man.

Levirate is also associated with the interest of the wife's agnatic kin. Her procreation and all its associated value enhancement are not exclusively the husband's. The whole lineage collected her bride wealth because of this community interest in her, and her continued presence and productivity is of vital interest to them. The Dinka say that the wife belongs to all people. In the interest of the agnatic group the genitor, being also the foster father, provides the widow with a home and her orphaned children with a father's care. Since levirate is primarily in the interest of the husband and his kin, the widow has to cohabit with a man of their choice. Sometimes, especially today, she is allowed to choose whom "to enter with"; however, her choice is limited to the relatives of her deceased husband.

This subordination of women underlying bride wealth and levirate was observed by the British government when it was still in charge of Sudan foreign relations. The government reported to the United Nations ad hoc Committee on Slavery that "A certain amount of purchase of wives and inheritance of widows by the heir of the deceased husband, involving subjection of a woman to a man not of her own choice, is inevitable in a country where by tradition women are regarded as inferior to men." [28] But the levirate can be compulsory to both parties.

27. Abyei, Ngok Dinka, Court (1946); Howell, "Ngok Dinka" 291.

28. United Kingdom, Reply to the Questionnaire on Slavery and Servitude, the Anglo-Egyptian Sudan, E/AC. 33/10/Add. 96 p. 2 (1952). The report added that "In the Southern Sudan no such subjection occurs!" Ibid. It is not clear whether the gov-

This is illustrated by *Adol Majith v. Col. Agwer*.[29] Adol's brother died, leaving a widow who was related to Col. She was inherited by Adol in levirate. Adol refused to live with her on the grounds that she had caused his brother's death. He brought an action claiming divorce for his late brother and the return of his brother's bride wealth. The court, considering the accusation against the widow unsubstantiated, refused the divorce. Adol was ordered to live with her or forfeit the bride wealth.

The dictum in this case illustrates that the levirate, like any other marriage, could be dissolved on legitimate grounds. Even the widow may initiate divorce. However, judicial attitude is strongly against the dissolution of marriage after the husband's death. To let things remain as the dead man left them seems to be the guiding principle. Even in situations where normal marriage might be dissolved, the court often refuses the dissolution of the levirate.

Although the dead man's agnatic group is interested in the procreation of the widow, her sexual relations are limited to the person chosen to cohabit with her. Any sexual relationships with her by a kinsman or a stranger is an offense against the legal heir to the wife as the representative of the dead man.

The sexual-affectional desires of those who cannot afford to marry are sometimes satisfied by the fulfillment of this procreation obligation to the older generations. This is why young men sometimes litigate over the inheritance of widows.

Once it is accepted that procreation justifies the continuance of marriage after death so that the dead man is provided with male issue, it follows that those men who die too young to be married, or who die leaving behind no male issue, should not be deprived of posterity. This is the foundation of ghost marriage. The heir of such a dead man must marry a wife for him. If the dead man was senior to the heir, even though he might have died as a baby, his ghost marriage must have priority. Apart from the legal problems that would arise, failure to fulfill his obligation is believed to inflict a curse, *acien,* on the living. The marriage creates a legal relationship between the woman and the dead man. Any children born are his legitimate children and are entitled to rights through him. Their relationship in the lineage structure is traced through him. As in levirate, he is the pater and the prohusband is the genitor and the foster father.

Ghost marriage may be performed by a woman if her husband dies

---

ernment meant that the institutions of bride wealth and levirate did not exist in the South or that they did not result in subjection even though they existed. In any case, either interpretation would not reflect the true situation.

29. Abyei, Ngok Dinka Court (1954).

leaving her without a son and she is past the childbearing age or is barren and her husband has no close agnates to discharge the ghost marriage obligation. She invites a man to cohabit with a woman and the children are her dead husband's.

The kinsmen on whose behalf a wife may be married are fathers, older brothers, paternal uncles, or maternal uncles. Generally, the system is not reversible, so that a man would not be obligated to marry for himself a wife to the name of his son, nor would a maternal uncle marry for the name of his sister's son. The system usually does not go back more than one generation, so a man would not marry for his grandfather, since that was for his father to do. These generational factors are significant. Not all those who die are thus privileged. Ghost marriage is widespread, owing to the high mortality rate among men, but the resources of the living do not always afford the discharge of this obligation. Priority is given to senior generations. It is not unusual that people who have begotten children biologically die without legal issue because they could not afford their own marriages.

The legal principles involved in ghost marriage are identical with those of levirate. The fundamental difference is that in ghost marriage, the relationship is created subsequent to the husband's death and the ceremonies of marriage are performed by the genitor, while in levirate the union continues as the dead man left it and no further formalities are necessary. Since in levirate, the marriage had not been contracted by the genitor and the woman had in most cases lived with the pater for some time, the genitor's control over her is less than in ghost marriage. In levirate, some of the children are usually the biological children of the pater, but in ghost marriage, none of the children are the dead man's biological children. Because of the closer association among the genitor, the wife, and the children in ghost marriage, it is conceived of as closer to a normal marriage. Children of the ghost marriage are referred to by the name of the genitor and, for most purposes, he is taken as the husband and the father. It is only on closer examination that their status becomes clear. The issue of the ghost marriage derive their rights from both the pater and the genitor, whereas the rights of the levirate children, except for the limited ones of guardianship, accrue through the pater only.

These traditional forms apply to educated Dinkas. However, they have been modified in the modern context. For example, simple legal marriage in the customary sense is widely practiced in mixed marriages involving Christian or Muslim Dinkas. Where a girl is the pagan, she is often though not always converted after the customary marriage, and a religious ceremony is performed. In the case of Christian girls marrying pagans, this does not happen and she often returns to tradition. In a recent case, however, a pagan father of a Catholic Dinka girl had arranged for her marriage to a young pagan. Hearing of this, the girl insisted that the formalities of canon law be observed. She went into the Catholic mission for refuge and the father of the bridegroom sued in the chief's court for her delivery. The presiding chief ruled that she could not be compelled to marry in a way which would anger her God and thereby endanger the marriage. The court accordingly ordered the return of the bride wealth if the bridegroom was unable or unwilling to carry out the requisite forms. This is not uniform, for cases are known in which mixed marriages between Christian girls and pagan men were upheld. The known cases are distinguished by the girls' consent to the union.

A similar trend goes on in levirate and ghost marriage. Although some educated people are compelled by family obligation, and others conform with pleasure, there is a tendency among educated Dinkas against these forms of marriage. Apart from economic difficulties, these Dinkas are Christians or Muslims and both religions object to such unions. Though biased for traditional law, there is evidence that traditional courts are responsive to these new perspectives. This is exemplified by a case previously cited in another context in which a Dinka chief's court permitted a postmortem divorce.[30] A Christian Dinka woman had been married to a Christian Dinka and had had children. When her husband died, she was asked to cohabit in the levirate with her husband's pagan heir. As a Christian she objected to the proposed union and asked for a divorce from her late husband to cut the agnatic bond between her and her brother-in-law. The court upheld her claim, provided that the bride wealth was returned and that she, though not her children, surrendered her claims to inheritance from her husband.

Broader changes have supplemented traditional simple legal marriages. These include Mohammedan marriage, marriage within an Excepted Community, marriage under the Non-Mohammedan Marriage Ordinance, and marriage "otherwise," which includes common-law marriage, marriage in diplomatic premises, marriage abroad, or marriage on board ships or aircraft. Though some have been only of theoretical interest to the Dinka in the past, they are assuming practical significance. The "cohabitation" of these marriages, to borrow Dr. Farran's term,[31] and the increasing number of mixed marriages pose conflicts of laws for which there have not been precedents. Whether these marriages are mixed in the sense that both parties are Dinkas,[32] or one party is a non-

30. See Chapter 3, p. 89.
31. See Farran vii.
32. Even if they had the same religion, their marriage may be mixed, for example, by the combination of customary marriage with one of the alternative marriages.

Dinka Sudanese, or one party is non-Sudanese, they raise secular and/or religious problems relevant to the Dinka context.

CAPACITY TO MARRY   Capacity to marry is determined by age and seniority in the family. Since the Dinka have no notion of age by years, there is no fixed age when a person may marry. Marriage cannot be concluded unless both parties have reached puberty. A man may betrothe a girl before he is initiated, but he cannot contract full marriage until after initiation. Betrothal before puberty is rare. Girls may be designated when little according to *mek,* "choice," and may be betrothed before puberty. Designation is not considered betrothal and does not involve payment of cattle. Expressing the choice will suffice, but usually the man puts a ring on the girl's wrist as evidence of his choice. Such choice is distinguished from betrothal in that betrothal confers certain legal rights and is considered a degree of marriage, conferring retroactive marital rights should the marriage be completed. Another distinction is the need for sacrificing an ox according to *agorot* in case of betrothal before the girl reaches puberty but not in *mek.* In both cases, such early engagement enhances the girl's status and gives her great pride. The fact that capacity to marry is determined by puberty is an illustration of the biological aspect of the myth of permanence as the basis of marriage. Contravention of this norm is believed to invite ancestral curse which might result in childlessness.

Among siblings, the older brother should marry before the younger, and sometimes the younger marries after the older has had a second wife. With half-brothers, the order is further determined by the seniority of their mothers. These circumstances may result in the late marriage of a junior son or the son of a junior wife. The rule is rigid and is generally observed. Occasionally, a younger brother may oblige his family to marry for him by committing offenses such as impregnation or elopement. The marriage of the older brother should follow quickly and usually his betrothal is promptly carried out.

Today, as people begin to acquire wealth independently, cases of younger brothers marrying prior to their older brothers are increasing, but the tendency is for the younger brother to aid the older in order to bring his turn nearer. Should he marry prior to his brother, the marriage will not be invalidated, but the court will compel the younger to aid the older in marriage. Should the younger brother have no remaining wealth, part of his bride wealth may be withdrawn to provide at least a betrothal wealth for the senior brother.

In the case of an educated Dinka employed away from home, his prior marriage is sometimes seen by the tribe as a necessity since, among other reasons, he lacks the female services available at home. This is so because the house of such a man often provides accommodation for many members of his traditional society. The fact that his problem is more acute does not normally exempt him from the rule, but it may lead to the betrothal of the senior son to open the way for the educated junior son to marry. The usual practice is for the educated man to purchase sufficient cattle to afford marriages for both his brother and himself. This tends to keep his standard of living in the modern sector quite low.

Priority based on age also applies to sisters, more so to siblings than to half-sisters, although not with the same intensity as to brothers. More important, because of the patrilineal nature of procreation, competitiveness among girls is less crucial to the basic principle. Consequently, although the rule of age priority is quite rigid among brothers, it may be contravened in the case of sisters, though the senior sister is paid *awec*, "appeasement payment," before her sister's marriage is completed.

An educated Dinka girl is not believed to require exemption from marriage priority; but because of her associations in school where men are not likely to be deterred by the fact that she is a junior daughter, she is more likely to be proposed to in disregard of the rule. If the marriage is in accordance with customary law, her senior sister is likely to be compensated for the insult.

Both the educated men and girls may avoid these impediments by using one of the alternative methods provided in the national law. However, Christian and Muslim marriages uncombined with traditional ceremonies are rare among the Dinka, and marriage by registration is even rarer. These alternative methods involve their own problems, especially in relation to religiously mixed marriages.[33]

CONSENT TO MARRIAGE Since consent is governed by the family stratification as the primary base in affection-shaping and -sharing, the consent of both the bridegroom and the bride is subordinate to the consent of their family superiors. Although a Dinka man has much greater freedom in the designation of his bride than has a Northern Sudanese, the bridegroom's father has to consent to his selection. Since many relatives are interested in the marriage of any kinsman, the range of people whose consent is obtained before marriage is very broad. However, the *sine qua non* is the consent of the bridegroom's "father," who is anyone responsible for a person's marriage, and may be one's uncle or one's brother. Normally, it is one's father.

The father may refuse his consent for any of several reasons. Usually it would be the reputation of the bride and her kin. Since marriage combines two groups of kin, it is important that they be people of good

33. For some of the theoretical problems posed by such mixed marriages, see Farran vii.

repute. This reputation, though centered on respect, is interlaced with other deference values. Wealth and skill become factors, and even enlightenment is considered. In well-being, the most obvious area of investigation is whether the bride's lineage is afflicted with certain infectious diseases, such as tuberculosis and leprosy. It will suffice that any member of her lineage, dead or alive, had the disease. These diseases are often linked with reputation, and tend to lower others' estimation of such persons. So serious are their consequences that they often form the subject matter of defamation suits. Rectitude may be a factor—the usual concern being whether a family has indulged in *peeth,* "black magic"—but it covers one's general righteousness and responsible conduct. In short, many values interplay in the exercise of consent, which confirms their being both objectives and bases in marriage.

While it may be argued that these considerations are only guidelines for the father and do not give a cause of action, the situation is more complex than that. Since many people are interested in the marriage and have a say, however subordinate, the man's relatives can demand the consent of his father in court if they feel that it is unreasonably withheld. The court then investigates the father's grounds for refusing consent. Should they prove unreasonable, the court will attempt to persuade the father to give in. What follows should he refuse to be persuaded is not clarified by available evidence. Some informants claim that the court will not compel the father to consent on the first occasion, but if he should unreasonably withhold his consent a second time, the court will compel him to consent. Others argue that even in the first instance, an unreasonable refusal may be invalidated. In any event, rather than force consent directly, the court will condone an otherwise illegal measure, usually elopement, on the side of the bridegroom and use it as a means of compelling his father to contract the marriage. The court may also authorize the withdrawal or the withholding of reciprocal kinship obligations by the dissatisfied kinsmen. Since this would mean forfeiting the father's role in the marriages of his kinsmen's children, it is an effective sanction.

It may also be asked whether the consent of the bridegroom is a condition to his marriage. The father may choose for his son a girl whom the son will not accept. Although the consent of the groom is considered more important than that of the bride, it is not essential for the validity of marriage. If a determined son refuses to consummate the marriage, an attempt may be made by the father and, if necessary, the court to persuade him to defer to his father. In practice, the boy is persuaded in the long run to give in. Maguei's [34] case was said by informants to be typical of such situations. Maguei, refused to marry the girl chosen by

34. Abyei, Ngok Dinka Court (1960).

his father, but the father, not considering his son's wishes, obtained the girl for a bride wealth of thirty-five cows. Maguei ran away from home. His friends, members of his family and clan, and other elders went to his residence and reasoned with him. Meanwhile, the girl had been installed in his father's house as his daughter-in-law. After a long period of persuasion, Maguei gave in, returned home, and settled with the wife.

The question of the bridegroom's consent has a new dimension for the educated class. They have little in common with uneducated women. While they may be obliged to marry from among them, they often insist on making their own choice. But the Dinka apply the rule which highlights the father's consent. Many are the cases in which educated men refused brides chosen by their parents but were in the last resort persuaded to marry them.

In Allor Biong's case, Allor's father chose a girl for Allor while Allor was studying in Egypt. Without waiting to learn his son's opinion, he proceeded with the marriage ceremonies. When Allor returned, he refused his consent. His father indignantly gave him two alternatives: acceptance or depending on himself for marriage. The second alternative must be seen in the light of the father's control of cattle and the implications of his repudiation of his paternal role, which is an important part of marriage negotiations. Allor took the case to family and clan elders, some of whom were chiefs. The elders tried to persuade Allor's father to reconsider his decision, but he would not. Instead, Allor was persuaded to accept.

A somewhat similar case is that of Deng Aguer. While Deng was in school, his widowed mother and his maternal uncle arranged a marriage for him. At school, Deng met an educated girl, a schoolteacher, and got engaged. When he returned on vacation, Deng was told of his arranged marriage and he told the family of his engagement. His mother and uncle tried in vain to persuade him to break the engagement and marry the girl of their choice, for whom cattle had already been paid. The matter was taken to the family and clan elders to decide, and all pressured Deng to accede to the word of his mother and uncle. After a very lengthy process of persuasion, Deng gave in. In the meantime, some uneducated Dinkas were competing in marriage for the schoolteacher, and her father permitted the competition against her consent. She wrote to Deng's cousin and younger brother explaining that, unless something was done, she would be forced to marry one of the competitors. Without telling anyone, even Deng, the cousin and the younger brother arranged for the girl to elope and come to Deng's family. She arrived soon after Deng had been persuaded to accept his elders' choice and give her up. Because diplomatic issues were involved, since she was the daughter of an important chief of another tribe, the family elders changed their decision in favor of Deng's marriage to her. The uneducated girl already betrothed was passed on to Deng's younger brother.

Dr. Farran reports a case in which "a Christian student complained that his father wanted him to marry a pagan girl. . . . Although he could refuse, the father would not give him his bridewealth essential to marry someone else. He estimated that at least fifteen years in Government service would be necessary before he could hope to save up an equivalent amount, and he was doubtful if the young lady of his choice would be willing to wait as long as that." [35]

It is possible for an educated Dinka to use alternative methods, such as marriage under the Ordinance (by the Protestant church or by the registrar of marriages), or by an Excepted Community, usually the Catholic church. The guardian's consent being necessary in a Muslim marriage, this might be an inadequate alternative. In practice, educated Dinkas rarely reject their fathers' wishes, because they are bound to traditional circumstances even though they may not reside at home for most of the year. Besides, there being an insufficient number of educated girls, they often seek uneducated girls who are more bound to tradition and their bride wealth-seeking relatives. There is an increasing tendency for educated Dinkas to marry from non-Dinka tribes where bride wealth is relatively small and more girls are educated.

In cases where a son defers to his father's authority, however, the result is often an unhappy married life, a factor behind increased divorce among educated Dinkas.

Since many people are involved, the question of whose consent in the bride's family is essential to marriage is not easily answered. It may be necessary for the bridegroom to appease by cattle payment some related elders who refuse to grant their consent on specific grounds, however minor. The person without whose consent marriage cannot be concluded is the "father" of the girl chosen to take charge of the marriage, and who may be her uncle even though her own father may be present. The choice is associated with the distribution of bride wealth. The relative to whom the girl is allotted at an earlier age is the one entitled to the lion's share of her forthcoming bride wealth and is the father for purposes of her marriage.

The bride's father may refuse his consent on grounds of respect, well-being, rectitude, or other values. Unless his refusal is reasonable, pressures similar to those used to obtain the consent of the bridegroom's father are applied. Because of incoming bride wealth involved in marriage, participation of kinsmen is marked and an unreasonable refusal to consent is likely to be defeated by their pressure outside or inside the court. If the father's refusal is the result of indignation caused by an incident involving the bridegroom or his kin and if there is the slightest

35. Farran 69–70.

element of justification, he is offered appeasement compensation rather than pressured to concede gratuitously. In the case of the marriage of Wor Abyei [36] the bride's father refused his consent because, long before Wor proposed marriage to his daughter, he had knocked at the gate of Wor's house and no one had responded, although he could distinctly hear people speaking inside the house. He would not give his daughter to a man who had shown disrespect for him. Wor did not remember not responding to a knock at his gate. He argued that the house was surrounded by a very large enclosure so that a knock at the gate might not be heard, especially if the people in the house were talking so loudly that the person at the gate could hear them. The matter was taken to Abyei Court by both Wor's kinsmen and the consenting elders of the girl. Abyei Court decided that Wor's plea was acceptable, but that Wor should pay appeasement cattle to the girl's father.

Once the girl's father has given his consent and cattle have been paid upon the faith of such consent, he cannot withdraw it without some legitimate cause. This is illustrated by *Ayii v. Allor*.[37] Allor's daughter was betrothed to Ayii, who paid a betrothal wealth of twenty cows. Allor, after having given his consent, decided to withdraw it on the ground that Ayii had given cows of the daughter's bride wealth to some relatives without consulting him. Since some of these relatives were chiefs, he felt that the effect of his son-in-law's action was to have him superseded in authority over his daughter's marriage, and, in protest, he sought to repudiate the marriage agreement. The court held that he could not give his consent and withdraw it without good cause. When he demonstrated determination to prevent his daughter from marrying Ayii, he was threatened with committal to jail. As an alternative, the court said that Allor might repudiate the betrothal if he promptly returned all the cows which Ayii had given him and compensated him for those he had given his relatives. As the alternative was too much for him, Allor was compelled to abide by his original consent.

There is another limitation to the father's right to refuse his consent. The Dinka say that consent should not be refused to a chief or any member of the chiefly clans. Rather than a rule of law which may give rise to a cause of action in today's Dinka courts, this is a rule which is backed by social pressures and by supernatural sanctions. One might recall Nyanaghar's case, which was described earlier in the story of succession to Chief Kwol Arob.[38] The relatives of Nyanaghar acted on her wish, probably because the importance of the marriage made forcing her seem inappropriate. Otherwise, the bride's consent is irrelevant despite the emphasis the Dinka place on courtship. Some fathers do not consider it

36. Abyei, Ngok Dinka Court (1944).
37. Abyei, Ngok Dinka Court (1959).
38. See pp. 77–84, supra.

necessary to consult with their daughters before accepting a proposal, but many do, for, just as a young man attempts to win her love if only in the interest of convenience, most fathers feel it desirable to consult their daughters. This consultation, to be more accurate, is merely information with the view to persuasion should she refuse her consent. Without her acceptance, marriage can hardly work. In practice, most girls accept the decision of their fathers, although perhaps with complaints. The desire to have a large bride wealth paid as their value also plays a part in their accepting men otherwise objectionable to them.[39] So attuned are Dinka girls to the fact that the choice is that of their male agnates that only those who detest their proposed husbands or are in love with other men insist on refusal.

Flirtation and courtship usually attract proposals which are not objectionable to the brides. This leads people to think that Dinka "men and girls choose their own mates," but that "in practice the girl does not accept a man who will bring disgrace on her by not being able to pay a proper marriage-price in cattle to her family." [40] In cases of a girl's refusal to consent, such pressures as beating and scolding are used by the males. Even the court may authorize such measures. It is in connection with such girls that "lawful rape," by which a man is authorized to consummate a marriage forcefully, is practiced. Other coercive measures may be used or resort may be had to the court. The following passage about an incident which took place about 1944 is quoted by Dr. Farran from the present writer.

> I remember as a child in our house (prisoners were then kept in the Chief's house) a girl who was refusing a proposed husband. She was lashed and tied up to a pole by both hands and legs so that she could not defend herself against mosquitoes which were terrible; and while she cried by night, a burly police-man kept on beating her. Her voice was calling for sympathy and telling the very truth within her; that she could not live with a man for whom she did not have the least feeling. The power of torture, however, overcame her truthfulness and she cried out in a voice denoting nothing but deceit, "I have loved him. Take me to him this very night." [41]

Such pressures are dangerous, for a determined girl has many ways by which she can deprive her kin of bride wealth. These include elopement, impregnation by a man of her own choice, or, rarely, suicide.

39. See O'Sullivan, "Dinka Law," 40 *Journal of the Royal Anthropological Institute* 180 (1910).

40. Buxton, "The Significance of Bridewealth and the Levirate among the Nilotic and Nilo-Hamatic Tribes of the Sudan, 2 *Anti-Slavery Reporter* 66–75 (1958).

41. Farran 72.

The sort of difficulties which may result from imposing marriage on a refusing girl are illustrated by *Akot Ral v. Lal Ayoum.*[42] Akot had paid a bride wealth of nearly a hundred cows for a girl who loved Lal Ayoum, with whom she eloped to the North. After some time, they were recovered and she was taken back to Akot's house, while Lal Ayoum was imprisoned and made to pay compensation to Akot. After his prison sentence, they escaped and were recovered again. The process of escape and recovery was repeated several times. During their escapes she gave birth to two children whose biological father was Lal but, being "children of the cows," they were legally those of Akot. In the final action, Akot claimed and was awarded the children, as well as compensation for adultery. Such cases occur quite frequently. Quoting the evidence and the cases collected by the writer from the Ngok Dinka, Dr. Farran adds that "students from other tribes knew of similar occurrences."[43] His interpretation of this evidence, however, is that it "points to a crude realization that the bride's consent is a prerequisite to a lawful marriage. Why otherwise would there be need for the beatings and scolding? The tribal marriage laws in effect require consent, but—at least in the past— some of them have not been scrupulous as to how such 'consent' was obtained."[44] O'Sullivan also observed, and, I submit, erroneously, "No girl is obliged to marry anyone unless she is herself willing . . . Fear of beating is used to influence a girl to consent, but such coercion is against tribal law."[45]

The objective of this interpretation seems more prescriptive rather than description. Even so, it is somewhat paradoxical that a system of law which requires consent would not only permit but enforce undue influence and coercive measures to obtain it. Dr. Farran himself admits that such torture is sometimes carried out "under the authority of a Chief's Court."[46] To call submission under such severe threats consent is a contradiction in terms. We prefer the interpretation that Dinka customary law does not regard the girl's consent as necessary but her acceptance facilitates marriage, for without it, consummation of the marriage would be difficult and the objective of the marriage might not be fulfilled. This is why a girl who refuses to marry the man chosen for her must be persuaded or coerced into accepting him, not because her consent is legally required.

Although the situations where educated girls are forced into marriage are rare because of their small number, they do occur. Usually, such

42. Abyei, Ngok Dinka Court (1954).
43. Farran 72.
44. Ibid.
45. O'Sullivan, supra note 39, at 180.
46. Farran 72.

marriages are arranged between educated girls and uneducated men. The case of Deng Aguer, cited earlier, although it ended in favor of both Deng Aguer and his educated bride, illustrates such forced marriages.

There are now available methods of defeating customary impositions. We have already cited marriage under the Ordinance and Excepted Communities as examples. Just as in the case of the groom, the bride would find not much improvement in Muslim marriage, for although Circular 54 of May 28, 1960 made the consent of the bride a *sine qua non* to a valid marriage, the consent of the *Wali,* the marriage guardian, is still necessary. There is, however, a practical problem for brides. More than educated men, Dinka girls are dependent on their parents and therefore on tradition. They are thus unlikely to rebel against their parents.

BARS TO MARRIAGE   Bars to marriage are based on affinity and alienage. Affinity includes relationship by blood, nursing, marriage, adoption, age-mate relationship, and friendship. Alienage covers relationships with feuding groups and with *juur,* "aliens," although the latter is more a prejudice than a legal impediment.

Any traceable blood relationship between the agnatic and cognatic sides is an impediment to marriage. Members of a clan separated long enough to fall within two tribes cannot intermarry. There is one exception to the rule: intermarriage of relatives falling beyond a certain degree of agnatic or cognatic relationship who are descended from a common male ancestor with intervening ancestresses on both sides is permitted.[47] The degrees of female intervention need not be the same. This is known as *kwot yeth,* literally "the neck of a gourd," symbolizing that the relationship becomes "too small," that is, remote.[48] The question of how many generations are necessary in order to reach *kwot yeth* is not certain. The Dinka merely say that "it must be far." The general opinion was that five or six generations would not suffice. The counting begins with the generation of the first intervening female. Despite the opinion of the informants, the marriage of Nyok and Akiyoi,[49] which involved five degrees, suggests a narrower range. Akiyoi and Nyok were descendants of Allor Monydhaang. Apart from herself Akiyoi's branch included a male, a female, a male and a female. Nyok's line, apart from himself, included a male, a female, and two males. Their marriage, which took place in 1956, was strongly opposed by some relatives on

47. The descendants of the intervening ancestresses are known as *anyaal* to the unbroken agnatic lineage.

48. The original symbol may be sharing from the same milk gourd, usually done by close relatives.

49. Abyei, Ngok Dinka Court (1956).

both sides, although the pivotal relatives favored it. With reluctance, the court upheld the marriage. It is therefore not clear whether the court decided that the relationship was sufficiently remote to warrant the marriage in violation of the rules of exogamy is not void but voidable only on the motion of the interested parties and not by outsiders or the court. Dr. Farran presents the latter as the presumably correct interpretation of Ngok Dinka law. Whatever the bases of decision, this case, the facts of which were gathered by the writer in 1960, is still controversial in Dinka society, and whether the couple would bear children was doubted by many elders at the time this information was obtained.[50]

In another case in which the facts were quite similar, the court upheld the marriage, but according to the report of the court members, it proved a failure, for it remained childless. In order to test the marriage, the wife cohabited outside wedlock and conceived. Since the Dinka often impute the responsibility for childlessness to the woman, this was proof of an ancestral curse against incest.

The exception of *kwot yeth* is significant. While males perpetuate the clan or the lineage directly, females provide bride wealth to be used in the marriages of agnates and extend affection circles. Although marriage takes them out of the group, they remain part of it and continue to share in the bride wealth of their descendants. At the excepted degree the descendants of a common ancestor no longer have claims to the bride wealth of their kinswomen. It thus becomes opportune to reaffiliate through marriages in order to revive mutual assistance in lineage perpetuation.

A nursing relationship occurs when a baby is suckled for any reason by a woman other than its mother. The baby is considered a relative of the wet nurse. If the baby should be a female, the suckling woman is entitled to share in her bride wealth. A marriage bar is created which prohibits marriage between the children of the wet nurse, the suckled child, and any other children whom she has suckled. The Dinka conceive of a fusion of blood in this relationship, and therefore, though limited to the second degree and descendants thereof, it becomes akin to blood relationship.

Another aspect of exogamy is "illegal conjunction," which introduces prohibitions into in-law relationships. Traditionally, the rule was that a man, his brothers, or his children could not marry into his wife's lineage. An apparent exception to this rule is the custom of substitution of a dead wife with her close relative who may be a sister.[51] Since the substituting party steps into the shoes of her dead relative, the union is not

50. Years after the marriage.
51. See *The Relatives of Salvatore Atem v. The Relatives of Athilueth*, pp. 178–79, infra.

a new marriage, but a perpetuation of the old marriage comparable to levirate, except that whereas the issue of levirate identify themselves with the dead pater, the dead wife is not considered by the issue of her relative as their mater. This is not deemed significant, since the fundamental objective is the perpetuation of the male line.

Innovation in Ngok society, particularly among the chiefs, who are both more innovating and more interested in marriages than the ordinary people, has affected prohibitions of illegal conjunction. The pioneering violation was by the paramount chief who married the full sister of the wife of his half-brother, who is also an important chief. Both sisters having procreated, more violations followed. One of the chief's sons and two of his nephews married the full sisters of his wives. This development is somewhat correlative with the increasing number of chiefly marriages. So much linked with the tribe through marriages have chiefly clans become that such a modification of illegal conjunction has probably become a necessity.

The next bar to marriage is adoption, a common practice among the Dinka. The ties between a man and his adopted child are socially and legally recognized as constituting full kinship. An instance is where a girl who has a child is married to a man other than the biological father and the biological father has not legitimated the child. Once adopted by the stepfather, such a child acquires his name and is affiliated with his kin. An illegal conjunction would therefore result from his marriage with a member of his stepfather's kin.

A form of adoption which is now obsolete, but remnants of which remain, is slavery. During the wars of slavery, the Ngok Dinka, although mainly the victims of Arab slavery, enslaved Arabs. Their leaders also rescued enslaved Southerners who decided to live with their redeemers either because they could not trace their origin or because they simply wished to stay. Both the captured Arabs and the rescued Southerners were affiliated into the capturing or the rescuing lineages. They were technically known, but were generally not referred to, as "slaves," *aloony*. They assumed the identity of the lineage into which they were affiliated. In the case of females, their bride wealth went to the lineage of the adopter, and the rules of exogamy were applied to those thus affiliated. The degree of their application is doubtful, however, for opinion is divided on the point. Some Dinka elders argue that it is identical with kinship, while others argue that it is not carried so far. There is no doubt that both opinions are influenced by the case of the marriage of Deng Majok and Nyanayuat, discussed earlier.[52] The authority of this decision is still disputed by many Dinkas, and one cannot deny the effect of Deng's

52. See Chapter 3, p. 97.

position on the outcome. In any case, it has established a widely publicized precedent. Although the Dinka are not easily led to disbelieve the
likelihood of danger merely because of the passage of time, the fact that
Nyanayuat has borne children and that she and her children are not
afflicted with the evils of ancestral curse may work in favor of the
precedent.

The Dinka make an exception in case of a male slave. He cannot
marry within the lineage of his adoption. Since the lineage is traced
through the male, the role of a male slave in the pursuit of permanent
identity and influence is direct and only depends on his marriage. The
female slave, on the other hand, contributes indirectly by attracting
bride wealth which may then be used by the males of the lineage for
marriage. If she is taken as a wife by her adopters, there is more gain
than is the case with male slaves, for she would have had to go
out of the lineage, while he would not. The Dinka thus choose between
two alternative ways of obtaining her contribution; either she does so
through bride wealth from outside the lineage, or through marriage
into the lineage. The facts indicate that different people choose according to the particular situation. This reasoning is similar to the exception
made for female agnates or cognates whose descendants, *anyaal,* after a
certain degree become *kwot yeth.* They are choosing intermarriage because their distant kinsmen would be unlikely to share in the bride
wealth of their females. Marriage thus helps bring them closer to the
lineage. *Kwot yeth* requires more degrees of descent than adoption by
slavery because of its stronger blood and marriage ties.

Another ground for exogamous bars is age-mate relationship. A man
may not carry the daughter of an age mate, for common initiation creates a solidarity comparable to kinship. We have seen that age mates are
closely involved in marriage and have certain entitlement by virtue of
their association. If a man were to marry the daughter of an age mate,
he would be his age mate's father-in-law, creating a discrepancy in status
directly opposed to relationship of age mates. Chiefs have married
daughters of age mates, instances regarded as violations by the Dinka;
but violations by leaders become innovations.

Akin to the barrier of age-mate relationship is friendship, particularly
the special "friendship agreement" discussed earlier. When confirmed
with the rite of blood fusion, it symbolizes kinship.

The rules of exogamy, whether based on blood, marriage, adoption,
age mate relationship, or friendship, are based on the notion of extending affection by compelling marriage outside the present circles. Contradictory to this are the prohibitions against marrying those considered
too distant from the kinship to be affiliated. The most articulate are

those with whom the kin group is in a feud. When a person commits homicide, culpable or accidental, a feud arises which requires vengeance unless ended by ritual conciliation, *peek*. This is more easily done where the killing is not culpable. Unless it is done, the two groups should not drink or eat in each other's homes, nor should they associate. This continues even after payment of blood wealth, although it no longer requires vengeance. Without *peek*, intermarriage is not permitted. If the feud has lasted for more than two generations and *peek* has not been performed, a special rite is performed to authorize intermarrige. First, more cows are paid to appease the deceased. They are paid to the person charged with the duty of marrying a ghost wife for the deceased and are known as *ghok kooj e nom*, "the cows of standing the head." They do not count as part of the bride wealth. A ram is sacrificed in ritual atonement.

The final bar is Dinka resentment of marriage outside their group. Even within Dinka society the Ngok Dinka, until recently, attached a stigma to the marriage of a Ngok girl outside the community, although it has always been acceptable for Ngokmen to marry from other Dinka tribes. Objection to non-Ngok Dinkas is waning since diplomatic marriages between chiefs and other prominent non-Ngok Dinkas with Ngok chiefly families paved the way.

Objections to marriages with non-Dinkas are more serious. A daughter of Chief Kwol is reported to have refused the paramount chief of the Homr Baggara Arabs, saying, "Babu's all right . . . but he's an Arab. I'm a Dinka. We don't marry outside our people." [53] The fact that no attempt to coerce or persuade her was made by her relatives implied their approval of her refusal. When the same girl refused to marry a Ngok Dinka, she was coerced into the marriage.

Great care is taken by the Dinka to avoid a breach of marriage prohibitions. When a boy and a girl meet, their introduction includes their paternal, lineal, and clan identifications. During the social processes of marriage, intense investigation is carried on by both sides to the proposed marriage. If the parents of the parties to a proposed "incestuous" union agree to it despite the opposition of less important relatives, those relatives are authorized to seize the bride wealth to prevent the marriage. Should the bridegroom demand the return of his cattle, the court may direct that the cattle taken be considered compensation to the relatives for the insult to their feelings caused by the undesirable union. Nowadays, seizure of cattle is dying out and the whole issue is fought in court.

When an incestuous union occurs, although the males make the de-

53. Henderson, *Sudan Reminiscences* 14 (1962).

cision, the females and their offspring are subject to spiritual contamination which may even result in death. The Dinka often judge whether
incest has been committed by the results. Among them is a serious skin
disease known as *akeeth,* which is also one of the words used for incest.[54]
Incest also is reputed to cause sterility. Should a woman be barren or die
in childbirth, one of the first areas investigated is the possibility of
incest. When people know or fear that incest has been committed, a
ceremony is performed to neutralize it retroactively.[55] This ceremony
or its variation may be performed prior to a proposed union in borderline cases where the parties are believed unrelated but it is considered
desirable to remove any doubt. When it is performed as a result of an
impediment discovered subsequent to a marriage, it does not authorize
the continuance of the union unless the relationship is so remote as to
approximate a borderline case. Normally, the marriage must be dissolved.

The rules of exogamy also apply to extramarital and illicit sexual relations. The wrong is aggravated by pregnancy, for the child is a permanent reminder of the wrong. As a result, the most severe measures
were taken in most Dinka tribes against such offspring. Dr. Farran reports that in some areas of Dinkaland, they were exposed to death.

> Among the ordinary Dinka, children born of such "incestuous"
> union are not merely illegitimate, but accursed, and are sometimes
> exposed in the open to die or brought up by strangers in an ig-
> nominious status akin to a sort of slavery. Among the Ngok Dinka,

54. The other term is *alaraan,* which simply means "relationship," usually kinship
relationships.

55. Dr. Lienhardt describes a ceremony for a man who had slept with one of his
father's junior wives. In such serious cases a bull is normally sacrificed, but in this
case a ram was used. A priest made several short invocations with the guilty couple
in front of him and their kinsmen standing around. The ram was held near. All
stepped into a pool of rainwater, pulling into it the guilty pair. They were ducked
and washed by their kinsmen. The ram was similarly treated, the idea being to
cleanse the parties and transfer their sin to the ram. The ram was then taken
from the pool and cut longitudinally while alive. It was particularly important that
the victim's sexual organs be separated longitudinally into halves. [Sometimes, especially in very minor cases, or in cricumstances where there is no beast available, the
Ngok use tobacco, in which case it is also divided into halves.] Dr. Lienhardt explains
this symbolic action as a part of the Dinka attempt to control their experience, for
it is the moral attributes of the wrong which cause illness. "That this is conscious
symbolism," writes Dr. Lienhardt, "and not a kind of materialist superstition that
the sin in some way actually goes into the water, is shown by the fact that all the
kin were also in the water. The sin was transferred only to the ram, according to
Dinka's symbolic intention." Lienhardt, *Divinity* 284–87. This creates a feeling of separation at the crucial period of wrong so that the sexual intercourse is conceived as
having occurred between an unrelated couple.

on the other hand, the issue of such a marriage is not considered to be illegitimate. This is presumably because the marriage is not void, but in the English sense of the term "voidable." [56]

Such treatment by the "ordinary Dinka" would not be tolerated by the national law today. It is still common among the Ngok for the relatives to pray for the death of such offspring, and curiously enough, they nearly always die. This may be seen as a result of calculated carelessness, or may be the outcome of defective care resulting from the mother's conviction that the child is accursed and must die.

There are miscellaneous considerations touching on an individual's social standing. The Dinka do not have disabilities on grounds similar to the Muslim doctrine of "equality in marriage," *kafa'a,*[57] the German "equality of birth" [58] which rendered a marriage "morganatic," or the Shilluk requirement [59] which forces princesses into the disguised celibacy of their woman-to-woman marriages. However, principles governing the approval of interested parties may be upheld or outruled by the court, though they are usually not matters for a law suit. A man in competition with a chief has no chance because of the moral or religious rule against refusing a chief. The character of the bride's or the groom's family counts. Working ability is another example.

> The Ngok gossip about me saying . . .
> "Do not give him this only girl
> He is a man who does not know to hold a hoe."

The housekeeping skill of the girl is particularly important. The Dinka word *ajiliu,* though covering several aspects of a woman's character, is especially focused on this. In well-being, the Dinka make specific diseases such as leprosy and tuberculosis impediments to marriage.[60] Theft is another example.[61]

There is no limitation to the number of wives permissible, although not everyone can afford to marry more than one wife because of the cost. The number of a chief's wives is generally determined by his importance. The present paramount chief has well over a hundred. This

56. Farran 73–74.
57. Fyzee, *Outlines of Mohammedan Law* 104–06 (1964).
58. Farran 79 note 16.
59. Id. at 79–80.
60. Curiously enough, illness in general tends to increase a moral obligation to give consent to marriage. If a man is epileptic, crippled, blind, or drastically deformed, it is considered spiritually dangerous to object to his marriage as it may inflict a curse on the refusing kin.
61. In Nyanluak's case, for instance, the bridegroom repudiated the bethrothal agreement on the grounds of an alleged theft involving a nominal object. Rectitude is, however, a more pervasive ground than these cases show.

is said by the Dinka to be a record. Average men have two, though the second is often a ghost wife or a levirate widow. It is this discrepancy between the rich and the poor that Stubbs observed when he stated, "In their present form the Dinka laws are essentially for the rich and not for the poor and in some respects need drastic amendment, especially as regards the collection and division of bride-price cattle." [62]

Polygyny is accepted by women, and a wife may even urge her husband to marry so that she can have a junior cowife under her authority. Since people who are polygynous have higher status than those who are not, junior wives may find marriage into a polygynous family gratifying. Because of stratification by marriage priority, women prefer being senior wives, and, if possible, the first. This is particularly true of daughters of important men who resent being subordinated to other wives.

Marriage bars work against the "progressives," especially the educated class, who desire their modification but lack the necessary bases to influence change. Since education among the Ngok was pioneered by a few families, most of whom are related, the few educated girls are from these families and therefore are related to most educated males. As educated men do not participate in the traditional activities which normally link unrelated youth, their opportunities for meeting uneducated girls are limited. Again, since the educated Dinka is less conscious of his kinship relationships, there is a certain feeling of remoteness from many relatives, which makes the rules of exogamy more arbitrary to them than to the traditionals.

Even more restrictive in the eyes of the educated class are the bars based on raciocultural alienage. Though the situation has changed since education was introduced, the educated are seen as culturally changed, and the social stigma that used to be attached to strangers in intersex relations is reflected on them. Indeed, they are sometimes referred to as *juur*, strangers. Girls could not associate with them without being scandalized. A song was quoted earlier in which a man scornfully dismissed an educated competitor in a marriage as so far below the dignity of the girl that the man should not even attempt to compete for her. In these lines, a man sings a warning to an unidentified girl against associating with educated men, whom he calls *juur*.

> Should you kill yourself some day
> To converse with the *juur*
> Hair will itch you till dawn [63]

62. Stubbs, "Customary Law of the Aweil Dinka," *Sudan Law Journal and Reports* 450, 451 (1962).

63. Dinkas, both men and women, pluck their pubic hair. Arabs and other non-Dinkas do not.

> Now that your friend will be gone
> Now that he will abandon you
> And go to the land of the Arabs
> With whom will you converse? [64]

The Dinka now realize the importance of education, and although there may be remnants of earlier attitudes the problem now is that the educated class is not content with traditional women.

Other factors have intervened against internally mixed marriages: Since Islam prohibits the marriage of a Muslim to a pagan, and of a Muslim woman to a non-Muslim man, and since Dinka society today is an amalgam of universal and traditional religions, the Islamic prohibition is bound to create problems. In a recent case a young Dinka Christian fell in love with a young Dinka Muslim girl whose parents objected to her marrying him unless he was converted to Islam. He did not change his religion, but the two eloped. The man was arrested and charged with a criminal offense under Section 316A of the penal code which penalizes a man who has had intercourse with a woman not his wife and under sixteen years of age, the lowest age of consent.

In another case Ahmed, a Muslim and son of the Ngok chief, wanted to marry a Catholic schoolteacher who was a daughter of a Dinka chief in Bahr-el-Ghazal Province. The missionaries in whose school the girl was teaching objected to the proposed union on the grounds of Ahmed's religion. The girl's relatives, some of whom were Christians, desired the union. Although the girl was sheltered by the missionaries and could not be reached, she was believed to be in favor of the proposed marriage. Ahmed, his father, and the girl's relatives brought an action against the missionaries for concealing the girl, demanding that her wish be ascertained in court. When the girl expressed her consent to the proposed marriage, the court restrained the missionaries from impeding the marriage, which was performed according to Dinka customary law.

Marriage bars on ethnic or raciocultural grounds are being abrogated in modern crossethnic, crosscultural, and crossracial circles. The previous tendency to see outsiders as strangers is disappearing and mixed marriages are increasing. Since Dinka fathers insist on cattle, mixed marriages in the Southern Sudan often involve a Dinka man and a non-Dinka girl whose parents' demands are more easily satisfied. Also, modern girls are more numerous among the non-Dinkas. Furthermore, there is the convenience in marrying where one is employed rather than going through the elaborate ceremonies of Dinka marriage which usually take

64. Conversation, *aleeng*, in Ngok Dinka usage, has something of the old common law meaning, although among the Dinka it normally means a relationship which has reached the degree of sharing the same bed, but without necessarily having sexual intercourse.

years. Other Nilotic cattle owners like the Nuer and the Shilluk are more likely to marry Dinka girls. The increasing number of mixed marriages in the South is a factor, however subtle, in the increase of affection circles within the South. In the North, Islamic prohibition against non-Muslims marrying Muslim girls, and against Muslim men marrying outside "The Book" is a factor, however subtle, in impeding South-North affection.

However, occasional marriages occur between Muslim men and converted (usually simultaneously) Dinka girls, and between converted Dinkas and Muslim girls. The obstacle of cattle is more likely to be overcome by the fact that neighboring Arab tribes possess cattle and the average Northerner is more able to purchase sufficient cattle for a Dinka marriage than the average non-Dinka Southerner. While impediments tend to weaken closer affection between the Southerners and the Northerners, one should not overlook the positive factor in whatever degree of intermarriage there is at present. There are several cases of Englishmen marrying Dinka girls according to Dinka customary law.

There are also some cases of Dinka men married to Western girls. This area is impeded by the Marriage of Officials and Students with Non-Sudanese (Control) Act, 1959, which restricts the marriage of Sudanese students abroad as well as government offcials inside the Sudan to non-Sudanese. Section 3 of the statute categorically states that "no student shall marry a non-Sudanese," but, according to Section 5, he can do so in expectation of deprivations. The deprivations, according to Dr. Farran, "are sufficiently drastic to deter all but the most lovesick student from his plan to marry a foreign sweetheart, implying the loss not only of very large sums of money but also of all hope of an honourable career in the Sudan." [65] Although he may marry a non-Sudanese on his return, he would be required to secure special permission or else to forfeit any chance of becoming head of a government department or of holding any "sensitive post" as defined by the statute.

Where mixed marriages involve Dinka girls, their dependence on their largely uneducated parents, though the girls themselves may be educated, often necessitates the performance of marriage according to Dinka law. There may be cases of emancipated girls or girls from educated backgrounds where Dinka forms may not be necessary; and, of course, Sudanese pluralism provides alternative forms.

Whatever way the trend of intermarriage and whichever laws govern this interaction, "It is said that in the Southern Sudan today intertribal marriages (formerly extremely rare, owing to a desire—conscious or unconscious—to preserve the 'purity' of the tribe) are tending to stimulate a wider feeling of being all Southerners and marriages of Northern

65. Farran 213.

Sudanese with Southern (Sudanese) similarly stimulate a yet wider, truly national common feeling of being Sudanese." [66] It has been argued that toward "the virtually important goal of welding the Sudan into a single, unified State and its people into a nation . . . internally mixed unions . . . should be encouraged." [67] Naturally, the same is true in the international context, and it is in this respect that the national statute restricting internationally mixed marriage is strongly criticized.

FORMALITIES OF MARRIAGE   In a system where the social and the legal processes intermingle, it is both difficult and undesirable to differentiate too rigidly. This is particularly the case in marriage formalities, many of which, though important, are not necessarily legal. Marriage among the Dinka is not a momentary ceremony, but a long social transaction stretching over not less than two years. The important components of this transaction are *ting nya,* "seeing the bride"; *leer atooc,* "conveyance of marriage proposal"; *leer amec,* "delivery of the betrothal consideration"; *kuen thiek,* "discussing the marriage"; and, finally, *geem nya,* "handing over the bride." There are also different procedures connected with such practices as competition in marriage, and wrongful but customary processes of effecting an impeded marriage.

Ting nya, "seeing the girl," may be performed by a prospective groom or by any of his relatives and friends. It is more than the simple fact of seeing, for it is associated with investigating the girl and her background, courting her by the man and his age-mate relatives in order to know her well, and agreeing within the family that she should be pursued. *Ting* thus begins with seeing and admiring, but covers a wide range of preliminary considerations leading to an affirmative family decision.

The question of who should designate the girl may depend on the seniority of the wife-to-be. If she is to be the first wife, more important relatives, such as the father and the paternal uncles, should be involved in seeing her. It is largely their consent which is relevant. The initial task of seeing the girl may be carried out by kinswomen, married or unmarried. It is in the area of "seeing the bride" that womenfolk most conspicuously participate in marriage decisions. Even here, however, a young man must avoid having a girl selected by his mother or even his full sister. This is an extension of the devices used to minimize their influence, which is associated with jealousy. The ideal kinswomen to recommend brides are paternal aunts, stepmothers, stepsisters, and such stepkinswomen. The most prominent role in initial *ting* is played by the prospective groom himself. A man may be expressly permitted to

66. Id. at 146–47.
67. Id. at 147.

look around for the girl he would like. Such permission was what this singer sought.

> Father, you will make me lose the name in Marial
> Let me go into the tribe
> To observe the girls of our Marial.

Dinka social life is conducive to the task of finding one's own bride, for young men and women associate quite freely in dances, feasts, and the like. In his everyday life, a Dinka mainly comes in contact with girls somehow related to him and therefore ineligible for marriage. Dances, especially large dances which are attended by people of various sections and subtribes, provide the best opportunity for contacts between unrelated people. Dinka youth use them for flirtation and courting. This, together with the idea of violence as a way of impressing girls, often provokes trouble at the dances and may lead to subtribal fights. After a dance a young man accompanies his dance partner hand in hand to her area of residence even in the eyes of her male relatives and the company of her female relatives. Such a walk may be for a long distance and a regular friendship may evolve. In courtship, *thuot,* the Dinka display a linguistic skill unique to the occasion and an important factor in social intercourse. What Dr. Howell said about the Nuer is true of the Dinka, namely that their courtship speeches are "full of subtle and suggestive phrases with a good deal of badinage," and "are spoken in a language which is almost poetic in form and difficult to understand." [68] Although such associations are not necessarily directed to marriage, most unarranged marriages based on mutual love originate from them.

The man is expected to familiarize himself with the girl through courtship. If the relatives of a girl see a man frequently visiting her, they normally hope that it might result in marriage, and unless they disapprove of him a priori, for instance because of known lack of cattle, they would not discourage the relationship. Dinka girls, accordingly, are brought up to be very courteous to men but to be also prudent. Since the status of a Dinka girl in her kin group and in the society depends largely on her marriage, the response of girls to courters often depends more on the prospects of marriage resulting from the friendship than on the mutuality of love. Some parents, especially mothers, instigate relationships with rich young men in the hope that marriage will result. This may result in a real or alleged illicit relationship, with the liability falling on the young man and his kin. Allegedly, such is the experience of this singer.

68. Howell, *Nuer Law* 80 note 2.

Anan Ayom Makuei, here I am
I am confused, I am confused
I am hurt by people's words,
I am hurt by the words of girls' fathers,
A man's daughter comes
She comes while her father sees.
You have chosen me,
But it is not my turn to marry
I am a younger brother
Too young to be killed with marriage,
If it is my ox, Makol (that you want)
It will be released; it will be released
To be a compensation for your daughter.
I have not touched your daughter.
When my father heard the case
In dismay he exclaimed,
"So the land has become the land of the government."
My father Ariath Maker is the son of Ariath Marol
State your case, state your case
I am not the son of a poor man
If it is only an ox
It will be given
It will compensate for your daughter.

Unscrupulous young men tend to exploit emphasis on marriage in courtship and profess to be courting for marriage. Such men are not highly regarded and they would probably not advertise their motive. A serious courter will invite his "best man" to accompany him in courtship and the girl will also invite her "bridesmaid" to keep company. Such courtship may include sharing a hut, though in expectation of propriety of conduct. Courtship continues and becomes even more overt after betrothal, when it involves more friends and age mates of both sides.

On the assumption that a mutual affection exists and the two wish to marry (it is more important that he wishes to wed her), the young man will declare his wish to his marriage "father" (who need not be his real father). This is, of course, necessary where the young man or someone else had done the "seeing" or where the father had made a suggestion conditional to his son's confirmation. When the matter has been settled between the young man and his father, many other significant kinsmen are informed. Not only will the bride wealth be gathered by them, but also, the broader the circle, the more facts about the girl and her kin group will be examined. Once informed, relatives explore various areas to see whether there exists any legal impediment to the marriage or whether it is desirable for the two to marry. The man's female relatives become especially active. They may engage someone who is related to the girl to observe her in her home when she is most natural and unlikely to put on such an impressive show as she is bound to display to them. The man himself may engage a male friend to observe her in this way. This intensive process of investigation and consultation among the relatives goes on for quite a long time until a consensus is reached or until at least the pivotal decision-makers agree.

Of course, things do not always go smoothly. The cases of Deng Aguer, Allor Biong and Maguei, are instances to the contrary. Even where the guardian authorizes his ward to look for a bride, he may refuse a number of the ward's alternative choices. This singer criticizes his guardian brother on these grounds.

> He tells me, "Look for a girl"
> Then he says, "I do not like this girl . . .
> Have you not seen Abyor, our tribe?
> My ox Marialjok, the thing is mockery
> That is what the older brother has done.
> He keeps telling me "Look for a girl"
> And then keeps telling me, "I do not like this girl"

Eventually, some agreement is reached and the second step, *leer atooc,* the conveyance of marriage proposal, follows.

Leer atooc begins with the man's kin sending word to the girl's kin announcing their intention to visit them. The girl's relatives will then fix a date for the visit. They must give themselves time to arrange for festivities. At the appointed time, the important relatives of the man, including his "father" or the representative of his father, visit the girl's relatives.[69] This may be for two or three days. The relatives of the prospective bridegroom must observe rigid restrictions on their movements in the bride's home, as they must always continue to do—an aspect of respect for relations-in-law which the Dinka consider very highly. They are not to enter the houses of the bride's people and must be clothed when moving in front of the female relatives of the girl. When the time for negotiation comes, each side plans who should say what and when before the meeting.

The assembly is then convened in the presence of *abathook,* the public, who will act as the court of arbitration. From then and throughout the marriage ceremonies, the prospective bridegroom's family is referred to as *koc moc,* "the people of the man," while that of the bride is *koc*

69. This is an occasion for slaughtering at least a ram and brewing beer, among other things.

nya, "the people of the girl"—descriptions which have acquired a technical usage and are consonant with the communal characteristic of Dinka marriage.

At the beginning of the negotiations, the people of the girl formally request the people of the man to state the purpose of their visit.[70] The man's kin then state their offer in modest terms. The theme is often something like this: "In our hearts is a lie we would like to attempt." By this, they mean that they are asking for a girl who might prove too expensive. It represents a kind of modesty which may be good manners or may be calculated to moderate the claims of the girl's relatives. Following their proposal, a lengthy dialogue follows which is typical of Dinka meetings, and which in the case of marriage is always carried out, however much in agreement the parties may secretly know themselves to be. One weakens one's bargaining position if one easily endorses the views of the other side, and yet one must treat relations-in-law with greatest deference. In most cases, therefore, the girl's relatives first refuse their consent even though they have planned to accept the offer. It may be that while the majority accept, at least one important relative objects. Though expected, such pretenses give marriage additional dignity in Dinka eyes, for they tend to augment the bride's value in the eyes of the man's kin.

The girl's relatives suggest the nature of their refusal. When their reasons are minor, particularly such nursed grievances as in the case of the marriage of Wor, they are more speedily given, while in case of serious grounds, such as infectious diseases, they may never be given. Between these two extremes are many grounds which are easily or reluctantly given. When they are resolvable, such as when some important kinsman is indignant, the *abathook* (i.e. the representatives of the public), will impose appeasement compensation and an agreement is reached. The *abathook* may not be able to resolve genuine and serious objections, but this may not end the proceedings. If the girl's relatives agree or it is apparent that their refusal is not seriously intended, the man's relatives then express their desire to return and send "a little something" (another gesture of modesty) as betrothal consideration. The girl's relatives in a combined acceptance-and-refusal manner reply, "Do the thing of your hearts, guests are not rebuffed," so that they permit them to bring the cattle while allegedly not committing themselves.

It is such things which make it difficult to decide what constitutes offer and acceptance in contract terms. The Dinka call this "the seating of the offer." It is a form of acceptance of the offer for the purposes of further negotiations, a kind of acceptance of the invitation to discuss

70. The girl's relatives, though known by the man's relatives to know, purport to be ignorant.

further rather than of the offer in the usual sense. The Dinka say that refusal does not really end the matter, for the man's relatives will go ahead on the presumption that no genuine refusal is meant, or that the girl's relatives can be persuaded to agree.

What approximates offer and acceptance follows with the next stage, *leer amec,* when the man's relatives return with the betrothal cattle. The number of the cattle will depend on the age of the girl. If she is below the age of puberty and it is expected that several years will pass before the marriage is concluded, a token payment of a few cows is made; if she is of age, the number is greater, depending on the estimated total bride wealth. It is desirable that among these cattle be special cows particularly selected for the most important mythical participants of the girl's lineage. The cows are driven by the bridegroom and his age mates, but the elders are the people who negotiate. The oxen in the herd are decorated with tassels, collars, and bells, and the young men and the women who meet them in the girl's home display their singing and dancing skills around the cattle and especially the oxen.

Great festivities follow, with slaughtering of beasts, brewing of beer, and much cooking. The prospective bridegroom, and his closest elders such as his father and uncles, do not partake of the food; they are to continue abstaining until "their mouths have been washed," according to the custom of *wak thok,* which means that an abstaining relative must be paid a cow or two by the bride's relatives before eating or drinking anything from the bride's home. The bridegroom does not eat or drink in the home of the bride until sometime after the marriage has been completed.

The occasion of *leer amec* is also one of social intercourse between the age mates of the couple, and courting goes on from which other marriages may result.

Negotiations are then resumed in which the girl's relatives are formally asked to accept the cattle. They then decide whether to accept the *amec* or reject them. The Dinka say that even if they should not be accepted, the man's relatives, if very interested in the girl, should not be provoked into taking them back but should leave them, and the girl's relatives, or at least some moderates among them, will look after them, pending final decision. This also indicates the anomalies of a Dinka marriage and the difficulty of deciding just when betrothal and even marriage may be considered concluded. This will be discussed later, but it is significant to note a point or two in this context. The Dinka word *amec* is used for cattle kept under any agreement analogous to bailment. Generally, it covers cattle possessed by one person but owned by another. We are thus led into thinking that the betrothal cattle, even when accepted, are still owned by the man's relatives. While this is so in theory, in practice the situation is more complex. Generally, they count as the property of the man's relatives for detrimental purposes and as those of the bride's relatives for beneficial purposes. Thus, should they die before the final settlement of bride wealth, they are considered the property of the man's relatives and are not counted as part of bride wealth. But should they increase naturally before the settlement, their offspring count as the property of the girl's relatives and will not be counted as part of the bride wealth.

After betrothal an important custom known as *mioc* may be followed. *Mioc* is the act of serving food to men by women. As a feature of marriage celebrations, the bride and several members of her age set visit the man's family carrying food. Although the idea is to bring food to the groom, these gifts are often distributed among relatives, since the groom cannot eat anything from the bride's home before "washing the mouth." *Mioc* is not an essential part of the marriage proceedings, and it is not always performed, but it is an important custom. In the past it conferred certain rights of "husband" and "wife" upon the betrothed couple which now depend on the mere fact of betrothal.

Following *leer amec,* the next important ceremony is *kuen thiek,* which is primarily concerned with the settlement of the bride wealth. *Kuen thiek* is done soon or long after *leer amec,* depending on the total length of the marriage celebrations. It is both a festive and "business-like" occasion. Several bulls and rams may be slaughtered and plenty of beer and food is prepared; dancing is at its highest.

Traditionally, *kuen thiek* is associated with the cattle byre, and is sometimes referred to as "entering" the cattle byre, a conception which associates the ceremony with the place of cattle. The parties sit opposite each other while *abathook,* the public, sit in the center. All those connected with the bride who claim a share in the bride wealth attend to voice their claims. Many of the groom's relatives who will be asked to contribute also attend. Each side utters invocations calling upon its ancestors and divinities to witness the negotiations and facilitate agreement. The bridegroom and the bride, together with their respective age mates, continue with celebrations and are thus excluded from the ordeal. The girl's people are then requested to state the number of cattle they claim. Their objective being to get the maximum possible, they are sure to aim high. The people of the bridegroom politely reject and counteroffer. Amid a lot of smoking, courtesy in demeanor, which should ideally mark the relations of relatives-in-law, gradually turns into clamor. Clamorous bargaining is not done by the fathers of both parties, but by other relatives. By this time, the relatives of the girl will already have investigated the cattle of the groom's relatives and will make demands specifying by color pattern what cattle they would like included in the marriage. One ox or cow may be pivotal in the negotiations. Usually, the best cattle are demanded for the ancestral spirits, *yieth*, but the father of the girl, and other relatives such as the girl's brother, also have specific claims for high-quality cattle. The people of the bridegroom are normally not reminded of the quality of the girl's mother's share which, though limited to a cow with a cow calf, is always among the best, a consideration for the attachment between the mother and the daughter. Negotiations usually end with a compromise. Once the amount of cattle is determined, the precise time of payment is then debated. Negotiations having ended, usually with a considerable compromise, all return to the festivities in a profoundly amicable fashion, for now the betrothal has attained a high degree of stability.

During the days of negotiations in which young men and women associate—eating, drinking, singing, and even sharing the same huts—badinage is at its highest, for usually it has become established that the bride and the groom accept each other. Sometimes, an occasion follows in which the bride and the groom, surrounded by dancing young men and girls, face each other singing a duet, with the bride finally anointing the groom with oil. The practice is something of a symbolic expression of the girl's consent and seems to be performed only in some marriages, especially important ones such as those of daughters of important men. In such marriages, since more status is involved and more is at stake, it is fitting to ensure the bride's consent.

The final stage is *geem nya*, literally "the giving away of the girl." On this occasion, the people of the man visit the people of the girl and formally request that she be given to them. Normally, unless an important condition in *kuen thiek* has not been fulfilled, there will be no further impediment. A promise being given that "their wife" will follow, the people of the man return to prepare themselves to receive her. Meanwhile, her kin perform a ritual ceremony in which a bull is sacrificed for the ancestral spirits who are invoked once again to bless the union. The bride then goes to the home of the bridegroom's father accompanied by a group of her age mates. As a safeguard against *tiel* and as an expression of solidarity, she stays in the house of the groom's stepmother or other stepkin, rather than in the house of his own mother. Another large celebration follows and the age mates of both parties have several days of badinage, eating, drinking, and singing—the festivities sometimes lasting all night. The bride and the groom share their first exclusive night and the marriage is consummated.[71]

We may now turn to the custom of *teer nya*, competition over the

71. To consummate a union in Dinka is *bi nya ruck*, literally "to dress the bride up," a further indication of how the Dinka traditionally associated being clothed with sexual exclusiveness.

bride. Once it is realized that a Dinka girl is primarily a source of wealth, competition is easily understood. For the same reason, and also because of the enmities it creates, it is avoided by the relatives of a man and is only resorted to when really necessary. It is more frequent among the rich. In case the competitors are related, one party is usually propitiated and persuaded to surrender. In competition, the cattle received as betrothal consideration are kept apart by the girl's kin, who are expected to inform the adverse group whenever one side increases its betrothal cattle. In response, the other group adds more cattle. The process goes on until one party is forced to surrender. In competition, there is no *kuen thiek,* that is, settlement of bride wealth. When one party is defeated, special cows from among the bride wealth are allotted to the ancestral spirits, the sacrifice to them is made, and *geem nya,* the handing over of the bride, concludes the ceremonies as in normal situations.

The process of competition is a very tense one in which the parties will use any means to defeat each other. In songs, anything that can destroy the reputation of the adversary is used. Open physical clashes, sometimes causing death, result. To minimize this, the right of courtship is regulated; the rule is that the first to betrothe the girl is the lawful bridegroom and the rights of betrothal accrue to him. He is thus the one entitled to courtship. One of the ways of determining the stage of validity of marriage is when sexual intercourse with other people counts as adultery, or when sexual intercourse of the girl and groom ceases to be wrongful. While sexual relationship is discouraged prior to the conclusion of the marriage, should it occur it is not an offense, and should the girl conceive, the issue is the lawful child of the marriage. In the case of competition, if the girl should conceive by the first suitor, even though he is eventually defeated he is not held liable and the child is his. The second groom, on the other hand, is not even permitted to court the girl. Should he do so, he commits an offense, as will be seen later under violation of rights in women. If he has sexual intercourse with her, he commits "adultery," and should he be defeated, he is supposed to compensate the winning suitor.

While most relatives of a girl welcome competition, the practice is not universal. Some fathers consider it disgraceful thus to put a daughter on the market. Indeed, the custom is waning, and, as is true of many other cases, the paramount chief has led the way. In one case, Acai, the daughter of Chief Deng Majok, was betrothed to a Ngok Dinka, and a betrothal wealth of about one hundred cows was paid. Chief Bol Col, one of the prominent chiefs of the Tuic Dinka, sought her for one of his sons. He offered one hundred and fifty cows for betrothal and undertook to pay a total bride wealth of two hundred. As in most marriages to the chief's daughters, the objective of Chief Bol was diplomatic. Deng

Majok's kin group were predominantly in favor of marrying the girl to
Bol Col's son on the grounds that, according to tradition, a girl is an
item of trade and higher payment should prevail. In this they were
supported by the tribe, who claimed that a daughter of the chief, especially in intertribal marriages, was a daughter of the tribe so that their
opinion should count. The matter went to Abyei court for arbitration.
Deng Majok argued that the bridegroom's father had died after the
betrothal, and that as the chief he had a general obligation to his needy
people and to the bridegroom, whose father had died believing his son
to be the chief's son-in-law. Secondly, he argued that his tribe would be
inviting an insult to him and therefore to themselves if they made him
accept a marriage on grounds of a more profitable offer. The court, convinced by the reasonableness of his grounds, persuaded his kin group
and the tribe to endorse it.

The preceding discussion of the process of marriage among the Dinka
shows that, although the individual parties are important, their fathers
and other kin are essential to the conclusion of the marriage. To obtain
their material and moral backing, a young man desirous of marriage has
to undergo one of the most trying experiences of his life. The Dinka say
that the process of marriage is one that must inevitably make the groom
gaunt, although this is the time when he should be most impressive
physically. It is partly for this reason that the custom of "hibernation,"
when men isolate themselves and drink much milk and eat meat, is
especially popular among bridegrooms who often appraise the attitude
of various relatives toward their marriage. Most critical songs in this
regard are composed during this cathartic period. The ordeal a bridegroom undergoes when lacking adequate family and kinship backing is
shown in these lines in which a young man mourns his father's death
because of the attitude of his uncle to his marriage.

> I have begun the wedding of Alai all alone
> And when I turned my face to see
> No one was there to follow me. . . .
> Is it cieng[72]; have I cieng badly? . . .
> Deng Kwol is pushing my claim away
> He has pushed my back into fire
> He has turned me into the legendary orphan of Kur.
> To what shall I liken this fate?
> That my bride should be left astray. . . .
> My father, Allor Kwol, left me
> In his last word, he said to me

72. See Chapter 2, pp. 24–25, for the many meanings of cieng. In this context, he
is asking whether he has been disrespectful in any way.

"My son, you will remain.
Deng, the brother of your father
Will marry a wife for you . . .
He will marry Alai for you."
When I ventured the daughter of Ajuong
I could not succeed
The wedding is delayed,
It is the treatment of an orphan
That is why Deng Makuei started
And even led my way.
Like a catfish followed by eels
And then dodging them,
He dodged me leaving me alone in the byre
I remained all alone in the byre of Alai.
Deng de Biong the stork of the marshes
A son of a man should not be left alone
To struggle with people
Like a black bull of the buffalo.[73]

The difficulties of traditional marriage, seen from both the man's and the girl's standpoints, prompt certain actions which the Dinka judge wrong but which, because of their frequency, become recognized as part of the marriage process in certain circumstances. These are elopement with an unbetrothed or betrothed girl, and abduction and/or forced intercourse with a married but an unwilling girl. Here we are not concerned with these acts as offenses, but as measures which Dinka youth take in order to influence marriage proceedings where they disapprove of the normal course.

Jon nya, elopement with an unbetrothed girl with a view to marriage where that is otherwise difficult or impossible, is considered the most serious, particularly if the elopement has been consummated. Depending on his assessment of his kinsmen's reaction, the man may take the girl to the home of the one in charge of his marriage, or even to the chief's home. This is naturally preferred to elopement to far-off areas, a practice which is on the increase as interaction with non-Ngok Sudanese increases. Whichever form it takes, elopement is a serious act. In the past, the girl's kin, if they desired the proposed union, would go armed into the cattle camp of the man's kin and seize all the cattle they could find. This is the custom known as *thel.* A serious, often fatal, fight ensued.

More prudent kinsmen of such a wrongdoer would not attempt obstruction. Instead, if they wanted their son to marry the girl, which would be preferable, they appealed to the chief to summon the girl's

---

73. The likening of marriage to a fight or a hunt, and of a person without kinship help to a lonely fighter or a hunter, comes out in these lines.

kin so that marriage could be discussed. On the appointed day, both sides came to the chief's court and a reasonable amount was fixed by the court as the bride wealth. A setoff was then made. If the cattle seized were less than the amount fixed, the difference was paid; if more, the excess was returned. If the girl's people insisted on her return they could do so but would not get compsensation unless there had been consummation, in which case they were given a cow called "the cow of the skirt." She then had to put on a bridal dress and continue to dress as a married woman whether married to this particular person or not. If she conceived, then additional compensation was paid. The relatives of the man might also refuse marriage and in theory similar measures as above are taken to restore the status quo, but in practice, settlement was rendered more difficult.

Elopement with a girl already betrothed to the man taking her is a less serious offense. This is implicit in the term the Dinka use for it, *jon tik,* literally "elopement with a wife," for once betrothed, she is thought of as a wife. Such elopement may occur for any of many reasons: inability to meet the bride wealth demands of the bride's kin or to secure the consent of some pivotal figure are examples. Usually, the bridegroom takes the bride to the home of his father. However, the couple may want to ensure their marriage by going beyond the reach of their relatives until their union will have been confirmed with children. *Jon tik* generally facilitates marriage in favor of the eloping parties. As in *jon nya,* negotiations are concluded in the chief's court and, except in a few cases, the return of the bride to her kin is not necessary. Should she be returned, marriage ceremonies are accelerated and previous impediments are greatly modified.

Where *jon nya* or *jon tik* takes place without the consent of the girl, it is called *guem,* "abduction." *Guem* is a most serious offense, and a bloody conflict is inevitable, whether there has been consummation or not. *Guem* may be authorized by the girl's relatives if after the conclusion of marriage ceremonies the girl still refuses her consent. Incredible brutalities can result from *guem.* The age mates of a bridegroom may seize the girl and physically force her into submission while he consummates the marriage. So embarrassing are the circumstances that some grooms fail to do so. Once consummation is effected, the girl is forced into dressing like a married woman and, it is hoped, would be too shamefaced to leave him. Many surrender, but some determined girls continue to reject their supposed husbands until they eventually secure a divorce.

In the course of their migration to urban centers, young Dinka men come in contact with Dinka girls in non-Dinka environments. Out of these may result marriages for which the traditional ceremonies cannot be adequately performed. Where the girl's relatives are present, the ceremonies may be greatly modified to suit the occasion. It is primarily in such situations that money is paid in lieu of cattle as bride wealth, though it serves the same function. Moreover, because of the absence of most kinsmen of both parties, the validity of such marriages is often questioned and most of them lack the stability of the traditional marriage. In some cases only initial betrothal is carried out and the rest of the ceremonies are postponed, to be performed back home. But even then, betrothal may be questioned. Where a man betrothes a girl in the tribe and then migrates, contact, and therefore courtship, is ended. Considering the length of the betrothal period, and the competitiveness of men over women, such betrothal often amounts to nothing.

These difficulties are especially acute in the case of educated Dinkas who are usually away from home and return periodically on vacations which are too short for the traditional marriage ceremonies. Even when he has fulfilled the traditional ceremonies, an educated Dinka, who is nearly always affiliated with one of the universal religions, is required to perform more social and religious celebrations. The celebrations add to the formal complexities of Dinka marriage. More important, subsequent religious ceremonies raise conflict-of-laws problems which are still matters of conjecture in Sudanese law. It may happen that the parties are not permitted by the religious law of one or both of them to contract a marriage by customary law or even at all. Assuming that they have the capacity to enter a Muslim, Christian, an Ordinance, or any other marriage, the question is raised as to whether that fact itself subjects them to the entire law of that marriage. It becomes significant whether the mere fact of religious adherence or of legal capacity to enter a marriage is a sufficient ground on which to alter radically the law that would otherwise govern one's status.

VALIDITY OF MARRIAGE   Although we later examine the validity of Dinka marriage in the context of legal pluralism, we are here concerned primarily with the stage at which customary marriage is recognized as valid and giving rise to rights and obligations. Since marriage ceremonies are so lengthy, this stage is not easily determined.

As betrothal is considered a degree of marriage among the Ngok Dinka, a betrothed man is said to have an action of "adultery" against third parties. A failure to appreciate the fact that betrothal is part of marriage in the customary laws of traditional African societies has led some writers to conclude that " 'adultery' here is used in a loose sense, for it covers sexual intercourse by wife before marriage." [74] Since the

74. Kasumu, "Integration of the Law of Husband and Wife in Western Nigeria," (paper delivered at the Conference on Integration of Customary and Modern Legal Systems, Ibadan, Nigeria, August 1964) p. 6.

protection of betrothal lies mostly in its anticipation of marriage rather than in the institution of betrothal itself, many societies require any compensation paid for adultery with a betrothed girl to be transferred to her relatives if the betrothal is subsequently broken. Among the Ngok, whoever weds her is entitled to it. Because of their misunderstanding of the true nature of such betrothal, some people are surprised to learn that "any child born to a betrothed woman 'belongs' to the intended husband." [75] For this reason, the man and his kin receive compensation for her injury. The same is true of any other rights over her which are violated. With these rights, the betrothed man and his kin also assume certain obligations for the girl. For instance, if she wrongs other people, the man and his kinsmen will pay compensation.

Identifying betrothal as a degree of marriage is only a starting point for delineating the stages of validity in the extensive proceedings of Dinka betrothal period. In this, Ngok law has undergone some changes. In the past, the validity of marriage giving rise to rights and duties was determined by one of two tests. The first was whether the cattle paid as a preliminary part of the marriage consideration included cattle dedicated to the bride's ancestral spirits and clan divinities. The second was whether the bride fulfilled the custom known as *mioc,* by which a betrothed girl visits her groom's home with gifts of food. Today, whether any cattle have been paid and accepted as *amec* is determinative.

In *Deng Ajith v. Magwith,*[76] Deng Ajith betrothed a girl and paid *amec.* Magwith eloped with the girl and went to a distant area. After begetting two children, they were caught and returned to the tribe. Deng brought an action of adultery against Magwith and claimed the children as "the children of the cows." Magwith pleaded that the girl had been his girlfriend long before she was betrothed to Deng. In fact, the first pregnancy occurred prior to the girl's engagement to Deng, a reason for their elopement. The court of first instance sentenced Magwith to six months' imprisonment for eloping with and impregnating "a married woman." The court also ordered the payment of six cows to Deng as compensation for the elopement and the adultery. The children were held to be his.

Magwith appealed to the chief's court of appeal on the ground that their first relationship had occurred prior to Deng's payment of the cattle of *amec* and therefore should not count as adultery to entitle Deng to compensation, nor should it entitle Deng to the offspring of that relationship. On proof of the facts, the court allowed his appeal. With respect to the first pregnancy, he was made to pay three cows compensation to the girl's relatives for the impregnation of an unmarried

75. Ibid.
76. Abyei, Ngok Dinka Appellate Court (1960).

woman, and was entitled to the child on further payment of legitimation wealth.[77]

As we saw in *Ayii v. Allor,* once the cows of *amec* have been paid not even the girl's father can interfere with the marriage. In *Koryom Arob v. Bol Duper,*[78] Koryom had paid thirty-nine cows as *amec* for the daughter of Bol. Bol subsequently gave the girl to another man who went outside the tribe with her. Bol was detained in jail while attempts were made to bring the girl back. Koryom, however, decided to "divorce" the girl and the court accepted his ground. As obiter dictum, the court said that had he wanted his wife back, he would have been entitled to an action of adultery and could have claimed any adulterous children as the offspring of his cattle. As it was, the court ordered immediate return of his betrothal wealth.

In the modern context, problems emerge as to the validity of mixed marriages. It is not the objective here to raise and answer the conflict-of-laws questions which result or are likely to result from legal pluralism. However, it is important to point out the incompetence of the tribal courts as now constituted, and the inadequacies of national law to deal with such issues. Dr. Farran, for instance, observes that while there are alternatives to polygynous marriages, Dinka chiefs' courts are not likely to realize them.

> When it is stated that tribal parties can marry in monogamous form, it is not so clear that this would be recognized as a valid marriage by the tribe and by the Chiefs' Court, which is its legal mouthpiece. Particularly would this be so if the marriage ran counter to an impediment known to the tribal law, but not to the general law. . . . Among such tribes as the Dinka, there is a feeling that any marriage without the delivery of bridewealth cattle is not a valid marriage so as to create agnatic ties with the clan for its issue. These considerations lead one to suppose that there may well be a marriage within the Sudan, which is lawful in the eyes of the Civil Courts, but illegal in the eyes of the courts which actually control family law in the area from which the couple comes and to which they may wish to return. This is a most unhappy and thoroughly undesirable situation.[79]

The same author has argued that the legal issues arising out of inter-tribal marriages are essentially identical with those of international con-

---

77. In *Akot Ral v. Lal Ayom,* (see p. 149, supra) we saw that the payment of the *amec* entitled Akot to two children who were physiologically Lal's and to compensation for elopement and impregnation of a married woman.

78. Abyei, Ngok Dinka Court (1953).

79. Farran 84–85.

flict of laws and that formalities should be governed by *lex loci con-tractus* and essentials by *lex domicilii*. He sees, however, the chiefs' lack of legal training and even general education as an impediment.

> It is too much to expect of the unlearned Chiefs' Courts that they should apply anything in the nature of conflict of laws rules. They simply apply their own tribal law . . . to all litigants coming be-fore them. As the married parties will normally reside in the hus-band's tribal area and litigate in his tribal court, his law will ordi-narily be that which governs the marriage after celebration. But presumably if a wife deserts him and returns to her own tribal area, he must sue for her restitution in her tribal court, which in turn will apply its own *lex fori*.[80]

Such observations can be made of other conflict-of-laws situations whether they concern Dinkas of different faiths or of the same faith but using different laws, or whether they involve Dinkas and non-Dinkas of whatever race or religion. In fairness to Ngok courts it must be said that they do make allowance for legal diversity. Since the bulk of the cele-brations take place in the girl's home, the requirements of her law must be fulfilled in order for the marriage to be valid. This approximates *lex loci contractus*. And since the wife automatically assumes the hus-band's domicile, any subsequent matters of essence are governed by his law. This fact recalls *lex domicilii*. Of course, both are approached from the male standpoint. For celebration, the girl's kin, who are then the primary beneficiaries, have to be satisfied in order to give their daugh-ter away. On the other side, the mere fact of the wife's adopting her husband's domicile is evidence of the supremacy of the husband and his kin. Ngok courts consider cases involving Christian and Muslim religions and therefore their laws. Whatever rules of conflict of laws the Ngok courts use, the hard fact remains that by virtue of their being unedu-cated, let alone legally untrained, they are incapable of handling these complex problems.

The national field does not present too different a picture. Although the lawyers, because of their training, are more enlightened (not neces-sarily about customary law), they are not free of cultural or religious bias.[81] Things tend to be seen in cultural and religious extremes. One is governed by either customary law, Islamic law, or imported Western law primarily according to one's religious affiliation or the ceremony

---

80. Id. at 181.

81. Dr. Farran explains why Northern judges are likely to apply these clauses with cultural bias: "It is by no means easy for anyone—even a judge—to put aside certain fundamental bases of thought: moral standards we may call them, if that term is not considered to be too amorphous in this context." Farran 16.

performed. The peculiarities of a crosscultural situation that would link tradition to modernity are not provided for.[82]

The problem requires adoption as well as rejection to suit the crosscultural situation. Let us take as an example marriages between Christian Dinkas. According to Section 6 of the Non-Mohammedan Marriage Ordinance of the Sudan, a subsequent celebration in church may turn a tribal marriage into a marriage under the Ordinance. If, for example, the community involved is Roman Catholic, the marriage would be governed by canon law in accordance with Section 5(1) of the Non-Mohammedan Marriage Ordinance and this would prohibit divorce under any circumstances. Divorce among the Dinka is difficult and rare, though it may be simple for a person who is willing to forfeit his bride wealth. Even then, a man would usually please himself with more marriages rather than divorce. Divorce proceedings are even more rarely initiated by women. Where a person is monogamous, as is true of most Dinka Christians [83] whatever the form of their marriage ceremony, absolute prohibition of divorce can be a serious deprivation. In one case,[84] the wife of a socially prominent devout Christian deserted him, leaving him with little children and an important home to manage. The man, having done in vain all within his power to bring her back, asked the church for a dispensation to divorce and remarry. This was not granted and he remained unmarried in a society which considers marriage a fundamental necessity. Of course, canon divorce law is only an example. The same can be said of any situation where harmonization of tradition with the realities of change is called for. In this respect, there is much room for creativity in the Sudanese legal system. This might tend to augment uncertainty in the law, but beneficial uncertainty is as much a virtue as detrimental certainty is a vice.

Dissolution of Marriage

Dissolution of marriage may be the result of the wife's death (not the husband's) or of divorce. Among the Dinka both are restricted. How-

82. There is nothing in Sudanese law, for instance, resembling the Christian Marriage and Divorce Ordinance of Kenya which states *inter alia* that: "Any African woman married in accordance with the provisions of this Ordinance or of the Marriage Ordinance or of the Native Christian Marriage Ordinance (now repealed), whether before or after the commencement of this Ordinance, shall be deemed to have attained her majority in widowhood, and shall not be bound to cohabit with the brother or any other relative of her deceased husband or any other person or to be at the disposal of such brother or other relative or other person, but she shall have the same right to support for herself and her children of such marriage from such brother or other relative as she would have had if she had not been married as aforesaid."

83. Some Dinka Christians are polygynous.

84. It is not important to reveal the names.

ever, a substantial amount of litigation in Dinka courts is concerned with the consequences of dissolving marriage. Under the current Ngok law, reference to court is necessary.

Disputes over dissolution on death are rather infrequent because the relations between the parties involved are not as strained as is usually the case with divorce. Unless there are unusual circumstances, there is often sympathy on both sides. As an example of such amicability, dissolution on death is the only situation where a man is not entitled to the cows of the bride wealth which are dead even if the wife's relatives had disposed of them for beneficial purposes.

Only the wife's death can justify a dissolution of marriage in that it may be used as a ground for a postmortem divorce. Because of levirate, the husband's death does not dissolve the marriage. Even the death of the wife is rarely a ground for divorce. Other considerations have to be made before a divorce decree may be granted; the most important is whether the woman died without issue. If she had two or more children, the marriage subsists and her widower will not be permitted to claim the return of the bride wealth. In such a case, the relatives of the dead wife are requested to pay him cattle of *duot yic,* literally "tying the belly." This expression originates in a mourning custom by which a man, who must not cry with tears but is believed to cry "inside," ties a piece of cloth or leather around his abdomen, a practice associated with controlling the expression of one's grief. Thus, the compensation paid by the wife's kin is in essence a gesture of sympathy and assistance. They may also help the man to marry again. While anybody may pay cattle of *adut,* as *duot yic* is sometimes called, payment by the wife's kin is compulsory. If a wife dies with only one child, the likelihood is that the marriage will not be dissolved, especially if that child is a male. However, should the widower desire its dissolution, he is entitled to it and will be returned his bride wealth with the exception of a number sufficient to retain his paternal rights over the child. Should he receive all the cows, he loses his rights over the child. In *Bol Malek v. the Relatives of Awut,*[85] Bol married Awut, who died not long after giving birth to a daughter. Bol sued for the return of his bride wealth in full, and recovered it. The daughter, Ajang Bol, though called by her father's name, was raised by the relatives of Awut. While he continued to be known as the father, Bol thus forefeited paternal rights over his daughter.

If a father who has lost his paternal rights over his orphan child wishes to reclaim him or her, he must "marry" the child. This notion applies whether the child is male or female. It recalls the fundamental base of Dinka marriage, and is a fictional restoration of the status quo ante so that the husband is in effect envisioned as remarrying his de-

85. Abyei, Ngok Dinka Court (1930).

ceased wife in order to reclaim his child—hence, "marrying" the child.
The number of cows a man needs to pay for his issue differs according
to the sex and age of the child.[86] In *Bol Malek v. the Maternal Kin of
Ajang Bol*,[87] the facts of *Bol Malek v. the Relatives of Awut* came to
the chief's court once more. When Ajang reached marriageable age, Bol
Malek reclaimed her. At this stage, when a daughter is about to attract
wealth, her father's wish to "marry" her is not easily accepted by her maternal kin. Ajang's maternal kin demanded more than Bol was willing to pay. Dispute arose over the matter and Bol brought an action for
the recovery of his daughter. The court held that in view of Ajang's age
and marriage potential, Bol should "marry" his daughter for twenty
cows in order to resume his paternal rights over her. This he did. Soon
after he recovered his daughter Ajang was married with a substantial
bride wealth.

Where a deceased wife leaves no children, dissolution is more likely to
be granted. This requires further qualification, for although there may
be dissolution of the marriage, the wife's kin and the husband with his
kin may perpetuate their in-law relationship by sororate, that is, by
substituting the deceased with another girl who may be her sister or a
relative. This is illustrated by *The Relatives of Salvatore Atem v. the
Relatives of Athilueth*.[88] Atem, a Roman Catholic, married Athilueth by
customary law. Athilueth died during her first childbirth. It was said
that one of the relatives of the girl who had unsuccessfully opposed the
marriage had inflicted a curse upon the marriage, saying that Athilueth
would never live to bear children to Atem. Her death therefore recalled
the curse. Atem's kin group sued for the return of their full bride
wealth. During the litigation, one of Atem's kinsmen proposed that a
girl be given to them as a substitute wife. Both sides agreed. Athilueth's
relatives suggested three girls, one a full sister and the others half-sisters
of Athilueth. Atem's relatives chose the full sister because she was educated, as was Atem. Atem, who was absent on government service, was
not informed of these measures. When the choice was made, the court
ordered that a nominal number of cattle be paid by Atem's relatives to
the girl's relatives as cows of *put*, that is, "cows of spraying with ashes"
—a blessing rite to establish the new union independently of the dead
wife and thus to avoid the implications of incest. This, it must be noted,

---

86. For a male, he pays the average of six cows, while for a female he pays the
average of ten. This may appear paradoxical since the objective is to prolong the
line through males. But in view of the fact that the daugther will probably be
married with cattle sufficient for her father to acquire a new wife who may beget
sons, one son is worth less than one daughter.

87. Abyei, Ngok Dinka Court (1954).

88. Abyei, Ngok Dinka Court (1958).

is different from the symbolic action of alleviating the evil consequences of experienced or feared incest. It is essentially indicative that the marriage of Atem and Athilueth had been dissolved by death and the relationship of in-laws could only be maintained by a new marriage.[89] This case illustrates the subordination of the individual parties to the marriage. Not only was Salvatore Atem not present at the proceedings, but the girl who was offered as a substitute was not there either and might not have been consulted.

Sororate must be distinguished from levirate and ghost marriage. Whereas in the levirate the previous marriage subsists, sororate is a new marriage. Ghost marriage may seem closer, but the union *inter vivos* is entered into in the name of the deceased; in sororate, death gives rise to a new marriage. In sororate, the objective is to perpetuate the name of the living and not the deceased, as in levirate. Indeed, if the deceased wife had children, sororate would not be possible, for they would then be a tangible symbol of the permanence and the success of the previous union.

Divorce presents more problems than dissolution on death. Since it involves undoing the complex network of relationships created by the collection and distribution of bride wealth, divorce is strongly opposed.

A man may claim divorce on any one of many grounds which the Dinka quote with consistency. Some of these can be seen from actual cases. The first and most obvious ground for divorce is the wife's barrenness, which in Dinka eyes is a failure to fulfill the fundamental obligation of marriage. The bride wealth is returned, with the exception of "a cow of the skirt" that is, compensation for having put her into her status as a married woman, which reduces her marriage potential. In *Mithiang Aguek v. Malek Deng*[90] Mithiang married Malek's sister, who proved barren. Mithiang sued for divorce. Malek counterclaimed compensation from Mithiang for having been cohabiting with his sister. The court held that Mithiang was entitled to divorce, but had to pay *weng biong*, "the cow of the skirt," to Malek. If the wife bears a child before her barrenness, sufficient cattle to preserve the legitimacy of the child will be left with her kin. If barrenness comes after the birth of two or more children, it would probably foreclose divorce. When a man's wife does not conceive, the Dinka usually suspect the woman of barrenness rather than the husband of sterility, and this is often linked with some

89. In accord with this, the court also ordered the payment of a few cows as *arueth*, a reverse payment made by the bride's kin to the bridegroom's kin which is equivalent to about one third of the total bride wealth. The court, however, made the girl's relatives pay more than one third of the new nominal bride wealth because it was to be considered *adut*, that is, cattle for soothing his grief.

90. Abyei, Ngok Dinka Court (1953).

indignation on the part of the mythical participants. If propitiation and appeasement rites have been carried out, the wife is either suspected of some wrong or simply believed barren.[91]

Analogous to barrenness is mortality of the wife's offspring. The woman is often suspected of hiding some evil, particularly a sexual offense, for which the death of children is a supernatural punishment.

The second ground for divorce is theft, which as we saw earlier, involves punitive measures by the age set of the alleged thief and is therefore a public scandal.

Habitual insults by the wife constitute a third ground for divorce. Such insults must be grievous and injurious to the reputation of the husband or his lineage, a question decided by the court in the light of all the circumstances.

The fourth ground is "badness of the mouth," *rac thok*. This is similar to the third ground, but *rac thok* does not need to entail actual insults; it concerns a wife who nags and grumbles so much that she wearies the husband to an unbearable extent. This is essentially a matter of character. It does not need to be directed toward the husband. It will suffice that the wife cannot get along with her associates. This ground requires such notoriety that proof is easy. Usually, even in court, people will be around who would be only too glad to testify in favor of divorce.

Adultery is another ground for divorce, but normally a man will prefer compensation rather than divorce unless the wife is persistently adulterous.

The sixth ground is witchcraft discovered after the marriage. If a man marries a woman knowing that she is reputed as a witch or that witchcraft is practiced within her lineage, he cannot use it as a ground for divorce. Even when subsequently discovered, witchcraft is rarely used as a ground for divorce because of the seriousness of imputing it and the difficulty of proving it. As the court becomes more empirically oriented, witchcraft becomes more difficult to prove and is therefore less utilized as a ground for divorce.

Mortal disease, of which tuberculosis and leprosy are typical examples, constitutes the seventh ground for divorce. However, the court usually persuades the husband against divorce on the ground that the disease is an act of God. Another obstacle is that imputing such diseases is often considered defamatory, and whatever the justification, the tendency is against such imputation. Only in the most obvious cases do people sue for divorce on this ground.

The eighth ground is *jiliiu* or *dejook*, which are very complex words.

91. Some wives deliberately have illicit sexual intercourse to challenge such imputations, and, of course, only get into further trouble.

A woman who is *ajiliu* or *adejook* is untidy, careless, ill-mannered, indecent, bad at cooking, at bringing up children, at keeping the house, and the like. The Dinka themselves say that *juliiu* and *dejook* cannot be easily defined. They are believed to be so intricate that sometimes the court has to rely entirely on the husband's subjectivities about his wife. These are sometimes better not said, but from the circumstances of each case, the Dinka believe that *juiliiu* or *dejook* may be objectively determined. The ground is rarely used because of the difficulty of proof, but when used, the court is likely to be sympathetic even without clear proof.

While *jiliiu* or *dejook* are essentially matters of general character, a ninth and somewhat similar ground for divorce relates to acts of gross indecency. This ground is wide and may include anything which in the opinion of the court is too unbecoming for the obligation of respect which a wife owes her husband, or which relatives-in-law owe each other. Like *jiliiu* or *dejook,* if the husband can substantiate his point without necessarily specifying his cause of grievance, the court may be lenient in its requirements for evidence in order to save him embarrassment. The act need not be by the wife herself: conduct of her close relatives may count against her, though in such a case the court is more likely to rule that instead of divorce, *awec,* conciliatory payment, be made to the offended husband. In *Madut Akoc v. Monytooc Deng,*[92] Madut was married to Monytooc's sister, Kuei. Monytooc, in conflict, with Madut, went to see him. Without adequate warning, he walked into the house to find Madut and Kuei in private circumstances. Madut sued for divorce. The court ruled that although Madut was justified in his claim, in view of his wife's innocence he should accept conciliatory payment and be reconciled. Madut accepted and Monytooc was made to pay him two cows.

The tenth ground for divorce is desertion. If a wife runs away with another man, the husband will probably have her returned and accept compensation from the man with whom she had eloped. But if she is not returned or she continually deserts, he would be entitled to a divorce. In *Mithiang Dut v. the Relatives of Adit,*[93] Adit, Mithiang's wife, bore six children, all of whom died. Believing the source of death to be with her husband, she brought a suit for divorce, but her claim was dismissed. She then eloped with another man. They were caught and she was returned to Mithiang. Her lover was made to pay compensation to Mithiang, and was sentenced to imprisonment. Soon after serving his prison sentence, they eloped again. The process was repeated so many

92. Abyei, Ngok Dinka Court (1953).
93. Abyei, Ngok Dinka Court (1960).

times that Mithiang became tired of litigation and asked for a divorce, which the court granted.[94]

The final ground is giving the wife away in marriage to someone else. It is obvious that such a transaction is not marriage, since the girl's relatives cannot contract another marriage while a valid one subsists. This is the case even if there has been only a betrothal. If, instead of enforcing his rights as a husband, a man prefers divorce, it will be granted. This ground is analogous to adultery and desertion; but it is contracting another marriage, though null and void, which constitutes the ground, as we saw in *Koryom Arob v. Bol Duper*.[95] In *Akuek v. Madut*,[96] Akuek was betrothed to a girl who did not like him and was determined not to live with him. When her refusal was dismissed, she indulged in illicit relationships to dissuade Akuek. When this strategy was not fruitful, she eloped with Madut. This time, her relatives felt themselves compelled to endorse her choice and contract a marriage with Madut. Though Akuek could have sued Madut for adultery and her relatives for giving his wife in marriage, he chose to sue Madut for the return of his bride wealth. The court held that, according to custom, in the event of a well-founded divorce and a subsequent marriage, the bride wealth is to be paid by the new husband, or the wife's relatives, or both, whichever is most conducive to prompt payment.

Although in most cases we have talked of the husband and the wife as parties in divorce actions, in fact the suits often involve kinship groups. Only if the husband can justify his cause to his kinsmen will they back him in his divorce proceedings. In most cases, a combination of grounds is necessary to establish good cause.

Divorce among the Ngok can only be effected through the court. In the past, this was not necessary, although the ritual of emancipating a divorced woman had to be performed by the chief. This change is linked with certain economic innovations. In the past, a Dinka would rarely part with his cattle except for marriage. For this reason, on the dissolution of a marriage, the restoration of the status quo ante was relatively simple. The actual cows which had been paid in bride wealth were returned with their offspring. If they were passed on in other marriages, they were traced and withdrawn. This was easy since in most cases the cattle would be within the Ngok territory. Where the actual cows could not be recovered, compensation was made from among the cows of the judgment creditor. This was also easy because cattle were much more

94. In *Akot Ral v. Lal Ayom* (see p. 149, supra) and *Gok Aguek v. Mabok and others* (see p. 194, infra) the husbands did not ask for a divorce although the continual desertion by their wives constituted sufficient grounds for divorce.
95. Abyei, Ngok Dinka Court (1953) (see p. 174, supra).
96. Abyei, Ngok Dinka Court (1960).

plentiful. Today, people dispose of cattle more freely and to distant areas where tracing them is unthinkable, although, as Dr. Howell has pointed out, there still is "often much argument as to the merits of the cattle concerned." [97] Besides, with the reduction in the number of cows a man has, compensation is not easily carried out. One wants to avoid discharging a debt as much as possible. Resort to the chief for execution has thus become necessary. The court has also assumed the right to decide whether the husband has good cause for divorce. Where the husband proves good cause and obtains a divorce, the wife's kin must return forthwith any cattle not disposed of, and compensate for those disposed of.

There are cases in which people still disregard the court's order, or attempt a divorce without resort to court. In such a case, the Ngok do not consider the husband's act truly a divorce. It becomes a form of desertion which may then entitle the wife to sue for divorce. Without such divorce, the wife is not ritually emancipated and the husband cannot recover his bride wealth. The court may, however, choose to accept divorce on the husband's insistence provided that, if the wife has borne him children, he forfeits the bride wealth. If the woman has no children, he waits until she is remarried, and he is repaid according to the amount of bride wealth obtained from the subsequent husband. This is always bound to be far less than he had paid, partly because the woman will be cheaper as a result of having been married once and partly because the cattle of the first marriage would have multiplied. With respect to the ownership and custody of children, they normally remain with the father even though he is to blame for the divorce. A child who is still being nursed is left in the mother's custody until he is old enough to rejoin the father. If the child was still in the mother's womb on divorce, the legal fatherhood goes to whoever marries the mother. The reason is that if the first husband had wanted the child, he would not have insisted on divorce. When the child is grown, and the father claims his or her return, the child will be asked to choose between the biological father and the adoptive father. If the child decides to go back to the original father, he may do so, provided that the original father pays the child's guardians, whether they be the mother's kin or the adoptive father.

The wife's grounds for divorce are fewer and often more compelling than those of the husband. Life with her husband has to be terribly hard for her to win the sympathy of her kin and the court. Her family obviously has much more to lose, not only because the cattle of her bride wealth will have multiplied far beyond the number they can pos-

97. Howell, "Ngok Dinka" 288.

sibly hope for in her remarriage, but also because her divorce often works against her chances for a good remarriage. The wife may, however, succeed on a number of grounds: the first is impotence and sterility. A man is rarely suspected of impotence and sterility especially if he has only one wife and there is no way of telling whether the defect is his or hers. Generally, women are embarrassed to adduce this as a ground for divorce, but it is sometimes a cause of wives' unfaithfulness. The singer was unfaithful because of her husband's inadequacy.

> There are women who say
> "What shall I do with the husband of another woman?" . . .
> A bewildering thing has appeared in my family
> I do not know what is killing the man
> He sleeps until it dawns.
> I will leave
> I hate such things
> "Man, get up,
> There is something at the door."
> But he would not wake
> He falls back to sleep
> I will leave
> I hate such things.

In normal cases, the impotence or sterility of the husband does not entitle the wife to divorce. Since the primary object is that she should procreate, the matter is secretly settled within the family, and a relative of the man may act as a genitor while the offspring are considered those of the husband. If the husband objects to such an arrangement, the wife would be entitled to divorce. Many husbands would rather have a genitor procreate with the wife than risk publicity over their impotence or sterility. This ground is, therefore, rarely used.

The second ground for divorce is incest by the husband. The Dinka believe the consequences of incest to fall on the wife and her issue. It is she and her kin, therefore, who are keenest on avoiding incest. If a man marries a girl related to the wife, the wife is entitled to divorce him. Even courting such a girl may give the wife good cause, although this is not settled. In *Bashir Deng v. John Ajuong*,[98] Bashir married the ward of Ajuong. Bashir and his wife quarreled frequently, and ultimately separated. Bashir later sued for the restitution of conjugal rights. Ajuong brought a counteraction demanding divorce on the ground that Bashir had courted Ajuong's sister. Ajuong's sister testified to this fact. The majority of the court were of the opinion that courtship short of mar-

98. Abyei, Ngok Dinka Court (1960).

riage or sexual intercourse was not a ground for divorce by the wife. Accordingly, divorce was denied, and Bashir was made to pay Ajuong a conciliatory fee. As an obiter dictum, the court held that if Ajuong was known to have sufficient cattle to repay the bride wealth, it might have been wiser to grant divorce. Their ground for this dictum was incompatibility resulting from frequent nagging and quarrels rather than from incest.

The wife's third ground for divorce is the husband's failure to provide maintenance. It is his duty to cultivate her fields and provide her with cows, sheep, and goats. The court will at first attempt to make the husband provide for his wife according to the wealth in his family. Should he be uncooperative, the wife may then be granted a divorce.

The wife may also be granted a divorce if the husband continually uses insults defamatory of his wife's relatives. This ground is somewhat similar to the one mentioned for the husband, but whereas insults against the husband personally would give him good cause, in the case under consideration the insult must touch on her lineage rather than her personally. Imputations of leprosy or witchcraft are examples. This ground rarely succeeds because the court would usually persuade the wronged party to accept a conciliatory fee and be reconciled.

The wife may also divorce on grounds of desertion. In most cases, however, she is requested to cohabit with one of the husband's relatives so that children may be begotten to the name of the lineage. On desertion, a woman may inform the chief, who will call upon her relatives to bring the husband back. If for one reason or another they fail to restore cohabitation, the wife will be entitled to select a genitor from among his close relatives. If, instead, she insists on divorce, it may be granted. If a man deserts his wife for long, especially without maintenance, and then turns up to restore cohabitation, the wife may justifiably insist on divorce. The singer in the following song had been deserted by her husband. She stayed at home with her little son whom she named Dhala, literally "I am scorned." On her husband's return, she sued for divorce. Although the court was reluctant to grant divorce, she won the case and then composed the song.

Why is the case not decided in haste
The case of my supposed husband, Awer Rial?
I would like to defeat the man in haste.
Why does he gaze into my eyes,
As though he is about to escape?
People say: "Aluel, the man still considers you his wife."
I answer: "Decide the case, his words are lies.
He knew I was his wife;

> Yet he went away as far as Anyaar.
> Do you call that a husband?"
> O my son, Dhala,
> I am scorned for my right cause.

Cruelty provides a further ground for divorce. Normally, a man has the right to reprimand and even beat his wife, and interference by her relatives would be reprehensible. However, if he persistently ill-treats her, or beats her without good cause, her relatives may intervene and divorce may ensue.

The wife, even more than the husband, relies largely on convincing her kin about suing for divorce. Her chances of convincing them are much poorer than those of the husband with his kin. Although her kin do not benefit from children as much as do her husband and his relatives, their most important consideration is that their daughter should procreate.

As is the case with the husband, the wife and her relatives may insist on a divorce contrary to the court decree. In such an event they will be compelled to repay the bride wealth promptly and only "the cow of the skirt" will be deducted, unless there is a child, in which case further reductions will be made equivalent to those of impregnation. If they have good grounds for divorce, the court will direct that the husband should wait for the wife's remarriage and that he be compensated from among the cattle paid by the new husband. The rules of ownership and custody of the children mentioned above are applicable.

Once a divorce decree has been granted to the spouse who claimed it, the ceremony known as *cuet arob,* "the spraying of the sacred ashes," is carried out to emancipate the wife from the status of a married woman. She is brought into the chief's court, and her legs are sprayed with ashes from the chief's cattle.

In explaining the infrequency of divorce among the Dinka, we must emphasize the complications of divorce and the multiplicity of people it affects. As Howell has observed, "It is . . . in the interest of all those persons to see that marriage is a successful and stable one and the system is one which makes for stability in marriage." [99] Usually, the greater the number of kinsmen who contribute bride wealth or who share in receiving it, the greater the stability of the marriage. In the past, these cattle were hardly ever sold, at least during the early years of the marriage, and since they had to be returned if the marriage was dissolved, they were a pledge that both sides were interested in ensuring its stability. According to Howell, the stability of Dinka marriage is largely due to the great care the Dinka place on choosing the right partner.

99. Howell, "Ngok Dinka" 288.

> The stability of marriage among the Ngok Dinka . . . cannot, however, be attributed solely to the deterrent effect of the complications involved in a divorce. . . . The main factor making for stability is to be found in the slow process of flirtation, courtship and marriage, which gives Dinka youths and girls the maximum opportunity to find the right mate. Occasionally, of course, girls are forced by their families to marry old and rich men whom they do not favour and it is sometimes said by the Ngork that it is difficult for a young man to get married at all. This does not, however, appear to be the rule, for although many old and important men have a large number of wives, most men of thirty have at least one wife.[100]

While Dr. Howell is correct on the role of courtship and long betrothal, his emphasis on the freedom of choice must be correlated with what was said earlier about the predisposition of most Dinka girls to accept whoever proposes to marry them unless cogent circumstances compel a refusal. It is true that this is often the same man or one of the men who would have been "dating" the girl, and it is also true that she can discourage anyone she particularly disapproves of from proposing; but it is equally true that she is often quite neutral so as not to repel a potential proposal. To understand the stability of Dinka marriage, one must understand the order of public policy issues facing a Dinka woman. First, she wants and is wanted, expects and is expected, to marry and ensure the stability of her marriage. Second, she is better off if she likes the person she marries and continues to like him.

In line with the conception of betrothal as a degree of marriage, breach of betrothal is considered divorce. But breach of betrothal is easier than the divorce of a fully married wife. It is necessary to distinguish the validity of betrothal as a degree of marriage from its indissolubility. Breach of betrothal implies disapproval by the "husband" and his relatives of the girl as a wife, thereby reducing her chances for a good marriage. However, other considerations are paramount. The betrothal relationship is less complex than a full marriage since the transfer and distribution of bride wealth as well as other gifts are less intensive, so that the bonds are not necessarily stabilized. In addition, a "divorced" fiancé in tribal society normally marries. Therefore, dissolution of betrothal does not usually alter the position of the parties substantially, and its problems are of less magnitude. If the husband-to-be is at fault, he is almost certain that the girl will easily find a substitute marriage and his cattle will be returned. When the relatives of the girl desire dissolution, the problem of collecting the cattle already

100. Ibid.

paid is mitigated, for the time interval since distribution is much shorter. But foremost is the fact that no children are normally begotten during betrothal so that, given lineal continuity as the base, betrothal is an unfulfilled relationship.

The importance of childbirth as the primary fulfillment of marriage led Professor Evans-Pritchard to remark on the kindred of the Dinka, the Nuer, that "Most broken marriages occur during or shortly after the nuptial ceremonies. One cannot properly speak of divorce at this stage because in Nuer eyes marriage is incomplete till a child has been born." [101] This observation is valid as an argument for the stability of marriage and not for its validity. As Howell argues, the use of the word "incomplete" is relative.

> If a "complete" marriage is one which is legally indissoluble, then this condition is reached only at a much later stage when at least two, and probably three, children have been born. If it is "complete" when the rights in the woman are legally transferred from her family to her husband, then this occurs much earlier in the proceedings. . . .[102]

Even in the first sense, completeness of a marriage would merely make dissolubility more difficult and not impossible.

The relative ease with which betrothal may be broken should not imply that breach of betrothal is frequent or approved. On the contrary, the Dinka believe that unless breach of betrothal is well grounded it leaves a curse which jeopardizes one's future betrothals and even marriages. Where the girl is rejected, her prospects for a good marriage are usually affected. The grievance of such a girl is shown in these lines. The singer was suddenly "divorced" with no known cause. In the song, she tells of her sorrow, pities her brother for her reduced value, condemns her heart for having led her to the man, and generally expresses loss of faith in marriage.

> Mine is the tale of the horse of Ajak [103]
> My brother, the Crested Crane, Matem.
> Ponder not, O my heart
> Do not curve your horns
> It was you who pushed my head into the bush [104]
> If I could pull you out to stand like a person
> I would grind you with a pestle

---

101. Evans-Pritchard, *Kinship and Marriage among the Nuer* 93 (1951).

102. Howell, *Nuer Law* 127.

103. Ajak is said to have jealously and carefully bred a horse that was suddenly killed and eaten by a lion before he even got to use it. She compares herself with the horse and her brother with Ajak.

104. To fall in love with him.

And I would burn you with fire
My case would be an example to all
Marriage would cease
And even the milk of goats would be abandoned.[105]
What about the beautiful thing smelling like ghee? [106]
I spend my nights musing with a confounded heart
Kerieth [107] of clan Pajok
We have bestowed a curse on ourselves.[108]
O Kerieth, son of clan Pajok
A man of your age once said,
"God is blamed for death
Yet God is never blamed."
So I blame you for the divorce
Yet, I will never blame you
Your head was spoiled by other men
To come and divorce me.

When the divorcée sang this song with her age mates in a woman's dance which happened to be attended by her ex-fiancé, he is said to have dropped tears and immediately taken his personality ox to her kin as symbolic of his desire to reinstitute the marriage. The marriage was accordingly recontracted.

Breach of betrothal, then, is not taken lightly but has principles comparable to those of marriage. Nor does its breach merely cause moral indignation. Cases were cited earlier [109] in which the court rejected breach of betrothal. In this regard, however, more cogency is required from the bride and her kin than is required from the groom and his kin.

Special problems are posed by acculturation. "Limping" marriages are often found among the people who migrate to urban centers. The marriage of an educated man to an uneducated girl is one cause of instability. This disparity in education, together with the fact that such marriages are often arranged, tends to increase such unbalanced unions. Many such arranged marriages hardly survive the betrothal period.

The conflict of laws resulting from the conversion of Dinkas to alien religions is another cause of instability in marriage. Earlier, we gave the

105. People would no longer believe in marriage even though through it they receive cattle for milk. Menstruating women drink only goat's milk or else suffer an impurity which is believed to affect their fertility. The singer also suggests that her example would discourage marriage and procreation, which is the objective of abstinence from cow's milk.

106. Clarified butter.

107. The bridegroom.

108. Because their conflict is without good cause, she believes they have provoked their ancestral spirits and therefore invited their curse.

109. For example, *Ayii v. Allor* (see p. 147, supra) and *Koryom Arob v. Bol Duper* (see p. 174, supra).

example of conversion of a tribal marriage into an Excepted Roman Catholic Community marriage where divorce is not permitted. Dinka Christians become more apprehensive as they witness the implications of such a marriage. While not necessarily expecting to divorce, they think of divorce as a possible outlet should their marriage present too many problems. Apprehensions about the impossibility of divorce in a statutory marriage of the kind illustrated make them fear commitment to the unconditional permanence of marriage and to monogamy. "One wife," Dinka elders tell their Christian children, "must be well selected"; but even when such choice is made, one party, usually the husband, often feels it necessary to have a "test" period of married life before marriage is confirmed with Christian celebrations. The wife, in turn, becomes insecure and apprehensive and, if she is a devout Christian, may put pressure on the husband to carry out the church rites. This in itself tends to work against the stability of marriage. Thus, prohibition of divorce augments divorce.[110]

Legitimacy of Children

The concept of illegitimacy is restricted in Dinka law. A child may be illegitimate in relation to a particular person but not in the sense that he occupies an independent status of illegitimacy. Children are the greatest treasure, and a child is at all times somebody's legitimate off-spring with all the rights implicit in that status. We have seen that the factors surrounding these affection institutions cause deprivations which in turn prompt violations of the norms. Consequently, universal legitimacy, though a very humane aspect of Dinka law, is marked with correlative deprivations and conflicts over children.

A child is legitimate if born during the subsistence of a marriage which is valid in accordance with the criteria described earlier. The stage of such validity is betrothal upon at least partial payment of bride wealth. Any children born to the bride after that are legitimate children of the intended husband regardless of their actual paternity. Because of the levirate and ghost marriage the "father" may have died when the child was conceived or even when the mother was married. If a man divorces his wife while she is pregnant, he loses the child, unless he

110. Whatever the validity of the maxim *ignoratia juris non excusat*, as a general rule a barely literate Christian Dinka without legal counsel cannot be expected to know the loophole provided by the ingenious *ratio decidendi* of *Bamboulis v. Bamboulis*, see Cases in Court of Appeal 76 (1954). In that case, the court held that although the non-Mohammedan Marriage Ordinance provides for the application of the religious law of the parties to the "effect" and "consequences" of their marriage, divorce is not an effect or a consequence and may therefore be granted on the basis of the general laws.

leaves sufficient cattle to retain his claim over the child, or unless the child himself later demands return to the original father, in which case he transfers his legitimacy by the father's payment of legitimation fee. It then becomes legitimacy by adoption and not by birth in lawful marriage. If a child is born of adultery, he is still the legitimate child of the marriage unless the mother is divorced while still pregnant with that child, in which case the legitimacy of the child is transferred either to the mother's kin or to the man who marries her subsequently.

Legitimation may be by the biological father or by a stranger. The first case usually occurs in connection with the impregnation of an unmarried woman. The biological father may legitimate the child by a subsequent marriage or by the payment of legitimation fee in addition to the damages on account of impregnation.[111] Failing adoption by the biological father, a child is adopted by anyone who subsequently marries the mother. A child who is not legitimate by birth or by adoption belongs to the maternal kin. He assumes all the obligations and is entitled to all the rights of a legitimate child.

By whatever means a person acquires his legitimacy, he is fully legitimate and no serious social stigmata are attached to the noncoincidence of biological and legal parentage. In certain cases, a child may suffer emotional strains and conflicts. Even an otherwise accursed child, once he survives, is entitled to the privileges of legitimacy. It is a serious wrong to remind a relative of the peculiarities of his legitimacy, whatever the provocation. Should any discrimination against him come to court, the judges are most likely to be biased for him and will reprimand his adversaries with unusual emphasis. He, in turn, is also reprimanded strongly if he tends to differentiate himself by attributing ordinary incidents of ill-treatment to the peculiarities of his status.

Despite their legal equality, such children may be discriminated against in subtle ways, and in any case are often emotionally insecure. This invocation by a master of a fishing spear indicates clearly this subtle discrimination and the resultant strains and conflicts

> . . . I am not a bastard coming with its mother, the bastard fathered by some stranger outside. If such a one prays, he calls upon no clan-divinity, because he is a child which comes with his mother alone and he will be unable to do anything in a case of sickness.[112]

Not infrequently a man who has been ill-treated by his father addresses himself to the lineage in songs with such words as "Am I not a

111. During the child's early years, a man pays up to six cows for a boy and up to ten cows for a girl. After the age of maturity, the rates increase to ten for the boy and twenty for the girl.

112. Lienhardt, *Divinity* 222.

son of the clan?" "Did I come with my mother?" "Was I adopted?" and the like. Since such a status is not rare, considerable problems of suspicion about the nature of their legitimacy by persons who feel discriminated against are to be expected. Because of this discrimination, however subtle, sons often return to their biological fathers who would at that stage be only too glad to legitimate them, thus bringing together biological and legal parentage. Since daughters change their residence and domicile, the problem is not so acute for them, and as a rule they do not seek their biological parentage. It is to be noted that once a child has been declared the legal child of someone other than the real father, all links are broken with the real father. The only exception is with regard to exogamy: a child cannot marry into the lineage of either the biological father or the pater.

Implicit in these practices are deprivations to the parents and children who are separated by the strict application of the legitimacy laws. The law approaches the whole matter from the viewpoint of the lineages of the parents involved and whether they can agree so that biological parentage may coincide with legal parentage. Failing such agreement, a parent and child are torn from each other with little or no regard of the consequences to the individuals involved. Such deprivations and the serious conflicts connected with them are frequent. Cases have already been cited which entailed taking away children from parents who had isolated themselves for years in secret illegal unions in the hope that if they begot children the people and the law would be sympathetic enough to legalize their marriage. Instead of cementing their love with marriage, they are further deprived of their affection as parents of their children. It is in such circumstances that a man says:

> What carries my children away?
> O Bird of the tribe, Awan,
> What takes my children across the land?

With the introduction of legal pluralism and the problems of conflict of laws already indicated, the concept of illegitimacy, though not yet adjudicated, is introduced into Dinka society by modern law. Since there are undoubtedly anomalous marriages the validity of which might be questioned by one in-law or the other, there is little doubt that undiscovered illegitimacy now exists.

Sexual Offenses

The Dinka emphasis on maintaining the male line implies that sexual wrongs are defined as those which interfere with the procreative process.

Such wrongs can therefore be committed only on women even though the moral responsibility of the female partner may be seen as greater than that of her male paramour. The categories of wrongs are adultery, seduction, and abduction.

ADULTERY Adultery is recognized as both a criminal offense and a civil wrong and is abhorred so much that it is believed to result in spiritual contamination likely to cause death to the woman, her children, or a relative unless it is redressed and certain rites are carried out. A woman who has committed adultery feels her guilt in physical pain of a religious significance which cannot be alleviated unless she confesses. Labor or illness in suspicious circumstances is sufficient to move older women into pressuring the woman to clear her conscience and confess any adulterous acts. It is believed that the presence of an adulterer near a sick person may be a fatal contamination. An adulterer runs the risk of serious injury or even death at the husband's hands. In the olden days, the wronged husband's lineage would rise and attack the seducer's lineage and a bloody fight might ensue. Today, criminal sanctions as well as compensation, more effectively enforced by modern administrations, have established a more peaceful solution than the traditional methods.

There is a tendency to take the wife's evidence as almost conclusive. The wife is placed under oath if there is a dispute over the facts. The presumption is that her evidence is correct. Theoretically, should she later be proved guilty of perjury by the curse of false oath manifesting itself in illness or death, and should she confess to having given false evidence, she will be purified ritually and the presumed adulterer may then have his cattle of compensation returned. In practice, however, the court will be reluctant to return the compensation. This is illustrated by *Matet Ayom v. Chol Monybaai*.[113]

In the past, once adultery had been confessed, the lineage of the injured person would go armed into the cattle camp of the paramour or his guardian and select any number of the best cattle to keep, pending arbitration by the chief. There was no imprisonment. Today, both the number of cattle and the prison sentence introduced are uniform within any chief's jurisdiction.[114] *Can de Malith v. Mathiang Ajing*[115] is a standard case. Mathiang committed adultery with Can's wife. Can brought action against Mathiang, and the chief sentenced Mathiang to

113. Cited in Chapter 3, p. 109.
114. Among the Ngok Dinka, in the absence of aggravating circumstances, the adulterer is made to pay three cows compensation and to serve six months' imprisonment.
115. Abyei, Ngok Dinka Court (1947). Cited in Howell, "Ngok Dinka" 290.

pay three head of cattle indemnity and to serve six months' imprisonment.[116]

Alienation of affection is not an actionable wrong, but it may be
evidence of an illicit relationship in an adultery action. Those who induce a wife to have wrongful relations with another man or to desert
her husband are subject to criminal punishment. Abduction and rape
are aggravating circumstances to liability for adultery. In the past, a
fight between the adversary kinfolk was inevitable. Today, severe penal-
ties are inflicted upon the culprit, although civil liability is not affected.
If the wife is abducted, adultery is strongly presumed, but the amount
of compensation is not increased.[117]

Abetting elopement with a married woman is a severe offense which
imposes on the abettor a penal sanction and an obligation to look for
the eloped parties if their whereabouts are unknown and bring them
before the court. This is so even if the abettor is the guardian of one of
the eloping parties and desires the dissolution of the existing marriage.
In *Gok Aguek v. Mabok and Others*,[118] Gok was married to the daughter
of Mabok. After years of married life, Gok's wife deserted her husband
and eloped with another man called Miyan. Several times they were
caught, Miyan was punished, and the woman was returned to her husband. One time when they were caught, Gok accompanied a policeman
sent to summon Miyan. While they were on their way to the court,
Miyan insulted Gok as a son of a leper, and a quarrel ensued. To avoid
a fight, the policeman told Gok to go separately while he walked with
Miyan. Miyan escaped from him, ran to where the woman was, and
eloped again. The policeman arrested the woman's guardian, Mabok,
and his wife on suspicion of abetting the elopement. The court also
summoned the relatives of Miyan on the same suspicion. They were
tried and found to have instigated the series of elopements in the hope
that Gok would divorce the woman and a marriage between her and
Miyan could be contracted. The court decided that they all should be

116. Where there are no aggravating circumstances, the three cows paid are described as *loc, yow,* and *nhian. Loc* literally means "the selected (cow)," and as the
name suggests, it is to be picked by the wronged party from among the herds of
the wrongdoer. It must be a pregnant cow; where there is no pregnant cow, a cow
with a calf is considered pregnant by a legal fiction. This calls to mind the procreative basis of liability. *Yow,* literally "the front (of the woman)," is a big cow. It
must not be pregnant, and if it is pregnant, the calf is returned to the adulterer
when it is born. *Nhian,* literally "testicles," must be a big bull, but should there be
no big bull, a young cow may be substituted. *Yow* and *nhian* are symbols of the
sexual relation by which the husband's procreative interests have been violated.

117. If pregnancy results from adultery, the amount of compensation automatically
increases to six head of cattle. In such a case, *loc, yow,* and *nhian* become two cows
each.

118. Abyei, Ngok Dinka Court (1960).

detained until the couple reported. It was believed that news of their elders' detention would move the eloped couple into returning. The question of the ultimate punishment to be inflicted on the abettors was left open pending the return of the couple.[119]

The Dinka conception of the nature of adultery suggests certain principles. For instance, although the adulterer may not use the husband's impotence as a defense, the wife is likely to adduce it as a justification for her unfaithfulness. Furthermore, we have seen that the attitude of the husband's and the wife's kin is that the wife's procreative power should not be allowed to be dormant. So, if she cannot bear children regularly, she may use this evidence to justify adultery from her point of view.

The fact that sex interests must be directed toward marital goals means that the husband cannot trade on his wife. Consequently, if a married woman's morals are such that she is a "loose woman," her husband cannot recover from an adulterer.

Adultery can be committed though the husband is dead. By the custom of levirate, the widow is not at liberty to cohabit with anyone, relative or not, before the genitor is chosen. Sometimes, more so today, a widow is allowed to choose the lover "to enter with"; however, her choice is usually limited to the relatives of her deceased husband. Once the choice is made, the rest of the husband's kinsmen are excluded. If any of them enter into a sexual relationship with her, it is an offense against the legal heir to the wife as the representative of the dead man. It may be that the deceased husband's legal heir delegates the right of cohabitation to another relative with the consent of the widow. The marital rights of a dead husband survive his death, and if a person commits adultery with the widow he is subject to criminal as well as tort liability. In *Deng v. Gwiny de Col*[120] a widow of Deng's father was living with a relative, Achwil, by agreement with Deng. Gwiny committed adultery with her. Deng, as the heir, and not Achwil, brought an adultery action against Gwiny. The court sentenced Gwiny to five months' imprisonment and ordered him to pay the traditional compensation of three head of cattle. Howell, then colonial officer in that area, states that the rank of the parties in this case must have influenced the outcome because "it is doubtful that in ordinary circumstances 'arwok' (compensation) would be enforced against a woman living in 'widow-concubinage.' "[121] Of course, there is an increasing tendency today to give the widow more freedom to decide her own destiny, but once she

119. The writer, having been unable to follow up the case, does not know the final outcome.

120. Abyei, Ngok Dinka Court (1946). Cited in Howell, "Ngok Dinka 291.

121. Ibid.

chooses to live in levirate, she is expected to be exclusive. For all intents and purposes the levirate widow has the ordinary matrimonial rights and duties of a wife.

What has been said about levirate is also generally applicable to ghost marriages. The woman is usually chosen by the genitor, he courts her as he would his normal bride, and he performs all the aspects of an ordinary marriage. His relationship with her is therefore more intense and personal than that of levirate. This fact is relevant only to the psychology of the vicarious relationship rather than the substance of the law. The levirate legal principles are theoretically applicable to ghost marriage, even though a genitor may overlook the adultery of his brother's widow more readily than that of his "ghost wife."

Although a blood relationship between the adulterer and the husband is legally considered as a mitigating factor in adultery, the gravity of the emotional injury to the husband arising from adultery between his wife and his relative may require special and more substantial redress. This is not contradictory when viewed from two different angles. If adultery is considered as a violation of the procreative rights of the husband, rights shared by the whole kinship, it would follow that adultery by a kinsman has a weaker basis as a tort. The adulterer is only interfering with the husband's portion of their joint interest in his wife. It has been argued, therefore, that the husband should be less indignant as his relationship to the adulterer comes closer. But it is analogous to incest, which is believed to cause serious spiritual impurity; therefore, all the other kinsmen who may be affected by any resulting evil strongly disapprove. In the second place, while the kinsman-adulterer has not interfered with the legitimate reproductive rights of the husband as much as an outside adulterer, there is still disapproval of the adultery because the husband is interested in maintaining the honor of his individual name quite apart from increasing the numbers of the kin group. While the rationale of an infringement of the husband's legal right to reproduction is weakened, the husband's moral indignation may be more intensified because the injured husband takes adultery more as a personal insult. The Ngok Dinka emphasize the aggravating aspect of adultery by a relative. The saying goes: "Except in her bedroom, a wife belongs to the whole kinfolk." The court will give the injured husband one of three choices: a purely legal remedy where the adulterer is ordered to pay the normal compensation (*rwok*); a family settlement where the adulterer is required to pay compensation in the form of a conciliatory payment (*awec*); or a spiritual curse where the adulterer is debased and the husband's compensation is the revenge he attains. The matter is normally settled by an assembly of family elders, but the courts may be asked to mediate. The amount of a conciliatory fee varies from case to case.[122] The wrongdoer will usually prefer reconciliation to a legal settlement in the interest of harmony among kinsmen; the plaintiff would also often prefer mediation because he is likely to receive more compensation. When the wronged husband has suffered extreme emotional injuries so that no amount of indemnity would gratify him, he may choose to inflict a curse upon the adulterer. A curse is much more effective as a deterrent. The need to remove the curse is thought to be so vital that it is usually effected after a passage of time. Sometimes the injured party will bequeath the spiritual power to remove the curse to his heir. When a removal power is requested, a much more substantial payment is made by the adulterer and ceremonial reconciliation is achieved.

Since betrothal is part of marriage, it is protected in the same way as marriage, and sexual intercourse with a third party gives rise to an action of adultery. In *Deng Ajith v. Maguith*,[123] Deng Ajith was betrothed to a girl by payment of some cattle toward her marriage consideration. Before she was betrothed, the girl had been Maguith's girlfriend. Soon after her betrothal the girl confessed to impregnation by Maguith, and Maguith eloped with her outside the tribe. Thereafter, the girl gave birth to two children by Maguith. Believing that Deng Ajith would no longer want her, Maguith returned to the tribe with the girl to regularize their union. Deng Ajith sued him, and the court made Maguith pay compensation for adultery and impregnation of a married woman, including the pregnancy which occurred before betrothal. Maguith appealed on the grounds that he had courted the girl with the intention of marrying her long before she was betrothed to Deng Ajith and that, if liable at all, he should at least not be liable in adultery for acts committed before the girl was betrothed. The court held that it was not sufficient to intend to marry; one must in fact pay at least part of the marriage consideration to manifest intention to marry. On the second issue, the relations between Maguith and the girl before formal betrothal were held not to constitute adultery but merely impregnation of an unmarried girl, for which the compensation was less.

Although flirtatious association with a betrothed girl is a criminal offense, certain circumstances may give rise to a defense. In *Dau v. Kwol Kon*,[124] Dau was betrothed to a girl whom Kwol Kon had wanted to

122. In *Acuil de Bulabek v. Kwol, Fajok, Miyan de Biong, and Deng Yol* (Abyei, Ngok Dinka Court; cited in Howell, "Ngok Dinka" 290) all the defendants were found to have committed adultery with Acuil de Bulabek's wife. Except for Deng Yol, the defendants were close relatives of the plaintiff. The court required each defendant to pay six cows as conciliatory payment, while Deng Yol was required to pay only three cows as the normal legal compensation for adultery.

123. Abyei, Ngok Dinka Appeals Court (1960).

124. Abyei, Ngok Dinka Court (1960).

marry but whose family had refused Kwol Kon. Subsequently, Dau eloped with a different girl whom he had wanted to marry. When they returned, the girl was taken from him, and the court ordered that, in the absence of cattle with which to compensate her relatives, Dau should deduct some cattle from his betrothal consideration. Although the relatives of the betrothed girl were offended, they decided to maintain the relationship if Dau would increase the marriage consideration (a demand which was not fulfilled at the time of the case). Meanwhile, Kwol Kon maintained his association with the betrothed girl. One day, Dau saw them in company and became so provoked that he attacked and injured Kwol Kon. The court, while conceding that Kwol was liable criminally for courting a betrothed girl, held, nevertheless, that Dau's conduct could mislead a person to think that he had intended to repudiate the betrothal agreement. Because of the peculiar circumstances, no criminal sentence was inflicted upon Kwol Kon but he was warned to keep away from the girl.

As with abduction of married women, elopement with betrothed girls calls for penal sanctions and raises a presumption of adultery in tort. Every act of elopement creates a new cause of action, as in *Akot Ral v. Lal Ayom*.[125]

If the betrothal relationship is broken, any compensation paid for adultery is returned to the girl's relatives. If the dissolution is because of the adultery, it does not count as adultery but as seduction of an unmarried woman. Since confession by girls not yet fully married follows pregnancy, such compensation would be for the impregnation of an unmarried woman, and the girl's relatives would be the people entitled to it, but the prison sentence will not be affected. Thus, in *Col Ajing v. Patal Abdullai*,[126] Col was betrothed and had completed the payment of most of the bride wealth, but the final ceremonies were not yet performed. The girl committed adultery with Patal and became pregnant. Col then repudiated the betrothal. The court sentenced Patal to six months' imprisonment and ordered him to pay the girl's relatives three head of cattle. As was said earlier, such compensation is transferred to whoever marries the girl.

Among the legal problems of adultery in modern situations of particular importance is "limping" marriage, a union which because of the absence of bride wealth or the inadequacy of marriage ceremonies is hardly recognized as marriage. A husband in such circumstances may be refused any remedy for an alleged adultery, although this has not yet been adjudicated. However, there is a tendency among the educated class not to sue in respect to adultery. Usually, divorce is resorted

---

125. See p. 149, supra.
126. Abyei, Ngok Dinka Court (1946). Cited in Howell, "Ngok Dinka" 290.

to. Even where they accept indemnification, the matter is usually pursued by the elders who are in charge of their traditional marriages. This trend must not be exaggerated, for while the prevalent attitude is toward not suing, it is a fact that most educated Dinkas are linked with traditional society and still conform.

SEDUCTION   In theory, the Dinka consider seduction of girls to be wrong, and compensation of three cows is demanded. Usually, however, they do not give any legal redress to seduction when it is not followed by pregnancy. In fact, the matter is not even brought to the court's attention. Yet if a complaint is made by the girl's relatives and there is evidence that they have suffered a loss, actual or potential, they should be compensated.

Potential loss to the family is estimated by the probable impairment of the girl's marriage chances if she acquires a reputation for promiscuity. Their own marriages depend at least in part on the value of her marriage in terms of cattle. The matter becomes a vicious circle because if she acquired a promiscuous reputation and her family brought a suit, the court might likely refuse remedy on the general ground of "looseness." Litigation over seduction of girls is therefore avoided unless, as when pregnancy results, the evidence is too strong and the consequences are too grave to be ignored.

Similarly, if a girl is wrongfully raped (as opposed to what we have termed institutionalized rape of married girls resisting consummation), whether it be by force, or by stealth (e.g. in sleep), the matter becomes too serious to be ignored.

It is a much more serious wrong if a man impregnates a girl. As in adultery with married women and betrothed girls, a pregnant girl has to confess the names of those suspected of being responsible for her condition. Failure to tell the truth is believed to result in her death or the death of her future children or any other relatives. The mere mention of the accused's name would in the past entitle the relatives to seize his cattle without resistance. After subsequent settlement, they might return some. Now the rights and wrongs are determined by the court. As with adultery, the woman is trusted so much that whoever is implicated in a confession is almost sure to be held liable. In disputed cases, her oath is sufficient evidence to support liability. This has the effect that several people may be liable for one conception. Thus, in Col Dau's case,[127] Col's sister confessed the names of four men as suspects for her pregnancy.

The association between procreation and the wrongfulness of seduction with unmarried women is seen in that confession is only associated

127. Col Dau v. Four Men, Abyei, Ngok Dinka Court (1953).

with pregnancy unless, as in rape, other factors are introduced. If a girl misses her menstrual period even for a short time, strong pressure is brought to bear on her to confess the man or men. A girl in such a situation sings:

> People rose against me
> Boys, old women, and girls
> They said: "The girl of men has conceived."
> It was because of blood which God had taken away.
> Because of a cow, I have met with bewilderment
> Afflicted with shame as though a monkey
> I have met with the loneliness of a speared animal
> In the camp of Dun de Kok.
> The daughter of my father said to me
> "Please tell me the man"
> Then I answered, "Not at all,
> O sister there is no man."
> I am holding mine with one heart
> And people come and color it with lies
> It has no legs to go wandering
> And meet with the gentleman it likes.

In seduction, unless there are aggravating circumstances, the culprit pays only compensation.[128] This indemnity is so important that if the wrongdoer has no cattle, cows may be withdrawn from his bride wealth or that of a close relative. The Dinka limit liability for pregnancy to grounds which show that the damage to the family is thought to be the impairment of the girl's marriage prospects. The girl's family cannot recover damages if they receive bride wealth for their daughter or give her in marriage with deferred payment before the final settlement in the case of pregnancy is reached. Settlement is determined not only by the court's judgment, but also by a ritual ceremony, *cuet wal*, performed before the court or the court's representative. In *Pandeng v. Manau*,[129] Manau was sued with other men for impregnating a girl. One of the seducers was absent; therefore, the court postponed judgment against those present until he came. In the meantime, the girl's relatives gave her in marriage to another person. The court held that the claim against her seducers was invalidated by the marriage.

The fact that marriage opportunities are the real issue is seen even more clearly in that such limitation does not apply to cases of adultery with married women and betrothed girls. For the same reason no lia-

---

128. The standard number of indemnity cattle is three, termed *loc, yow,* and *nhian* as in adultery.

129. Abyei, Ngok Dinka Court (1957).

bility is imposed if the seducer decides to marry the girl as a settlement. His payment then takes the form of bride wealth and the offspring becomes his legal child. If the girl is subsequently married to another man, the seducer may lose the child to the husband if it has not already been legitimized by payment of the prescribed number of cattle.

The emphasis on the elimination of the chances of marriage as the loss incurred in cases of pregnancy should be viewed from the perspective of the ultimate reproductive purpose of marriage.

In recent years, with the emigration of young men and women to towns in search of work, cases of seduction have increased. The checks of the traditional society are missing; the girls are less aware of the communal demands of their lineage regarding potential bride wealth; and this emigrant community often has little wealth. As cases of seduction and pregnancy multiplied, the chief-in-council passed an order to the effect that any guardian who allowed his female relative to go into the urban community would not be permitted to bring a law suit in respect to seduction occurring during her urban stay. The objective of this order was to discourage migration. It is doubtful whether it was meant to be executed seriously, and despite the fact that it was well publicized, the writer is unaware of any cases in which remedy was refused on the basis of it.

ABDUCTION   A man may entice his fiancée away from her relatives if he is having difficulty in completing the marriage ceremonies, either because his relatives are uncooperative or because her family demands more cattle than he can afford to pay promptly. Abduction or elopement may also occur where the parties are not engaged. The motive is usually to evade various obstacles to their marriage. The idea is to reduce the girl's worth for marriage save to the man who has abducted her; therefore, she would usually be made to assume the costume of a married woman as an indication of the fact that the proposed marriage has already been consummated.

In the past, a fight between the two families often resulted from such provocation. It was, however, more civil for the girl's family to seize all the cattle in the possession of the man's family, and a fight would ensue only if this action met with resistance. The man's relatives were supposed to be submissive and beg for negotiations on the question of marriage. The provocation was much more serious where abduction was effected against the girl's will; a fight in such cases was inevitable.

Today, the battle is fought in court, and the outcome is more likely to be reconciliation. Marriage is usually arranged unless the circumstances make it highly undesirable. In *Ajing Nyok v. Akol Kur* [130] the

130. Abyei, Ngok Dinka Court (1960).

defendant's brother impregnated a girl and subsequently eloped with her before paying compensation to her relatives. It was understood that the defendant had approved of the abduction, and there was reason to believe that he knew where the couple had fled. The court ordered his arrest and detention until he swore to find his brother and the girl and to arrange for their marriage. Such cases do not always end in marriage, for the man may lack the required number of cattle and the girl's family may choose to marry her to a wealthier person. When there is no marriage the man will be made to pay compensation, particularly if he has consummated the relationship, or criminal sanctions may be inflicted instead of damages.

A culprit is better off if he is economically competent to marry. Thus, abduction is not so much a wrong in itself as it is a disruption of the vested interests of the girl's family in her marriage opportunities. The procreative prospects are so dominant in all torts relating to an unmarried girl that her own interests are ruthlessly obstructed unless they are conducive to the family goals.

As in the case of seduction, abduction is also on the increase among the Dinkas who migrate into the urban centers to find work. The restrictive order mentioned under seduction applies to abduction: a guardian who permits his daughter to migrate for labor forfeits his right of action. As was said earlier, this order was calculated to be a deterrent to migration, especially of women, and is probably not strictly applied.

PARTIES ENTITLED TO SUE   In sexual wrongs, Dinka law recognizes only the male interests. Women are not liable for sexual offenses except socially and morally. This implies that a woman cannot sue another woman for adultery with her husband. The nonliability of women is sometimes explained in terms of male aggressiveness and female susceptibility. As an elder put it, "It is men who lead women in these matters." The Dinka word for adultery is "seeking (another man's wife)," *akor*. The Dinka do not, however, deny the fact that a woman can be the aggressive party. A man who had committed adultery with his father's junior wife, Akuc, sings:

> Wek Agoth asked me
> "Who told you to do it?"
> I said, "It is Akuc
> She trapped me with a rope
> And said, 'Son,[131] come
> Let us go to lie on the river side

131. The wife of any relative senior in degree might call a person "son" without regard to their respective ages.

Then we shall think.' "
The thing, we truly did
Then we thought.
I lay on her
We were found entangled.
When I said to her,
"Akuc, let us move away"
She said, "I refuse"
So I must say it was Akuc
She trapped me with a rope.
Is mine the only wrong?
What about that of Akuc
Is it also not a wrong?
That she should tell me
"Son, come
Let us go to lie on the river side
Then we shall think."

Another man, who was accused and convicted of adultery, reveals the enticing role of the woman and his initial reluctance.

I saw a woman accompanied by two men
My ox, Adol of my father, she was accompanied by two
They accompanied her toward the *toc*.
And when I reached them
She was handed over to me
"Please take the woman across the river
Since you are paddling across."
I thought I was taking the mother of a girl
So I paddled my canoe.
Then she began to smile.
I wondered why the woman watched my eyes
And her face filled with smiles . . .
We had said nothing funny
Nothing to make one laugh so much that she lay down.
She exposed herself
She spread her legs
And put her skirt away,
The hornless one remained exposed
The hornless one which cuts through the heart of a man.
But I refused to be tempted
I fastened my heart very tight
I went on paddling my canoe.
Then she dared to hold the horn of the moon

She caught and held my horn—the horn of the buffalo.
Then she said: "Please do not refuse
O son of the clan of Alic
Try, so that I may sleep tonight
And today
I will never say a word.
Try.
I have had no man for three years
No one sleeps with me
Thiep, Crested Crane, son of 'The Snake' [132]
Try."
Then I said: "Are we crocodiles to sleep in the river?"
I said: "Are we fish to sleep in the river?
Have we become fish and frogs?"
I went on paddling my canoe
Until I crossed the river, Lol.
I am the man who paddles the canoe
And cover myself with sweat.

The myth of female susceptibility to male aggressiveness is correlated with the position of males as the primary beneficiaries in procreation, so that any sex violation is a damage to males by other males. Adultery, seduction, and abduction are all regarded as wrongs against the husband, father, or guardian respectively. These roles may of course coincide in one person—the head of the family. But, since the head of the family is the custodian or the principal manager of the family property, whatever benefits him derivatively benefits his family. Again, his position may be affected by broader family connections such as the reciprocal interests of the extended family or the kinship.

In the case of adultery, the husband is normally the person entitled to sue. In a polygynous family, if the adultery involves a young wife and the husband has a son, the son may bring the action in his father's name.[133] The brother of the husband may recover for adultery in the name of the husband and may take the compensation for himself. In such a case the husband has no further claim. In cases of adultery with betrothed girls, the plaintiff may be the guardian of the injured boy

132. Metaphoric names of praise.
133. It is considered most undesirable for a person to sue in respect of his own mother's adultery. The writer is not aware of such cases ever occurring. In any case, one hardly even hears of adultery with the mothers of adults. This is mainly because mothers are careful to avoid embarrassment to their children, and therefore do not commit adultery. But it might also be because the matter is dropped, inasmuch as the mother would have already fulfilled the purpose of her marriage (i.e. childbirth).

responsible for the marriage. Compensation may then go to the bride-groom or it may be used by the guardian. In rare cases, a senior widow may sue for the adultery of a junior cowidow or the wife of her son. Such women will have assumed a status of responsibility quite comparable to that of a family head. In cases of wrongs with respect to unmarried women, the guardian of the girl is the person rightly entitled to bring the action. The guardian may be the father or any relative who is allotted the paternal obligations and rights in respect to her marriage.

Whoever pleads the case does not necessarily take the proceeds to the exclusion of the other members of the family. As there is only one right of action, the family head is the primary beneficiary, but the family may decide how to distribute the indemnity. Any disagreement is usually arbitrated in front of the family or kinship elders, or even in front of the chiefs. Serious conflicts may be officially adjudicated.

The association of indemnity with procreation is further illustrated by the fact that the husband, father, or guardian is supposed to dispose of the cattle in marriage or as a gift to a relative. At least, he himself must not drink their milk, eat their butter, meat, or any food produced by them even indirectly, as when a cow is sold and the money used to buy grain.

In the light of Dinka emphasis on procreation as the basis of liability in sex offenses, we may speculate that the plaintiff views the wrongful act primarily as a violation of his procreative rights in a woman which demands material indemnification, rather than as an alienation of her affections which is too emotionally injurious to be soothed by compensation. This is particularly so if his wife has already fulfilled the role of procreation. We have seen that mutual "love" in the Western sense is not a prerequisite to Dinka marriage. Consequently, the fact that a wife has been unfaithful does not necessarily imply the insult that her husband has failed to maintain her affections. His marriage success is proved by the mere fact of having children. If he is betrayed during betrothal, he could not yet have been a failure. This notion is supported by the fact that where a man is impotent or sterile and cannot produce children, he will normally avoid litigation so as not to advertise his failure in marriage. Even if he insists on suing, he might be denied remedy. The same may be said of seduction and other sexual torts relating to unmarried women. Such torts are regarded as resulting in the reduction of the girl's marriage value in terms of the amount of bride wealth obtainable. With this economic possibility is linked the chances of maintaining the male line.

One may explain the tendency of the educated class not to sue for sex offenses in terms of its increasing emphasis on mutual affection in matrimony. The moral indignation of an educated husband is enhanced by the fact that he regards himself as unsuccessful in retaining the affections of his wife. Thus deeply hurt, he is not likely to advertise this failure.

Vicarious Liability

Among the Dinka, the ultimate ownership of family property is vested in the head of the family. He is responsible for indemnifying for torts committed by any member of his family. Although his wife and children are protected against extremely unreasonable conduct leading to their deprivation, and although he would normally consult them, the powers of the head of the family in respect to property are almost unqualified.

The head of a family is considered the guardian of his unmarried brothers if their father is dead. Similarly, a man may assume guardianship of his dead brother's unmarried children and will be considered responsible for their torts.

The emphasis on the family as an agency for procreation has the effect that capacity is determined by marriage. Once a man is married, the status of matrimony bestows upon him full capacity with rights and obligations. Male children, as long as they are unmarried and attached to the parents' home, are regarded as infants. The parents are supposed to control and protect them, and a child's bad behavior is attributable to the parents. The cause of action itself may be against the child; but once the child is held liable, the father is ordered to pay for the damage and may be compelled to do so. Cases where the father refuses to pay seldom arise. Where a child has become particularly notorious or has hopelessly and deliberately failed to observe his duties to his father, the relationship may be severed provided the child is old enough to be emancipated or another relative is willing to assume his protection. The severance is done by ritually breaking grasses in front of the chief. After severance the father will be asked to give the son his due share of property, and for all legal purposes they cease to be father and son. Such extreme measures are detested and will rarely be allowed.

The relations between a married son and his parents are by no means entirely severed. If the parents are old and with insufficient means, he must support them and assume responsibility where they cannot discharge it. The child also inherits his dead parents' liability, as was the case in *Chol v. Ring Aguer*.[134]

The situation is different for girls. Women remain in a position of dependence forever. An unmarried woman, just as her male counterpart, lives under the control and protection of her own kin group until marriage. Marriage conveys her control and protection to her husband

134. Abyei, Ngok Dinka Court (1960). See p. 110, supra.

and his kin, and it is he and they who benefit from rights and incur liabilities connected with her.

The scope of the family varies with the nature of the liability. Only the head of the immediate family would be responsible for minor torts of the members, but cases of homicide would require the contribution of the entire kinfolk.

Intrafamily Liability

The solidarities in the Dinka family preclude any tort liability between family members. Children are considered a projection of their father's personality and the wife is a means to that end. All unite to form one legal entity in the person of the father. Generally, therefore, the spouses cannot sue each other, nor children their parents, nor brothers and sisters one another. This is not to say that disputes do not arise within the family, but whatever conflicts arise are normally settled as family matters even by courts.

There may be matrimonial complaints between spouses. Where such complaints concern minor injustices, they are usually referred to elderly kinfolk who act as mediators. In more serious cases, however, a wife's own family will come to her assistance. Thus, in matrimonial causes like divorce on grounds of impotence, cruelty, or neglect, her kin would join to assist her in the action against her husband. Indeed, the case is normally between the respective kin groups rather than the spouses, although a wife may sue alone. In short, it is unlikely that Dinka courts would entertain ordinary suits brought by one spouse against another.

Domestic disputes between parents and children often take the form of a male child seeking to establish his rights. Daughters, being destined to be severed sooner or later, are usually less militant. It is considered admirably courageous for a son to face his father about his rights as he sees them, and the senior relatives of the family will always be quick to appreciate the son's claim and support him. If the family elders fail to settle the dispute and it proceeds to court, they will aid the son if they find him in the right, and the father is likely to be defeated. Should the son be found in the wrong by the council of elders or by the court, he will be reprimanded severely and made to submit to his father's authority.

Disputes between children are very unlikely during their father's lifetime, since any claims they may have are directed against and to the father as the manager of family affairs. In a polygynous family, however, there are often potential conflicts which materialize upon the father's death. Here again, senior kin members are consulted and their advice is usually persuasive. If reconciliation cannot be effected, the case is taken to court for further mediation. It is important to keep in mind that intrafamily disputes over reciprocal family rights and obligations are connected with aid in marriage payment and maintenance; they are not in the nature of tort actions. These familial causes are usually settled by arbitration, but the court may legally enforce a settlement.

5. Respect

Respect, *atheek,* is crucial for the maintenance of a good name, and a good name is an important factor in the principle of permanent identity and influence. Consequently, the Dinka lay a great deal of stress on respect for oneself and for others. In the first is rooted their striking pride, and in the second may be found notions of stratification in their hierarchy of respect.

The subjective elements of honor and pride, as well as their outward appearance and bearing, are grounded in a concept called *dheeng,* which has many meanings. As a noun, *dheeng* means such things as dignity, beauty, nobility, handsomeness, elegance, charm, grace, gentleness, richness, hospitality, generosity, and kindness. Except in prayer or on certain religious occasions, the Dinka refer to singing as *dheeng.* The way a man walks, runs, talks, eats, or dresses affects his *dheeng.* The adjective form of the nouns associated with *dheeng* is provided by the word *adheng,* which may also be used as a noun and is often used to mean "gentleman."

The high-ranking positions of pride and honor in the Dinka value system have been stressed by observers. After an intimate association with various African peoples, Major Court Treatt wrote that "The Dinka . . . is a gentleman. He possesses a high sense of honour, rarely telling a lie" and "a rare dignity of bearing and outlook." [1] Linked with this is a striking sensitivity to insult or anything touching on one's sense of honor, dignity, or pride. Club and spear fights, sometimes to the death, may be provoked by incidents not always significant. Major Treatt characterizes the Dinka as "highly temperamental, alternating almost hysterical joy with . . . depression and gentleness with violent temper." [2] But the Dinka reinforces his high sense of honor "with a golden gift of humour; indeed, he often works these virtues in double harness." [3] Many a time, one sees men and women, young or old, ex-

1. Treatt, Out of the Beaten Track 115 (1931).
2. Id. at 116.
3. Id. at 115.

changing insults, talking, or singing to the amusement of their hilar-
ious audience, with the one provoking the most laughter as the win-
ner.

The Dinka sense of pride, which makes them see themselves as the
standard of what is dignified and honorable and therefore the best, may
be illustrated by the fact that to emphasize the value of a human being,
a Dinka will speak with pride of *raan macar* or *raan col,* "black man."
It is not uncommon to hear a protest against an outrageous treatment
expressed in the words "How can a black man be treated like this?" and
needless to say, they do not think of all the black people, but of themselves. It is also significant that the Dinka call themselves *Jaang,* "the
people," or *Monyjang,* literally "the husband of the people" or "the
man of the people." Non-Dinkas are referred to as "the others," or *juur,*
"foreigners." By these terms, the Dinka do not claim to have power over
others, but as many other proud people, they take themselves as the
standard of what is "normally human" and, therefore, superior.

Respect for others is more directly expressed by the Dinka word
atheek, which has strands of meaning appearing somewhat unrelated but
stemming from the same root. One strand might be called "good manners," [4] which emphasizes self-control and nonaggression. This sense is
closest to the English word "respect." The second range of meaning
might be summed up as "avoidance." Avoidance between relatives-in-law
and between senior son and father are instances. In this sense, *atheek*
may apply to situations where the English word "respect" does not. The
Dinka conceive of respect in this sense as embodying both voluntary
deference and that which is required by the relationship between the
parties. It is significant, for instance, that *ryoc,* a verb which means "to
fear," is also used to denote "respect." It is difficult to distinguish voluntary respect from mandatory respect, but in certain cases, especially
those of avoidance, the evidence is clear. For instance, "respecting" a
menstruating woman is directly connected with fear of spiritual contamination. The same is true of "respecting" clan divinities and em-

---

4. To illustrate: "An ill-mannered or aggressive child, without decorum in the presence of those senior to him in age and status, is said to have no respect. A man
who behaves with respect is courteous to his elders and superiors. He will join an
assembly of senior men or strangers in a markedly quiet and self-effacing way, gently
snapping his fingers to indicate when he wishes to pass, and taking care not to
jostle anyone as he takes his place. When approaching a homestead such a man will
pause before entering its central court-yard and clap his hands to announce his
presence and ask permission to enter. Teasing, joking, and horseplay, which are not
inappropriate between those who regard themselves as familiar equals and perhaps
in some sense rivals, are improper between those who practise *thek* (or *atheek*)." Lienhardt, *Divinity* 125.

blems. Killing them or being in a situation where there are any acts of violence against them is very dangerous.[5]

Seeing respect as both voluntary and mandatory is important because it explains the stratified shaping and sharing of respect and its divine and secular sanctions.[6] It is the right of those whose life is being perpetuated through the younger generations to be shown respect, for only thus can their participation be adequately immortalized. The giving of respect is a condition for receiving it. If a man shows no respect to people who owe him greater respect, he would be shown only mandatory respect and, in extreme cases, none.

The clan divinity is respected as the source of life of the clan. Respect for him as well as other mythicals is shown in prayers, sacrifices, dedication of beasts, and the like. Representative of the mythical is the patriarch, the highest figure in the family respect process.

Because respect is approached through lineal continuity, a man is often referred to by his senior child's name (e.g. as "father of Deng"). The wife, especially if she is not in her later years, must address the husband this way.[7] While offering food to her husband, a wife kneels. In most cases, a junior wife avoids being seen eating by her husband. While talking with him, she avoids looking into his face. Should he insult her, her best resort is to cry and not to retaliate.[8]

As is true of affection, children must show great reverence to their father. They must never refer to him by his name. They must not insult or argue with him. They must obey him. If he clearly wrongs them, they may complain to him or, in serious cases, to elders or even chiefs. Most young men's songs are exaltations of their fathers.

The position of sons and daughters in relation to their father exalts sons as the patriarchs of future families which will perpetuate the agnatic line. For instance, with personality oxen allotted to them earlier through distribution of color patterns but formally accruing to them

---

5. "To be touched by the blood of the emblem of one's clan-divinity is one of the greatest misfortunes that can happen. I have known a man of a clan respecting Crocodile refuse to travel along a path where part of a dead crocodile had been carried some time previously, and to kill a man's emblem in a river prevents him from entering the water until he assumes that every trace of its blood has been carried away. It is supposed that the blood of the emblem of a clan-divinity causes, in the clansman who comes in contact with it, a skin-disease akin to leprosy called *akeeth*, and perhaps lameness and blindness." Id. at 128.

6. The basis of this stratification is the perpetuation myth.

7. While she also has this privilege vis-à-vis society at large, her husband does not normally address her in a corresponding way, though he might say, *"man mith,"* "mother of the children."

8. The same applies if he should beat her.

on initiation, sons acquire the symbolic capacity to hold property, a privilege daughters do not have. On marriage a son becomes sui juris, while a daughter merely transfers dependence to her husband's lineage. Should the marriage fail, she reverts to her original dependence. The respect position among children of the same sex is dependent on the marriage order of the mother in polygynous families, since a mother's seniority determines her children's status.

A son's position is enhanced by his courage, aggressiveness, and use of violence as means of ensuring the protection of family values.[9] As children grow up being unruly and aggressive, they transgress the bounds of legitimate courage and may even show disrespect to their offended and yet admiring seniors.

The mother-child relationship is different from the father-child relationship. Children, especially sons, are expected to call the mother by her name rather than "Mother." It is not unusual for children to insult their mothers, but it is unthinkable for a child to insult its father. It is considered virtuous for children, especially sons, to disobey their mothers. They should command their mothers and be obeyed. It is not usual for a child to praise a mother, even by song, but a father is frequently praised by all means. The disrespect children show to the mother is almost formalized as a method to minimize the influence of women. When a son demonstrates such disrespect, he may know, and it may be known, that he in fact respects her. It does not seem to matter to the Dinka that the reality is quite different from the appearance. To them the symbols are significant insurance against the harmful influence of women. Since the unity of the clan is more important among its permanent members, disrespect for the mother is more marked among sons than among daughters. The more senior the wife and the child, the more they are shown respect. Nonetheless, wives and children form groups in which competitiveness impedes respect. Jealousies between co-wives are reflected through their children, especially daughters. Insults and fights which are characteristic of Dinka children show the same point. In contrast, the elders are expected to, and in fact do, show a high measure of self-respect and respect for other elders.

The agnatic kin of wives and mothers occupy a special respect position. This is because of their primacy in the lives of women and the arrangement of their marriages. The respect which a bridegroom is expected to show toward the bride's family, and which is most formal in the avoidance practiced with his mother-in-law, is extended in the next

9. Most of the fighting which is engineered by senior men (though usually not by elders) consists of falsely informing a son that his father has been insulted by another boy. The other boy will back this false information in order to demonstrate his own courage. In nearly all cases, a fight is inevitable.

generation to the respect between a man and his maternal uncle. The maternal uncle is considered the guardian of his sister and the one to whom a child is expected to show gratitude for his mother. Moreover, the Dinka frequently remark that the maternal uncle marries with his nephew's father's cattle. "Hence, in the Dinka way of thinking, when two families have a marriage between them, each has provided the means for the continuation of the other," [10] and therefore deserves respect. A man should be particularly grateful to his wife's mother for educating her daughter as a wife. The wife's mother is thus a primary source of the continuation of the husband's lineage.

The emergence of new criteria for respect is disturbing the traditional equilibrium. Young men and women with modern skills and enlightenment not only view themselves as deserving greater respect but, by and large, receive it. Yet, the traditional concepts of age stratification remain intact. The result is competitiveness in which the patriarch is still preeminent. The moderns are acquiring recognition which is so limited in view of the magnitude of their demands that it creates greater demands. The result is a respect conflict between the traditional elites and their modern dependents.

On the tribal level, individual members may acquire special reputations because of their wealth, skills, rectitude, or any other value, but on the whole one's standing is dependent on one's agnatic or cognatic descent. The formal in-law avoidance finds its extension into all the categories of people who could be one's potential relatives-in-law.

Respect is one of the foundations of the age-set system. Uninitiated men are *dhak*, "boys," while initiated men are *adheeng*, "gentlemen." It is the uninitiated men who must do the day-to-day work of cattle husbandry, and only in exceptional circumstances, such as an area where ferocious animals might be, are initiated men expected to herd.[11] An uninitiated man may be sent at any time by an initiated man even though the latter may be younger. The life of an uninitiated man in relation to initiated men is one of servitude. Hence, initiation is one of the greatest ambitions of Dinka youth, and is the most festive and ceremonial occasion in the life of a Dinka. While children stratify their own age sets through mock fighting and initiation, formal initiation takes place at about the ages of sixteen to eighteen. Since physical courage is the qualification for adulthood, initiation is a brutal and bloody custom. Because of this, it is conceived of as a war of emancipation. These lines from initiation songs illustrate its goriness and its martial symbolism.

10. Lienhardt, *Divinity* 129.

11. Uninitiated men must milk cows for adults. Should it be necessary for adults to milk, they milk for one another. No male adult can drink milk that he himself has drawn.

My *dheeng* [12] shocked the Arab to hold his head
My *dheeng* shocked the Arab to bite his lip
My *dheeng* shocked the Arab to close his eyes
"O, the thing is death," he said.
No, it is our ancient deed. . . .
Myandeeng de Koor, chase the dogs away
And fill in the holes [13]
The dogs are lapping the blood.
In my war with the Pelican, there is death.
Chief Dorjok, bless the hand of Ayom's father.

The knife turned red like tanned leather,
We lie for pain in the home of the Crested Crane.
Initiation is the thing which redeems a man from slavery:
I will not run
I would rather die on the flank.

When the morning star appears, I will not run,
I will kneel and sing a song of war
Gray of the Dancing Head, [14] I scorn its pain.
Son of Col, Potrial Ajak,
If I run from the knife, slaughter me.
Grandfather, son of the clan of Kon d'Ayong
Grandfather of Deng, "The Swimmer Over the Reeds" [15]
O son of the clan of Kon d'Ayong
My head will be scourged in the morning.
Man, endure the pain
Your father is dancing with joy,
The whole of Abyor is dancing with joy.
The wife of my father is dancing,
She approaches us burning houses. [16]
Agany, Bol, on the right flank
I defeat the people,
I will not fear.
Marial de Col talks to me pointing into my eyes [17]

12. *Dheeng* here means both the initiation rites and the happiness of the occasion.
13. For each initiate a hole is dug to collect the blood pouring from his head as he is initiated.
14. Gray is the ox color-pattern of the man praised and the Dancing Head is the Crested Crane, the ox color-pattern of the father of the initiate.
15. The Pelican. The ox of the singer shows the same color-pattern.
16. A customary distinction in expression of joy for which compensation is expected to be made.
17. He shakes his finger in admonition.

I hate being a boy.
I will not remain a boy this year.
Father, Marial, O Father Marial
The Knife sharpened by the son of Rialjok,
Will cut my veins for the sake of pride.

Initiation may cause death, though rarely. As evident in the songs, to have endured the pain of initiation is to give joy to relatives and friends. A great deal of damage is done in the name of this joy. Houses of others may be burned, though with the intention of compensating them. Other people's livestock may be killed. All this excitement gives the impression that fear is expected on the side of those to be initiated. It is said that in the past the relatives of the initiate-to-be would stand armed to see to it that they killed their man if he shamed them with fear. However, there seems to have been no case of killing nor of such fear.

The mere fact of initiation, though it causes a radical change in the respect position of the initiate, does not resolve intergenerational competitiveness: it intensifies the conflict—hence, the insult songs by the age set immediately following the youngest warrior age set.[18] Such songs are partly responsible for the institutionalized fights between successive age sets. The implications of such aggravated violence are much graver than the fact that violence leads to interage-group conflicts. The age sets of subtribes find it a symbol of respect to demonstrate courage by pro-

18. According to custom, after initiation an age set is temporarily prohibited from drinking beer, the only alcoholic beverage of traditional Dinka society. Several years later, it is permitted to drink and this is done with great festivity. This song by Aliab age set tells how Cuor, the age set immediately following it, drank so much that Pieng, an important member of the age set, became drunk. The facts are undoubtedly exaggerated to debase Pieng and consequently his age set.

The women of that Noong [see gloss] came running to the pool,
And the women of the other Noong came heading for the pool,
Pieng has fallen;
Pajok, cover him, I see shame coming.
My first time to see a man pay for beer,
Nyannyok, you have cursed the people [see gloss].
What I saw will not remain unknown,
What Aliab saw will not remain unknown;
He sat with a bulging stomach as though pregnant with beer;
Pieng sat on the meat of maternal aunt [see gloss]
And women closed their eyes.

Gloss: (1) Noong was the traditional home of both Deng Majok and Deng Makuei before the latter left it. Their homes were divided by a pool. (2) The child Nyannyok, is said to have been maltreated by members of the age set. The curse of drunkenness is attributed to her. (3) In ritual distribution of sacrificial animals, the hip is given to maternal uncles and aunts.

voking wars. Such provocation may take the form of songs defamatory of each other or of each other's elders. In this way, respect deprivation enhances the belligerent characteristic of Dinka society.

In somewhat the same category as the warrior age groups is the educated class. This is none other than a collectivization of the educated members of families. They now receive more respect from both the traditionals and the Northerners than their traditional counterparts do, but this indulgence merely prompts demands which are extended into modern national situations where the inferiority of their respect position vis-à-vis the Northerners is easily seen in the Northern use of the term "slaves" to mean Southerners.

In the words of two Southern political leaders, "Segregation marks the relationship between Northern and Southern Sudanese. The reason for this segregation seems to arise from the fact that the Northerner considers himself as belonging to a privileged class while the Southerner occupies the lower stratum of Sudanese society." [19] That this attitude is an important factor in the South-North animosities is obvious from the report of the commission of enquiry into the 1955 revolt.[20] The reaction of the Southerner against second-class citizenship has intensified since 1955. Well-meaning Northerners are candid about their responsibility to improve the status of the Southern Sudanese. One, for instance, writes, "We Northerners have committed some serious mistakes in the South. Our forefathers were slave raiders and the South was their hunting ground. . . . We are determined to make good their mistakes in terms of material assistance and progress of our Southern countrymen. . . . The recent record speaks for itself." [21]

To many Southern Sudanese, there has been "no change of heart." [22] Among other things, they see disrespect in the Northern attempt to mold the South in the Northern cultural image. In the words of Southern leaders, "Since 1955 [the Northern attitude] has merely become more general, more arrogant and hateful as the Northerner increases his grip on the South." [23] It has been said that "the present social relations between the Arab North and the South spell out a return to the old days of the slave trade." [24] While the two eras cannot be considered identical, the reality of a race war in which the Southerners are weaker, if only for the inferiority of their weapons, brings to mind many similarities.

19. Deng and Oduho, *The Problem of the Southern Sudan* 53 (1962).
20. Sudan Government, *Southern Sudan Disturbances* 123–25 (1956).
21. Said, *The Sudan* 151 (1965).
22. *The Vigilant,* June 27, 1965, p. 1 ff.
23. Deng and Oduho, op. cit. supra note 19, at 55.
24. Id. at 54.

RESPECT AND THE LAW

Defamation in General

Although respect has a pervasive significance to law, we select defamation to illustrate some of the major aspects of the legal expression of the respect process. The goals of unity and harmony can only be approximated in an atmosphere of mutual respect. Moreover, permanent identity and influence is directly linked with the maintenance and the perpetuation of a good name. Respect for a man's name is part of his immortality. Members of society owe each other the duty not to "spoil" another man's name, and calumny is a serious matter. Because of the family orientation of the society, anything which degrades a man threatens to reflect on his family, and the gravity of the offense is largely determined by the descent and the generational factors involved, with the result that defamation is graver the higher the stratification of descent and age. In relation to women, its seriousness is greatest in situations of in-law relations. Among the warrior youth, personal imputations are hardly recognized as defamatory, but what is basically personal may still bring shame on a descent group, as when a man is accused of theft or indecent practices. Most insulting to the name of descent groups are those statements which directly touch on ancestors.

In former times, defamatory utterances led to breach of the peace—especially by the youth of the descent groups involved. Today, they are normally brought to court where civil or criminal measures, or both, may be taken against the wrongdoer, but the youth still resort to violence. Defamation is one of those things the Dinka do not ignore; however trifling the matter, the court will take corrective measures. The name of the complainant does not have to be actually spoiled; as long as it could be spoiled by what is said, an action will lie. Thus, it is not essential that people believe the imputation or alter their attitude toward the defamed.[25]

Generally, the defendant's intention is immaterial, but in certain circumstances relief may be refused on the ground that, considering the status and the relationship of the parties, no defamation exists. It is, for instance, customary that members of an age set, especially young men, jokingly insult one another. There is often a competition in such insults, and one tries to be creative and amusing in ridiculing the adversary; the audience, by laughter or the like, acts as umpire. Where it has been habitual to insult playfully and nothing unusual happens to change this

25. This is in contrast with Anglo-American law, where incurring damages is generally a condition to entertaining an action.

understanding, the court will dismiss the action. This is presumably because no breach of the peace is expected, nor is the name "spoilable" while a game of creativity, distortion, and hyperbole is being played. Should the particular occasion be unsuitable, such as among strangers, or people with whom the plaintiff, to the knowledge of the defendant, has a special respect relationship (e.g. relatives-in-law), or if the insults are made in such a way that they are likely to be taken seriously by the listeners, the defendant will be held liable.

Modes of Defamation

The mode of defamation is significant in assessing its magnitude. Depending on the circumstances in which the defamatory statements were uttered, the Dinka speak of direct imputations, imputations by way of "gossip," and imputations through songs.

Direct imputations are those addressed to the person defamed, though they should be heard by third parties. This form of defamation is considered grave because it is likely to cause breach of the peace. It is immaterial that the imputation is not about the person addressed, as long as it is about a person so related to him as to justify his indignation. Nor is the plaintiff necessarily the person addressed. A relative who is defamed by such a statement may bring an action, but there is only one cause of action. The statement does not have to be specific, as long as it brings or is feared to bring shame or embarrassment to the person addressed or to those about whom it is made. Such statements as "If I insult you, you will cry," [26] have been held defamatory. Direct defamation is so serious that, even where the wrong is trifling, the court will at least award nominal damages, inflict a nominal penalty, or reprimand the defendant and warn him against such conduct.

Defamation may arise out of repeating a defamatory statement to someone other than the person to whom it was addressed, or to the defamed person himself, or it may be an original statement to a person other than the one defamed. These may be somewhat arbitrarily called "gossip." For repetition to give rise to a cause of action, it must be *mala fides* and unprivileged. When a person hears a defamatory statement, he should not repeat it except in court as a witness or to a person to whom he owes a duty. For instance, in marriage, a father refusing his consent because of things he has heard about the girl's family may repeat that information to his son. A person may report to the chief anything which is a threat to security and order. Where a person, provoked by a statement about another, repeats it to someone else in condemnation of the

26. *Juac v. Mior Col,* Abyei, Ngok Dinka Court (1960).

person who originally made the statement, or in support of the person defamed, he is considered acting in good faith. He might, however, be told that the situation is better served by silence. It is no defense that the statement has been accurately repeated, but, if the statement is distorted, the offense is aggravated.

Generally, repetitions to persons other than the defamed are not likely to cause a breach of the peace. However, word may eventually reach the defamed person and a breach of the peace may result. Thus, a repeater both defames a person and instigates breach of the peace. Where the repetition is made to the defamed person, the defendant is deemed directly responsible for any breach of the peace that may ensue. A particularly detested person is one who gossips with both sides. He might be encouraging the defendant to confide in him in order to inform the plaintiff. Apart from being tortiously and criminally liable, he would be hated, shunned, or ridiculed. An original statement constitutes a less serious defamation than repetition. While a person who repeats what he hears is also to blame, first utterance is single defamation.

Defamation through songs is aggravated by the fact that it is addressed to the society as a whole. Defamatory songs may be women's songs, ox songs, age-set insult songs, war songs, or other types of songs. In *Macok and Maguith Malual v. Matiok Nyok*,[27] Macok's brother, Maguith, wanted to marry a girl in whom Matiok was also interested. Maguith's relatives betrothed the girl to him. Matiok, who was wealthier than the brothers, decided to compete in marriage and paid more cattle to the girl's relatives than they had given. Provoked by Matiok's attitude, Macok and Maguith composed songs imputing tuberculosis to Matiok's family. Matiok retaliated by composing songs imputing "evil eye" to Macok and Maguith's family. The two brothers then brought a case in defamation against Matiok, who pleaded provocation by defamation. The court held them all guilty of defamation and fined them. No one was compensated.

Defamation through songs acquires its widest dimension in age-set insult songs and war songs, which often provoke the violence between age sets and territorial units.

Objects of Defamation

By object we mean the person against whom the defamatory statement is made. He may be the plaintiff himself or his relative. Groups may be involved through individuals or directly in different degrees according to the nature of the imputation and the status of the person against

27. Abyei, Ngok Dinka Court (1959).

whom it is made. Whether the imputation is against the plaintiff personally, his relative, or his group, age and descent are important factors in determining the gravity of the offense.

Although personal imputations against the plaintiff may lead to a breach of the peace, the fact that they do not touch on descent makes them less serious than imputations against relatives or families which implicate the plaintiff as a member of the group. Thus, if a young man is insulted as a thief or accused of indecent conduct, the defamation is basically against him individually. In *Wol Miyan v. Mareng*,[28] Mareng was enamored of Wol's girlfriend but she did not return his love. Hostility developed between the two men and Mareng accused Wol of seducing the girl in the forest. In the trial that followed, Mareng admitted his statement to be false. He was held liable for defaming both the plaintiff and the girl, and was sentenced to three months' imprisonment.

Imputations which are essentially connected with descent are usually of diseases believed to be inherited, such as leprosy and tuberculosis. Witchcraft and evil eye are also linked with descent.[29] Imputations of this nature may be alleged against the plaintiff himself, his relative, or the descent group. In the case of a senior member, not only is the family defamed, but, in addition, the rule against abusing anyone who is a senior in age or rank is violated. The offense is even more serious where the senior man is a chief or of chiefly descent. The person defamed need not be a living member of the family. The logic of maintaining the name of a dead man means that he can be defamed in death. Furthermore, permanent identity and influence means that his defamation implicates his living relatives, and the more senior he is, the graver the offense.

The interdependence of the individual, his relatives, and the family as a whole and the underlying principles of lineal continuity are illustrated by *Juac v. Mior Col*.[30] Juac gave Mior a goat in satisfaction of a debt. Subsequently, Mior married a girl related to Juac. According to custom, if a man owns property which once belonged to his fiancée's relative, that relative may reclaim the property as part of marriage consideration, even though he might not have shared in the distribution of the bride wealth in normal circumstances. Juac reclaimed the goat. Mior insulted Juac by saying that, as he was not marrying Juac's mother, but only a distant relative, he was not willing to return it. Juac was provoked and answered that it was the same reckless talk which had made Mior's father a very repulsive and lonely man all his life. Mior retaliated, "If I insult you, you will cry." Juac asked what that insult

28. Abyei, Ngok Dinka Court (1958).
29. *Macok and Maguith Malual v. Matiok Nyok*, supra p. 119, is a case in point.
30. Supra note 26.

could be. Mior said Juac would be better off not hearing it. Juac answered, "You cannot compare yourself with me; none of our lineage has
ever had an evil eye." Mior said that he could not see how Juac could
be better than he when his father had died of starvation. Juac then
brought action on defamation. The members of the court, who had
known the fathers of both parties, expressed indignation at their assertions. Both were sentenced to eight months' imprisonment, commuted
on appeal to a fine.

Defamation touching on descent groups, whether directly or through
individual members, is a much more serious offense than personal defamation because it affects a wider range of people. If a grandfather is
said to have leprosy or tuberculosis, for instance, his grandchildren are
affected. This partially explains why it is more serious to defame an
elderly man or woman. There are many imputations against groups
which are not taken seriously and rarely give rise to litigation. A man
may sing against maltreatment by the police, tax collectors, clan heads,
or court members with impunity, depending on the generality of the
defamation and the degree of group spirit it is likely to arouse. If the
subtribal chiefs are insulted as a group, partly because of their small
number, but mainly because of the sensitivity of the society to their integrity, the chances are that the wrongdoer will be convicted.

Because of the violent disposition of warrior age sets, group defamation is serious among them. Within the subtribe we have seen that a
senior warrior set composes songs defamatory of a junior age set either
about individual members or about the group. This is one of the usual
causes of interage-set fights within the subtribe, but it is so institutionalized that it is hardly ever litigated. Age-set sensitivity to defamation becomes acute in subtribal situations. Subtribal identity rotates around
unity behind the territorial chiefs and the age-set system. Competition
is most dramatic between the corresponding age sets of the different subtribes. Defamatory war songs are often a cause of subtribal wars. There
have been recent administrative attempts to discourage such songs.
When a song is obviously defamatory of another subtribe, it is forbidden in war dances. This has induced an attempt to disguise the insults.
A typical example is where the age set of one subtribe hunts and kills
a wild animal, after which the adversary age set is named. The adversary
then composes insulting songs about the animal, exaggerating incidents
that had occurred in a prior war with the enemy subtribe. As representative of a territorial group, an age set is provoked by songs defamatory
not only of them as individual members or as a group, but of a chief
or elder.[31]

31. In May 1960, the age sets of Acueng subtribe composed songs defamatory of
Abyor's warrior groups, elders, and chiefs. Before the songs were used at an open

Age-set defamation does not always take place through songs, nor is it necessarily by groups. A statement or any conduct may constitute a group insult, and as long as the individual responsible for it is seen as a member of a group, indignation may be aroused against his group. This incident will illustrate the point. Among the Dinka, it is customary that young men confront a girl or girls they meet and compel each girl to choose which man attracts her the most. The custom is practiced on social occasions which bring girls and boys together, but it is extended to strangers. In this case, a young man of one subtribe was traveling with his sister across the territory of another subtribe. They were approached by a few young men of that subtribe, and both his sister and himself were asked to choose from among the men. Asking him to choose meant that he, his age set, and his subtribe were insulted as "women" in relation to the other subtribe—cowards, in other words. When he refused, he was badly beaten and then let go. Hearing of the incident, his age set waged an attack which was stopped by the authorities in time to avoid a war. The initiators of the crisis were punished.

The Necessity of Publication to a Third Party

The Dinka say that until recently a statement did not constitute a cause of action in defamation unless it was heard by a third party, *neen*.[32] *Neen* must actually have heard the statement from the defendant. Where there was no *neen*, the court maintained that the plaintiff, by complaining to the court, had defamed himself.

The basis of this requirement is uncertain. The maintenance of a name implies that one's name is known in society, and the name cannot be "spoiled" without the society hearing the defamatory information. On the other hand, it may be argued that, in most cases, the defendant's allegation implies his knowledge or at least his belief that the allegation

---

dance, word of their composition came to Abyor warrior groups. Rumors of the Abyor group's secretly planned attack were received by Acueng, and both sides started moving to strategic points. At this stage, word was brought to the chief, who immediately sent the police to pacify the situation. For three days and nights, the police struggled in the forest with several thousand intractable warriors. It was not until the paramount chief himself joined the police force that the situation was normalized. During the trial that followed, the court decided that the songs not be repeated in court, but the members of the court were informed of the essence of the songs in secrecy. The songs were banned, and the individuals responsible received varying sentences of imprisonment, up to one and a half years. The composers were among those who received the maximum. The subtribes were fined and later paid conciliation fees to the elders and chiefs insulted in the songs.

32. It is significant to note the verb "heard" because defamation has generally been slander and not libel, owing to the lack of writing in traditional society. The significance of writing has not yet been adjudicated.

is founded. This is not substantially different from the third party hearing the statement. Where the defendant makes an original statement knowing that it is false but calculating to shame the plaintiff, the plaintiff's name does not suffer unless the statement is heard by a third party. The requirement of *neen* has recently been made evidentiary rather than necessary. Only if the defendant denies making the statement is *neen* required.

Justification

The defense of justification requires that the defendant maintain or show sufficient reason for having made the defamatory statement. It is particularly concerned with the truth of the statement. Dinka law has no rigid rules about the defense of justification, but whether truth is a defense or not depends on the necessity to protect society by revealing the truth. Legal or moral guilt requires verification. But where the imputed evil does not endanger society, justification will not be allowed as a defense. We illustrate the first category with theft and the second with tuberculosis and leprosy.

It is important to point thieves out because they are dangerous to society and must be punished. To facilitate this, truth is a defense. In the case of tuberculosis and leprosy, there is no legal or moral guilt attached to them to require punishment. Yet, the knowledge of their existence makes one's reputation suffer seriously. It may be argued that it is in the interest of the society that such diseases be exposed in order to be avoided. However, the Dinka do not believe they are contagious. They are thought to be hereditary. For this reason, there is a defense of privilege where a father or anyone *in loco parentis* imputes such diseases to dissuade his child from marrying into a family afflicted with them. The argument could be pushed further that, for the relatives to know and avoid marrying into such families, it is expedient that the diseases be exposed. Here there is a balance of gain and loss. A person interested in marrying is expected to make a thorough study of the family he wants to marry into, but in a small society there is no need for unnecessary exposition to learn about people. The loss for the families accused of such diseases would be much greater than the interest of the society in terms of marriage.

Privilege

The defense of privilege exempts the defendant from liability on the grounds that he made the statement in the performance of a duty, whether this duty is political, judicial, social, or personal. As in justification, the Dinka have no definite principles about privilege as a defense. A person *in loco parentis* is permitted to inform his ward of any mortal diseases in the lineage of his or her intended spouse. What is said in good faith or in the interest of the plantiff is also privileged. Furthermore, in court defamatory statements are repeated in the interest of justice.

Privilege must be exercised sparingly. It is said that a person should avoid making the defamatory statement in the course of duty unless he cannot discharge it otherwise. Good faith and the plaintiff's interest as defenses are interpreted narrowly. When songs, especially group songs, are repeated in court, security measures must be taken to prevent the outbreak of violence.

Redress

The form of redress varies with the nature of the defamatory matter and the relationship of the parties. Here we classify defamatory matter into imputations other than wrongs and those of wrongs. Relationship classifies parties into relatives and nonrelatives. Those who are senior in status compose a special category.

When a person is allegedly defamed, he complains to the chief, who summons the alleged wrongdoer. In the trial the plaintiff restates his claim. Where the defamatory matter is contained in a song, the court may direct that the song be sung in court, if, considering the circumstances, it deems it fit.[33]

Since imputations other than wrongs often concern diseases like leprosy and tuberculosis, it is considered undesirable to investigate the truth of the imputation. In the past, however, the plaintiff took an oath in denial of the allegation before the defendant was held liable. It is said that the reason for this was merely to exonerate the plaintiff of the allegation. It did not imply recognition of truth as a defense. In practice, it seems to have made truth a defense; only those who knew that the imputation was false would litigate, since litigation itself caused wider publication.[34] The oath having been taken, the court usually levied conciliatory compensation, *awec*, payable in cattle. *Kueng*, a ceremony of reconciliation, was then carried out by the chief in court. By this ceremony, the chief willed that misfortune should fall upon the party who would initiate further conflict.

33. In certain cases, such as defamation against an important chief, it is most unlikely that the song will be sung in court. In intergroup defamation, hostilities may develop from the singing of songs in court, and preventive measures are usually taken in anticipation.
34. This is why plaintiffs always took the oath.

The requirement of oath-taking has now been abolished. If the statement is proved to have been made, the defendant is held liable. Instead of conciliatory compensation, which is still maintained in special circumstances, such as where the parties are relatives or the plaintiff is a chief, a prison sentence is now imposed.

Imputations of wrongs called for a different treatment. Examples of such wrongs are the possession of an "evil eye," *peeth,* and theft. When a person is accused of an evil eye, the accusation is usually associated with his lineage. The liability of the defendant is contingent on the plaintiff's proving that he knows of no evil eye in his lineage. In the past he did this through an ordeal called *lau,* by which he picked up a stone from the bottom of a pot of boiling water or oil. The belief was that only if he was wrong would he be burned. Conciliatory compensation and the ceremony of reconciliation then followed.

Theft among the Dinka is very rare and when it occurs it is strongly condemned and the offender is subjected to severe sanctions. To impute theft on a person alerts the society against a grave offense and defames the alleged offender seriously. It has already been mentioned that once theft was alleged, the age set of the alleged offender would seize his personality ox as a way of compelling him to clear his name and therefore theirs, or as a punishment if he actually committed the offense. If the alleged thief desired to clear his name, his age set joined him in the proceedings against the person accusing him. The court would then investigate the truth of the statement. If the plaintiff won the case, he was compensated by both the age set and the defendant, and his age set was entitled to an ox from the defendant. If the plaintiff lost, then, apart from the general alienation from society, the brutal skewering of his personality ox by his age set remained uncorrected as a punishment. There was no imprisonment. However small the object alleged to have been stolen, the consequences were the same. A small gourdful of butter and a pipeful of tobacco were sufficient to initiate the proceedings. Where the age set had no reason to believe that their member had committed theft, they would refrain from seizing his personality ox and might even initiate proceedings against the person making the allegation on the grounds that a personal defamation of an age mate amounts to age-set defamation.

The introduction of modern criminal proceedings and the weakening of the age-set system have affected the consequences of alleging theft. Age-set seizure of a personality ox is discouraged and made contingent on proof of theft.[35] During the defamation suit that follows, truth would be a defense and would, when proved, entitle the age set to seize the plaintiff's personality ox. The defendant is also made to compensate

35. See Nyanluak's case cited in Chapter 3, p. 99.

the plaintiff and the age set for the insult. Where theft is proved, criminal proceedings may or may not follow, depending on whether the court deems traditional measures adequate or not.

The relationship of the parties may affect the nature of damages payable to a successful plaintiff and may also determine whether imprisonment is more appropriate. Where the parties are relatives, conciliatory compensation is the most appropriate. Since the objective is to reconcile the relatives, such compensation is payable even in cases which might otherwise be justifiable. In such cases, no imprisonment is imposed on the wrongdoer. It is said that by the defamation of a relative, the defendant has also defamed himself. This is especially true in cases of imputations essentially associated with descent, but goes beyond that. In Kuac Kwot's [36] case, Kuac saw his cousin quarreling with a man and reprimanded her for her bad manners. She got provoked by this and said, "You son of a promiscuous woman. I know the heritage of your evil eyes." Kuac sued her in defamation. His mother, the girl's aunt, told the court that she was not in favor of the litigation, and that although she had been insulted, she was willing to forgive her niece. Despite her forgiveness the court ordered the payment of a heifer to her in conciliation.[37]

When the parties are not related, imprisonment or fine, or something analogous to it, such as payment of an ox to the plaintiff's age set, is imposed. The defendant may request that he be allowed to make conciliatory payment and to be reconciled with the plaintiff. The court may permit this, but the amount would be much higher than is normal. In practice, the descent orientation of the society does not make conciliation between nonrelatives imperative. Relatives, being in more intense interaction, must be more united and in harmony to lead normal lives.

The defamation of a person higher in status, such as a chief, is a very serious offense which often calls for both imprisonment and heavy conciliatory payment.

36. Abyei, Ngok Dinka Court (1960).
37. There was no separate compensation to the plaintiff

6. Rectitude

Rectitude is concerned with responsible conduct; its primary institution is religion. The discussion of overriding goals and other deference values has shown the intense and pervading effect of Dinka religion. Dinka religion is not merely an affair of the "soul"; it is rooted in experience and expedience. Out of experience, the Dinka realize what is conducive to their ends. They fail to understand the rules of natural phenomena and they attribute them to a superior being, unknown and yet seen in the realities of life.

Experience gives life to Dinka religion, makes it dynamic, and focuses its attention upon mankind in a living society rather than upon individual survival after death. The Dinka call upon God to give *wei*, "life," in its full value sense—spiritual and physical, individual and social. The dead are important because their world is a projection of, and into, the present world. In traditional Dinka society, therefore, religious beliefs include metaphysical, cosmological, moral, and political theories.

Although Divinity in the sense of one God is believed to embrace all men, the Dinka recognize that different men have different divinities and, consequently, different religions. It is said that the Arab has his God, and the European his God; and in fact, each individual human being may have his own God, for each is an individual with peculiar experiences, though belonging to the unity of mankind. As a corollary, it is understood that the Dinka divinities have limited power over Arabs or Europeans. Likewise, European and Arab gods have limited power over the Dinka. This parochial conception is a factor in the narrowness of the Dinka rectitude process, especially outside Dinka culture.

As heads of their descent groups, mythical participants are believed to ensure responsible conduct in human society. Through rectitude, they influence all values, achieve rectitude through all values, and see to it that a similar reciprocity exists among men. This they do by using basically persuasive strategies but, when necessary, resorting to coercion rooted in the self-scrutiny of the living and manifested in illness or other deprivations. Dr. Lienhardt observes the paternal symbol of divine sanction and the awe for the unknown which reinforces rectitude.

> Divinity is held ultimately to reveal truth and falsehood, and in doing so provides a sanction for justice between men. Cruelty, lying, cheating, and all other forms of injustice are hated by Divinity, and the Dinka suppose that, in some way, if concealed by men, they will be revealed by him. . . . Divinity is made the final judge of right and wrong, even when men feel sure that they are in the right. Divinity is thus the guardian of truth—and sometimes signifies to men what really is the case, behind or beyond their errors and falsehoods.
>
> . . . The Dinka have no problem of the prospering sinner, for they are sure that Divinity will ultimately bring justice. Since among them every man at some time must meet with suffering or misfortune, death or disease among his family or his cattle, there is always evidence, for those who wish to refer to it, of divine justice. It is a serious matter when a man calls on Divinity to judge between him and another, so serious that only a fool would take the risks involved if he knew he was in the wrong, and to call upon Divinity as witness gives the man who does so an initial presumption of being in the right.[1]

Whether in direct confrontation with men or in regulating relations among them, mythical participants are generally right. However, being part of human experience, they are not entirely infallible and may be criticized as capricious. Ultimately, however, man must submit to them and pay for reconciliation. That he shoulders the ultimate responsibility is symbolized by the myth imputing to him the wrong leading to God's withdrawal and the infliction of harm on man.[2]

The leadership of the mythical participants is expressed in the primacy of the patriarch. He is the recipient of greatest rectitude deference and, at least in theory, the most upright. With his divine and secular powers, both of which are derived from ancestral heritage, he is expected to enforce rectitude within his family and in situations involving his group. To subject his wife and her children to the mythical participants through him, he includes in the bride wealth cattle dedicated to these mythical participants. The blessing of the wife's agnatic relatives is ensured by their sharing in her bride wealth. She thus retains her deference to her agnates while also deferring to her husband's.

Just as man is less virtuous in comparison to mythicals, so women are

1. Lienhardt, *Divinity* 46–47.
2. Id. at 4.

less virtuous in comparison to men. While in sexual wrongs it is the man who must pay and receive indemnity, the spiritual impurities of the wrong are on the woman, who must confess or invite evil on herself or her children. Most acts of witchcraft are attributed to women. The original sin leading to the suffering of man is imputed to them. Indeed, women are associated with negative aspects in all values. Their negation of the overriding goals of unity and harmony is obvious in their jealousies. A man sings:

> Mabior, do not let the son of your father stray
> Men do not join the words of women
> It is they who break the clans.

Because of their alleged impurities, women are prohibited from drinking the milk or eating the dairy products of cows dedicated to mythical participants. Furthermore, women do not partake in dedications and sacrifices to the mythicals unless there is no male present.

With a position approximating his father's, the son represents his father in the latter's absence. As a woman, the daughter's rectitude position is low, but she is considered less afflicted with such evils as jealousies than are the wives. That both the sons and daughters are considered superior to the mothers is demonstrated by the fact that mothers are virtually incapacitated from cursing wrongdoing children, which is the privilege of male seniors.

Ritual functions are carried out by the eldest son of the first wife, *kai,* and in his absence by the second, and so on. The youngest son, *kun,* supersedes the middle sons, although his position is not identical with that of the eldest. The Dinka say, *kun e jok,* "the youngest son is a power," to show his unique spiritual strength. Together with this special rectitude position are other indulgences. For instance, while the eldest son inherits from the father materially, the youngest son acquires the mother's share in her daughters' marriages.

The subordination of youth on the ground of age results in practices negativing rectitude. The discussion of other deference value processes has already shown this negative role expressed, at its climax, in aggressiveness and violence. This negation of rectitude tends to be greater among the youth in their dealings with one another, since reciprocal deference is more emphasized in their relations with older generations, but the negatives are reflected in the whole society, for the wrongs of youth cause conflicts between wider groups and the elders.

The religious basis of traditional rectitude shaping and sharing in the Dinka family has been affected by the impact of alien religions, especially Christianity and, less so, Islam. Since it was the policy of the condominium to interfere with the traditional systems as little as possible,[3] while "civilizing" through Christianity, there were more changes in the spiritual sense than in the material sense.[4] The convert embraced Christianity but his material environment remained almost unchanged. The few who received missionary education usually drifted back into economic conditions which were not much improved. Indeed, missionary education itself was designed to make the child remain in his traditional setup, lest he become "materialistic." [5]

Of course the fact that missionaries were mainly concerned with spiritual values did not entirely prevent concomitant changes in other aspects of culture. From the purely religious standpoint, converts conceived of traditional religion as primitive and, indeed, irreligious. Deference to elders still existed; however, adherence to the religious guidance of traditional divinities, ancestors, and elders was radically affected. Although this was accepted as a natural consequence of education, it caused serious conflicts. The educated became considered "spiritual strangers," and were dismissed in consequence, thus limiting their influence in society.

Since Islam was considered Northern and was discouraged in the South, its impact on the family level has been minimal. There are, however, Dinka Muslims. The degree to which their conversion causes basic changes and conflicts depends largely on whether they were converted through educational or noneducational methods, for in the latter case, Islam differs from Christianity in important respects. The technique adopted by Islam was to advance itself along preexisting indigenous lines. Rather than obliterate animistic ideas and institutions, it cloaked them with the concepts and outward, but highly ritualized, symbols of Islam. Even today the noneducational Islamizer pursues this approach. Whereas the Christian proselytizer is interested in intensive religious instruction as a prerequisite to baptism, the Islamizer is more interested in the recital by the convert of the words "There is no God but The God, and Mohammed is His Prophet." As Dr. Farran points out, "No other test is necessary and it would not matter if he had never heard of

3. In January 1930, the civil secretary, under the instructions of the governor-general, restated the new policy in the following terms: "The policy of the Government in the Southern Sudan is to build up a series of self-contained racial or tribal units with the structure and organization based, to whatever extent the requirement of equity and good government permit, upon the indigenous customs, traditional usage and beliefs." No. CS/1 C. 1, Central Archives Office, Ministry of the Interior, Khartoum. See also Sir Stewart Symes' memorandum dated May 1938 in Trimingham, *The Christian Approach to Islam in the Sudan* 71–72 (1948).

4. Indeed, missionary education was such as to minimize material desires in its converts. The way the children were required to dress, the food they ate, and the like were calculated to achieve this result.

5. Christian Mission Society, *The Southern Sudan Then and Now* 11 (1950).

Mecca or even of the Koran." [6] This leaves the pagan with much room for pursuing his traditional mode of life under the pretext of adhering to Islam. Thus, by its noneducational methods, Islam does not accelerate modernization, though it may rapidly cease to be regarded as alien. The educational methods of Islamization, on the other hand, cause radical disaffiliation from Dinka culture just as Christianity did. But the real impact of Islam on the modernization of the Dinka comes on the national level where it clashes with Christianity in the South-North problem.

Family roles may be projected to the tribal level with the head chief, his subordinate chiefs, and elders leading in that order; the warrior groups in a lower category; and the educated class culturally disaffiliated and confronted with new rectitude problems on the modern level. The role of the chief and his subordinates as divine leaders and ideally the most upright has been sufficiently discussed under power and related values. In that capacity they receive the greatest deference which is sanctioned by the mythicals in whose name they guide the tribe. Today, alien religions have reduced the divine powers of the chief. He is no longer quite the man who brings peace, order, and harmony through a cool mouth and a cool heart. The rectitude position of youth age sets is a collectivity of the low positions of youth at the family level epitomized by aggressiveness and violence but covering a much wider range of activities. The disruption caused by these activities is exacerbated by the increased size of youth organizations on territorial bases.

The new religious outlook of the educated class as a group is in conflict with traditional religion, especially the divine prerogative of the chief. They see in him some of the evils of "paganism" and the exploitation of ignorance. Their attitudes set an example to traditional tribesmen, and the divine prerogative of the chief becomes a topic of controversy. He in turn makes use of his new force. He becomes suspicious of the educated class. Modern ideas turn his fatherly attitude into one of struggle for survival; the language of persuasion is replaced by that of force and arrests. Authoritarianism results.

The problem is more than one of irreverence toward the chief. Cowdung ashes, which in traditional society were used for oaths, have lost the respect of the converts. At least theoretically, adultery need no longer be confessed, except perhaps to the priests who keep it a confessional secret, and those wronged are left without remedy.

Even more explosive is the confrontation of the educated class with the central government. The encouragement of Christianity in the South is seen by the North as part of British colonial strategy of dividing to rule; Islam is therefore encouraged and Christianity discouraged.

6. Farran 227.

Southern Christians see this as a violation of freedom of religion, while the North views it as a governmental responsibility for national integration.

The religious controversies between the Muslim North and the non-Muslim South derive not only from their adherence to different religions, but also from the divergent methods adopted for the assimilation of these religions. This explains, for instance, the differences between the views of Northerners and educated Southerners on the relationship between religious institutions and the state. The perception of the Northerner is that "Islam is not merely a creed or worship absorbed or exercised by habit or imitation . . . it is a creed and a regulation at the same time, i.e. a Religion and a State which can never be severed." [7] The Southerner maintains that "Religion is a matter of individual consciousness" [8] and he cannot understand why "Islamization of the South is perhaps the most pre-occupying concern of the Sudanese Arabs both as a Government and as individuals." [9]

In the South, Christianity supplanted the traditional social system. The convert no longer aspired to the tribal religion, which is woven into the social fabric. Religion became disentangled from politics as a matter of individual concern. Although the condominium government favored Christianity, its policy toward the Christian missionary societies, which represented various denominations, was one of "strict and tolerant impartiality." [10] The abandonment of the relationship between politics and religion in traditional society, and the separation between the new faith and national politics, created a belief in the separation of religion and politics. Religious segmentation into pagans, Catholics, Protestants, and some Muslims made the Southerners believe in national unity despite religious diversity.

Islam aims at supplementing, rather than replacing, the religion of the animist, a fact which encourages its assimilation. Today, a glance at the Northern Sudan shows that "Islam . . . has so filled the lives of its inhabitants and acquired such tenacious hold that it renders them (not only) impervious to other influences but intolerant of any competition in proselytization." [11]

The assimilation of Islam was particularly augmented where traditional patterns were similar to Islamic principles. In such a case, the position was one not merely of mutual tolerance but of identity. This was so in the relationship between religion and the state. Politics and

7. Madather, Grand Kadi (Chief of Muslim Justice) of the Sudan, *A Memorandum for the Enactment of a Constitution Devised from the Principles of Islam* 19 (1956).
8. *Petition to the United Nations by Sudan African Closed Districts National Union* [later SANU] *on Behalf of the People of Southern Sudan* 19 (1963).
9. Deng and Oduho, *The Problem of the Southern Sudan* 55 (1962).
10. Cash, *Changing Sudan* 54 (1930).
11. Trimingham, op. cit. supra note 3, at 44.

religion are welded. The convergence of these identical conceptions enhanced the present Northern Sudanese perspective about the role of religion in public order. So strong is this theocratic phase of Northern culture that it withstood and survived the secularizing forces of European administration. Indeed, the British attuned themselves to it.

Important also is the unity fostered by Islam. As a universal religion, Islam extended the vision of the Sudanese solidarities beyond their tribal horizons without abrogating their institutions. It has been said of Islam that group solidarity is its real God. *Din* (religion) in Islam means a spirit of devotion to the ideal of social unity shown in the *Umma* (community or nation).[12] It was this broadened aspiration intensified to fanaticism which made it possible for Mohammed Ahmed, the Mahdi, to excite devoted support for his religious-political revolution against Turko-Egyptian rule in the Sudan.[13] This theory of Islam explains its use by Northerners as a strategy of unification.

Even more pervasive is the impact of Muslim-Arab civilization, which is considered by most people as superior to the animistic cultures of traditional Africa and is consequently conceived by the Northern Sudanese as the national civilization with which modernization must begin. Addressing the 1965 Round Table Conference on the Problem of the Southern Sudan, Sayed Ismail el Azhari, the President of the Republic at the time of writing, spoke of the northern Sudanese pride in their Arabic-Islamic identity.

> I feel at this juncture obliged to declare that we are proud of our Arab origin, of our Arabism and of being Moslems. The Arabs came to this continent, as pioneers, to disseminate a genuine culture, and promote sound principles which have shed enlightenment and civilization throughout Africa at a time when Europe was plunged into the abyss of darkness, ignorance and doctrinal and scholarly backwardness. It is our ancestors who held the torch high and led the caravan of liberation and advancement; and it is they who provided a superior melting-pot for Greek, Persian and Indian culture, giving them the chance to re-act with all that was noble in Arab culture, and handing them back to the rest of the world as a guide to those who wished to extend the frontiers of learning.[14]

12. Ibid.

13. Since the Mahdist rule was both religious and nationalistic, the fact that the Egyptians and the Turks were Muslims did not make much difference. Partly because of their corruption and partly because of their being aliens, the Turks and the Egyptians were almost regarded as non-Muslims.

14. Statement by Sayed Ismail el Azhari at 2–4. It was during Sayed Ismael el Azhari's premiership that the South revolted in 1955. He is now the president of the Republic by virtue of being the permanent president of the five-man supreme commission.

This cultural ethnocentrism is an important factor in the South-North problem. In its attack on the Euro-American Christian missionaries and the type of civilization they introduced to the Southern Sudanese, the Sudan government said, "They [the Christian Missionaries] embarked upon the introduction of superficial rudiments of a new civilization and culture different from what is prevailing in other parts of the country." [15] As the missionaries pointed out, "what are the other parts of the country? The North. And what is the culture that prevails in the North? Islamic." [16]

One must add the qualification that the more modernized Northerners, especially the youth, maintain a dual attitude. On the one hand, if they are Muslims, they consider it an individual affair. Not too infrequently one hears educated Northerners saying, *"A-Din Lil-Lahi Wal-Watan Lil-Jamie,"* "Religion to God, and the Nation to All." On the other hand, they seem to regard religion as inseverable from public life.[17] This inconsistent approach is subjective in that the two attitudes probably coexist in most educated Northerners; but it is also used as a device to meet the demands of the still "unsophisticated" populace.

The Northern decision-maker, ignoring the differences in cultural outlook, and undermining the influence of the Southern educated elite, equates the Southerners with the Northern masses, and feels sure of winning their favor through Muslim "brotherhood" or Islamic "unity." The use of religion as a means of solving the South-North problem has made religion one of the most conspicuous aspects of the problem and has led to the breakdown of rectitude.

RECTITUDE AND THE LAW

The association between rectitude and the law is striking in Dinka society and is pervasively expressed in the relationship between religion and the law. The effectiveness of the Dinka legal system is ultimately based on religious sanction. This reveals itself in the various branches of Dinka law discussed and still to be discussed. The point of emphasis here will be freedom of religion, which will be traced to the national level to see its connection to the South-North crisis.

In traditional Dinka society, one is born into a cult which obligates one to adhere to ancestral spirits, clan divinities, and other deities, by whose authority the worldly power structure is sanctioned. What is right or wrong, how the law protects or penalizes, and who benefits or

15. Sudan Government *Expulsion of Foreign Missionaries and Priests from the Southern Provinces* 3 (1964).

16. Verona Fathers, *The Black Book of the Sudan* 53 (1964).

17. Trimingham, op. cit. supra note 3, at 61.

loses in this process are all predetermined and subject to little or no change. Since there is a high degree of homogeneity in traditional society, conflicts over freedom of religion were not at issue, though religious stratification had consequences detrimental to rectitude.

It is on the national level that the problem of religious freedom is most pertinent. Cultural continuity works in favor of Islam as the national religion and is a catalyst for national integration. The functions of the Department of Religious Affairs concern this objective.[18]

A typical example is the day of rest. Throughout modern history Sunday had been the day in the South. However, in February 1960, the Council of Ministers resolved that Friday instead of Sunday should be the official resting day. This action met with general opposition in the South. All Southern schools including Muslim schools went on strike in protest. The government retaliated strongly. In *Sudan Government v. Paulino Logale and Others*,[19] for instance, a native priest, Paulino Logale, was sentenced to twelve years' imprisonment, and two secondary school students to ten years each, for distributing leaflets with the "object . . . to incite opposition and bring discredit to the Government." [20]

The major steps taken by the government to accelerate integration have been in the field of Christian missionary activities. Since independence, the Northern Sudanese skepticism about the role of missionaries in the South has manifested itself in restrictions on missionary activities. The conflict is fundamental. According to the government, "the majority of the population knew, for years, about the dangerous role which had been played by the missions in executing the colonial policy of separation." [21]

In 1962, the Missionary Societies Act was passed to regulate missionary activities, including social and health services and religious functions. Section 3 of the act provides that:

> No missionary society or any member thereof shall do any missionary act in the Sudan except in accordance with the terms of a license granted by the Council of Ministers. Such license shall be in the prescribed form and shall specify the religion, sect or belief of the missionary society, and the regions or places in which it may operate

18. Urging the Northern Sudanese to join efforts with the government in proselytizing Islam in the South, the daily *Rai el Amm* of April 8, 1960 stated: "There is no doubt that many of this country know how much need Islam has in the South of efforts on the part of the government. The administrative authorities and men of the Ministry of Education and of the Department of Religious Affairs continue to make gigantic efforts; but this by itself is not enough."

19. *Sudan Law Journal and Reports* 83 (1962).

20. Ibid.

21. Sudan Government, op. cit. supra note 15, at 6.

and in addition may impose whatever conditions the Council of Ministers may think fit either generally or in any specific case. [22]

By Section 6 the Council of Ministers may refuse to grant or review or may even revoke a license at its discretion. Section 7 not only imposes spatial limitations, but also prohibits a missionary society from doing "any missionary act towards any person or persons professing any religion or sect or belief thereof other than that specified in its license." It is also not allowed to "practice any social activities except within the limits and in the manner laid down from time to time by regulations." By Section 8 "No missionary society shall bring up in any religion or admit to any religious order, any person under the age of eighteen years without the consent of his lawful guardian. Such consent shall be reduced to writing before a person appointed for that purpose by the Province Authority." This means that Christian parents must receive state permission for the baptism of their own children. Section 9 provides that "no missionary society shall adopt, protect, or maintain an abandoned child without the consent of the Province Authority. . . ." Formation of clubs, the establishment of societies, organization of social activities, collection of money, famine and flood relief, the holding of land, and the publication and distribution of papers, pamphlets, or books are all subjected to ministerial regulations. In short, the act practically froze the activities of the missionaries to a standstill.

Commenting on the act, the government declared that it "came to provide the missions with a legal status and regulate their religious work. . . . (It) particularly stipulated the right to freedom of religion, and the right of the missions to preach their sacred Faith without restriction." [23] If that were the case, then the provisions of the act seem to betray its purpose. The act was certainly a political device to impede Christianity and enhance the progress of Islam in the Southern Sudan in order to achieve political unity. Correlated with impeding Christianity is the objective of disabling the foreign missionaries who became suspect as partners and patrons in the Southerners' antigovernment movement.[24] The contention that Christianity and Christian missionaries were the targets of government restrictions was dramatically demon-

22. The text of the act also appears in the Verona Fathers, op. cit. supra note 16, at 209.

23. Sudan Government, op. cit. supra note 15, at 11.

24. This motive is articulated in the following government statement:

It is clear that the missionary organizations have directed most of their internal and external efforts against the national government. Their main objective has been to have the confidence in the Government shaken and the unity of the nation undermined. It became necessary, therefore, to pass an Act aiming at the regularization of the work of the missions.

strated in March 1964 when the Sudan government expelled all foreign missionaries from the Southern Sudan.[25] The Sudan became exposed to severe criticism in world opinion, while in the Southern Sudan itself, tensions rose even higher.[26]

The belief of the government that the legal restrictions on Christian missions would maximize the prospects of unity has proved a miscalculation. The present situation in the country shows that animosity has been intensified. The Southerners consider themselves bereft of the rights to religious liberty, and the missionaries to have been "made the scape-goats of political blunders."[27] The attributing of their political consciousness to foreign influence is embittering. "To say that the people of the South cannot think for themselves without the British administrator and Missionaries is grossly to underestimate our intelligence,"[28] wrote two Southern political leaders.

In 1955, the commission set up to investigate the reasons for the revolt in the Southern Sudan commented: "We find on evidence that the real trouble in the South is political and not religious. . . . Christians, pagans, as well as Muslims took part: in fact some of the leaders of anti-Northern propaganda are Southern Muslims."[29] Today, however, the religious problem has become so entangled in South-North politics that the solution of the one necessarily implies the solution of the other.

25. On that occasion the government stated: "It has now been proved beyond doubt that the foreign Missionary organizations have gone beyond the limits of their sacred mission. . . . They . . . exploited the name of religion to impact [sic] hatred and implant fear and animosity in the minds of the Southerners against their fellow-countrymen in the North with the clear object of encouraging the setting up of a separate political status for the Southern Provinces thus endangering the integrity and unity of the country." Sudan Government, op. cit. supra note 15, at 16–17.

26. "Human Rights in the Sudan," *America*, May 23, 1964.

27. SANU, op. cit. supra note 8, at 24.

28. Ibid.

29. Sudan Government, *Southern Sudan Disturbances* 6 (1956).

Part III

Welfare Values

7. Wealth

THE PROCESS OF WEALTH

Although the Dinka are among the economically backward in modern Sudan, their animal and agricultural resources are among the main potentials for Sudanese economic development.[1] Animal husbandry and a pastoral life are primary features of Dinka economy. They keep cattle, sheep, goats, fowl, and pets like dogs and cats. By far the most important are cattle. They are an essential part of their food supply and from them needed objects are manufactured.[2] Cattle provide the most important medium of exchange. They are the subject matter of constant litigation in customary courts, although one must allow for the radical changes now taking place with the introduction of cash economy.

Cattle have a significance beyond their economic value. The fact that they are used as marriage consideration means that they are linked with the maintenance of lineage. These lines show the point.

> Tell the family of Atong
> If they should cease to have herds
> They will be extinct.

The cattle paid for a daughter are used to provide a wife for her brother. Most complaints in songs are by young men denied cattle for marriage by their senior kinsmen, or by poor men without cattle. The cattle given by the bridegroom's family are shared among the bride's relations, including those so distant that in most societies they would not be regarded as related at all. Cattle are thus used to strengthen the ties between the married couple and their relations on both sides and to further ties among all the bride's kinsmen. The cattle are not just "bride price" but are regarded as symbols of these highly valued human ties, so that they themselves acquire something of the reverence involved.

---

1. See Sudan Government, *The Ten Year Plan of Economic and Social Development* 1960/61–1970/71.

2. For instance, their horns become snuffboxes or are carved into spoons or other utensils. Their dung is used as both fuel and fertilizer.

Important also is the religious significance attached to cattle. Cattle are the medium of reconciliation between man confronting God and ancestral spirits through the mechanism of dedication and sacrifice. Thus, the interlinkage with the mythical participants is maintained and well-being ensured. A Dinka who had recovered from an illness believed fatal but for the sacrifice of his favorite ox sings thus:

> It is one's bull that redeems a man,
> It is one's bull that redeems a man from death,
> Mading Nyiel, you will go into the byre
> In the byre of Divinity, you will sleep.

Cattle are also paid as compensation for homicide to be used in ghost marriage.[3] Most male names are bull names based on their color patterns, and most female names are cow names.

The way in which various values come into play with cattle to enhance one's status, and the underlying significance of the principle of self-perpetuation, are evident in these lines.

> Ring Giir, The Great Flower-White
> My father Ring was called by his father
> He seated him by his side
> Caressed him, and said these words,
> "Son, Ring, there are the cattle
> There are the cattle, O son,
> Cattle are the prosperity of man."
> My great father had a cattle camp
> His camp became rich with herds and men
> The cattle byres full of cows
> My ancestor Akol is an elephant
> And Ring, my father, is an elephant.

Cattle are the dearest possessions of the Dinka and men sometimes die to acquire or defend them. The Dinka have a story which explains their suffering for cattle. It is said that man had hunted and killed the mother of the buffalo and the cow, who vowed to take revenge. They decided that the buffalo should remain in the forest to kill man whenever he came in sight, while the cow should become domesticated so that men should labor and kill themselves for her. The cow provides for the

3. Explaining the importance of cattle to human relationships, Dr. Lienhardt says: "Perhaps the clearest example of the way in which cattle represent not only human beings but human relationships may be seen in the division of the sacrificial meat when a beast is killed. 'The people are put together as a bull is put together,' said a Dinka chief on one occasion '. . . [W]hen the beast has been sacrificed, most of it is divided according to the division of groups within a kinship system, leaving some over for the community in general, distinguished according to sex and age." Lienhardt, *Divinity* 23.

continuation of the Dinka family and, in turn, the punishment they deserve for the deprivation man inflicted on her family. This implies attaching significance to continuity among cattle as well. The Dinka attach great importance to the ancestry of individual beasts. In certain cases, the law prescribes that the cow to be paid must be pregnant or suckling its calf. Should there be no pregnant cow where such is required, by a legal fiction a calf is said to be put into the cow's womb. Where a cow should be "empty," but only a pregnant cow is available, the progeny should revert to the original owner. When a beast has been sacrificed, a child subsequently born may be named after it.[4] Except for a few highly regarded purposes, the cattle with a history in the lineage were hardly disposed of; "the continuity of generation in cattle thus being balanced against the continuity of human generation." [5]

The value of cattle in Dinka society "is that of something to which men have assimilated themselves, dwelling upon them in reflection, imitating them in stylized action, and regarding them as interchangeable with human life in many social situations." [6] The Dinka often apply the word *aciek,* "creator," to cattle, though not in the sense it is applied to God. It is significant to note that terms of social and political identification are derived from cattle names.[7]

Although sheep and goats do not occupy the same position as cattle, some of the same reverence is extended to them. In addition to their economic significance, they are used in sacrifice to represent cattle in minor crises. Indeed, the Dinka sometimes say that *thok,* a goat or sheep, is *weng,* a cow.

"But if the Dinka has been mainly known to the outside world as a devoted owner of cattle, [he] . . . deserves also to be known as a cultivator, and this is a combination which is rare among primitive people." [8] It is often asserted that the Dinka lead a seminomadic life. This is only

4. Dr. Lienhardt writes about the application of the principle of procreation to cattle: "In compensating the beast for its death by naming the next child after it, they are preserving its memory in a way which is very characteristic of their thought about perpetuating the names of their families' dead in naming the living. They complain that in the government herds of cattle which have been taken as fines, it is wrong that the cattle of different families should be all mixed together, for cattle 'have their own names'—their own affiliations and groupings in relation to human groupings—and are not merely so many individual 'head of cattle' as they are officially regarded." Id. at 22.

5. Id. at 25–26.

6. Id. at 27.

7. *Wut,* "tribe," "subtribe," or "section," also means "cattle camp," and *gol,* "clan," means also "cattle hearth." This gives a rough idea of the dominant position cattle occupy not only in people's economic life, but also in shaping spirit and political institutions.

8. Stubbs & Morrison, "*Land and Agriculture of the Western Dinka,*" 21 *Sudan Notes and Records* 251 (1938).

true if by seminomadic it is meant that a proportion of the population accompanies the cattle in temporary camps in search of better grazing areas. The Dinka are much more sedentary than is commonly supposed. "The villages are in every sense of the world permanent, and are always inhabited by the older men and women who remain there even when the younger people are away with the bulk of the cattle on the far off grazings." [9]

Land has intrinsic value. The significance of its perpetual nature is shown by its association with the ancestors. A Dinka will swear on land to establish his truthfulness, thus symbolizing his submission to the judgment of the ancestors. This connotation has a bearing on the rules favoring perpetuity in traditional land tenure.

There are inferior forms of wealth. Examples are chickens, fish, grain, canoes, tobacco, bull collars, shields of hide, ivory bangles, iron hoes, bull bells, ox tassels, fishing and fighting spears and spear shafts, hut furniture, and utensils. Included in a man's property are claims. Rights over all these forms of property are much more personal in character than are rights over cattle or land.

Another form of property is the possession of spirits or medicines which have supernatural qualities to protect people, to cure sick persons or cattle, or to diagnose and explain evil and its remedy. In exercising these powers, the possessor acquires material gain. Some objects, the possession of which gives rise to supernatural powers, may be purchased for cattle, although in general they are owned by groups like the clan or the lineage. Those which can be sold are regarded as of an inferior quality.

Some objects are valued because of their ritual associations rather than their economic properties. These are the heirlooms of social, political, or religious groups. Although they are kept by the individual heads of these groups, their use must be directed toward the common good. An example of these objects are the sacred spears, or sacred ornaments.

The right to control and use the various forms of wealth is determined by one's position in the lineal order. Perhaps the most obvious key to this order with regard to movables is the institution of bride wealth. If a man must pay in order to start and maintain a family, then the society must afford him the necessary control over wealth. Herein lies the foundation of male dominance. It is a chicken and egg riddle to wonder whether the male is dominant because he pays or whether he pays because he is dominant. But if it is assumed that values are conditioned by the principle of permanent identity and influence, it is logical to assume the priority of this over a man's economic primacy.

The association between payment of bride wealth and powers of

9. Id. at 253.

control over wealth can also be inferred from the difference between the rules relating to cattle and those relating to land. Although cattle are used as a medium of exchange, their main function is the payment of bride wealth. Land is not thus exploited. Consequently, the power to alienate land is more limited than the power to dispose of chattels.

Since permanent identity and influence is both communal and individual, rights over property are also communal and individual. Even the mythicals, who are often referred to as a collectivity, have claims as individuals. It is important to expose the true balance between individual and social interests in wealth and the factors conditioning their expression.

The mythicals have transcendent control over wealth.

> Cattle and children are gifts from Divinity and from the clan-divinity and they always ultimately belong to Divinity, the clan-divinity, and the whole agnatic descent-group of which the clan-divinity is the tutelary spirit. Any owner's or father's relationship to his cattle or his children is thus a more temporary expression of a transcending relationship between human group, its herd, and its divinity, which persists through the generations. . . . This aspect of the Dinkas' attitude towards cattle is of . . . importance for an understanding of the dedication of cattle to Divinity or other Powers.[10]

The association of the mythical participants with land is dramatized by the fact that ancestors are buried in the earth, making it a monument of continuity.

Among the living, it is the patriarch who is charged with the payment of bride wealth. The dependent members of the family are economically sheltered by him. Their rights are his rights and it is he who will recover any compensation due to them; their obligations are his obligations, and it is he who will discharge their liability. His main obligation is to continue his genealogy: he must incur material losses to create a family, to maintain it, and to marry his children off. Corresponding to this obligation is material interest in the members of the family—the son should continue the genealogy by begetting his own children; the daughter should bring wealth to be used for family marriages and maintenance; and the wife should bear him children. Any interference with these interests calls for material recovery.

While the dependent members of the family are deprived of control over cattle, wives and dependent sons preoccupy themselves with cattle symbolized by their husbands' or their own personality oxen. These oxen, though of little utilitarian value, are symbols of personality and

10. Lienhardt, *Divinity* 23.

status for men and their wives. This preoccupation may justifiably be called an obsession. For male youth, status is enhanced not only by the man's identification with his personality ox, but by the exaltation of his ancestry and the lineage through which he acquires the ox. The importance of identification with a personality ox is expressed by a young man thus:

> My Mijok is important to me
> Like tobacco and a pipe
> When there is no tobacco
> The pipe goes out
> His pace and mine are the same

Furthermore, the name by which a young man is known in both intimate and formal situations is often a metaphor derived from the color pattern of his personality ox.[11] The following is an example of a song a man may compose to honor his ox.

> How grow the horns spreading?
> How grow the horns sweeping the earth?
> The horns of Mangar are going astray;
> The horns of Mangar are going astray like a lost man.
> The horns go to greet the things above.
> The rafter-horned Jok, I call him "The Breaker of Ropes."
> The ropes of "The Flour" [12] thunder like guns on rifle ranges.
> The "Curve-Horned" who trots has a voice like trumpets
> And like a gourd blown by the wind.

The emotional involvement a man feels for his ox and its significance as a symbol of himself and his social relationships is evident in this song by a man whose ox, Mijok, nearly died at a place called Gok. The ox had accrued to him through *anyial*, female agnates, with whom his father had asked him on his deathbed to keep good relations. In the song, he prays to his father to save the ox which symbolized the relationship his father had willed.

> My Mijok went into the byre
> Then groaned like a dying man
> And I prayed moaning,
> "In the byre of the son of Guiny
> Will my Mijok remain behind
> Father, Son of the Decorated One
> Father, Son of the One like the Giraffe,

11. Ibid.
12. Referring to Mijok's white parts. Mijok is white and black normally.

> The last word you said to me
> That I should live with the *anyial*
> *Anyial* will slip my Hand if Mijok should die."
> The tragedy of unforeseeable things
> I would not have come to Gok.

Women express their pride by the oxen of their husbands or suitors. A woman singing in praise of her husband's or boy friend's ox or wealth in general satisfies her ego by occasional reference to her husband as "I" and thus identifies herself with him and his wealth.

It is this devotion to oxen which motivates young men and women to endure the hardships of going to distant camps in search of better grazing—suffering hunger, confronting wild beasts, and engaging in, or defending against, raids. In many songs, young men who undergo these hardships adduce pursuit of good grass for their oxen or the defense of them as their motive. In fact they always herd many other cattle as well. Wealth, from a young man's point of view, is thus represented by his ox or oxen.

The symbolic significance of oxen, as opposed to bulls (which are of less esthetic significance), is the combination of bullish aggressiveness and courage with the amenability and submissiveness which are required of a dependent son. The beauty, the gentleness, and the sensuality of the ox and the toughness and virility of the bull are thus combined to symbolize the personality of a young man. This combination is then cast onto his descent and the whole image is primarily aimed at attracting girls.[13]

Although display of personality oxen provides compensation for the deprivation the youth undergo, and although the youth have the expectation of being the elders of the future, there is a certain amount of com-

---

13. While dancing, people curve their arms as horns. Dr. Lienhardt describes this phenomenon in relation to one type of dance: "It is clearly based upon the theme of the running of oxen with cows in the herd. Display-oxen are the equivalents of young warriors in the camp. The whole bull, the centre and sire of the herd, is associated with the father of a family and senior man of a camp. It is display-oxen, and not bulls, which are bedecked with tassels and hung with balls. They represent the unmated rising generation of the herd and the camp, of which the bull is the begetter and master. In the *gar* dance, the men advance and retreat, guiding or driving their female partners backwards and forwards and stamping and crying out before them. The young men regard themselves in this dance as oxen, and their girls as cows. The stamping and cries of the men are stylizations of the sounds and vigorous movements of bulls and oxen. The rhythmical repetitions of the cry *"eyi, eyi"* which men make when imitating oxen are not attempts to reproduce the actual sound which the beasts make, but they represent and express the whole rhythm of the beasts' movements, with their powerful ambling gait and swaying heads." Lienhardt, *Divinity* 17.

petition and hostility created by stratification in wealth. The opposition of the young men to their seniors is symbolized by the recurrent theme of opposition between display oxen and full bulls. In songs, the display oxen are represented as violently aggressive against the bulls in competition over cows.

The obsession with oxen does not cease with age. However, the older a man becomes and the more his children join the scene as young men and women, the more they replace him in its demonstration. An old man would still have display oxen, but he would no longer display them, though his wives, particularly the junior ones, may still be much involved with them.

Since the primary value of cattle is not economic, sale of cattle was traditionally shameful. It is still considered as evidence of social disintegration. This attitude is greater among young men and women, but is universally shared. A young man whose senior female relative attempted to sell his personality ox sings:

> Mother of Wor,
> Mother of Wor Mijok
> Never have I found so daring a woman
> How she ventured to sell the ox of a gentleman
> What evils the market has brought into the land
> That a young man breeds the ox of his pride
> Then comes a woman and wants him for sale.
> My Malith, I will never surrender . . .
> I clear him like the seed of a fruit
> He will remain in our sacred camp.

Since bride wealth is not paid in land, inequality in its use among the family members is reduced, but the pivotal position of the husband and father is not eliminated. He remains at least the "trustee" of the property, and no transactions can be validated without his consent.

Agricultural use of the land is minimized by the fact that young men and women devote little time to agriculture. Their attachment to land is seen primarily from the standpoint of cattle economy. There is a continuous struggle between the younger and the older generations, with the former wanting to herd far away and the latter requiring their assistance in activities such as clearing the fields, sawing, weeding, and building. Although there are sufficient pressures against them to cause a certain amount of conformity to the expectations of senior men, the conflict is generally acknowledged. During what we have called the cathartic period, it is considered a matter of pride for a young man to be exempted from agricultural labor, to retire with cattle, fatten himself, and have songs composed for him concerning his loved one, his lineage, or any matter of significance to him. Those who have had something to do with his exemption from cultivation are especially acknowledged and praised.[14]

While there are other factors, such as climatic conditions, preoccupation with cattle explains why the Dinka are not enthusiastic agriculturists.[15] People take pride in the possession of numerous cattle to be used for the enlargement of their families, but they want merely enough grain for subsistence. Even with an unusual amount of assistance from friends, agemates, or festive parties, people cultivate the same fields they have always cultivated. With the hazards of nature, the actual produce is sometimes insufficient and must be supplemented with such things as fishing, fruit collection, and, nowadays, purchase of grain from Arab merchants. To buy, the Dinka have to sell their livestock, an alternative which is becoming increasingly accepted but which is still unattractive.[16]

Some uneducated men are beginning to attribute more economic worth to cattle and are willing to sell even oxen. Admittedly, the attitude revealed by the following song is most unusual, and the singer might well be sardonic. However, it shows something of this change. It is significant that the singer sees selling oxen as a tearing apart of the tribe.

> Our oxen are driven into the market
> Arob Allor has driven his curve-horned into the market
> His curve-horned Miyan
> And I will drive my Maper into the market:
> My curve-horned Maper is bought by the Arabs

14. In this song, a man praises his stepmother and his older brother's wife.

> Nyanyaath of clan Pabong
> Has hidden my hoe
> She has thrown my hoe away
> Nyanyaath has released cows for me
> The woman takes care of me
> And Agorot, the wife of my father
> She has also thrown my hoe away.

15. See Howell, "Ngok Dinka" 245.

16. Dr. Howell suggests that the frustration of agriculture by unfavorable climatic conditions is the cause of preoccupation with cattle rather than the other way round: "The vagaries of rainfall and the endless chapters of disaster which are the result, are sufficient discouragement even without the counter attraction of cattle and are enough to inculcate an almost instinctive dislike for back-breaking agricultural processes which often give little in return. Grain is necessary for beer and for existence, but the Ngok cut the effort involved to a minimum." Ibid.

Whichever came first, observation shows the dominance of cattle today. Success in agriculture is regarded as much lower than fortune in cattle. Even if the hardships of agriculture were behind the present obsession with cattle, it is valid to consider it an impediment to agriculture and economic utilization of cattle.

They paid in flying money called notes
O Arob Joktuong,[17] what the Arabs have done
They have deprived us of coins.
We took our oxen into the market
And the market became rich with oxen,
Then our cattle camp at Maker remained without oxen.
Abyor has decided to sell their oxen
Our subtribe Abyor
If we put it in order, it is ours
If we tear it apart, it is ours.
Why is it not ours
Is it not our ancestor who holds the horns of the tribe? [18]

It is the same class of people who, when they earn money, do not think only in terms of buying cattle. For agriculture, they may use cash to hire labor to increase production. By and large, the demands of kin obligations are so great that their attempts to accumulate wealth do not succeed.

More innovating are the educated. They paid for their education by selling cattle, and through education they lose their preoccupation with cattle. They see the economic value of cattle but cannot exploit it because they lack control. Nor do they have the capital to exploit land.

On the tribal level, class structure based on wealth is hereditary and is largely stabilized. We have seen that *bany,* "chiefs," a term collectively applied to chiefly clans, when used as an adjective means "rich," and *kic,* the commoners, means those who acquired possession of the land by association with the chiefly lineages. It does not necessarily follow that the owners of the land are also the richest in cattle, although this is generally true.

The chief has an overall control of the resources and wealth, though this control is largely symbolic and ritual. Under him are experts in cattle, fish, and grain.[19] A cattle expert is a descendant of a lineage or

17. Arob's praise name.
18. The singer is of Pajok lineage.
19. Dr. Lienhardt writes of the functions of fish and crop experts: "All over Dinka-land at places chosen for major fish there are . . . masters of the river. They may come from spear-master clans or from warrior clans, and they may or may not be from spear-master lineages dominant in the sub-tribal areas in which they function. They are traditionally controllers of the river . . . and their task is to drown a bound beast . . . in the river before the fishing begins. This drowning is accompanied by prayers that the fishing may prosper. . . .

". . . Other minor experts are known as *bany rap,* masters of the grain. Like the masters of the river, they do not function for defined political groups, but for people in their neighborhoods who call them in if insects or birds are ruining the crops. They may belong to any clan which in a given locality traditionally performs this function." Lienhardt, *Divinity* 278.

clan traditionally empowered to purify cattle as a preventive or curative measure against disease.

While there are social classes determined generally by wealth, there are no social barriers between these classes. There is respect for the wealthy, but the strong spirit of equality among the Dinka does not permit the rich to look down on the poor or the poor to look up to the rich. The privileged have sympathy and regard for the less privileged, who in their turn bear little or no grudge against the rich. We must admit that this is a difficult phenomenon to explain. However, it is a conspicuous feature of Dinka society that the emphasis on the human element in personal relations bridges class barriers which nonetheless exist. In this way, the evils of class differentiation are concealed. Wealth, with consequent social prestige, carries commensurate social responsibilities. The extent to which a wealthy man wins influence and prestige depends on his social conscience. A rich and generous man attracts various dependents and retainers; to these, other members of the community, the strangers passing by, he offers hospitality. He also must be prepared to assist the needy. These indulgences promote his respect. The Dinka words *adheng* and *ajak*, which mean "rich," may also be translated as "kind," "generous," "gentle," or, in a word, "noble." To call a man "rich" is therefore to describe what is expected of his relations with other people.

Thus the need for the individual to maintain himself and his family corresponds to his obligation to assist hungry kinsmen, friends, and neighbors. His need to secure a wife for himself corresponds to his obligation to assist others in paying their bride wealth; his need to protect himself from evil by sacrificing a beast corresponds to his obligation to help other relatives do the same; his success in promoting his influence and prestige depends among other things on his generosity and hospitality to other people; and so on. The personal aspect of the system must be emphasized. Even in the case of the chief, benefits are given to individuals conceiving of him as the father of all. The relations of man to man and man to community are such that the individual is naturally conscious and responsive to the needs of others. In confronting individuals conditioned by these values, the decision-maker, whether tribal, subtribal, or familial, puts emphasis on persuasion rather than on coercion. But this deferential aspect of wealth is negated by the restricted basis of the wealth process. To give, one must have, and Dinka economic practices limit having.

The overindulgence of family youth in cattle takes the form of collective sectional or subtrial activities on the territorial levels. Adventure and violence as expressions of masculinity in cattle life are reflected in far-off herding, sometimes in disobedience to the chief's demands of maximum use of manpower in cultivation. Cattle raiding or defense of cattle and grazing areas frequently occur. Nearly every year there are intersubtribal attempts at fights, and actual intertribal wars. The war songs composed about such incidents often represent the warrior groups as serving the chief in defense of the land of his ancestors and therefore his land, even though in modern Sudan there is state machinery for handling such territorial violations. Wars nearly always end with the winning side capturing the herds of the losing side; but, today, the herds are always returned and any damage done is redressed.[20]

The literate class is disentangled from the traditional obsession with cattle and looks to modern cash economy. To their mothers who object to education, schoolchildren sing, advocating money and education over cattle:

> Should I propitiate you with a white cow?
> What about the White One of the Market
> And my pen?

Their education is not oriented toward utilizing resources. The less educated seek white-collar jobs in urban centers, but since most of them are not qualified for these, they settle for inferior jobs, such as domestic service, or remain unemployed in the towns. The more educated Dinkas, who are generally government employed and the spokesmen for the less educated, see economic stagnation in governmental policies and seek control over planning. This is an important feature of the South-North problem. As a spokesman for the Southern Front in the 1965 Round Table Conference said, "All plans for development have been either shelved or abandoned." The government adduces traditional social processes as a factor in the impediments facing economic development. On the occasion of the presentation of the Ten Year Plan of Economic and Social Development, the Minister of Finance and Economics listed among the most important characteristics of Sudan economy that "Traditional societies in the South, the East and the West . . . represent in their total a big idle manpower" and that there was "lack of full use of the known natural and human resources." [21] The plan itself gives the attitude of the people as the reason for the inadequate utilization of livestock.

> Livestock constitutes one of the main potential sources of income of the country. . . . The development of livestock has been hampered by the social habits of livestock rearing population,

20. See the incident recounted in Farran 88 note 18.
21. Sudan Government, op. cit. supra note 1, at 6.

mostly nomadic and semi-nomadic, to whom possession of livestock is more a sign of social prestige than of economic value.[22]

Consequently, one of the targets of the plan as stated is "removing the barriers which prevent population of the backward areas from participating in the modern monetary sector and laying the necessary foundation for a multilateral basis facilitating quick development and progress." [23] To the Southerner, all this is talk without action, and the impediments of traditional society are used simply as a justification for governmental neglect.[24] The resentment of the educated class of governmental attitudes toward economic development in the South is an important factor in the Southern problem.[25]

The civil war and the breakdown of order in turn frustrate development. One Northern Sudanese urges the Southerners to realize this point and to help halt the rebellion:

No progress can be achieved in any part of the world if there is no stability and tranquillity. The Southern Sudan was not, is not and will not be the exception. Responsible Southerners must have

22. Ibid.
23. Ibid.
24. One Southerner states about the animal wealth potential of the Southern Sudan: "One really feels disgusted from the monotonous saying amongst the educated circles connected with livestock or agriculture in the North [that] 'Nilotic cattle are very poor,' 'the Southern cattle are poor milkers,' 'the Dinka do not want to sell their cattle,' 'the social aspect among the Nilotic people' and the like. This is but an inherited outlook from the previous British rulers who were mostly interested in the 'human zoo' policy. The present rulers are no better, if not worse. If the British were as interested in livestock as they were in cotton I don't think the livestock of this country would have been at this very same stage. . . . By European standards these animals are of inferior quality. But, are we to fold our hands and do nothing? No, at least not for a Southerner at heart." *The Vigilant*, July 8, 1965, p. 2.
25. In their speech at the Round Table Conference, the Southern Front had these examples to give about the shelving or abandonment of economic plans for the South: "The growing of sugarcane in Mangalla and Malakal areas and the building of a refinery by a joint partnership of the Sudan government and the Boxall Company have been abandoned in favor of a poor alternative scheme in Ganeid. The plans for paper and tobacco factories in the South, where raw material is available, were frustrated by the decision of the government to set them up in the Northern Sudan. Similar fate goes with the recommendations of an investigation team into the natural resources and development potential in the Southern provinces. That report recommended:
a) Setting up of marketing boards for crops and livestock.
b) Opening of an agricultural school at Malakal. Instead, the only agricultural school at Yambia was closed down.
c) Construction of a 150-mile all-weather road between Rumbek and Shambe Port."

no illusion about this fact. They must use their influence to contribute to the cause of tranquillity in their country, not to play
into the hands of some of the opportunists. Trouble and progress
don't mix.[26]

For this reason, not only do projects remain unimplemented but those
which had been commenced have been terminated. But to many Southerners, no change of heart is apparent on the Northern side to justify
Southern reliance on the North's promise of reconstruction. The vicious
cycle is thus perpetuated to the deterioration of not only the Southern
economy but also that of the country at large.

WEALTH AND THE LAW

The importance of wealth as a subject matter of legal processes permeates Dinka law. Wealth is a means of satisfying claims by way of
damages or fines. It is also the subject matter of much of the law of
contract. Here, we discuss the institution of bride wealth, the law of
inheritance, certain contractual transactions, gifts, theft (as an example
of interference with property rights), acquisition and rights of ownership, and, finally, labor and produce. Although the institution of blood
wealth is one of the fundamental aspects of the interaction of wealth
and the law and has much in common with bride wealth for purposes of
perpetuation, it is better left to the chapter on well-being since it is
primarily retributive rather than a means of wealth distribution.

Bride Wealth

THE NATURE OF BRIDE WEALTH   The Dinka family is founded on bride
wealth. Its payment before, accompanying, or after the marriage ceremonies is a *sine qua non* to the validity of marriage. Misconception of
its meaning has led some people to consider bride wealth in purely
economic terms. It has been given the misnomer "bride price" to indicate that marriage is the sale and purchase of the bride and her potential
offspring.[27]

---

26. Said, *The Sudan* 151 (1965).
27. For instance, in his compendium on Dinka law, O'Sullivan speaks of "the purchase of wives by means of cattle (O'Sullivan, "Dinka Law," 40 *Journal of the Royal
Anthropological Institute* 175 (1910) as one of the bases of Dinka laws. Hartland, in
his introduction to O'Sullivan's work, states that "it is usually the payment of the
brideprice that authorizes [the husband] to reckon the children to his stock and gives
him control over them to the exclusion of any claim by the wife's kindred," although
he qualifies that "all this comes very far short of vesting their absolute ownership in
him. They are not slaves, however servile their status may appear to superficial ob-

One cannot, of course, defend the institution of bride wealth un-reservedly. Indeed, it is unfortunate that the recent defense of the insti-tutions and concepts of African traditional societies has tended to shelter much of what even the traditionalists might be skeptical about. Bride wealth has implications which tend to lower the status of women, but this is different from the assertion that every transaction of marriage represents a sale. Rather, it is an honor, and the greater the amount of the bride wealth, the greater the honor. Many songs by both men and women praise female agnates through whose marriages men acquired their personality oxen. The ox may be referred to as the ox of the girl for whose bride wealth it was paid, and she is praised for possessing the virtues that attracted the man to marry her. In her article "The Sig-nificance of Bridewealth and the Levirate among the Nilotic and Nilo-Hamitic Tribes of the Southern Sudan," Dr. Jean Buxton observes that "Girls like to be married for a lot of cattle, and will boast about this. Cattle reflect the girl's value, her beauty and social position, intelligence, popularity and so forth; ugly and inferior girls cannot command many cattle. A girl likes to do better than her age-mates and see their envy." [28] Admittedly, the mere fact that the higher the bride wealth, the higher the status attached to a woman, does not mean that she has not been purchased. However, the implications of bride wealth are quite different from those of purchase. Marriage binds the two families or bodies of kin among whom the bride wealth is collected and distributed.[29] This link may even survive a divorce and the woman's return to her kin. In any case, a woman cannot be considered "sold" if, as happens, her kin retain the right to protect her if her husband should mistreat her. Furthermore, the family of the bride has to make a counterpayment equal to approximately one-third of the bride wealth.

This suggests that bride wealth is more complex than an economic institution; it has a legal significance which permeates the kinship sys-tem. First, it legalizes the union between man and woman with the primary objective of establishing the legal paternity of the offspring. Second, it brings together formerly unrelated groups and gives emphasis and legality to their reciprocal obligations. Third, it stabilizes the mar-riage. If the girl or her relatives are responsible for the failure of the

servation." Id. at 172. Under the heading "Laws of Property," O'Sullivan includes among a man's property his wives and other dependents. According to him, "No woman can possess property, she being herself property." Id. at 178.

28. Buxton, "The Significance of Bridewealth and the Levirate among the Nilotic and Nilo-Hamitic Tribes of the Sudan," *Anti-Slavery Reporter* 66–75 (1958).

29. "The inter-relationships are maintained by a reciprocal system of bride-wealth distribution and the obligation to assist in the collection of bride-wealth." Howell, "Ngok Dinka" 280.

marriage, they are expected to return the bride wealth promptly, with certain reductions for children. Since the cattle will have been distributed far and wide, this is a task to be avoided. If the man is at fault, he forfeits his cattle unless the woman is remarried to someone who can afford to compensate him. Since his cattle would have multiplied, it is difficult to compensate a former husband. If he has sufficient wealth for another marriage and does not need the return of his cattle, he might better be a polygynist than divorce. If he can not afford marriage without the return of his cattle, then to divorce is to abandon the only hope for progeny. Divorce is therefore very rare. Fourth, bride wealth is a compensation for the loss of a member. When a woman is married, her lineage lose her and her contribution to their value maximization. Bride wealth compensates them, and introduces them to wider circles and other compensatory values through these circles. It makes it possible for her brother or other agnates to marry. It is in this sense that bride wealth and blood wealth are somewhat identical. Usually they are of the same value and are collected and distributed by identical sets of relatives. But it is important to qualify this identification of the compensatory nature of bride wealth and blood wealth. While the former is primarily a means of wealth distribution, and the loss which necessitates compensation is self-imposed for other supposedly more beneficial purposes, the latter is an externally imposed deprivation of a punitive nature. In a way then, it parallels other compensations for injury.[30] Fifth, by including in the bride wealth cattle dedicated to the man's ancestral spirits, and by giving the woman's ancestral spirits their share in the bride wealth through dedication, the dead are symbolically linked with the living, and their blessing is secured.

PARTICIPATION IN BRIDE-WEALTH COLLECTION The collection of bride wealth is the task of the bridegroom or his father with the help of kinsmen on his father's and mother's sides, as well as of relatives-in-law. The assistance is reciprocal, so that, generally speaking, those who give are the same who would receive in a reverse situation. Between friends of a special contractual category, there is also a reciprocal understanding to assist in each other's marriages. Reciprocity is nowadays enforced by the chief's court.

The following are the standardized contributors in bride-wealth collection.

Father: The "father," as the elder in charge of the marriage is called,[31] pays the bulk of the bride wealth, just as the bride's father receives the

---

30. Such as bodily injuries.

31. We said earlier that he need not be the real father, though he often is. An uncle may be appointed even when the father is alive. Such an arrangement affirms solidarity.

lion's share. The amount paid depends on the amount of help received from kinsmen and friends. Where the father is the normal father and there is a division of the family wealth according to houses, the cattle payable are those which by virtue of his position in the family and according to the rules of distribution and inheritance are the bridegroom's. Other houses, too, must contribute.

Paternal uncle: A paternal uncle may be the "father" appointed to arrange the marriage with the obligations of the normal father. Otherwise, the uncle following the bridegroom's father in seniority contributes about ten cows. Other uncles may pay eight or fewer cows, according to the estimated total bride wealth and their own relative wealth.

Maternal uncle: The maternal uncle is expected to pay a lactating cow with its calf. He may, however, pay more, and in doing so, he may be influenced by the amount paid for the bridegroom's mother, and also by his relationship with his sister's son. Only one uncle is obliged to assist, though others may choose to do so. Which one should assist depends on the corresponding position of the uncle and the nephew in the order of seniority in their respective families.

Paternal aunt: The paternal aunt (i.e. her husband) is expected to pay a lactating cow with its cow calf.

Maternal aunt: The husband of the maternal aunt is also expected to pay a lactating cow with its cow calf. As is the case with maternal uncles, only one pays, and the arrangement is similarly one of corresponding aunt and nephew.

Paternal half-uncle: The paternal half-uncle is expected to contribute five cows to the nephew corresponding to him in seniority. For the rest of the nephews, help is optional.

Maternal half-uncle: The maternal half-uncle is not obligated to assist, though he may choose to do so.

Sisters: Both full and half-sisters, (i.e. their husbands) must help. Help is on the principle of corresponding relationship. If there is only one brother, then all the sisters must help him. A sister pays a cow and a cow calf.

Relatives and friends: Other relatives and friends may choose to help, but in such a case they are also entitled to be helped on the occasion of their personal marriage or marriages for which they are responsible. Failure to observe this reciprocity may lead to the withdrawal of prior assistance. This is an aspect of gift withdrawal already mentioned. It will be pursued further under "Gifts."

AMOUNT OF BRIDE WEALTH The amount of bride wealth among the Ngok is unlimited and varies according to the size of the cattle population and the social and political importance of the bride's family. Dr.

Howell reports that "A man may hand over as many as forty, fifty or even a hundred head of cattle for the daughter of an important man, but the average appears to be between twenty-five and thirty. This is on the whole higher than the Nuer average." [32] There are cases in which daughters of chiefs have been married for two hundred cows. Although the average today might be doubtful because of the decrease in cattle, traditionally an average of twenty-five to thirty would seem a very conservative estimation.

Sometimes a girl is given in marriage to a poor man after a nominal payment on the grounds that sooner or later his female relatives will be married or somehow he will acquire wealth to enable him to discharge the bride-wealth debt. In such cases, the amount is not discussed. If the husband acquires wealth and there is disagreement on the amount to be paid, the court will fix a reasonable amount. There must always be prompt, even if partial, payment to validate the union. If a girl is given on deferred payment with a nominal validating fee, her relatives will not be permitted to revoke the agreement. If it is proved that the husband can afford to pay but does not want to, he can be forced to pay, but the woman's family would then be given the option of repudiating the marriage agreement.

DEATH OF CATTLE DURING BETROTHAL Since betrothal cattle belong to the bridegroom's kin for detrimental purposes, and to the bride's kin for beneficial purposes, a cow dying during betrothal, that is, before the formal handing over of the bride to the bridegroom's kin, is not counted as paid. The only exception to this rule is where the bridegroom's family has used the cow in a beneficial transaction.

NATURAL INCREASE DURING BETROTHAL Since, for beneficial purposes, title in betrothal wealth passes to the bride's kin, any increase is theirs and therefore not counted as part of the bride wealth. Although betrothal is concluded by the payment and acceptance of betrothal cattle, the principle of benefit to the bride's kin is emphasized so much that if a calf is born on the way to the bride's kin, that is, prior to any agreement, the increase accrues to them nonetheless and is not regarded as an increase of the betrothal wealth.[33] Bulls, be they large or small, do not count, though big bulls, full or castrated, have their own importance in facilitating agreement. Thus, if a man pays one hundred cows and ten bulls as bride wealth, the girl is said to have been married for one hundred cows, though, in determining reverse payment, or return of cattle in case of breach of betrothal, the bulls are considered.

32. Howell, "Ngok Dinka" 280.
33. We give the example of birth because the Dinka count a cow with a calf as two cows.

MONEY IN BRIDE WEALTH   Generally, bride wealth must be paid in cattle. Even sheep and goats are regarded as inferior for marriage. Until recently, money was entirely unthinkable, but with its increasing importance, the Ngok are beginning to employ it.[34] The practice is only resorted to in special circumstances and is not common. Payment of money in lieu of cattle is detrimental to the bridegroom's kin; for while cattle multiply, no interest is accorded to money, and should there be divorce, the same amount or its equivalent is refundable. If an amount is paid which is too small for a cow, it is considered a gift not forming part of the bride wealth, but should there be divorce, the amount may be reclaimed.

DISTRIBUTION OF BRIDE WEALTH   Distribution of bride wealth covers relatives of the paternal, maternal, and in-law sides according to an accepted pattern of rights. Just as the paternal kin pay the bulk of the bride wealth, they receive most of the incoming bride wealth. The pattern of participants and their shares are as follows:

Father: The bride's father need not be the biological or legal father; he is the person in charge of the marriage. In the marriage of the eldest daughter, and only in her case, the eldest half-uncle is the "father," and he receives the bulk of the bride wealth in that capacity. With the next daughters, full uncles become "fathers" to nieces of corresponding positions of seniority. After all the uncles have shared in the daughters' bride wealth, the normal father becomes the marriage father for the rest of his daughters and takes the bulk of their bride wealth. Where he is not the marriage father, the normal father is allotted shares varying according to the marriage father's choice and the total amount of bride wealth. However, he is always given a cow, a cow calf, and an ox which he may then pass on to one of his sons. In addition, he receives the cattle of divinities and ancestral spirits, three or more in number, to be distributed among the bride's uterine brothers and half-brothers.

Mother: The bride's mother is entitled to a cow and a cow calf, which go to the youngest maternal uncle, if he is still resident with her; otherwise, the cattle, with their natural increase, accrue to her sons. If her daughters are married after her death, her share is still provided but it goes undivided to her youngest son. The mother's share must be provided in all her daughters' marriages.

Paternal grandfather, alive or deceased, is entitled to a cow with a cow calf, usually inherited by one of his own sons (e.g. the bride's father himself or one of his full brothers).

---

34. Dr. Farran, citing the present writer, says, "Among some of the Dinka, although bridewealth is still necessarily assessed in varying numbers of cows, a tendency is just commencing to pay over the cash value of some of them instead of the animals themselves." Farran 286.

Paternal grandmother, alive or deceased, receives a cow with a cow calf, usually inherited by one of her own son's (e.g. the bride's father himself or one of his uterine brothers).

Maternal grandfather, alive or deceased, receives a cow with a cow calf and a bull to be inherited by one of his sons by another wife (e.g. the bride's mother's half-brothers).

Maternal grandmother, alive or deceased, receives a cow with a cow calf to go to her own sons (i.e. brothers of the bride's mother).

Paternal uncle, alive or deceased, if not the marriage father, receives a cow and a cow calf.

Maternal uncle, alive or deceased, takes five cows and a bull. The eldest maternal uncle receives his share and then distributes it among his brothers. If there are more than five uncles, the bridegroom may increase their share at his option, and thus increase the total bride wealth. It is significant to bear in mind the strong spiritual power of the maternal uncle. This was discussed earlier as a projection of the strong but repressed deference to the mother being reflected through her agnatic kin, or as evidence of male supremacy following on to her progeny. The maternal uncle rarely sues for his share. It is nearly always paid promptly or else the marriage is accursed.

Paternal aunt, alive or deceased, is entitled to a cow with a cow calf, which accrue to her sons and therefore outside the lineage of the bride's father. If the bride wealth is insufficient, she receives a pregnant cow. If there are two or more aunts, each receives in turn according to corresponding seniority.

Maternal aunt, alive or deceased, receives a cow with a cow calf to go to her own sons and therefore outside the lineage of the bride's mother.

Sisters' shares, *ariek,* go to their husbands, and depend on the bride wealth these husbands paid for the sisters. Since, in most cases, sisters receive from the bride wealth of their age-mate sisters or those younger, the problem of their share accruing prior to their bride wealth hardly arises. If it does, a reasonable share is allotted which affects what the sister's future husband will be asked to pay.[35]

A bridegroom may claim his fiancée's share in her sister's bride wealth soon after a betrothal agreement is reached between him and her relatives. It is immaterial how many cows he has already paid, as long as the total bride wealth to be paid justifies the amount he claims, for his

35. Dr. Howell explains the complexities of the relationships and the expectations involved in such payments: "Superficially, this is similar to the . . . paternal aunt's portion . . . but further analysis shows that it is a separate transaction which is also reciprocal. It is, moreover, the woman's husband who is the actual claimant, thus establishing a link between the bridegroom and his wife's eldest sister's husband, and finally his wife's younger sister's husband, because he can in turn claim a similar number from the latter." Howell, "Ngok Dinka" 286.

share anticipates his completing the payment of the agreed amount. In Maguith's case,[36] Maguith had paid six betrothal cows of which two were still in his possession, though the title had passed to his relatives-in-law. Before the completion of the marriage, Maguith eloped with the girl. The girl's relatives brought the matter to court, which decided to consider the marriage completed on the understanding that Maguith's relatives should pay an additional sixteen cows promptly. This they agreed to do when their cattle were back from the dry-season camp. In the meantime, a sister of the bride was betrothed with betrothal wealth of thirty cows. Maguith claimed a share of three, which was proportional to the twenty cows agreed upon. His relatives-in-law rejected his claim on the ground that his payment of the additional sixteen was a condition precedent to his sharing in his sister-in-law's bride wealth. The court held it immaterial whether a person had actually paid or not, provided the amount was settled and would be paid. In accordance with the amity demanded by the custom of a man's sharing in his sister-in-law's bride wealth, Maguith was authorized to select three cows from among the thirty. The court then turned to Maguith and urged him to pay the sixteen cows as soon as his herds were back from the camp.

Friends receive according to the nature of the friendship. A woman who has suckled a child is entitled to a cow. Anyone who has assisted the girl or her mother in a notable manner may claim a share. Thus, if the girl or her mother was saved by the blessing of a remote relative, or a friend, or by that relative's or friend's sacrificing a beast, that relative or friend may claim a share of a cow or so, though he would not have been entitled to do so in ordinary circumstances. Furthermore, a friend who has assisted the bridegroom's father or brother in the payment of bride wealth may claim a share depending on the value of his prior assistance. Even a friend who might not have done any particular favor may claim a share and this would entitle the bride's father or sister to share in a subsequent bride wealth of that friend's sister or daughter.

ENFORCEMENT OF BRIDE WEALTH   Bride wealth may be enforced by the action of the bride's kin or by a court decree. The bride's kin may seize cattle from the bridegroom's kin in such cases as elopement. If the girl is already given in marriage, they may invite her for a visit, hold her, and insist on the payment of bride wealth as a condition for her return. Of course, she would be regarded as married, so that no other marriage could be contracted. After the lapse of a reasonable time, her relatives may be entitled to sue for divorce and welcome new bidders. The man himself may use this as a ground for divorce and claim the return of whatever he has already given in part payment of the bride wealth. In

36. Abyei, Ngok Dinka Court (1960).

either case, the court is more likely to enforce the bride wealth rather than grant a divorce. In *Pajok Monytooc v. Matiok Atem*,[37] Pajok married Matiok's daughter and received her before completing payment. On Pajok's failure to pay the remaining portion in reasonable time, Matiok took his daughter and her three children to his home, threatening to retain them until Pajok discharged the bride wealth debt. Instead of paying or demanding their return, Pajok left the tribe for a number of years. On his return, Matiok sued for divorce. The court ordered Pajok to pay Matiok nine cows promptly as a condition for the return of his wife and children.

Instead of withdrawing the woman and her children, the wife's relatives may sue for the rest of the bride wealth and the court may compel the husband to pay. Since the court judgments are now enforceable by police force, this is a more effective alternative.

REVERSE PAYMENTS   There are a number of payments which the bride's kin must make to the bridegroom's relatives and his age mates. They must pay the bridegroom's kin a certain fraction of the total bride wealth from their own cattle, and not from the cattle given them by the bridegroom's kin. This is called *arueth*. There are no rules for calculating the amount payable. The Dinka themselves do not use any fixed proportion, but they will readily give the corresponding reverse value of any amount of bride wealth given them as an example. Thus, they will say that forty corresponds to one hundred, and six to forty, though it is not explained how these figures are arrived at.[38]

The purpose of this reverse payment is not clear. Originally, it was to help found a herd for the bridegroom, who would then have become more independent. Now the cattle are distributed among his kinsmen according to their shares in the collection of his bride wealth. A person will assist a friend or a relative to increase the amount of bride wealth for the purpose of enhancing the bridegroom's status on the understanding that he will be refunded from the reverse payment. Reverse payment is compulsory. Indeed, a great deal of litigation concerns failure to discharge the obligation.

The second payment, *wak thok*, literally "the washing of the mouth," is a payment of a cow or more to the husband which formally requests him to eat and drink for the first time in the homes of his relatives-in-law. Such abstention, we said earlier, is a gesture of respect for oneself and for the relatives-in-law. It reinforces the rules of avoidance. Its duration varies according to when the wife's kin pay the cow or cows of

37. Abyei, Ngok Dinka Court (1960).
38. Reverse payment "consists of approximately one third of the total bridewealth paid." Howell, "Ngok Dinka" 287.

"washing the mouth." It may follow soon after the conclusion of the marriage or may last for years after the marriage. Apart from her immediate family, the circles of his wife's kin in which a man wants to abstain are usually a matter of his choice. These circles may be multiple, in which case each of the relatives pays a cow to break the abstention in his own home. Where the in-law relationship is remote, a sheep or a goat will suffice. The husband's relatives may also abstain from eating or drinking in the homes of his wife's relatives and may receive payments of "washing the mouth" differing in value according to the relative importance of those involved and the proximity of their relationship. *Wak thok* is optional, though refusal to pay can strain the marriage and catalyze conflicts.[39]

There are two further payments. The first is *biol,* which is an ox of hospitality paid to the bridegroom's age set to be slaughtered for meat. The other is *akuath thiek,* literally "the driving of bride wealth," also an ox, supposedly a gesture of appreciation to the age set for driving the bride wealth cattle to the bride's family. It is immaterial whether they actually did so or whether an ox was slaughtered for those who did if other than the age set.

Inheritance

If, as we have maintained, the principle of permanent identity and influence is at the core of Dinka economic life, inheritance must be conceived of as a perpetuation of the deceased's ownership through his heirs. Thus, the ownership of the chain of ancestors is continued. Inheritance is therefore a "stepping into the shoes" of the deceased, who had also stepped into the shoes of those before him.[40] This determines who should inherit what rights and obligations. The system being patriarchal, the sons are the rightful heirs, and failing them, their sons. Stratification within these circles is based on the seniority of the mother and of the son. Within the broader lineal circles, and in the territorial units, descent determines succession.

Although there are broad principles governing who should inherit what, the will of the deceased, though too limited to affect descent stratification, has some significance. Except for specific objects of ritual significance, which automatically accrue to specific heirs, a man distributes most of his wealth in his lifetime to his family units, that is,

39. Despite the expression, the custom does not entail physically washing the mouth. Only payment is required.

40. Although the expression "stepping into the shoes" is alien to the Dinka, the eldest heir inherits the shoes of the deceased, thus symbolizing the nature of inheritance.

his wives and through them his children. Although basic stratification is governed by the order of seniority in the family, the quantum of what a man allocates to his wives and their children is largely a matter of his whim. Sometimes, this results in a junior wife receiving more than a senior wife. This would, however, be a violation of the norms and would probably affect only the lower segments of the pyramid. While he distributes his wealth, he remains the owner and can dispose of the property, though often in consultation with the wives and children to whom it had been allotted.[41]

The Dinka revere the last will of a dying man, and relatives will gather to catch every word he says. This is called *cien*. It governs how the family should be run after his death and what basic reorganizations or changes need to be made. Through gifts similar to *donatio mortis causa,* he may allocate that part of his wealth which is not yet allocated. But if the father has treated any one of his sons unfairly, other brothers may be compelled to make good the father's injustice. Since the idea is to perpetuate lineage ownership through his progeny, a man cannot make a legacy to outsiders. Generally, his ownership was from the group, for, excepting recent innovations, wealth normally accrues through inheritance or through bride wealth. A man may, of course, make reciprocal donations *inter vivos,* provided they are not extravagantly depriving to his family, but this right is eliminated on his deathbed.

Heirs inherit not only a man's wealth, but also his claims and liabilities. A dying person may distribute these claims and liabilities; otherwise, they normally fall on the eldest son, who may then distribute them among the heirs.

The eldest son inherits what is allotted to him in his father's lifetime. But, if of age, he is the representative and the executor of his father, and must see to it that his last instructions are carried out and his affairs settled. It is the eldest son who inherits *panom,* the homestead of his father where shrines of their clan divinities and ancestors are built and where major sacrifices to them are made. Even if the eldest son has a separate residence, on his father's death he must transfer to his father's *panom.* He also inherits other objects of ritual significance, such as the heirlooms of the family. Furthermore, the eldest son, through primogeniture, succeeds to any administrative or ritual position his father might have held.

Where a man dies unmarried, we have seen that he leaves behind an obligation to have a wife married to bear him children. Connected with this obligation is succession of his property. It passes to the person whose

41. It may be said that the wife and her children have a usufruct over the property. We prefer to call it a limited ownership owing to the hierarchical rights of ownership among the Dinka.

duty it is to marry him a wife, and those objects which can be traded are sold or exchanged and ultimately converted into cattle to be used toward the payment of the deceased's bride wealth.

Inheritance among the Dinka is thus an aspect of family continuity implicit in the myth of continuity. Just as wealth is acquired through the lineage, it is passed on through the lineage, and except within these confines, the will of the deceased has little or no consequence.

Barter and Sale

Prior to the introduction of money, the Dinka traded by exchanging various commodities. This is essentially barter, but the concept of sale also existed. The Dinka distinguish exchange of livestock of one kind, usually based on the sex of the animals, from exchange of different kinds of livestock or of different commodities. The former is *dil*, "barter," and the latter is *ghoc*, "sale." Most cases of *dil* concern exchanging bulls for cow calves and rams or billy goats for ewes or goats. They occur mostly in situations requiring the killing of a male animal (e.g. for hospitality or sacrifice). The reason may also be to acquire a personality ox. If both animals are available, they are exchanged immediately; otherwise, a specific animal not immediately available is designated, or the transfer of the bull is made on a promise to give in exchange any animal of a certain description. The agreement may be to give the first cow calf to be born by a specified cow. Should no cow calf be born, alternatives may then be discussed. A man may promise payment on the marriage of his female relative. There is a great deal of litigation out of such postponed payments, since most people are reluctant to pay when the time comes. Another disadvantage of postponed payment is that there is no profit unless an animal was first designated and left in the possession of the transferor, who subsequently disposes of it for a different purpose. In such a case, the natural increase of the animal is traced and either it reverts to the first person entitled or its equivalent is paid. If the animal cannot be traced, a reasonable increase is assessed by the court.

While *dil* primarily concerns animals of the same kind, there are a few cases when rams and billy goats may be exchanged for bulls. These are cases where a man desperately needs a ram or a billy goat and either is obliged to benefit the person providing it or pays more in appreciation of his assistance. In most of such cases, there is no immediate payment of the bull. The owner of the ram is also expected to give *ajuek*, a payment, usually of a female sheep or goat, in addition to the ram or billy goat. Both the payment of the bull and of *ajuek* are often deferred. If a particular bull is designated but then disposed of before delivery, profit may be dependent on how it was used. Thus, if it were exchanged for a cow calf, the debtor would pay the value including the increase.[42]

Sale, *ghoc,* concerned such exchanges as sheep or goats for a cow or bull, chickens, hoes and spears, ornaments, and the like for a sheep or a goat. A few people who grew a surplus of grain also traded it for cattle, sheep, or goats. with the introduction of money, most of these objects are now purchased in cash, though a man often must sell a cow, a sheep, or a goat to acquire it. While the Dinka are still reserved about selling their livestock, their animal population is decreasing rapidly because of the very low prices paid by merchants who then sell them in the North at great profit and buy goods they then sell to the Dinka at exorbitant prices. This applies to other commodities and is especially severe in the case of grain, which the merchants buy very cheaply from the Dinka during harvest and then sell at very high prices during the lean seasons. This is behind the present restrictions by the chief against sales of grain.

Custody of Livestock

The Dinka have a common contract by which a person entrusts his animals to the custody of another for a definite or indefinite purpose or period. This custom is known as *mac,* "tethering," which implies that the custodian has only the possession and not the ownership of the animals.

Giving cattle for custody may be done for any one of several reasons. A person may want an expert on animal husbandry to take charge of some of his animals. A friend or a relative may need milk cows for his family. A man may want to disguise his wealth to escape the risk of his cattle being claimed in discharge of kinship or other obligations or the envy of less fortunate people. A young man may want to accumulate independent wealth unknown to his seniors. Or custody may be prompted by lack of space for one's herd.

There are two main classes of such agreements: those which confer possession to the custodian for a definite purpose and period, and those which specify no terms except to keep the cattle. In the former case, the agreement comes to an end when the condition has been fulfilled. For

42. In *Mading v. Mayol* (Abyei, Ngok Dinka Court [1957]), Mayol needed a ram to sacrifice on the occasion of his son's illness. Mading gave him a ram in exchange for a bull then still nursing. Shortly afterward Mading paid Mayol a sheep as *ajuek.* Mayol, however, disposed of the bull when it stopped nursing and promised Mading a cow calf on the occasion of the forthcoming marriage of his niece. When bethrothal wealth was paid, he designated a nursing cow calf for Mading. The cow calf grew into a cow in Mayol's possession, and eventually Mayol disposed of it. Mading then sued Mayol. During the trial, the cow, then in someone else's ownership and possession, had given birth to a cow calf and was pregnant. The court held that Mayol should pay a pregnant cow and a cow calf.

example, A gives B a lactating cow to provide milk for B's family. The cow must be returned when dry, unless the agreement anticipated a long-term provision of milk, in which case it would continue into the cow's next lactation period. A might have given a cow to B to assist him during a famine. In such a case it should be returned when the famine is over, whether dry or not. In unspecified conditions, it is implied that the custodian will keep the animal for a long period during which he takes the milk for his own use. Generally, he must not use it for purposes detrimental to the owner; but in cases of need, the custodian, usually a relative or a friend, may use the property with the view of restitution. For example, if one of his family is dangerously ill and a sacrifice for which he has no animal is needed, he may sacrifice the animal under his custody but he must report the matter to the owner. They then decide whether it was a loan [43] or a gift.

Since the purpose of such long-term custody agreements is to encourage the increase of the animals and to discourage the owner's being tempted to alienate them, the custodian may trade with them. Thus he can exchange cattle for goats or bulls for cows. If done in good faith, the fact that he ultimately loses does not obligate him to the owner. On the other hand, if he incurs a loss to the owner in his own unjustified interest, he must account for the loss.[44]

43. Relatives often do not compensate for one another.

44. In *Deng v. Dan Bol* (Abyei, Ngok Dinka Court [1960]), Mading, the son of Deng, while a child in 1944, took two sheep to the son of Dan Bol, a young boy of Mading's age. Mading and Dan Bol's family were relatives. No conditions were made concerning the nature or duration of custody. It was understood that Dan Bol would keep the sheep to multiply and be a source of wealth to Mading when he was grown. As Mading grew up, he forgot that he had sheep with Dan Bol's family, a fact which left the latter a great measure of freedom over the sheep. The sheep multiplied. Dan Bol sacrificed a few of them on occasions of illness in his family. Then came a disease which killed most of the sheep. Dan Bol decided to exchange them for a bull which he later exchanged for a cow calf. He put the cow calf into the herds of a nephew whose father had died leaving him under Dan Bol's guardianship. The nephew, then on bad terms with his uncle, fled with his herds, including some of his uncle's, to another Dinka tribe where he disposed of the cow calf as part of his bride wealth. Later, the cow calf was traced and found to have increased to four cows. At this point, Mading's father, Deng, who until then had not known of the arrangement between Mading and Dan Bol's family, brought an action against Dan Bol for the recovery of the four cows. The court held that Deng could recover three out of the four cows. One cow was left unclaimed in accordance with the custom that when the owner ultimately reclaims his animals, he leaves at least one of them to the custodian in appreciation or in reward for his services.

Deng v. Dan Bol also illustrates the intricacies of Dinka transactions and the underlying family relationships together with those determinants giving the heads of families family rights and obligations. Deng benefited from his son's transaction, while Dan Bol lost on account of his nephew's act. That Deng did not know of his son's transaction shows his son's desire to accumulate wealth independent of his father's control, a motive not infrequently behind custody agreements. That Dan Bol's nephew

Gifts

The Dinka say, "What is given circulates, and what is consumed is wasted." This explains much about the reciprocal nature of gifts among the Dinka. While the Dinka are very generous, gifts are made on the tacit understanding that the donee will assist the donor in a future need. This is derived from the fact that gifts are often in the form of cattle, and that cattle have a peculiar significance to permanent identity and influence, so that ancestral claims intervene to supersede the donor's right to dispose of property without consideration.

A Dinka will not hesitate to "beg" a relative or a friend for help, because the concept of begging in their society, except for certain items, lacks connotations of indignity. There is nearly always a special relationship between the beggar and the person he approaches. Professional begging is unknown. A man whose personality ox dies may take the rope and approach the chief, a prominent elder, or a relative, asking for a substitute ox. A man whose favorite cow is dead will take the meat to the family of a female agnate, who, by accepting it, obligate themselves to pay that relative a cow either immediately or from a daughter's bride wealth to which he would otherwise not be entitled. Asking for help is extended to members of society who in the judgment of the beggar are able to satisfy his need.

There are kinds and degrees of requests for material help, but the major ones which come to court are those relating to assistance in bride-wealth payment. Gifts are also exchanged in the special form of "contractual" friendship discussed earlier. Since such gifts are reciprocal, they may be withdrawn if there is later a substantial breach of the friendship obligation on the side of the donee. The friendship is then dissolved and the status quo ante restored. This return of the gifts exchanged is termed *dhiel*. The Dinka defend *dhiel* on the ground that cattle are divine and "to throw them away" without valuable consideration is to invite ancestral curse manifested in illness or poverty. While *dhiel* originated in the social importance of cattle, it was extended to other types of wealth, like sheep and goats, to which the divine attributes of cattle are extended. It must not be assumed that the Dinka are likely to withdraw any gifts where withdrawal is justified. The custom applies only to those types of property endowed with special attributes. Even then, it is not universal to reclaim gifts on the dissolution of friendship.

In *Matet Ayom v. Deng Majok*,[45] this customary law was invalidated.

---

fled with the herds also shows a similar conflict implicit in the inequities of procreational stratification.

45. Abyei, Ngok Dinka Court (1955). See also *Nyuong v. Wor*, Chapter 3, p. 99 *n.* Despite the abrogation of the custom by judicial authority, the Dinka are still largely unaware of the change.

Matet Ayom, a sectional chief and a close friend of Chief Deng Majok, was held vicariously liable for his brother's elopement with Deng Majok's half-sister. Matet, offended by Deng Majok's attitude, began to agitate politically, whereupon he was arrested and convicted. After serving a prison sentence, Matet claimed formal severance of his friendship with Deng Majok and the return of cattle he had contributed to the bride wealth of Deng Majok's marriages. His claim was rejected by the Abyei chief's court on the ground that as Deng Majok would not claim the return of anything, although it was common knowledge that he had helped Matet far more than Matet had helped him, it was not equitable for Matet to have his cattle returned. Matet appealed to the district commissioner, Sayed Mohammed Ibrahim, who said in dismissing the appeal that if the custom were upheld, he for one would be reluctant to accept even a cup of tea from a Dinka.

Theft

The Dinka distinguish between theft of ordinary property, ordinary theft of cattle, and theft of cattle in self-help. The term *cuer* is applied to the first two, which are not only strongly condemned but are very rare. The last is called *kap*, "seizing," by the Ngok and is hardly considered theft.

In an earlier discussion of age-set activities, we saw that theft of ordinary objects gives rise to the skewering of one's personality ox or, as in *Nyanluak's* case,[46] the ox of one's brother. The stolen object, depending on its value, may then be forgotten or restored.

Ordinary theft of cattle, sheep, and goats is even rarer than that of ordinary objects. The obvious reason is that it is not easy to conceal the crime. The Dinka are well informed about a neighbor's stock and the source of a new animal would almost certainly be investigated, if only for curiosity. This is why most thefts of cattle, sheep, and goats are accompanied by the slaughtering of the beast for meat. Even in such a case, it may not be easy to utilize the skin, for its origin would be of interest to associates. A more serious reason arises from the attribute of cattle as divine animals closely associated with human life. Stealing them is said to invite spiritual contamination which might cause death to the thief or a relative. Since some ordinary objects are exchangeable for cattle, sheep, or goats, a somewhat similar feeling is applicable to them, though to a much lesser degree.

Theft of cattle in self-help is more frequent, but does not provoke the ordinary moral disapproval of ordinary theft. The origins of this, as of self-help in general, have already been attributed to the ineffectiveness of traditional judicial process. There was the need to compel an unco-

46. See Chapter 3, p. 99.

operative defendant to appear in court, to speed up litigation, and to execute court judgment. Seizing a cow thus facilitated the process of claims. It was not regarded as an offense, though the likelihood of violence was great if the person was caught in the act. Usually one seizing for rightful cause would take it to the chief's home, pending final settlement. Most seizures, however, were instigated by one's own sense of right and wrong which might be in conflict with the opinion of the court. This has now been greatly modified but not eliminated. The seizure of cattle continues. Partly because its rationale has disappeared and partly because of administrative misunderstanding of its true nature, seizure of cattle is now regarded as an ordinary case of theft, and receives the newly introduced prison sentence of six months. Nonetheless, the society still considers it different from ordinary theft. Even the court does not entirely equate them. The ordinary rules governing theft and the sentence normally inflicted on thieves will only apply in cases where the circumstances of seizure are aggravating. Thus, in Manyuol Dongbek's case,[47] Manyuol seized a cow and took it outside the tribe. On a charge of theft, the court held him guilty but promised release if he would promise on oath to return the cow. Manyuol refused to do so and was sentenced to six months' imprisonment.

Acquisition and Rights of Ownership

The Dinka recognize the concept of ownership as distinct from limited rights such as possession. The nature of ownership, conditioned by the cumulative interests inherent in the principle of perpetual identity and influence, is both collective and individual in a hierarchical sense. This fact must not blur the distinction drawn between ownership and limited rights, though it also limits the rights of ownership.

The Dinka do not have a single word for the English word "ownership." Instead, they use such expressions as "It is mine," "It is yours," "It is ours," or "It is theirs." It would be an unnecessary repetition to say, as in English, "I own it, so it is mine." The Dinka can dispose of that which is his at will, subject to any limited claims there might be. A cow might, for example, have been pledged as security for a debt, or paid as betrothal wealth, pending the completion of marriage.[48]

Because of the collective-individual nature of agnatic acquisition and rights of ownership, a man may say, "It is mine" when his claim to it is part of a wider common claim. Thus, if a son of a component family unit speaks of cattle allotted to his mother as "his," his claim to owner-

---

47. Abyei, Ngok Dinka Court (1960).

48. As we said earlier, for detrimental purposes, title does not pass to the bride's kin.

ship is to be seen in the light of his father's overriding claims, which must in turn be seen in the light of ancestral claims. Being the highest worldly owner, the patriarch has greater effective control over wealth than his dead superiors.[49]

That ownership is recognized as distinct from limited rights is obvious in that a Dinka will not say, "It is mine" where he is keeping another person's property either as security for a debt, as betrothal wealth, or in similar situations. A man would rather say that it is a cow of "a debt," or "marriage," or "custody," or merely of a named person.[50] An owner will say, "It is mine" even if the property is in someone else's possession.

The hierarchic structure of ownership means that the Dinka concept of ownership is more limited than the Western concept. This is especially the case with land, which, because of its immovability and its closer association with ancestors, is more in line with lineal continuity than movable property. In discussing acquisition and rights of ownership, therefore, we should treat land, livestock, and other types of property separately.

LAND The land of the Dinka was originally occupied either by peaceful settlement where there were no prior inhabitants or by conquest. In their migrations the Dinka were led by members of dominant clans whose lineages founded (and still hold) tribal or sectional chieftainships. The conquering leader in a tribe distributed land among his original followers and thereby formed the subtribes. The heads of these subtribes redivided the land among their internal groups, and so on, according to the segmentation mentioned earlier. Thus, rights in land, grazing, and fishing and drinking pools are held by the descendants of the original settlers of the area. Those who followed only acquire rights by association with these lineages. This is not of much practical significance today. So complicated and intricate are the problems associated with land tenure that to use words like "ownership" loosely is futile.

Today, every Dinka has the right within his section to settle and cultivate a piece of land, provided that it has not been occupied by any other person. Grazing areas are usually used by the members of the section in common. These areas may be near residential land, or may be in the far-off *toc* or *gok* where only young men and women go with cattle.

As various rights to land are vested in a hierarchy of social and politi-

49. Who intervene only from time to time and over a more definitive and limited portion of the total wealth than his living subordinates do.

50. If ownership is disputed, a man may say that "it is *amani*," which expresses the uncertainty pertaining to its ownership.

cal institutions, the nature of interests in real property is confused. Although the individual member of the community is relatively free to acquire land subject to territorial division, theoretical control, at least, is vested in the chief. It is he who allocates land to newcomers; it is he who protects the land against outsiders; and it is he who by virtue of divine power controls elements destructive to production (e.g. rain, birds, and locusts). He should not eat of new crops until he thanks God and ancestral spirits through a ceremony called *mioc piny,* "offering to the land," which though observed by every family is most elaborate and festive in the chief's family.

The control of the Chief over land is minimal with respect to members of his tribe. There is no need for allocation among them, since there is land for everyone to occupy without friction. Disputes about boundaries do, of course, arise, but they are often solved by local headmen. Only those concerning sectional grazing areas reach the head chief.

In whatever manner the possession of arable or residential land is acquired, a man and his family have the exclusive right to use that land. It is inherited from generation to generation. In a compound family, each house, with its cowives, owns and cultivates certain fields collectively. Each of the cowives usually has her own plot of land. In such polygynous families the head usually has cattle byres and fields which are commonly owned by the family; in addition, each wife within the family has her own huts and fields with her children and dependent cowives. The husband cannot interfere with these.

The right of the individual over his residential land is so strong among the Ngok that even if abandoned the land must be kept unoccupied unless he consents. A long-abandoned, unoccupied area is still referred to by the name of the owner who had once occupied it. Even if someone else is allowed to use the unoccupied land in the absence of the owner, on his return it must be surrendered to him. Continuous use is not a prerequisite to maintaining ownership.

In Dinka law no one can sell land. Land has strong religious significance, particularly the link with ancestral spirits and clan divinities. Objects sacrificed to God, ancestors, or divinities are offered to the earth, or to the river for the spirits of the water. Land can therefore not be evaluated in material terms alone. By analogy, cattle dedicated to God or spirits cannot be alienated in any way except in marriage and similar considerations of perpetuation. Furthermore, although a piece of arable land may be known as the land of someone, all of the relatives of that person have potential or actual interests in the land which qualify the person's ownership and right of alienation.

Huts and cattle byres can be sold. In such a case, they are either dismantled and their rafters and grass used for building elsewhere, or they are used where they stand on the understanding that when they fall the purchaser must leave. In Dinka law, houses are not real property.

The individual can, however, make a gift of his land, residential or arable, to a member of his group in the hierarchy of the social structure given earlier. Any change of residence from one section to another must be with the permission of the chiefs of the sections concerned and of the head chief. Since family and lineage members tend to live together for defense purposes, and since intrusion by anyone outside the group may be resented, gifts of land are made either to close relatives or to neighbors who have become affiliated with the group. Such gifts may be for short or indefinite terms, but normally the owner has the right to reclaim the land at any time, subject to the rights of the donee over the fruits of his labor, even if still attached to the land, as in the case of crops before harvest. In Dinka law, crops are not real property.

Rights over land are inherited by children from their parents. Generally, any child who comes of age and marries ceases to be a dependent and acquires independent residential and arable land for his new family. But the eldest son of the first wife inherits the father's land.

Generally, hunting rights are exercised in common by all the members of the tribal community. The same is true of the collection of wild fruits and honey, unless, in the latter case, the beehive is marked as private property. Trees may be cut anywhere except within the vicinity of the settlement of another group. Even within the group, religious belief works against cutting certain trees near areas of settlement.

LIVESTOCK The customs governing cattle differ from those relating to land. Whereas rights in land are more communal in nature, ownership of cattle is more personal. Such ownership is vested in the head of the family, subject to the use of family members. Cattle are allocated by him according to the seniority of the houses. Within a house, cattle are redivided among the individual wives, but needs of individuals are provided for by whoever can afford to meet them. Any cattle that are not allocated by the head of the household are collective property of the family. The sons of each house inherit from their father the cattle under their control. While the father is alive, neither the wives nor the children can dispose of cattle without his consent. The means by which the individual acquires property in cattle is often connected with his kinship. The cow comes to him through the kinship structure and will be paid to some kinsmen in discharging an obligation or will be passed on in marriage.[51] The manner in which a person acquires cattle corresponds to his reciprocal obligations to his kinsmen. Cattle are in constant circulation. A man receives cattle as marriage consideration only to dispose

51. Titherington 164.

of them in marriage; he gets help from a relative or a friend only to return the favor another time. A Dinka will refer to his own cattle as "cattle of my grandfather" or "cattle of my father," another demonstration of the lineal attributes of acquisition. Cattle could be captured in wars and distributed according to family units. This method is often used by warrior age sets, but recent raids on cattle and their subsequent return by the government have demonstrated that the practice is obsolete. Bride wealth is another means of acquisition. Akin to that is blood wealth. In both cases the cattle are distributed among relatives, and in the latter case each kinsman receives his share on both lineage and family levels. Gifts of cattle may be made by friends or by the head of the family. In the latter case, a junior wife is either specifically allotted cattle, or the cattle are kept by the wife under whose control she falls.

There is a significant custom by which each son is allocated a color pattern, *kit*, according to the seniority of his mother and a known hierarchy of color patterns. The eldest son of the first wife gets the most senior color pattern.[52] When a bull calf is born from a cow belonging to any member of the family, or when it comes to the family as marriage consideration, the son whose color pattern it bears will claim it. The color patterns are so intricate among the Dinka that frequent litigation centers on their determination. Although the allocation of a color pattern is determined by birth, it is officially effective when a young man is initiated. From his color pattern he derives his ox name, *mior*, by which he is known and addressed. Apart from its proprietary significance, the color pattern becomes a symbol of a man's social position.

Other ways of acquiring cattle are by trade (e.g. exchange of cattle for grain) or loans on interest (the loan of a ram might be repaid by a small bull). They are also received as compensation arising out of violation of rights in wives or daughters. Finally, they may be obtained for services. Poor men may obtain cattle by serving as herdsmen. There is usually a link, however remote, between the herdsman and his employer, except where the employer is a political authority. Another way of acquiring property is in the form of reverse payment in marriage, *arueth*.[53]

The fact that kinship is the normal source of acquisition does not exclude individual ownership; rather, it strengthens the individual's sense of obligation toward his kinsmen. For practical purposes a person

52. Mijok, that is, black head and shoulders with white body and either black or white hindquarters. The hierarchy of colors is not uniform among the Dinka tribes. Marial, which has a different pattern of black and white and which the Ngok allocate to the first son of the second wife, is considered the first among some tribes.

53. Somewhat similar to *arueth* are the cows for washing the mouth and oxen given to the groom's age set.

can dispose of his cattle without the consent of the dependent members of his family, but in the exercise of his powers he is governed by his obligations toward his kinsmen. There has recently been a general tendency among people to individualize their self-acquired property, so much so that courts have had to enforce kinship obligations, a necessity which would have been regarded as scandalous in the past.

There has been some recent regulation of the sale of cattle. Registration must be made with the market clerk in any sale. The purpose is to trace the seller in case his title is subsequently questioned and to trace the cow should the buyer lose it and it returns to the seller.

OTHER PERSONAL WEALTH The ownership of personal property other than livestock, unless it be of spiritual or ritual significance such as a sacred spear, is rarely a matter of claims in Dinka courts. It is in this field that ownership in its ordinary sense is least limited by perpetuity. However, even here kinship claims are strong, depending on the parties' positions in the lineal hierarchy. Dr. Farran, cites the present writer on the effect of marriage on a woman's property.

> . . . Evidence suggests that among the Ngork Dinka at least the harsh old English rule applies: a bride's beads or other trinkets or pieces of household equipment (whatever small property she has) are ostentatiously taken from her by her husband after the marriage ceremony and given to her mother-in-law or a senior wife (if such there be).[54]

According to Dr. Farran, this is "to show that she is in subjection to her husband's wishes, in this, as in other matters." One may add that it is not merely a question of subjection to the husband, but also a symbolic action emphasizing the group spirit embodied in the principle of permanent identity and influence. The bride's property is given to another wife, and she is given new property or that of another wife. Ideally, what a man acquires is that of his father, brother, or any other relative. Similarly, the property of a father belongs to a son, though in subordination to his father. In these lines, for instance, a man identifying himself with his ox uses his father's ownership and his own ownership interchangeably.

> Tinkle the bell my Curve-horned,
> The black bell of my father Arialbeek
> Even if you should break it, Mijok, it is yours,
> Even if the iron breaks, who will claim it?
> You will have spoiled the bell of your father, Deng.

54. Farran 279.

Giving to a kinsman what one acquires is balanced by receiving what a kinsman acquires. While the process of counterclaims by kinsmen is continuous and common interest in the property is encouraged by the kinship source of acquisition, individual identity in ownership is marked. Although the acquisition and rights of ownership of personal property other than livestock are less complex than those of more valuable kinds of property, they are governed by the identical group-individual combination.

Labor and Produce

LAND USE AND CULTIVATION A family usually works its own land and builds its own huts and cattle byres. They may hire others to help to cut grass for thatching or poles for rafters, and even to build. Such employment may be settled by pay or by inviting friends to a feast of beer and food. The exception in this is work for the chief, whose huts are built by the age sets of the various subtribes. Even then, he gives them beer and beasts for meat. But whether a hut is built by a wife herself or by the whole family for her, she is entitled to it.

Each house in a family cultivates its own field. The head of the household often cultivates his fields separately from those of his wives, although he usually assists them. A man or a woman can always get help by giving a feast with beer, meat, and other food to which he or she may invite friends or neighbors. Gratuitous aid of blood relations or relations-in-law may also be obtained. The chief may ask any age set to work his fields and may also be assisted by litigants awaiting their turn in his court during the cultivation period. The reason behind this custom is that the chief has no time for his own work since his judicial and administrative duties occupy so much of his time. Besides, his respect position exempts him from menial work.

In cultivation there may be a division of labor. Some young men regularly go to far-off cattle posts with the herds, leaving the older people to work in the fields. This practice is sometimes employed to exempt from work young men whose relatives wish them to *toc,* that is, "to lie down," during the cathartic period. This custom is now restricted by the chief in order that all may work to increase agricultural production.

Each family is entitled to the crops reaped from its fields. A defunct custom decreed that some of the corn reaped by a family must be presented to the chief. This went to the chief's household because it was understood that he was also responsible for the poor. Furthermore, his court, as the tribal meeting place, had to provide food for the tribe. Although these responsibilities of the chief have remained, the custom has been abolished. Within the family each wife owns the crops from her fields. The crops reaped by the head of the household in his fields are common property, but he must discharge obligations to assist kinsmen. This obligation is extended to neighbors whose crops have failed. Apart from specific obligations toward kinsmen and neighbors, there is a general obligation of hospitality to all in need. This was based on the expectation of reciprocity, for the giver today might expect to be the receiver tomorrow. Refusal to assist hungry kinsmen might lead to fission and the severence of relationship. Nowadays, hospitality may be enforced, and the Ngok chief's court has honored many such claims.

Apart from these rights, a person has the right to deal with his crops in any way he thinks fit. He can exchange corn for cattle, sheep, goats, domestic utensils, etc. A husband cannot sell corn from the field of a wife or dispose of it without her permission. Nor can a wife sell her corn without his consent. Cattle or other objects bought with a wife's corn belong to her household and can be inherited by her children; but her husband's right in the property amounts to ownership by him.[55] A wife may make gifts of hospitality without her husband's consent, but if a gift is extravagant, he can interfere, though at the risk of being disapproved of as a miser. Men are generally believed to be more extravagant in hospitality, and a female miser is more tolerated than a parsimonious male (except with respect to cattle, when parsimony is a lesser evil).

ANIMAL HUSBANDRY Herding of cattle is generally collective except for the few cows kept permanently at home for milk. A single family cannot protect its cattle alone, so the cooperation of territorial groups becomes necessary. Cattle are usually herded together, within either the section of the tribe or the subsection. The group may, collectively or by families, use cattle to fertilize the soil. Dinka cattle are tethered together, each to its own peg, so that field after field receives a sufficient deposit of dung and urine. This, with the rapid breaking down which the climate en-

55. This case, although decided by the Shilluk court, illustrates the respective rights of a wife and her husband over the produce of her field in Dinka law as well. A wife had her own field separate from that of her husband. They consumed together the produce from her husband's field. She bought a cow with her own grain. In time the progeny of the cow amounted to six head of cattle. Payment of her marriage wealth had not been completed by her husband. When the wife and her husband were enriched by her daughter's marriage, the wife's brother (the daughter's maternal uncle) came to claim the balance of his sister's marriage consideration. Her husband gave his wife's brother the cows earned from her own produce. The wife and her brother maintained that the cows belonged to her so that her husband could not use them for her own marriage consideration. The case went to the court, which held that the cows belonged to the husband and could therefore be given by him to her brother as part of the bride wealth. Evidence of Mr. Natale O. Akolawin, LL.B., LL.M. Lecturer, Faculty of Law, University of Khartoum.

sures, maintains the fertility of the soil. Thousands of cattle may be tethered in this manner. Within this collective herding, each person has to tether and care for his own cattle except during grazing, when they may be tended by members of the group in turn.

Every wife can produce butter from the cattle of her own house. With this she trades and buys more cows. Among the Dinka, butter produced from cattle dedicated to God or ancestral spirits may not be disposed of to strangers.

When a beast is slaughtered, the meat is divided between kinsmen according to strict rules. An age set shares cattle which accrue to it as a body, as when a beast is seized from a member who has disgraced the age set, or when the age set is awarded a festive beast by the bride's relatives in honor of the marriage of one of its number.

HUNTING AND FISHING   The Dinka are not keen hunters or fishermen, as these are considered the poor man's occupations, but they do hunt and fish to supplement their diet. Hunting and fishing are done collectively. Meat from hunting is distributed among the hunters. Ivory is subject to more definite rules since it is a valuable commodity which is often exchanged for cattle. The Dinka also use ivory for bracelets and bangles which are highly regarded.[56] In fishing, every person takes his own catch. But there is a custom known as *dom* by which the first man to grasp the fisherman's spear after the fish is speared gets the fish. He need not physically seize the spear as long as he states his claim. The claim is subject to the acceptance of the spearer who has the right to refuse, but who usually would not, as that would be ungentlemanly.

COLLECTION OF WILD FRUITS AND HONEY   When collecting wild fruits or honey in a far-off place, people usually go in groups for the sake of protection, but each person is entitled to his own collection. A person may make a beehive, or mark any tree where bees are likely to swarm, thereby ensuring that any honey produced is his private property.

56. The first person to spear an elephant is entitled to the right tusk and the second person to the left tusk, even if the wounds they inflict do not lead to the death of the animal.

8.   Well-being

The Dinka are among the more deprived of modern medicine and the benefits of health facilities in the Sudan. They conceive of health in deferential terms, and explain disease largely as resulting from discord. This emphasis on deference implies their neglect of physical cures and explains the stratification of well-being according to the principles of permanent identity and influence.

Well-being among the Dinka is intimately associated with *wei,* "breath," and although all living creatures have it, it normally refers to the spirit of life in human beings. As cattle are important animals and are sometimes sacrificed to save the lives of human beings or to compensate for them as in blood wealth, they are also believed to have *wei.* *Wei* is sometimes translated as "soul" or "spirit" by Christian theologians, mainly because it leaves the body after death, but as Dr. Lienhardt points out, *"wei* in Dinka is not, as 'soul' or 'spirit' tend to be in popular English, a kind of dematerialized replica of the personality. Consequently, we cannot speak in Dinka of the 'souls of the dead,' but only of their 'ghosts,' or of the 'life' which has left them." [1] When "life" leaves a person or an animal, it is believed to be transmittable to others. In sacrifices, for instance, the vitality of the sacrificial beast is symbolically transferred to the sick person.[2] This symbolic action is important as an analogy to the myth of immortality. The life of the dead is not lost. If their line is maintained, their *wei* is transmitted through posterity so that the dead are rendered immortal. Because of this link with the dead and other mythical participants, the well-being process is basically magico-religious.

Every living person has control over *wei* in proportion to his position in the social structure. This power implies giving and taking life as well

1. Lienhardt, *Divinity* 207.

2. "It is important for an understanding of what the Dinka suppose to occur at their sacrifices to recognize that when a beast moves vigorously in its death agonies its life is not being 'lost.' Released from the particular confines of its body, its vitality is made available to others." Ibid.

as possessing life. This force in any person can also be dangerous, so that there is a dual nature to life-giving and -taking. Who gives, weakens, or withdraws whose life depends on the relationship of the parties and the degree to which the expectations of the relationship are fulfilled or unfulfilled.

God, lesser divinities, and ancestors are conceived of as the producers and custodians of life, and their role is envisioned in familial terms. The creative force of God leads the Dinka to refer to Him as the real and ultimate husband of women and cattle, the complementary agents of creativity. As the Creator, God is also the ultimate protector. This prayer for twins recorded by the Seligmens,[3] shows the attribution of both functions to God and other mythical participants.

> Thou *Nhialic,* it is Thou alone who created them,
> Thou alone didst bring them; no man hates them.
> Thou *Nhialic,* look on life [mercifully]; no man is
>   mighty, Thou art mighty.
> Accept the bull, I have paid you the wage, let them live.

About the following hymn, Dr. Lienhardt comments:

> Here Divinity is clearly represented as the head of a homestead, a husband and father barring the door of his huts (*gar-gar ghot thok*) against the dangers of the night. "To bar the door," which is metaphorically used for this action, and "Divinity (who) bars the door, (who) protects," represent the father's care for his home and children.[4]

> You [Divinity] protect the homestead
> Shall I not propitiate You with a cow
> Divinity, father, you protect the home
> Husband of the cows
> Husband of the women
> It is you who protects the home.[5]

The following hymn might be sung when people are frightened by thunderstorms, for thunder is considered the angry voice of Divinity and lightning the glittering club with which He strikes the evils of this world.

> The Great Lord thunders in the byre [6]
> Thundering in the byre, He is angry with the ants [7]

3. Seligman and Seligman, *Pagan Tribes of the Nilotic Sudan* 166 (1932).
4. Lienhardt, *Divinity* p. 44.
5. Ibid. Poem translated by Dr. Lienhardt.
6. Enormous huts in which men sleep and keep cattle during the rainy season.
7. Human beings are considered ants in proportion to God.

> The Great Lord has brought death upon the earth
> The master whose heart has no grudge
> He attracts all the ants of the world
> People collect at his feet, and also on his head
> Great Lord of the Gourd [8] put right our home
> The home is shaken.
> If the earth is bitterly cold
> If the earth blows with cold wind
> It is the wind of Divinity.

The Dinka explain the suffering of man by a myth representing God as having once been physically connected with the world. Everything was then Goodness. The connection with God was severed owing to the fault of the original parents. In anger, God withdrew from man and willed that the world be immersed in suffering and misery—as it is today. A recurring theme in Dinka religion is the imploring of God to restore harmony. The need for this becomes especially manifest when man suffers the misfortunes of sickness and death consequential to the separation. These hymns collected and translated by Dr. Lienhardt [9] illustrate the point.

> Leave your home in the sky and come to work in our home
> Make our country to become clean like the original home of Deng [10]
> Come make our country as one the country of Akwol [11]
> It is not as one whether by night or by day
> The child called Deng, his face has become sad
> The children of Akwol have bewildered their chief's mind.[12]

> The strangers came with muskets
> And the aeroplane flew and evil followed [13]
> Does Divinity laugh and injure?
> Alas, ants of the earth
> Divinity laughs, Creator, alas!
> Deng brings the rope of the finch [14]
> That we may meet on one boundary
> We and the moon and Divinity

8. Gourds are used in some religious rituals.

9. Lienhardt, *Divinity* 37–38, 103.

10. One of the most important divinities common to all clans. See id. at 90–103.

11. An important female mythical participant of the singer's lineage.

12. Though seen as the child of God, Deng is also symbolized as the child of the human beings.

13. Reference here is to the wars against the Anglo-Egyptian regime.

14. In one of the myths of division the connecting rope is said to have been cut by the finch.

> Give the rope of the finch
> That we may meet on one boundary with the moon.

A Dinka strives to maintain unity and harmony between himself and the world outside, and he reads cosmological discord into all the mishaps of his life. Unity and harmony often fail, but they must be restored through such rites and ceremonies as may be recommended by a diviner. Harmony is best achieved by attuning one's demands and desires to the mythicals, living superiors, and other fellowmen.[15]

The Dinka who is visited by illness or disaster explores the depths of his inner self or that of a close relative in the hope of finding the sin which has brought on the discord. Even when the physical "cause" of an injury is clear, as when a man falls from a tree and breaks his arm, the Dinka often look beyond the evasive notion of "accident" and attribute the mishap to a supernatural force. In searching for a sin which might have provoked a mythical participant, the chances are that he will find some fault on his side.[16] The Dinka postulate that Divinity has the transcendent right to expect man to yield to His will; but, when His legitimate expectations are satisfied, He is supposed to rid man of evil. [17]

But Divinity is not always predictable. Consequently, it is not always possible to explain His harshness; nor is it always possible to appease Him. Since the notion of an anthropomorphic God is revealed through the realities of Dinka experience, He may display a nature which is both

15. Dr. Taylor explains the interplay between one's well-being and one's ability to harmonize with the cosmic totality: "A man's well-being consists in keeping in harmony with the cosmic totality. When things go well with him he knows that he is at peace, and of a piece, with the scheme of things, and there can be no greater good than that. If things go wrong, then somewhere he has fallen out of step. He feels lost. The totality has become hostile and, if he has a run of bad luck, he falls a prey to acute insecurity and anxiety. The whole system of divination exists to discover the point at which the harmony has been broken and how it may be restored." Taylor, *The Primal Vision* 74 (1963).

16. The remark "It is your right, Grandfather" is frequently heard even when God has been violently harsh with man—for example, when a person has been struck and killed by lightning. In some cases this is more a concealment of criticism in fear of worse consequences than it is a sincere and full appreciation of God's invariable goodness.

17. Appeasement is commonly accomplished by the sacrifice or the dedication of cattle.

> If I wrong him, I propitiate him
> If I wrong him, I appease him
> I will not tire, I will not despair
> I will not tire of appeasing Deng
> The divinity of my forefathers
> Ayuel Longar, Master of the Earth
> If I wrong Divinity, I propitiate him.

harsh and gentle, cruel and kind. The Dinka are occasionally forced to say, "Divinity has no heart," or "Divinity's eyes have no tears." Such extreme judgments are passed only where a disaster occurs for which man cannot find justification, or when divinities capriciously refuse to be reconciled by propitiation or to help in any situation where they are implored to do so.[18] The Dinka are thus a submissive people, living in a world they cannot control and subject to the will of a whimsical God.[19]

A Dinka has very little concern for physical cures without mysticism. As Titherington put it, "Ignorance of cause and effect, and a credulity which never ceases to astonish the observer, cloud his life with the constant dread that he has neglected some precaution against the malevolence of man, spirit or nature, and he hardly distinguishes the last two." [20] Yet, the Dinka do complain against unjustified malevolence. "As complaints are obliquely addressed to the human father in songs," writes Dr. Lienhardt, "and are also often intermingled with pleasing praise (lec nhom, literally 'to praise the head'), so hymns to Divinity and divinities also include the complaint of an anxious child." [21]

A man's well-being is the concern of the whole family and the kinship group, because the role of each individual in the interdependencies and solidarities of the group is a vital one. "Illness, catch me that I may see my people" is a popular saying. When a person is sick, relatives and friends cluster around him either in prayer or in silent watch.[22] When an animal is to be sacrificed, a group of people form a circle invoking spirits. With one person speaking at a time, the rest repeat after him in chorus. The concern of the community for the patient is symbolized by the division of the sacrificial beast in the manner described earlier. This unity of interrelated and interdependent families is essentially a corollary of the myth of perpetual identity and influence. By constantly calling upon "that of the fathers" [23] they are demanding the help of their entire heritage. "The fact that, despite the difficulties and dangers of human life, they are themselves living and multiplying, testifies to some-

18. See songs in Lienhardt, Divinity 38, 39, 45, 54, 55.

19. See Seligman, op. cit. supra note 3, at 178.

20. Titherington 170.

21. He continues: "Such a tone of complaint, which, if resigned, is not without an element of resentful accusation, is a common feature of Dinka prayers and hymns. The divinities in particular are asked why they treat their children so badly, why they are unresponsive on occasions to prayer and sacrifice, and whether they love suffering. To say "I am your child" is a usual way of urging one's claims upon a superior of any sort, and the father-son relationship is that upon which all relationships of dependence upon a controlling authority are modelled." Lienhardt, Divinity 44.

22. For a typical example of a prayer on such an occasion and the significance of procreation as the theme, see id. at 223–24.

23. Ancestral spirits.

thing in that inheritance which is stronger than the forces of death and sterility which constantly threaten its transmission." [24] Although "that of the mother" may also be invoked, emphasis is on agnatic heredity. [25]

Mythical participants, divinities, or ancestors may be the cause of illness whether justifiably or unjustifiably, in which case they are called upon to correct the situation. The cause of illness may be one mythical participant, in which case other mythical participants are asked to mediate. If the infliction of harm is a just retribution by a wronged person, the matter is settled with that person, but if it is an unjustified evil deed, then the divinities are called upon to cure the sick man and punish the evildoer. If it is discovered that a wrong committed by the sick person or his kinsman is the cause of the malady, confession is made as a step toward readjustment. A diviner is called to diagnose the grounds for sickness or diabolical possession only when the patient has not been able to do so. Sometimes, the power behind the illness may make itself manifest through the patient's mouth. The diviner may discover the grounds either by going into a trancelike condition or by inducing such a condition in the sufferer or his kin, or both. [26]

The power of the mythical participants over well-being devolves on the living in various degrees according to their proximity to the divinities and ancestors. Apart from direct devolution from the mythical participants, every person is believed to have inherent divine power, but the strength of this power varies according to one's position in terms of descent, sex, and generation.

Since the supremacy of divinities and ancestors is symbolized as patriarchal, it follows that the living patriarch gives and takes life. He gives life not only by begetting children, but also by being the most efficacious in prayer to the mythical participants for help in cases of illness. It is the patriarch who is the best qualified to make offerings, sacrifices, and dedications to the mythical participants. He takes life either by willing so, for instance, in prayer, *lam,* or as a natural consequence of a dependent's gross irreverence toward him. The patriarch possesses this power over life and death in relation to all his dependents, wives and children alike, but it is greatest in relation to the children. [27] The power of the father over well-being is not purely spiritual. The fact that he is pivotal in all value processes means that he can deprive a dependent

24. Lienhardt, *Divinity* 239.

25. This is obvious in such expressions as "I am not a bastard coming with its mother"; "help my people now as in the past my father looked after you," and "you my prayer, and you prayer of the long distant past, prayer of my ancestors, you are spoken now." Id. at 239–40.

26. Id. at 152–53.

27. In Chapter 3 (p. 35), we saw how the authority of the father or anyone in his position is sanctioned by this threat.

of values crucial to his well-being. It is obvious, for instance, that a wife and her children who fall out of the patriarch's favor may lack adequate cows for milk, the most nutritious food for the Dinka. Again, if they fall ill, the patriarch may be reluctant to sacrifice a beast. Even the mere lack of deference may itself be a cause of mental ill-health. *Muk*, which includes caring for, feeding, protecting, and the like is an essential feature of dependence on the patriarch, and its withdrawal implies physical and mental jeopardy.

The ultimate indulgence and deprivation of well-being from the patriarch concerns lineal continuity. Both the wife and children represent a means of life prolongation for him. The woman not only bears him children but also brings them up according to the goal of permanent identity and influence. Apart from being a revitalization of his worldly life, they must support him in his weakening years. The patriarch is obligated to give his wives the right to procreate and he must marry his children off so that the sons beget children in the interest of both the lineage and themselves, while the daughters bring in cattle which will become a security. The daughters' progeny continue the link with their maternal kin in a way sometimes stronger than those of the paternal kin. The special power of the maternal kin to curse is in part an aspect of the extension of the female agnatic commitment. It is a serious threat to a daughter and her offspring for her or them to offend her agnatic kin, or for their share in bride wealth to be denied or delayed.

Of course, it is expected that the patriarch within the family or in circles extended by females should exercise his power of life and death scrupulously. Unless his indignation is justified, or believed to be justified, his power is likely to be impotent. This is easily conceivable once it is realized that the effectiveness of his power lies in the "guilt" of the wrongdoer.

While the wife-mother is crucial in generating and preserving life, her legitimate spiritual power over the life and death of the husband and children is minimal. Of course, around women and cattle rotate Dinka ambitions and fears of life and death. Through them lie the chances of prosperity, abundance, and fertility, and the fears of barrenness, sterility, and misfortune. These two themes of life-giver and life-taker are recurrent in Dinka myths about the role of women. Their attitude toward women is therefore ambivalent. In most versions of the myth about the withdrawal of Divinity with the consequence of death and suffering, the woman is said to have committed the original sin. Furthermore, it is the woman who caused the division into clans and tribes with the resultant hostilities which are constantly a source of insecurity to life. Yet, it is through them that communities multiply, flourish, and ensure the survival of the lineage. Their life-taking evil is countervailed by their general lack of spiritual power (except for a few instances of senior women like grandmothers and mothers-in-law) to inflict harm. But this deprivation in the legitimate control of life in turn leads to their being considered depriving of well-being through black magic.[28]

Children have greater power over the family well-being than women have, no matter how old the women may be. In offerings of various objects, including sacrifices of animals, and in prayers, whether during sickness or as a matter of course, sons, and not wives or mothers, represent the patriarch if the latter is away. A wife can always pray as an individual, but the child, especially the son, overrides her. Yet, among the children, it has been seen that priority depends on one's mother's position and, among children of the same mother, on age. The eldest son represents the father as the father represents Divinity in its multiplicity. The order of representation is maintained down to the youngest son of the last wife.

While children, whether in relation to the father or to each other, are a prolongation of life, they are nonetheless destructive to life. The role of sons comprises fighting skills and courage as a means of protecting the family values. This, as a means of self-enhancement, assumes a dimension out of proportion to the legitimate expectations of their seniors. Fighting is an obvious threat to life. The youth also assume roles which invite the indignation of the seniors and therefore their curse. Unless atonement is effected, such curse may be transmitted through posterity, afflicting the lineage with the continuous threat of death.

While these participants are generally stratified on identical principles, the educated class, by repudiating the magicoreligious bases of the family well-being process, represents a new perspective. Education, secular or religious, undermines the norms of traditional religion. A child is encouraged to kill the animals which symbolize divinities. He is taught not to accept the blessings of pagan priests or elders. He is instructed not to consent to pagan divination or immolation to divinities and ancestors. When a sacrifice is made, he is enjoined to abstain from sharing in the sacrificial meat.

Tribal leaders and the public have been invited on parent's day in schools to see plays which disparage traditional bases of health. Typically, they picture a Dinka diviner failing to cure a sick person, while a convert who has openly denounced the diviner is cured by modern medicine. Of course, the parents admire the achievement of education. But they also develop the feeling that the schoolboy is changed into a different person, no longer Dinka in spirit. He is regarded as belonging to the new spiritual world of the missionaries. In many Dinka dialects the word for schoolboy is "the son of the missionary." He is not interfered with in his Christian practice, but that is because he is regarded as spiritually differ-

28. Hence such accusations as practice of witchcraft.

ent. The following prayer is reconstructed from the many prayers the writer has heard Dinkas say for their schoolboys—lost as they are.

> Divinities of my father, God of my father, it is not for a bad thing that I call the word; it is a good word that I want. When we sent them to school, we did not say that they should disclaim you; it was for a good thing. But if they have been changed, then you my ancestors, spirits of our fathers, and you Flesh of my father, there is nothing bad; your names are still great and we are here to grant you your wants. Cool your hearts, because we, their fathers, have not forsaken you. We shall honor your names still, so bring breath and coolness, you that of our fathers.

Tribal hierarchy is headed by the chiefs, whose functions from this perspective "are summed up in the expression *'aa muk weikua,'* they [the chiefs] carry (support) our life." [29] Like the eldest son in relation to the father and brothers, the chief is the representative of his people to God, the supreme father, to clan divinities, and to his ancestors. He also personifies these mythical participants to his people. It is in this capacity that the chief is believed able to curse a serious wrongdoer and perhaps even cause him to die. It is considered fatal to a person for the chief to point a finger at him in anger. Similarly, the chief can cure the sick and enhance the general well-being of his people by controlling human, animal, and crop diseases or other mishaps.

Among the most potent of the spirits behind the chief's power over life and death is *Ring,* Flesh, which is common to all chiefly lineages, and which is, as the word indicates, connected with life itself. Because of this the Ngok Dinka chief is known as *Bany de Ring,* Chief of the Flesh. As a Dinka expressed it, "Flesh is in a man's body, and it was in his father's body and the bodies of his ancestors from . . . the first master of the fishing-spear, and from Divinity, who gave it in the beginning. It is on their bodies and it is in their spears." [30] The paramountcy of the chiefs is further symbolized by the quality of their share in the sacrificial meat.[31] The reliance of the Dinka on the chief as the ultimate worldly supporter of well-being by derivation from mythical participants is shown in the following hymn. A few years ago, a young man of the Pajok clan fell ill. After his recovery, he did not resume normal life, but became "a man of God." In this hymn, he asks the chief to turn to God to save the tribe from the famine which had prevailed for several years because of continuous crop failures.

29. Lienhardt, *Divinity* 206.
30. Id. at 146.
31. Id. at 208.

We have become lean;
Big Chief, pray to God.
Our buttocks have wrinkled;
Big Chief, pray to God.
Our faces are in misery;
Big Chief, pray to God.
Will dances be held at night,
As though they were dances of spirits? [32]
Do-doo do-doo
Big Chief, pray to God.

In order to give life, the chief must have life himself. His personal well-being is therefore a matter of prime importance to the whole society. For this reason among others,[33] he is to be sheltered from physical danger such as war or wild animals. When a chief falls ill, however minor the illness, news of his condition swiftly circulates in the tribe. As he lies on his deathbed, relatives and strangers alike cluster around him. He must not die a normal death, and until the custom was abolished by the British, he had to be buried alive. Only on the death of the Chief do the Ngok Dinka have burial dances which show no marked difference from ordinary dances. In other words, they depict no obvious sorrow, for the Chief is not really dead. He will live in his people's memory and through his heirs, ideally his eldest son who steps into his stead soon after his death. Even ordinary cries, especially common among women on the death of a relative, must be repressed. Nonetheless, men and cattle must feel the pain of the Chief's illness and death. On the day of his death, no one should cook or eat. Children must not suck at their mothers' breasts. Cattle must not graze, and cows must not suckle their young.

Though their spiritual power is less marked than that of the Chief, all lesser chiefs are believed endowed with this power of life and death. There are also other functionaries who are more specialized in various aspects of societal welfare. There are specialists in cattle and animal diseases, land productivity, and the like. Their power may be individually acquired but it is generally inherited. Even if the former is the case, it usually accrues to their descendants. Apart from Chiefs and special religious functionaries, people are generally believed to possess the power to bless or curse, differing in degree according to the nature of the relationship involved, descent, and age.

Apart from legitimate means, there are evil practices of life-taking or life-protection which may be individually acquired or inherited and

32. Most adult dances are held in the daytime. He means that they will be too ashamed of their appearance to dance when they can be seen.

33. For example, his role as a peacemaker.

which are more common among the commoners. Typical of these are the evil eye, *peeth,* and evil medicine, *wal,* the power of which is contained in fetish bundles which are distinguished from the herbs ordinarily used for curative purposes by spiritually authorized people. *Wiel* is a more inclusive practice of symbolic action desired to bring death or some misfortune to whomever it is directed against. These various practices may be utilized by a genuine victim to punish a wrongdoer, but they are loathed and deplored. This is because they are believed to victimize innocent people and to counteract legitimate power. Many of these evil practices, especially the use of fetishes, are considered originally non-Dinka, being attributed to the Sudanic peoples farther south.

Also significant on the tribal level is the role of youth as a collectivity. Just as youth on the family level, they have little or no power over life. As the family youth engage in activities destructive of well-being, so do the youth age sets. This is especially the case in their excessive use of violence. For instance, traditionally they complemented the prayers of the Chiefs and priests by hunting wild animals, like lions, which often threatened the security of man. Nowadays, if a lion proves to be a threat, the Government sends the police to shoot it. The warrior groups, in order to demonstrate their courage, nonetheless prefer to hunt with spears in open disobedience to the authorities. The result is often an unnecessary loss of lives before the animal is subdued.

In the same manner, the warrior sets are excessive in protecting themselves from other warring units, so that defense and aggression become confused. As in all wars, taking life becomes a virtue, and, at least traditionally, this moralized evil was frequent. Furthermore, the pervasive preoccupation of youth with peccant deeds, which on the family level invites punishment, only assumes a wider dimension on the tribal level.[34]

Although we have presented the Dinka as dependent on superstition for physical and mental well-being, this should not imply that their

34. A story illustrates the point, though in an extreme form: One version is contained in an official record in Tonj, Bahr-el-Ghazal Province. The record reports that the young men of one subtribe, fat with milk and in display of their strength, once decided that only Divinity Himself was a great enough adversary for them. So they attacked the rain (as a manifestation of God) in a way not specified by the report. All except one were killed. The father of a man who is still alive is reported to have seen, in his childhood, the remaining rebel with a hole in his thigh from the incident. See Lienhardt, *Divinity* 43–44 for the Rek version. The Ngok version says that while young men were in an unusually large day-dance, it suddenly began to rain. Offended at God's act, they decided to battle with the rain by darting it with spears. Gradually, they sank into the earth while their drums beat. The spectators survived and stood hearing the drums until the dancing group disappeared. It is said that there is now a pool where they sank, and some people who claim spiritual insight allege that they sometimes hear the sounds of drums from that pool still beating at night.

approach to well-being has no secular aspects. To illustrate with a popular story, a Ngok was visiting another Dinka tribe. There he found that cattle and sheep were tethered outside without a fence to protect them from wild animals. When he asked why this was so, the people replied that their clan divinity, Atem, was protecting them. To this, the Ngok remarked, "Atem should be combined with a fence."

In addition to the use of herbs for medication, some experts are skilled in surgery. Even where the approach is clearly magicoreligious, the interconnections of the psychic well-being with the physical well-being are secularly significant. Diseases or other evils are not always corrected successfully. In such a case, the Dinka find an easy answer in the refusal of the mythical participants to be appeased, or perhaps in the failure of the diviner to have discovered the real cause. Where the organic disease is one which psychological cure cannot affect, or where the patient's condition is too serious, the diviner's psychological cure is likely to be ineffective. In such cases, some diviners are honest enough to tell the relatives that they can do nothing.

The association of disease and misfortune with lineal continuity, that is, the attribution to inheritance or lineage of the evils of the lineage members, has the effect that in the event of death the relatives of the deceased avoid, and are avoided by, outsiders. There is a taboo against their drinking or eating in the homes of outsiders or mixing with others on social occasions until they have been ceremonially cleansed.[35]

The Dinka have been somewhat affected by modern medicine. Among the Ngok, modern medicine was first introduced by the Government, followed by the missionaries. Among most Dinkas, innovation was by the missionaries who continued to render health services until they were prohibited from doing so by the Missionary Societies Act of 1962, preceding their final expulsion from the South in 1964. Dinka acceptance of missionary medicine was intrinsically linked with the missionaries' association of medicine with religion. Though it was hard to break the initial barrier, once the missionary had the opportunity to demonstrate the magic of his medicine, it became highly valued. Occasionally his medicine failed, and fear of traditional divinities arose. In many cases this failure was due to the patient's unreasonable delay in seeking medical

35. This is done through *cuol*, a ceremony which takes place on the third day of the death of a male, or the fourth day of the death of a female. The spirit of death is symbolically disassociated from the living. The people then shave their heads. Then they allow their hair to grow back for a year, during which time a certain measure of avoidance and retirement must be exercised. This period is known as the period of *cuol nom*, "black head," because of the taboo against dyeing their hair blond as Dinka youth generally do. The final ceremony, "shaving the head," *muot nom*, is performed at the end of the year to mark the final purification and the lifting of the taboos. For a chief, this period is only three months.

attention from the missionary. Eventually the missionaries won the confidence of the people.[36]

This success in missionary health programs did not directly cause any basic revolution in Dinka religious thought. Instead of repudiating their religious concepts of disease, they tended to associate modern medicine with religion. The missionary, in his turn, was able to use this association of God with the powers of his medicine: he became known not only as man of physical abilities for curing the sick but as one endowed with spiritual powers to cleanse the diseased. The reputation of his spiritual powers spread swiftly across the tribe. Occasionally, a person who was cured, or one interested in the cure, was so impressed that he immediately embraced Christianity. A cured child grew up being reminded of his savior, the missionary. By and large, the medical services did not produce such dramatic results, although they did help to establish a link of confidence between the missionary and the people, thereby affording him a better opportunity to spread the word of his God. Sometimes even baptism was looked upon by the people as a curative measure. A dying man was brought to the missionaries for baptism in the hope that it would heal him. In one case a child at the point of death was given the sacrament of extreme unction. He survived and his people regarded the missionary as his savior.

These and similar governmental health measures have contributed to a change of Dinka attitude toward modern medicine. It is obvious that people are turning more and more toward hospitals rather than relying entirely on traditional cures. Only a few years ago, modern medicine, both for animals and for people, was believed to worsen the situation. The chief, who in relation to traditionals is more receptive of modernity, would compel people under threat of imprisonment to accept vaccination or similar treatment both for themselves and for their livestock. If a person was dangerously ill and his relatives opposed modern medicine, the chief might coerce them (through modern administrative machinery) to submit. The diviners are also attuning themselves to the modern changes. Until recently, they considered divinities and ancestors as particularly sensitive about modern medicine, especially if it was mixed with divination and traditional cure.[37] Today, some of them encourage the combination. Many diviners now say that both they and the modern doctors are concerned with the well-being of men and that they do not mind a joint effort toward that end.[38]

36. It became common to see people near missionary health centers, thus revealing their new confidence in European medicine.

37. Modern medicine was resisted and resorted to only after the diviners had despaired, and quite often that meant that the patient was beyond help.

38. Lienhardt, *Divinity* 231, 280.

The educated class has largely repudiated traditional well-being practices and has turned toward alien religions and modern medicine for its spiritual and physical well-being, which it sees as welded together—a carry-over from traditional outlook.[39] In the light of the changing attitude of the Dinka in favor of modern medicine, the major issue today is not so much the resistance of the Dinka as it is the lack of facilities and guidance. In this factor rests the hostile disposition of the educated class against the national government, which it sees as withholding the requisite resources; as the hostilities intensify between the South and the North, the well-being of both sides and especially the weaker Southern side suffers even more.

WELL-BEING AND THE LAW

Because of the interconnections of all values, well-being permeates Dinka legal processes; however, the objective here is merely to illustrate the principles underlying the legal expression of well-being. Toward this end we select homicide, animal liability, employment of curers, and some notions of public health service.

Homicide

GENERAL NATURE OF HOMICIDE   Although the capital aspect of homicide has ceased to be governed by customary law, its tortious aspect is left to local courts to be governed by appropriate customs where the circumstances permit (e.g. where the accused is not sentenced to death). In homicide the broadest familial identifications come into perspective. Broad solidarities were vital since the effectiveness of social control was not sufficient to provide security amid widespread hostilities between various units of Dinka society.

An act of homicide immediately gave rise to a blood feud and the need for vengeance. The idea of a life for a life rarely led to peace, for the honor and pride of the victim's group dictated that even the life of a murderer required the taking of another life. The basic obligation to avenge fell on the dead man's kin but might extend to territorial groups, depending on the circumstances of the homicide. An entire subtribe might remain hostile to another, irrespective of the kinship relations of their members. If the vendetta was settled by payment of blood wealth, collection fell only on those who could trace paternal kinship to the killer, although maternal kinship and marriage affinity sometimes created the obligation to assist. Thus, the duty of vengeance was not necessarily correlative to the obligation to assist in the payment of blood wealth.

39. This theme recurs frequently in schoolchildren's songs.

While vengeance was usually carried out by youth, whether as relatives of the deceased or as warrior groups, the settlement of a vendetta and the compensatory payment were the duties of the senior members of the lineages or the territorial groups involved, with the overall mediation of the chief.

Nowadays, retaliation is replaced by state action, but homicide still gives rise to feuds that must be settled on traditional lines. This customary settlement still takes the form of blood wealth payable in cattle. Underlying blood wealth is the fundamental principle that the deceased's wife will beget children with a genitor to continue his name and his participation in the lineage structure.[40]

Of course, the dead man's group loses in ways other than those connected with procreation, but the dominant factor is that his procreative potential, both for his own sake and for his contribution to the kin group, has suddenly been terminated. He must therefore be married with the cattle paid as compensation by the killer's kin. This is clear in the manner of collection and distribution of the compensation. Contribution on the side of the killer is generally made by the same persons who would assist in marriage, and the distribution among the relatives of the dead is also quite similar to the distribution of bride wealth. Above all, the remainder go to the man whose duty it is to marry a wife to the deceased. Normally, he will wait for the remaining cattle to increase and complete a bride wealth. As soon as he can afford it, he is expected to carry out the obligation, lest the curse of the dead man befall him.

The discriminatory aspects of procreation are also encountered in the settlement of homicide. Stubbs reports of the Awiel Dinka that the amount of compensation in the past depended on the value of the deceased to his clan, assessable according to his age at the time of death.[41] The decrease of value with old age may seem inconsistent with the pivotal position of the patriarch in well-being. However, seen from the standpoint of permanent identity and influence, an old man will have, or should have, fulfilled the primary purpose of the family—procreation. This is why, although the youth provoke wars, the real fighters, once the war is in process, are, ideally, middle-aged men who have the strength to fight and the children to leave behind in case of death.

Female children were graded as boys until they reached the age of puberty, when they were valued at their bride wealth less the *arueth*, that is, the reverse payment made by the girl's relatives. If the woman was unmarried these estimates were made and given to her family; if she was married, then her husband's kin received the compensation.

40. Howell, "Ngok Dinka" 274; Howell, *Nuer Law* 41.
41. Stubbs, "Customary Law of the Aweil Dinkas," *Sudan Law Journal and Reports* 464 (1962). See also Howell, *Nuer Law* 465.

The association between blood wealth and bride wealth has the effect that if blood wealth is more than her husband had paid in marriage, he will be expected to keep only a number of cattle proportionate to what he paid. The rest of the compensation goes to her family.

A man does not pay compensation if he kills his own wife, for he would have to pay it to himself. He will, however, be expected to pay two or three cows to her kinsmen to reestablish peaceful relations with them. These cows are known as "the cattle of blood," *ghok riem*. If a woman kills someone, her husband, with the assistance of her kinsmen, is responsible for the compensation. As in other torts, payment by a wrong-doing kinsman is generally regarded as a fee of appeasement. It varies in value according to the circumstances of the case and may be more or less than the rate of normal compensation. In cases involving relatives the matter is more localized, and is determined by the nuclear or extended families involved rather than the kinship at large.

FORMS OF HOMICIDE   The Dinka recognize various forms of homicide, determined largely by the manner of commission, which affects the gravity of the offense and the indignation of the dead man's kin. They may be summarized as secret killing, *loc piny;* killing by stealth, *dheng piny;* killing by magic, *awok, wiel, wal,* or *peeth;* ordinary intentional killing, *nak raan;* negligent and accidental killing, *weec;* and death incidental to other wrongs such as breach of taboo.

Loc piny occurs when a person kills secretly and conceals the offense. This is very serious, for apart from its depriving the victim's relatives of their member and their due compensation, it invites spiritual contamination on the kin groups of both parties and might cause death. A blood feud creates a spiritual barrier between the groups concerned and gives rise to observances and taboos which, if broken even in ignorance of their existence, constitute a serious threat to all concerned. An incident is recorded in which a person was believed to have been contaminated by a secret murder committed by his long dead grandfather.[42] A man must therefore confess any homicide to enable those concerned to follow the necessary observations and taboos. If a man is later compelled by the evil consequences of concealment to confess or he is somehow detected, a higher scale of compensation is demanded. The indignation provoked by such behavior calls for greater punishment and more pecuniary benefit to appease the wronged group.

Dheng piny occurs when a person takes unfair advantage of his victim, thereby giving him no opportunity for self-defense. Such a cold-blooded murder outrages the Dinka sense of dignity and honor. Appeasement is difficult in such circumstances, and only a higher scale of compensational punishment can atone for the wrong.

42. Such murder is usually detected by a diviner.

Killing by various magical charms, though difficult to prove, is also very serious. The Dinka explain in detail how evil medicine, *wal*, evil eye, *peeth*, and other such antisocial practices affect the victim. The symptoms of each of these are so clearly established that the difficulty is not so much what kind of death is involved as who has caused it. Usually, people suspect those who might have had a motive, such as those who were on bad terms with the victim or with his close relatives. Should any additional circumstantial evidence lead to a reasonable conclusion as to the identity of the killer, he would be personally attacked and killed. In the past, a fight was bound to occur between his relatives and those of the victim. Compensation for death caused by magic is difficult to settle. Since magic is strongly associated with descent, to admit that a member has caused death by magic is so serious that it is hardly ever done. The present writer knows of no case of such death settled by compensation, though cases were cited in which retaliatory violence resulted between the groups involved. However, Stubbs in his collection of Awiel Dinka customary laws says that when death was attributed to magic, compensation of ten cows (later reduced to five cows) was paid if the wrongdoer was a stranger. If the victim was a kinsman, one cow was paid as conciliation fee, *awec*.[43]

By ordinary intentional homicide we mean such cases as killing in a fair fight, individual or group. This is the standard case in the absence of aggravating or mitigating circumstances.

Weec covers cases of both negligent and accidental killings. The former is less serious than intentional killing and graver than the latter. In determining negligence, the Dinka use a concept comparable to the Anglo-American "reasonable man." In an interview with the chiefs and elders, an English lecturer who, with the present writer, was investigating Dinka customary law asked them whether the Dinka law had the concept of the "reasonable man." The question was interpreted into something like "When you judge a person do you consider what a man of proper conduct would have done?" Their reaction could nearly be described as "What a silly question! Of course we do." One chief went on to give an example based on actual cases. If one saw cornstalks waving in a field immediately behind the huts during a season when corn is ripe and assumed that there was an animal destroying crops and speared it, but it turned out to be a human being, his assumption would not be a good defense because "a man with a head," *raan de nom*, should have known that a person might be in the field picking corn.

In one of the cases from which the example was derived, a man killed his neighbor's wife in a durra field a few miles away from the homestead. He had been on friendly terms with the deceased and her family, and used to eat with her husband. When the incident occurred, her husband

43. Stubbs, supra note 41.

was away and she was cooking for this man since he was unmarried. One afternoon, he went to guard his fields from birds and animals. Before he left, he saw the hut of the woman closed but did not wonder whether she was inside or had gone somewhere. On reaching his fields, he saw the durra stalks moving in the adjacent fields of his neighbors. Thinking that monkeys were destroying the crops, he threw a spear at the direction of the movement and fatally injured his neighbor's wife. He was tried by a major court and convicted of negligent homicide. After he had been sentenced to imprisonment, the Abyei chief's court tried the tortious aspect and assessed the compensation on the basis of negligent homicide. The plea of accidental death was dismissed on the grounds that he should have known that the woman might also be guarding her field, especially when he had seen her hut closed.

Another case showed a clearer instance of negligence. A man saw the stalks of durra and corn waving in a field immediately behind the homestead. Believing it to be jackals spoiling the crops, he threw a spear at the area and killed a small child. The Ngok usually plant fast-ripening durra and corn in such nearby fields to supply food before the main crops ripen. Although the crops were not entirely ripe, they were sufficiently ripe for children to gather corn or sugarcane. The man was held guilty of negligent homicide by both the major court and the chief's court. Being a kinsman of the child, he was made to pay *awec,* conciliation fee, and not *puk,* blood wealth. Since *awec* is often greater than compensation, and the child's father in this case was the paramount chief, the amount paid was much greater than usual.

Accidental homicide is the least serious, and requires compensation on a greatly reduced scale, usually only six head of cattle. It is difficult to substantiate "pure" accident without an element of negligence, but in extreme cases, liability may result only in nominal compensation for the purpose of ritual atonement.

Death resulting from breach of taboo or other observances may give rise to liability, depending on whether the defendant was the sole wrongdoer or whether he shared the wrong with the deceased or a relative of the deceased. An example of the first is *thiang,* whereby sexual intercourse with a nursing woman may cause death to the suckling baby or the baby of a neighbor. There would be liability to such a neighbor. If, on the other hand, a person commits adultery with a woman who does not confess, thus causing death to herself, her children, or any other relative, the adulterer is not liable for such death since there is an intervening obligation on her part to avoid the death.

There are other circumstances which affect liability for homicide. For instance, where two or more people are involved and death was caused by spears, the man to inflict the first wound, however trivial, is alone held liable. To spear first epitomizes the intention to kill and therefore calls for severer punitive measures. This is consistent with the benefits of the first spearer in hunting. In the case of elephants, for instance, the right tusk goes to the first spearer. Where injuries are inflicted with clubs and not spears, death subsequent to recovery calls for compensation at a reduced rate. The Dinka believe that, once cured, injury inflicted with spears does not return, while club injuries often do.[44]

The preceding forms of homicide substantiate the point that the Dinka consider *mens rea,* that is, criminal intent, as relevant and that the nature of compensation is not merely restitutive but also punitive.

SETTLEMENT OF BLOOD FEUDS   In the past, the administrative and judicial system was largely ineffective and pursuance of a feud was dominant, but in most cases, payment of blood wealth and reconciliation by the chief eventually followed. Feuds between those who were too distant, that is, in different tribes, were rarely settled in this manner, but those between local lineages or groups were usually settled.

When a man commits homicide, a feud automatically arises between his kinsmen and those of the deceased. He himself must immediately undergo a personal ritual of atonement, secretly carried out by his own kin. The ceremony involves the sacrifice of an animal and scratching of the killer's shoulder with a fishing spear to let blood flow. The kinsmen on both sides are not permitted to partake of food or drink together, for to do so might cause contamination leading to death. This taboo must continue until full settlement and possibly longer. One of the leading chiefs, who knows of the case, then intervenes in person or through a representative of his lineage.[45]

The chief calls upon the relatives of the deceased, sacrifices a bull known as *mior de kueng,* "the bull of peace settlement," and asks the aggrieved group to take an oath to keep peace and avoid vengeance. The chief then asks the relatives of the killer to collect the blood-wealth cattle and hand them over to him. On an appointed day, the two groups are convened and a bull known as *mior de yuom,* "the bull of the bone" is sacrificed. The chief, or one of his relatives acting on his behalf, takes the bones of the right hind leg of the animal, breaks them in two, and throws one half to the killer's kin group and the other to the relatives of the

44. Usually only six head of cattle are demanded for such subsequent death, provided that at the time the injury was inflicted the guilty party had paid the sheep of *athiol* and the cow calf of *nhiem* to express his regrets and good wishes for the injured person's recovery. If this had not been done, more, usually ten, cattle are demanded.

45. If death was caused by spear, which is usually the case in subtribal wars, the jurisdiction lies with the Pajok lineage; if by clubs, the jurisdiction is that of the Dhiendior, who now have the vice-presidency and deputy paramount chieftainship.

deceased, who must at first show resistance and wage a mock attack of vengeance on the killer's relatives until they are persuaded by the chief to accept the settlement. Being interested in the well-being of all his people, the chief receives one cow from the bloodwealth and hands over the rest to the relatives of the deceased, who usually leave them to increase undivided. A portion is then used to marry a wife for the deceased while the rest are distributed in a manner similar to that of bride-wealth distribution.[46]

Thus, the divine aspect of well-being, the pivotal role of the chiefly lineages, the need for forceful retaliation prompted by their traditional ineffectiveness, and the realization of the higher value of unity and harmony they stand for, all combine in the ceremonies of feud settlement.

Bodily Injuries

Depending on their gravity, personal injuries not resulting in death are matters of less concern to the respective groups of the conflicting parties than cases of homicide. If the injuries are severe, they may provoke group violence; otherwise the matter is usually settled by the court's imposing liability for reasonable compensation on the assailant, with or without penal sanctions.

For certain injuries[47] there are traditional rates of compensation to guide the court in reaching a settlement which will restore the equilibrium. If an injury is inflicted by a kinsman, payment takes the form of a conciliation fee rather than compensation.

The Dinka often fear the reoccurrence of injuries caused by means other than spears, and a considerable number of deaths are attributed to early injuries. In such a case, it would be material that *athiol* and *riem* cattle had been paid as a demonstration of good will toward the injured. Under such circumstances, compensation in the event of death is reduced. This anticipation of full loss of life is significant, for while injury deserves compensation for its own sake, focus is on elimination or weakening of life as a self-generating force. For this reason, cattle paid in compensation of injury are ideally used for marriage.[48]

46. Lienhardt, *Divinity* 287–88.

47. Such as injuries to the eyes, limbs, or teeth.

48. The primary importance of procreative potential in relation to other aspects of bodily well-being is illustrated by the story about which several songs have been composed. The singer, courter of Akuol, one of the two girls critically appraised in the songs, went with the girls to sleep in a hut. According to Dinka customs, such sharing of the room, and perhaps the bed, is not necessarily acceptance of sexual intercourse. While in the hut, he attempted to force sexual intercourse with Akuol, who cried to her friend Ajok for help. Ajok in turn squeezed the genitals of the

Such proceeds as are recoverable in personal injuries usually benefit the family as a whole, for if the injured party is a dependent member (e.g. a child or a wife), he or she would be expected to hand the compensation over to the guardian, and if he is a family head, then it naturally forms part of the family property. Indeed, if there is no material dispute as to the facts, the Dinka practice is that the case may be brought by one member of the family for the benefit of all or of any one member agreed upon by the family.

Liability for Animals

Here we are concerned only with liability for personal injuries by animals. The distinction between domesticated animals (*domitae naturae*) and naturally tamed animals (*mansuetae naturae*) on the one hand and those naturally wild (*ferae naturae*) on the other seems to be recognized by the Dinka. Liability attaches to the former and not to the latter. Apart from the obvious case of intentional injuries, the owner of a domesticated or naturally tame animal is liable if he knows of a dangerous propensity in his animal and unreasonably neglects to keep it under control or to give adequate warning to those within its zone of danger. Such duty of care as is imposed seems to focus on imminent danger. Thus, an aggressive cow is stopped when attacking a stranger or the stranger is warned against the cow on the spot. Similarly, a vicious dog has to be held when a stranger approaches or else he is told to avoid the danger. But a cow which is aggressive against people is not necessarily kept from grazing with the herds in fear of its harming passersby. Nor is an occasionally vicious dog necessarily kept in bondage. But if a cow becomes ferocious, which is extremely rare, or a dog becomes rabid, which is more common, it must be destroyed.

In cases of negligence, reasonable damages are assessed by the court depending on the harm done, the degree of negligence, and the relations of the parties. In the absence of negligence, strict but nominal liability is imposed and the injuring animal itself must be surrendered to the injured party or, if he has been killed, to his heirs as nominal damages. The beast is then used for marriage, either immediately or after it has increased naturally or through trade.

The Dinka do not impose liability for naturally wild animals, perhaps because they are normally not owned. However, a form of ownership and possession attaches to a number of wild creatures which symbolize

---

man to subdue him and hurt him grievously. In the songs, the injured man complains to the chiefs about the possibility of not begetting children and not about any other injury.

divinities, *yieth:* these are snakes, lions, hyenas, crocodiles, and the like. An animal representing a divinity of a lineage must not be killed by that lineage. The animal may be aware of the friendliness of that particular group and be gentle toward them. Thus, cases are cited in which lions have come into the homes of their "relatives" and received offerings of cows, sheep, or goats.[49]

Snakes, some of which are deadly, are frequently accommodated by the Dinka, given butter to lick, anointed and patted on the back, carefully persuaded to enter a basket, and moved by the elder members of the family, who declare that it is for the snakes' own protection from accidental injury that they are returned to the forest. While the snakes are often gentle under such treatment, they are unpredictable and may bite when a person stumbles over them or frightens them in any manner. When a snake or any other totemic animal injures a person related to it, the matter is easily explained in terms of a wrong committed by that person or any other member of his kin group. Propitiation of the creature and ritual atonement must be done.

The protection of totemic creatures is one of the early areas of conflict between the educated Dinkas and their traditional elders. The snake being the symbol of evil in Christian mythology,[50] young converts often demonstrated their repudiation of paganism by killing them, thus causing spiritual contamination manifested in illness. In one case, an educated youth killed a puff adder near the hut of his stepmother whose agnatic kin group was related to the snake. The four daughters of his stepmother immediately fell ill with identical symptoms. Their illness was divined to be the curse of the puff adder's death, and sacrifices and dedications were recommended and carried out. Soon after this was done, the girls recovered. The writer knows a number of cases in which schoolchildren were beaten by their seniors for violating the taboo against injuring totemic creatures.

Thus, while the Dinka consider domestic animals as causing nominal liability to their owners unless the owners are negligent, their religious

49. An instance appearing to have been witnessed by the European who reported it in the Sudan Intelligence Report confirms the point: "The appearance of a seven-foot-long crocodile in the Dinka village of Aweil (Northern District, Bahr-el-Ghazal) gave occasion for a practical demonstration of totemistic belief. The animal was taken charge of by a man of the crocodile totem. It spent the night in his hut, where it was supplied with a meal of two goats. It showed no fear and made no attempt to attack human beings. In the morning it was escorted by its host back to the swamp, killing and eating a cat on the way. An analogous case occurred some years ago in the same district, when a man clearly demonstrated his ability to call birds." Quoted in Lienhardt, *Divinity* 132.

50. But Ngok Dinka word for snake is *ke rac,* "bad thing." In many Dinka dialects it is called *ke piny,* "thing of the ground."

thought makes them accommodate dangerous creatures, a practice which leaves these creatures secure and generally in harmony with men. But should this harmony fail and they injure people, the Dinka attach no liability to injuries caused by them. Instead, liability is imposed on their "hosts" if they are injured, for not only must they be ceremonially buried, if killed, but sacrifices and dedications must be made to them in compensation and appeasement.

Employment of Curers

The Dinka are still largely dependent on magical cures, and while divine rulers like the chiefs and prophets do not demand remuneration (though they may welcome gifts), other curers are generally professionals who are paid for their services. They undertake divination, blessing, herbal treatment, and other aspects of doctoring people, crops, and livestock. Their skills are mostly hereditary, but there is training within the group.

When summoned, a diviner or a curer often demands an honorarium *in limine*, in the form of a coin, a spear, or an animal.[51] The actual fee for services performed differs according to the nature of the work done and the seriousness of the illness. It varies from money to cattle of ranging value. Generally speaking, the fee is paid after the services have been effectively performed, but the amount is agreed upon before services are rendered; where the employer is a man of wealth and the practitioner has no reason to fear default in payment, he may render services on the tacit understanding that a reasonable amount will be paid.[52] Some well-reputed functionaries refuse payment prior to their success. Others, even when successful, insist on only a nominal fee without which the divinities and ancestors are believed to be unhelpful.

The less interested in material gain a curer is, the more divine he is believed to be and the more popular his services are. But since the success of their cure is generally a condition precedent to their remuneration and recognition, all diviners and curers are very concerned about their patients' recovery. If successful, a curer may sue for his fee, and the court will enforce it. If the fee has not been agreed upon before the practitioner's performance, the court will assess a reasonable amount. Usually,

51. As *agut piny,* the coin, the spear, or cow of "hitting the earth" derived from the practice of darting on the ground a sacred spear to assist divination or cure. Unless this is paid, not only is the practitioner likely to withhold his services, but if his services are rendered, they are believed to be ineffective.

52. Some professionals, however, insist on advance payment. This may be the result of fear that they will not be paid or an attempt to avoid what appears to be a universal practice that no fee is paid if the treatment is unsuccessful.

disputes do not arise over the value or the payment of the fee, because the practitioner's dissatisfaction is believed to invoke his divinities and ancestors to undo the cure or inflict a new evil on the cured person or another relative. Moreover, there is always the expectation that his services will be needed again. Since the success of divination and cure is largely dependent on the diviner's understanding of the social environment of the patient and the possible psychological cause of discord, a local diviner, who would be more interested in such a social environment for this very purpose, could be more effective than a stranger.

The fact that traditionally the Dinka pay for medical services has recently been extended to modern medicine and has been taken advantage of by local medical assistants and dressers. The Dinka sometimes pay for services due to them from the state. The projection of traditional practices and the abuse of these by the modern medical men have so interacted that many Dinka genuinely believe that a government medical officer cannot treat a person adequately unless paid. Some keep out of hospitals on account of this belief. Others receive services they have no faith in because they have offered no money to their doctors. The writer is informed by medical practitioners that they are not infrequently forced to treat Dinka patients in their private clinics instead of in state clinics on the request of the patients. A doctor is then obliged either to receive much less than his services are worth because of the poverty of the people, or to render cheaper and less useful services than the patient could have received in a state clinic without payment.

"Health Insurance"

The Dinka practice of paying for medical services should not imply lack of public "health insurance" in traditional society. But it does show the importance of individualism in lineal communalism. Health protection for the individual took various forms, from ancestral protection to mutual dependence among the living. We noted earlier that a Dinka sometimes calls upon illness to visit him so that he may distinguish between those who are "really his people" and those who are not. A sick, aged, or otherwise needy person must be taken care of by his relatives or friends. The circle of such people usually extends to neighbors and even strangers, with reciprocity as one of the incentives.[53]

53. The Dinka illustrate the importance of reciprocity with a story. A black cobra bit Ajang's cow and Ajang speared the cobra with the spear of Akol Adiangbar, a neighbor. The cobra escaped down a hole in an anthill, still carrying the spear. Akol was told of the incident and was offered another spear as compensation. He refused the spear and insisted that his own spear be returned. Ajang therefore tunneled into the anthill, looking for the spear, until he reached the land of the cobras. There

During illness, a man in need of an animal to sacrifice may seize any-one's beast, if necessary without the owner's consent, though on the understanding that it will be compensated for. A similar practice is authorized where there is danger of starvation, or any case of imminent peril. Collective herding and protection against external animal or hu-man aggression are other aspects of mutual dependence.

Legitimate obligations to fellowmen, relatives, friends, neighbors, or even strangers may be enforced by the chief. A sick or poor man without an able relative may trust in the chief's care. In numerous ways, the chief himself receives material benefits from his people so that they in-directly finance such public services.

---

he found the cow which the cobra had bitten and the cobra itself, bearing the wound inflicted by the spear. Asked what he had come for, he asked for the spear, putting himself at their mercy and insisting that they either kill him, keep him there, or return the spear, but that he would never return without it. Impressed by his courage, the cobras decided to return the spear and give him a girl for his wife. While Ajang was away from home, Akol Adiangbar's son died, and Akol buried him in Ajang's sleeping hide. When Ajang returned, he insisted that his hide be returned. Akol dug up his son from the grave and returned the hide to Ajang. The two clans of Ajang and Akol Adiangbar, Pajieng and Padiangbar, respectively, are now believed to be still enemies. Their enmity, referred to as *ater koth biok,* "the feud in which the hide was dug from the grave," is often used by the Dinka to illustrate the evils that can result from lack of reciprocity.

9. Skills

Formal education, through which modern skills are largely introduced, is minimal among the Dinka. Existing skills are predominantly traditional and aimed at the continuance of familial occupations. The list of skills on the traditional level includes mediation, agriculture, animal husbandry, ritual performances, magicoreligious practices, smithery, fishing, building, weaving, leather-working, dancing, singing, warring, and so on. Some skills are specialized, while others are broadly shared as part of the generally self-sufficient way of life. The more specialized a skill, the more important its hereditary value, although the undifferentiated skills are also hereditary in the more general sense of Dinka cultural continuity. Thus, cattle being the most important part of Dinka wealth process, the skill of herding and caring for cattle is broadly shared and is an important part of a child's education. The richer in cattle a family is, the more emphasized the skills associated with them.

Whether a skill is specialized or widespread, its function as an aspect of cultural continuity implies following the ways of the forebears. The lead of the divinities and ancestors in this respect is most apparent in skills of a religious nature. Even in those skills which appear to be individual, a man finds it elating to identify his ability with those of the senior members of his lineage back to his forefathers. Because of this attachment to the past, Dinka skills are interfused with mysticism and monopolized by those for whom they are an ancient legacy, and skills which are highly embued with mysticism tend to be viewed as hereditary.

The hierarchy of efficiency and role differentiation in the particular skills of a family depends upon a member's position in the family. The living patriarch, who is closest to the source of skills in the ancestors, should be the most qualified. Furthermore, he has had longer experience. Even when certain aspects of a profession need the vitality of youth, the patriarch retains overall supervision.

The wife is usually not incorporated into the skills of her marital family though she may carry over those of her agnatic kin which she may then pass on to posterity. Although certain skills overlap, there is division of roles on the basis of sex. Thus, while men take care of cattle, women milk cows and make dairy products. When sowing, men often prepare the ground while women plant the seeds. When both are doing the same work, as is often the case in weeding, women work part-time and return home to cook and keep the house. Women are largely independent in the exercise of their specialized skills and in instructing their children, especially daughters, in these skills, but men retain the overall supervisory function.

In order that the children, particularly the sons, may perpetuate the family skills, much attention is given to their practicing these skills from early days. As little children, their games are designed to teach them the skills required in adult Dinka life. They build little huts, make cattle out of mud or shells, and build cattle camps fully equipped with fires and cow-dung smoke to keep out flies; they have mock courtships and marriages; they constitute moots for the settling of cattle cases and emphasize the ability to speak both as a litigant and a persuasive judge. As they grow older, children transfer these games into reality. Their work is concentrated on attending to animals. At about the age of seven, they are given charge of sheep and goats and at about the age of twelve start cattle care.[1] A Dinka boy, if old enough, does most of the work connected with cattle. Once initiated, he stops most of these tasks and only herds in far-off grazing areas where conditions may be too hazardous for children. Even there, adult males concern themselves only with the daily tasks of taking cattle to grazing, driving the cattle when the camp moves, and protecting the herds from wild animals. Their preoccupation is with the esthetic aspect of cattle, especially their personality oxen.

If, as we maintain, skills are primarily conditioned by the cultural continuity implicit in the principle of perpetual identity and influence, then the children must practice these skills for educational purposes, and those who have founded families must practice them as their familial responsibility. This leaves the youth, who are generally unmarried, poised between having learned the skills as apprentices or servants to their seniors and taking charge of what they have learned by later stepping into the shoes of these seniors. This situation produces consequences comparable to the familiar implications of family stratification. Young males

1. They release the animals in the morning, clean the cattlebyre or other place where the animals are kept, spread the cow dung to dry from which smoke fires are made, attend to the sheep and goats or to calves in order to keep them from sucking the cows during grazing, and, if older, to the cows, return and tether the animals, each by its own rope and to its own peg, tether the calves after the cows have been milked and the calves have nursed, and keep alert in the night to attend to any animal which might break a peg or a rope or in any manner need attendance.

conceive of childhood labor as "slavery" and initiation into adulthood, despite its agony, as a way out. It is followed by a period of "hibernation" in which the skills most desired are the esthetic skills which give pleasure to the practitioner and win him popularity and respect in society—especially among girls. Thus a young man maximizes his chances in marriage, and may succeed however limited his wealth, since bride-wealth requirements are sometimes frustrated by such acts as elopement and impregnation. It is for this reason that young men preoccupy themselves with personality oxen and the skills of singing and dancing, among others. Uninitiated youth are not permitted to own personality oxen officially, nor may they sing in display of oxen, or dance with girls formally belonging to an age set corresponding to an initiated male age set.

This preoccupation with cattle is accompanied by the creativity in ox names expressed by young men when they reach manhood through initiation. Once initiated, a young man is identified with an ox which he proudly displays before the girls. He praises his ox in songs and delights in inventing new ways of describing its appearance and introducing in songs imagery suited to the color of the ox.[2] Creating new imagery based upon the color names of cattle is regarded as a mark of intelligence in a young man, and attempted by all.

When a young man displays his ox at home or in the cattle camp, singing about it as he precedes or follows it, the attention of the girls is drawn as much to the ox and the songs as to the man. That singing and dancing are directed toward enhancing one's position in society is apparent in these lines from a young man's song.

> When I dance to the drums
> I do not dance with a girl who goes out of step;
> The confused girl who disrupts harmony
> The bad [fisherman's] girl who lives on the river [3]

2. The kind of imagery used in connection with ox names may be illustrated by the following names of a man with a black personality-ox. In song, or when addressed by his age mates as a gesture of intimacy, as well as by strangers as a sign of respect, it is not the simple name for a black ox, *micar*, which will be used, but some metaphoric expression based on that color which he or his intimate friend will have invented. He may be referred to as *tim atiep*, "tree with a shade"; or *kor acom*, "the lion of snails," after the black ibis which hunts for snails; or *bun anyaar*, "thicket of the buffalo," suggesting the darkness of the forest where the buffalo resides; or *akiu yak thok*, "one who cries in the drought," after *ajiec*, a small black bird which gives its characteristic cries during this time of the year; or *areec luk*, "spoiler of the court assembly," after the clouds which threaten a downpour of rain and force a court meeting, which is usually held under a tree, to break.

3. Although all Dinkas fish to supplement their diet, they look down on those tribes which live primarily on fishing and have few or no cattle. See Seligman and Seligman, *Pagan Tribes of the Nilotic Sudan* 136 (1932).

I dance with a polished girl.
I am not simple at dancing to the drums
I am not simple
I am never challenged in our tribe
I cannot be dribbled around at Akot
I am respected as an officer.

The significance of songs as a method of influence in society is discussed elsewhere. It will suffice here to emphasize their distinct importance as a skill of Dinka youth, an aspect of the youths' overindulgence in unproductive skills.[4] Nor is this the only problem. The dissatisfaction of youth expresses itself in excessive fighting and bravery, as in hunting wild animals, going to distant places [5] in search of objects of beautification such as beads or ivory, or felling trees for drums.[6]

Because of the importance of continuity in skills, young men identify their skills with those of their elders and ancestors, even though their roles vary. Since these predecessors once occupied the positions held by their descendants, the identification is justified. In the following song, a young man praises his lineage members and himself for their skill in cattle husbandry and singing.

Mabor, our herds are herds tethered by Maper Nyok
Lorjok of my father is skilled in making ropes
Polcok is an ancient expert on cattle
Atekbai is an ancient expert on cattle

4. That the period following initiation but prior to marriage is one of leisure and engagement in unproductive skills is further illustrated by the custom of lying, *toc* (mentioned in Chapter 7, pp. 248–49, 276), which most young men practice annually and for the sake of which they seek exemption from cultivation and other menial tasks at home.

5. Usually to other Dinka tribes. In the past, when communications were more difficult, such journeys might take weeks or months.

6. In this song, an age set boasts of its expedition to a distant land to fell a tree for a drum and sees the achievement as an object of envy by other age sets.

I took my axe
I, Yom
I walked toward the land of the Arabs
And brought the ebony of Pakir
I brought the drum
And the tribes made jealous noises,
I brought it into the land.
I hate careless talk
A man will defecate at my hands
I, Yom,
Tribes with dark bottoms
If it were not for Kwol d'Arob
I would do what the tribes do not know.

Rumaduer has a surpassing skill
I am told that I do not know cattle
Has any of my fathers ever been ignorant of cattle
Or do you hear it only of me?
When I rise to sing, gossipers disappear [7]
When I rise to sing, gossipers disperse
I rise and make them swallow their words
My words are never questioned
I am like my forefathers.
I rise to be seen by my fathers
I rise to be seen by my ancient fathers
And also by the passersby
I rise to be seen walking with pride
As it was in the distant past
Where our clan was born.

One even takes pride in identifying one's violent disposition with that of his father or ancestor. This is often expressed in terms of reference to one's father or ancestor as "the bull." [8]

Unproductivity is also observed in the skills of women. Apart from their occupation in the utilitarian skills in which they complement men, a large portion of their time is consumed with esthetic skills: for instance, decorating gourds, sifters, leather skirts, bell collars, and the like. Like young men and girls, married women are preoccupied with personality oxen, singing, and dancing.[9] The negative implications of women's skills are also observable in ritual practices. Most black-magic skills are attributed to women, including "diabolical" possession.[10]

With the impact of Western civilization, the skill practices of the Dinka are undergoing change. This is most observable among traditional and modern youth. The former now see and seek new individual opportunities in a cash economy; but because of the association of young men's position with esthetic rather than menial or materially productive skills as a way of influencing women, they prefer to go to far-off areas for temporary employment to avoid being seen by Dinka girls. Rather than produce cash crops in their own land, they sometimes go and culti-

7. His skill cannot be questioned.

8. See the song cited in Chapter 3 (p. 57) in which a young man praised his father not only for his warring skill but for his disrespect for authority, a mark of courage common only among youth warrior groups.

9. There are occupations such as milking which only children and women do.

10. We saw above in Chapter 3 (p. 35) that possession is common among women. This may be called a form of skill. The fact that possession shows a kind of self-assertion is confirmed by the obviously deprived condition of most women who become possessed, whatever the nature of their deprivation. Rarely does a woman without apparent malcontent become possessed.

vate for pay in distant rural areas. In towns they learn new skills, some of which they feel very ashamed of when judged by traditional criteria. A man who had lived in town as a prisoner sings about the humiliating conditions of urban labor and the scornful attitude of the girls in the tribe. Since he labored as a prisoner, it is not clear how working for money applies to him. We may assume that he sings as an observer.

> The words of the girls of our land are bad
> They are displeasing to God
> God is the person who settles words
> Even if words are hidden.
> Money likes slavery
> Slavery in which gentlemen are ordered
> Money likes slavery,
> Even if it is taken to a graveyard,
> The heart will follow.
> Dinkas are right to complain
> I exclaimed, O my ox Miyar
> There is something which stinks like a latrine [11]
> Dinkas are right to complain.

Modern skills, though very limited, have been introduced through education. Literacy was the first. Initially, people disapproved of education. When the first school in Abyei was opened in 1944, almost all the pupils were sons or relatives of the paramount chief and his deputies. Even in these circles, there was much criticism—especially of the paramount chief, who sent all his sons to school. The idea of leaving no one to look after cattle was a matter for criticism. This attitude changed when the Dinka began to see the fruits of education—the miraculous wonders of reading and writing. For the Dinka, who see linkage between skills and mysticism, writing and reading quickly assumed a respected place in their value system.[12] The educated themselves came to feel the superiority of their skills,[13] and sometimes saw the new skills as additions

11. He presumably worked in the sanitation department emptying latrine buckets.

12. This song is about Nyong de Kwol, son of the late chief Kwol Arob and one of the earliest to receive modern education. The singer praises his skill in writing receipts and his usefulness in the collection of the poll tax.

> Nyong de Kwol Dorjok
> The gentlemen has put the land in order.
> He writes four lines on paper
> And ends with a zigzag, [signature]
> The poll tax comes to an easy end
> Like a falling tree.

13. In addition to reading and writing, other modern skills in such fields as carpentry, building, and agriculture were introduced, especially by Christian missionaries who set up technical schools for that particular purpose.

rather than as substitutes for the traditional skills, thus using them to augment their position in traditional society. A young man sings of himself,

> The gentleman knows all things
> He knows how to write
> And knows how to dance to the drums
> Both are things of pride
> I have put tassels on my bull.

While alienation from traditional society generally resulted from modern education, it was less acute during the colonial era when Dinka teachers ran the schools. They attempted to orient school activities to certain aspects of Dinka social conditions. As demonstrated by this school poem, children were encouraged to cultivate.[14]

> See my field
> I grew it myself
> The rain watered it for me
> And made it grow.
> I see it every morning
> I see it every evening
> And when I see it
> It adds to the pleasure of my heart.

Many children who left school during those days were able to practice traditional skills but lacked adequate modern skills to introduce any improvements.

Most educated Dinkas today, however, do not conceive of their skills as complementary to Dinka society but as revolutionary. Consequently, they are at variance with the system. This appears to be the result of the academic emphasis in education and the relative disregard of practical skills suited to environmental requirements. The detachment of school activities from the child's background tends to increase the gulf between the old and the new skills, a fact which encourages migration into urban centers where there are fewer or less satisfactory jobs than the educational system appears to promise.

On the tribal level, the chief occupies the role of the tribal patriarch and thus assumes the chiefly skills of his family's heritage. The elders represent the collectivity of their fathers, while the warrior groups form the collectivity of family youth. The negative implications of generational classification are also reflected on the tribal level. The warrior

14. Composed by a schoolteacher and collectively recited by the pupils on special occasions.

"father" gives his group an intensive training in various skills after their initiation, most important of which is warring. A warrior age set sings:

> I killed a man and cut him open
> I am Miyar who has subdued the tribes.
> I am a child instructed by his father
> I proudly display myself with my spears.

Certain changes have been introduced into warrior skills and among the more important of these is their utilization in constructive work. This was first seen as governmental compulsion, but later became accepted as expressing traditional warrior spirit. The war dance song shows the competitiveness of subtribal warrior groups in this respect.

> I pride myself with my axe
> I Miyan, I am like a lion
> The storm arose
> The tribe with a hollow bottom
> Held the road for ten days
> The castrated bull has gone
> I took over the road from a tired man
> . . . .
> Tribes, surrender
> I have defeated you
> I, Malek, the flank of the Almighty
> Even if it rains
> I continue working on the road of the government
> Other tribes work with their hearts at home

Of building, an age set sings:

> I took the axe in the evening
> I walked in the dark all night
> I was on my way to Paandit
> I, Mithiang, the Mighty One
> I was away for two days
> Then I returned, I did not delay
> Ours is the land of Deng Arialbeek [15]
> I built the home of the *jur* [16]

The revolutionary perspectives and migratory practices of educated youth from the tribe also have repercussions. An official report evaluates the education system from which evolved such perspectives.

15. Praise name for Deng Majok.
16. This term which normally means "foreigner" is also used to mean "government" and is sometimes applied to the chief.

It has been claimed by all authorities that our system of education in the South is at the root of all the problems and should thus be subjected to a searching review and severe reappraisal. Students are offered a standard of living unobtainable outside the schools' walls, along with this they are offered academic education for the most part allowing them little or no future employment opportunities. The result of such education is the mass production of misfits, making it impossible for them to go back to the family . . . to develop their village community and not qualifying them to find jobs in town, a horde of discontented odd men out for mischief.[17]

Their reaction against unemployment and quantitatively and qualitatively inadequate education causes them to react against governmental educational policies, especially the abolishment of missionary education in the South.

According to this official government report, the Abboud military regime sent a mission to the South in 1964 to determine "unemployment among the Southerners; to register the skilled unemployed and place them in suitable vacancies in the South and if possible in the North; and to impress upon employers in the Public and Private Sectors the Government Policy of giving priority of employment in the South to the Southerners." [18] The minister of local government stated that the mission was necessitated by the fact that "unemployment . . . is detrimental to the life of the citizens in this part." [19] The mission found that unemployment in the South was due mainly to three things: "lack of skills in the lower categories of labourer; lack of qualifications among those boys who did not complete their education; meager chances of employment and the need to extend schemes, agricultural and industrial, to absorb the unemployed." [20] The solution suggested by the mission was a complete reversal of the situation.

A quick remedy for this is the conversion of all (or at least 80%) of the intermediate schools to technical education. Academic education should be stopped and new schools . . . should be diverted to technical education. This will help the Southerners to help themselves and shall reserve for the country a huge reservoir of skilled manpower, whose interests and future might well be in the North.[21]

The extremism of the measures recommended would alter the unemployment point of conflict but would not alleviate the South-North

17. Sudan Government, *Survey Report of Employment of Southerners* 4 (1964).
18. Id. at 1.
19. Ibid.
20. Id. at 2.
21. Id. at 4.

problem, whose complexity is not fully comprehended by the report. Other factors must be weighed. For instance, as a pioneer, the educated Southerner demands much more recognition than his Northern counterpart. Instead, he gets much less out of his education because of the emphasis given to Arabic and seniority. Besides, the eradication of the British colonial system which had solidified itself in the South, and the substitution of the Northern regime, is seen by the educated Southerner as "flinging back the South to the nineteenth century," [22] and widening the gulf between the school and the home. The use of vernacular in the elementary schools and the staffing of these schools with local teachers used to mitigate the problem during the colonial era.

The change also means that, in the eyes of the Northerner, a Southerner educated in the old system is "half-educated." "The old Southern elite," write Southern political leaders, "is now considered illiterate by Sudanese standards, and one of the main difficulties confronting Southerners in finding jobs is a lack of knowledge of how to read and write Arabic." [23] This evaluation of the educated Southerner is officially acknowledged. Thus, a government publication says, "The missions' failure to educate and project inherent Southern talent according to required standard has had, of course, its aftereffects. Many of their school graduates were not qualified to compete for work." [24] Most of the Southern leadership was educated in missionary schools. The change has led to the loss of vital resources for aiding education in the south, a fact which was demonstrated by the take-over of missionary schools and the expulsion of all foreign missionaries. Furthermore, the educated Southerner sees a colonial element in the molding of his culture to suit the rulers' objectives. These factors combine to cause the oppositional reaction of the South. From the Northern Sudanese standpoint, even those improvements which they plan cannot be implemented without order. Southerners, on the other hand, regard improvement as a condition for order. Violence and disorder are thus perpetuated.

SKILLS AND THE LAW

The law applicable to skills pervades the Dinka legal process as a whole, and is generally expressed in various kinds of contracts and quasi-contracts with indulgences and deprivations reflecting the stratification discussed above. The ritual skill of the chief in the settlement of feuds calls for a fee of a cow or cows. A form of litigation fee which used to be

22. Deng and Oduho, *The Problems of the Southern Sudan* 47 (1962).
23. Ibid.
24. Sudan Government, *Basic Facts about the Southern Provinces of the Sudan* 6 (1964).

paid by the winning party as a token of gratitude for the settlement of a conflict is now fixed and is paid to the government. In property, there are various contracts involving such skills as building and thatching the roof of houses, clearing a field for cultivation, seeding, and herding of cattle. In certain cases, such as building a cattle byre or a hut, there are fixed rates for pay. Apart from employing individuals, one may request the services of a group of people or an age set to do collective service for pay. Usually, such pay is more social than economic. A person may have beer brewed, an ox slaughtered, or food made for the group hired. In rectitude and well-being, the examples are employment of diviners and medicine men. These are usually more substantially compensated, though some demand little or no fee. Divination similarly creates a contract in enlightenment insofar as the diviner enlightens the patient and his relatives about the source of illness or any misfortune. Experts in song composition are employed to compose certain types of songs which it is permissible to have another person compose for one. Even in affection, *aben,* an expert on winning a girl's affection for another man, is usually regarded as one who must be given much for his services. This is often put as an expression of appreciation and affection for his assistance but is comparable to a fee. In short, whether there is a clearly expressed agreement or not, the exercise of skills in the interest of another results in an obligation to pay for services rendered. There are, of course, free services, but these are generally not issues for litigation.

10. Enlightenment

THE PROCESS OF ENLIGHTENMENT

Enlightenment in the Sudan, whether on the traditional or the modern level, is a strategic value geared toward the dominance of a certain culture and those privileged by it: traditionally, it is Dinka heritage which dominated, while on the national level it is predominantly Arab civilization complemented by Western knowledge. In both cases, not only are there discrepancies in the sharing of knowledge but there are also clashes between the elites endowed with the various kinds of knowledge.

Traditional enlightenment must be seen in the context of the era before literacy where such media as the radio, newspapers, books, and the cinema were lacking. Residence was spread over a wide area with a few families situated several miles from the next settlement. People traveled on foot to carry news. Special alarms warning of war or attack by wild animals were transmitted from one settlement to another by identifiable cries [1] or drums. These conditions are expressed in the past tense but to a large extent they still exist.

Among the Dinka, enlightenment in general is expressed in the term *nginy wel*, "knowledge of the words." This entails not only accumulation of information, but also the use of that information to attain social objectives. To say that "a man knows the words," *raan angic wel*, may mean that he is wise, generally well informed, considerate, tactful, and diplomatic. A man who does not know the words, *raan kuc wel*, is unwise, aggressive, obstreperous, and insensitive.

"Knowledge of the words" is a function of education. Traditional education largely consists of information transmitted orally from generation to generation. *Weet*, which may be translated as "instruction," or "advice," or "information," is an educational process which is both informative and normative. *Kuen wel*, "counting the words," is another example of such normatively informative expressions: used as an intransitive verb, to *weet* or *kuen* a person is to enlighten him in human

---

1. The vocal quality of the sounds and the flatness and openness of the land may be factors in making this possible.

relations with the view to influencing him to follow a righteous way; *weet, kuen,* and related terms imply inequality between the instructor and the instructed. Information on the community process is a phenomenon, but especially revered is information pertaining to past trends. *Wel theer,* "ancient words," or *ka theer,* "ancient things," are often the subject matter of the most solemn conversations between younger men and their seniors. The farther back in time oral literature goes, the more mythical and the more revered it becomes. This introduces us to the peak of the enlightenment process, the mythical participants.

Since the mythical participants are not involved in day-to-day education, their primacy is not easily apparent. However, their participation depends on the remembrance and application of their principles in contemporary society. Knowledge of these principles is therefore crucial. While this knowledge is passed on by the living, the mythicals themselves are believed to intervene from time to time to enlighten the living elders, revealing their instructions through various media such as dreams and divination.

The primacy of the mythical participants in enlightenment may be exemplified by the significance in enlightenment of the divinity Ring (Flesh). The Dinka sometimes allege that in the past only God, Nhialic, and Ring supported them, though now many other deities have become recognized. Ring, however, remains the most superior divinity, second only to God. "Flesh," said a Dinka, "is one word. Our ancestors knew about it, but none knew everything about it. Some say they have seen it. It is a single word, it is of the further past, what has always been." [2] By "one word," *Wet tok,* the Dinka mean the true and decisive word. Although the Dinka admire knowledge of many words, and eloquence, they prize the ability to be effective with few words. A man who speaks in the name of Flesh is supposed to be absolutely truthful. This knowledge is symbolized by illumination through which man sees and comes to know. The only man-made source of illumination in Dinka society is fire, hence the connection between the divinity Flesh and fire. In a line from a hymn, "The Flesh kindles like Fire." [3] The divinity Deng (also the word for "rain"), is also associated with illumination, the connection being that one of the characteristic phenomena of Deng is "lightning." [4]

Divinities are only examples of the enlightening function of all mythical participants, including ancestors, whether manifested in dreams,

2. Lienhardt, *Divinity* 138.

3. Id. at 136, 227.

4. The same power of illumination is attributed to Garang, who is alleged to be the son of Deng: "The shining master has fallen to the byre / Garang, son of Deng." Id. at 87.

divination, or otherwise. Divine enlightenment is the source of the primacy of the family head, who has received knowledge from the mythicals and must transmit it to his dependents. The patriarch's supremacy in enlightenment is also attributable to his being the link between the family and the outside world. He is the first to receive information from an incomer, and by representing the family in outside processes, he is exposed to wider information.

The wife-mother's enlightenment is partially acquired in her agnatic home and is further enhanced by her knowledge of the tradition of her marital family, especially important for the education of the children. Children's education is more directly the function of their mothers during their early years. In the case of daughters, the mother's educational role continues since she prepares them to be wives and even guides them after marriage.

Children are, of course, the central recipients of education. The subject matter of learning comprises such things as recitation of the father's genealogy, identification of various clan divinities and their emblems, cattle life, and the code of Dinka behavior according to status and relationship. Apart from direct instructions, the children learn through such media as songs, fairy tales, legends, and play. The special importance of songs in the comprehensive sense—that is, words, rhythm, and occasion of presentation—is impressed upon a child very early. A child is often held and jounced up and down to the rhythm of songs to represent dancing. When a child cries, the mother, or whoever is taking care of it, sings at the top of her voice, even in the middle of the night, with the music of a gourd containing grain accompanying her. Such songs are by no means lullabies in the Western sense. Any song is a lullaby to the Dinka. Since words do not provide the whole meaning of a Dinka song, it is not too important that a child is below the age of cognition. But the educational significance of Dinka songs goes beyond the child's being put to sleep. While such a child may successfully be made to sleep, older children and adults sharing the hut and in other village huts are almost inevitably awakened. They may enjoy the songs or at least listen to them. As Dinka songs cover a wide range of subjects, a cognizant child gets deep insight into Dinka culture by listening to such songs in the quietness of rural nights.

Fairy tales have an even more direct impact on children. The traditional import of such tales is epitomized by their opening expression, *ke ghon ka,* literally "There is an ancient event." In these stories, the world of beasts and inanimate beings is often welded with that of man. Fairy tales in Ngok Dinka dialect are known as *koor,* "lion," because of the frequency with which lions appear in them. In fairy tales the Dinka are not much concerned with approximating truth literally.[5] The truth included is a truth which though superficially unreal has a deeper reality. Where human conditions interact with natural phenomena, the world must be envisioned as a unity in which all animate and inanimate beings communicate, as illustrated by this popular story.

There is an ancient event. A small rain fell at the beginning of the rainy season. Angiic, a small brown ant, came out to cool her children after the rain, because the world had become cool. When Angiic returned to her hut to do something, the bird called Awec came and ate her children. As he was about to take the last child, Angiic saw him and when she saw such a thing, she poured salty water into his eyes. Awec ran blindly and sat on a tree called Adhot. Adhot fell because Awec was too heavy for him. He injured an animal called Amuk which was under him. Amuk ran wildly and entered the house of the chief's wife. He knocked down the chief's wife who was sitting in the doorway and broke her teeth. He was then brought to court to be tried.

Asked by the court why he had done such a thing, Amuk [sic passim] said, "How can such a big tree as Adhot fall on a person and the person still be expected not to run?" The court turned to Adhot and asked him why he had fallen on Amuk. In answer he said, "How can a person not fall when a big bird like Awec sits on him?" The court turned to Awec, saying, "Why did you sit on Adhot when you knew that he too had breath?" Awec answered, "How can a person see when such a lot of salty water is poured into his eyes? I did not know where I was sitting." Angiic was then asked why she had poured salty water into Awec's eyes, and she answered, "When it had rained, bringing a cool breeze, how could one be expected not to cool her children in the breeze? And when one's children are then eaten, how can one be expected not to pour salty water on the person eating them?" "Rain, why did you fall?" asked the court. "When peoples' crops were drying up," answered the rain, "how could a person be asked not to water them?" The court asked the crops, "Why did you go dry?" In answer, the crops said, "When a big animal like Arou (the tortoise) excretes on people, how can they be expected not to dry up?" "Arou," the court asked, "are crops your forest where you excrete?" Arou answered, "When such a large animal like Akoon, the elephant, steps on a person unexpectedly,

5. That these tales are not subjected to the usual test of "truth" is indicated by the fact that the Dinka do not speak of "telling" a fairy tale but of *paar*, which is a difficult word to translate but carries the notion of uncertainty. *Paar* is very close to guessing, but implies an attempt to construct as much of the truth as is possible from the scanty information available.

how could he be expected not to excrete?" Then Akoon was asked, "Why did you step on Arou?" He answered, "When drums beat so loud and well, how could a person be expected not to run to the dance? I was overwhelmed by the happiness of dancing and knew nothing else." Then the court addressed the drum, "Why did you sound so loud and well?" In answer the drum said, "When a person is beaten by two drumsticks (*theet*) how can he help sounding loud and well?" The court asked the drumsticks, "Why did you beat the drum?" The sticks gave no answer and were held liable.

The Dinka who told the story said that the explanation of the sticks, to the effect that they had been forced to beat the drum, was not accepted, thus evidencing how, in confrontation with "the others," people favor themselves. Nonetheless, man is aware of his interaction and interdependence with the cosmic totality. This is why animals, birds, trees, and the like still symbolize divinities and are considered "relatives." Thus, even though he favors himself, a Dinka sees himself as a part, and not a master, of the cosmic totality.

Fairy tales have a variety of themes in which virtue often prevails. Courage and strength form a recurrent theme of fairy tales. One of the most common themes is the need for affection and for curtailing cowives and stepkin jealousies.[6]

There are also legends which tell of the achievement of various participants, thus providing a basis for the status of their living representatives, as a class or as individuals. Many songs are about claims to status by virtue of such past achievements. Often, the younger generations, who have not yet fully assumed adult roles, brag the most about

6. A man had two wives. The first had remained for long without a child and the husband decided to marry again. Although he did not divorce his first wife, he was becoming less fond of her in consequence of her barrenness. Soon after her marriage, the second wife became pregnant. She delivered in the middle of the night and the senior wife did the midwifery. As the mother slept, the senior wife took the baby, put it in a gourd, and threw it in the river, leaving a piece of wood in its place. The next morning she reported that the wife had given birth to a piece of wood but that she had not wanted to distress her with the truth. The mother was confronted with the "truth" and although she insisted that she herself had heard the baby cry, she was not believed. On account of this she was divorced. Her agnatic kin also rejected her as a carrier of a curse. Everywhere she turned, she was rebuffed until one maternal aunt took pity on her and took her in. Since giving birth, she had worn torn clothes and had covered herself with dirt as do mourning women. Meanwhile, her son had been carried by the water to a distant shore where he had been picked up and brought up by an old couple as their son. When he was fully grown, they told him what they knew about him. One day a singing young man spoke in his ox song of a woman who was alleged to have borne a piece of wood despite her assertion that she had had a living child. Later, the man went over to the singer to investigate the story. He then found his mother.

the achievements of their legendary heroes to satisfy their own egos and enhance their status. Nor need these heroes be men of distinction. Each young man praises his ancestors even if their deeds have no real importance to the society at large.

There is no contradiction between the exaltation of aggressiveness in seniors by their juniors and the peacefulness of their role, since contemporary elders themselves were once youth who occupied the role now filled by their sons, and the sons' success rests in part on living up to the vitality the seniors had when they were young. It is customary for a Dinka father to critically appraise his son in such comparative terms as "When I was your age, I used to . . ." or "At your age, I would never have . . ."

Another means of education for children is games. Apart from the pleasures children derive from them, games give an insight into the Dinka way of life. In addition to acting such adult roles as cattle-camp life, family life, litigation, initiation, singing, dancing, and war, children play games which are less obviously informative but which are of great educational value. In a game played in the river, one child dives into the water surrounded by a circle of children beating with their hands on the water above him and singing:

> The diviner of that day
> From where did he come?
> The diviner of Man-Nyandeeng
> Is that why my mother must die
> My little buffalo, rest in peace
> Mankind is passing on.

On the face of it, the song is not clear. The allegation may be that the diviner is evil and may bring a curse on the mother. He may, however, have divined the source of evil and concluded that death is inevitable. The actions of the children are clear because they symbolize burial. Whatever interpretation children give to the words is not as important as the effect of the game in its full context including the melody, the rhythm, and the mystery of a person under water. This prepares fertile soil for the roots of Dinka magicoreligious beliefs in the face of such tragedies as death.

In another game, children sit in a circle beating their hands on their laps while singing. In the center is a girl who sits on her knees as she vigorously hops and turns, beating the ground with her hands and participating in this song.

> Girl who is courted
> Girl who is courted in the camp of Riaungol [7]

7. Usually, the ox name of the father of the girl in the center.

Riaungol has refused,
"I will not number my herds.
My head is confused
Which of my daughters is that?
Is that not my daughter, Abul? [8]
Abul, my curse will fall on you.
Bring the cow Rial
With it, my butter gourd will shake
Girl for whom I have never received a cow."
Father, claim your cause
Claim your cause, O father
The gentleman has a cool heart
The gentleman has smiles of perfect teeth.

As the girl in the center increases her excitement, she may become possessed. Should that happen, she retires from the game, or the game is stopped. Again, it is apparent that the words in themselves do not say much, but the whole context imprints on the child such vital norms as the spiritual danger of not giving senior relatives their share in bride wealth, and diabolical possession as evidence of the guilt that such a situation causes to women. At the same time, the game provides a kind of training to dispose the girl psychologically to inducing or being receptive to possession in appropriate circumstances.

Conditioned by his education, a child follows in the footsteps of his parents. It is from his father that a son acquires such knowledge as is necessary for a male of his age. While he is a child this is bound to emphasize agressiveness. In addition to collective male characteristics, the Dinka attribute most good or evil traits to a man's father, or male ancestor, and many are the songs to this effect.[9] The mother's influence over her daughter being greater, a daughter tends to reflect her.[10] This becomes collectivized into a role of characteristic attributes, of which the negatives, such as jealousies arising from women's inferior status, have already been discussed.

The education of a child is not confined to his agnatic group. Since ties with the maternal kin are highly regarded, it is important that a child should be informed about them. He should know the people in those circles; he must revere their divinities and their ancestral heritage. This knowledge is acquired very early during the years of weaning when a child is sent to live with the maternal kin. This partly explains the psychological power of the maternal kin, seen by the Dinka in magico-religious terms.

8. Usually, the name of the girl in the center.
9. Especially in ox songs.
10. For example, a man whose wife had been seduced by a fisherman attributes the evil to the fact that she had been educated by a promiscuous mother.

The conformity of traditional enlightenment is now confronted with the innovating disposition of modern formal education and other enlightenment media such as the radio, television, newspapers, libraries, museums, and cinemas. Here, the pioneering work of the Christian missionaries is important. Children returned from their schools with new concepts of God, new human horizons, new medicine, new interpretation of the cosmic reality—in short, new enlightenment. The missionaries produced local newspapers in the vernacular, showed documentary movies in schools and villages, and demonstrated the magic of phonographs and tape recorders. They introduced their pupils and others to modern enlightenment, although the number reached was minimal. Formal education coexisted with other measures so that the educated were also the most enlightened. To these young men, the past was darkness. This is one of many songs in point.

> Learning is good, learning is good
> Brothers in learning, let us rise early
> Learning is good.
> Open our minds, masters,
> Open our minds
> Our minds like rocks, our minds like rocks
> Our minds like earth, our minds like earth
> We shall enlighten them with rays of light.

But to the traditionalists, the new light was meaningless. Many questioned education especially because it was closely associated with a new faith they dismissed as alien. Even the miracle of reading and writing was considered a tool for expressing one's natural knowledge and was not in itself a source of new knowledge. It was not until later that traditionalists saw the wealth of knowledge and even wisdom that came with education. But since education was not oriented to the child's living conditions, modern knowledge and wisdom were seen by both the traditionalists and the educated to be well apart from traditional knowledge and wisdom. Enlightenment caused disparity of participation and culture in that few people obtained new enlightenment which was unoriented to the receiving culture. The participants and cultures were thus envisioned as opponents, with the new elite attempting to change the situation and the traditionalists resisting change.

Determined to assert the leading role their education had conditioned them to expect, the educated children saw revolution as the alternative. With respect to the whole country, K. D. D. Henderson, once a province governor, wrote about youthful social revolution that came with modern education.

It was for the disappearance of this traditional discipline that the Sudanese used to blame us bitterly. Our whole twentieth century educational bias was against it, with its anxiety that a boy be taught to think for himself. "The young men," they would say, "are drunk with freedom and pride of learning. They scorn their parents, they argue with the elders, they smoke and drink and live . . . [a wretched life], and of course they are against the government." [11]

The Sudanese elders overstated the point, for on the family level individuals became subdued by traditional discipline and repressed revolutionary expressions. Thus, while most Sudanese, especially Muslim Northerners coming from families where drinking and smoking is prohibited, find emancipation in breaking the family code, they usually dare not do so in of their family elders. If asked, they misrepresent the truth. A certain amount of cooperation exists in which the educated guide their traditional seniors. But the nonutilization of their qualifications in a satisfactory way forces the educated members of the family into modern urban centers where often new associations come into being among people with similar problems. Whether they form new associations or not, whether they direct their energies constructively or destructively, these men generally suffer the frustrations of being disassociated from tradition and of confronting a new type of tradition. This failure to provide adequate substitutes and bridges led Henderson to scrutinize education in both England and the Sudan.

The snag about our present system of education is that the product is so often rootless and unhappy, without ballast and without respect for anything in the way of principles of traditions. The exceptions, in the Sudan and in England, are the products of sound homes, not of the system.[12]

Apart from the formally educated, young men who migrate for temporary employment in towns also acquire enlightenment through such media as the radio, the cinema, night classes, and, more recently, television. They, too, find alleviation from the traditional milieu and consider themselves better qualified for modernization. However, the generational disqualifications of traditional society work against them even more than against the formally educated. Consequently, conflicts between them and their elders occur which contribute to their moving continuously between the town and the village. As these young men become enlightened, they develop an interest in politics and acquire

11. Henderson, *Sudan Reminiscences* 17 (1962).
12. Ibid.

the attitudes of the educated but sometimes express them with greater militancy, in accordance with their traditional predisposition.

The preceding roles, both traditional and modern, have been largely concerned with family participants extending into broader contexts. Through such extensions, identical stratification is encountered on the tribal and the national levels with the chiefs, warrior age sets, and the educated as a group. With the guidance of mythical participants, the chief is the most enlightened of the traditionals. The divinity Flesh "is the principal inspiration of masters of the fishing-spear, the grounds of their ability ideally to 'light the way,' to pronounce and define truth, to prevail in prayers, and to reconcile conflicting groups and interests." [13] They are likened to lamps, the sun, the moon, and such sources of illumination.[14] At night, when everyone is asleep, masters of the spear are said to "call the word," *long col,* indicating their request for knowledge from their mythical participants. Flesh sometimes reveals itself to them in the form of light. One master of the fishing spear explained his experience to Dr. Lienhardt.

> Flesh comes to me in the middle of the night, when I am lying in my hut and the hut is dark. Flesh shines like a lamp for me, like a fire. I can see my wife and everything in the hut as if there were a lamp there. Others do not see a light like this, it is only those who have the divinity Flesh who see it lighting up the hut at night.[15]

This assertion is by no means unique. The symbolic spears of the Ngok chief of the Flesh, also the modern government chief, are believed to

13. Lienhardt, *Divinity* 146.

14. It is in this sense the Kwol, in a story cited earlier (see p. 47), was referred to as the "Ray to lighten," "the light to brighten the path," and "The light to show . . . the words of truth." A Dinka said to Dr. Lienhardt: "See our masters of the fishing spear are like that lamp. Look now it gives a bright light, and we see each other and we see what is on the table. If the lamp goes dim, we shall not see each other so well, and we shall not see what is on the table . . . (God) made our masters of the fishing spear thus to be the lamps of the Dinka." Lienhardt, *Divinity* 140.

These lines further show how prophets and God are associated with illumination.

My father Cyer Deng, hold the country
A master like the sun and moon.
. . . .
My father Longar is like a comet
Encircles the earth like a rainbow
. . . .
Divinity my father, you are prayed to
You will wax like the moon

Id. at 141.

15. Ibid.

shine brightly at night if they want to draw the chief's attention to something. The information may accompany the illumination or the illumination may draw his attention, with the truth subsequently divined.[16]

This divine enlightenment of the chief is complemented by his intergroup and crosscultural involvements. He is the meeting point of all the most knowledgeable and wise of his tribe, both traditional and modern. Perhaps only he among traditionals owns a radio. Since his family pioneered education, members of his family are among the more educated. Through them he receives information from the enlightenment media accessible to them. During his not infrequent visits to urban centers, he has access to some of these (e.g. the cinema). To justify their leadership, members of chiefly lineages must have and demonstrate knowledge of their lineage history with its heroism. These often constitute the subject matter of their youth songs. It is also the chiefly clans who remember the longest genealogies. However, the chief and his subordinates remain unenlightened in modern terms.

Enlightenment for youth age sets is concerned with such areas of their activities as cattle life, war, relations between the sexes, and other esthetic preoccupations discussed earlier. As we have seen on the family level, the educated class is not enlightened about tradition and the resources of its modern education are wasted or are inadequately utilized. On the family level, we saw the problems resulting from lack of educational orientation and the fact that the system does not offer what it promises.[17] We have also seen how the resulting revolutionary spirit is repressed on the family level but finds more freedom on the collective level in the modern sector. As this takes the form of South-North politics, enlightenment suffers in consequence. Missionary education has disappeared. The Arabization of the system and the evaluation of enlightenment in Arabic terms make the Southerner who is educated under the old system a less

16. The association of the divinity Flesh with enlightenment and illumination is further demonstrated by the control it is supposed to have over sight. When offended, Ring is sometimes believed to inflict harm on the eyesight of the wrongdoer or one of his relatives. Conversely, he is expected to alleviate eye trouble when called upon. This song is by a man who recovered from an eye disease.

> I called upon the Flesh and Deng
> Divinities of clan Payaath
> Why have you let me stray?
> Dhunydhuol nearly peeled my eyes
> Like the male of the grouse
> My eye would shimmer like a hippo.

17. The clash between the desire for change and the continuity at all levels produces the attitude expressed in the lines from the schoolboy's collective song quoted (pp. 62–63).

enlightened person in official eyes than he believes himself to be. He opposes the introduction of enlightenment which will undermine both his traditional and his acquired cultures. Northern teachers feel insecure in the South, and most Southern schools are closed. The television, newspapers, government information publications, and the like turn to propaganda instead of enlightenment. The only Southern newspaper, *The Vigilant,* unable to repress its anti-North undertones, suffers governmental restrictions. Communications between North and South became impeded and, within the South, break down. The educated Southerner, "the eyes" of his people, if not himself a rebel or a refugee, feels safer in the North. Most inhabitants of the villages thus remain isolated and unenlightened.

ENLIGHTENMENT AND THE LAW

Enlightenment is a strategic value for the continuance of ancestral heritage, and is primarily acquired during early childhood through family education. While education is basically homogeneous, each descent group has its own heritage. Consequently, there is neither tribe-wide formal education nor prescriptions regarding the type of education a child should receive at home. There are instructions to age sets on a subtribal basis, but these are essentially an extension of the familial instructions through the age-set father and are therefore private.

The principles of education on both descent and territorial levels are sanctioned by the authority of whoever is in control according to the context, but because of conformity or the privacy of the system, matters arising out of these principles are not brought to community-wide decision matters, though such matters as who should be the guardian of a child in case of a divorce come to court. This means that according to Dinka customary law, education is utilized for community purposes, but only through the narrower descent and age-set circles. As in skills, the higher up one is on the hierarchal ladder, the more pivotal he is in education. It is this ancestral conditioning of traditional education that modern education has radically undermined.

Part IV

Policy Considerations

11. Evaluation and Recommendations

In view of the dynamics of Western modernity with its notions of freedom and equality, our analysis indicates that future trends are bound to emphasize emancipation, either by the recognized decision-makers or by the self-assertion of the less privileged participants. In the former case, the law may emancipate the subjugated but it may also become entrenched in inconsistencies and paradoxes. In the latter case, the deprived are likely to use strategies fundamentally repugnant to both the posited goal of human dignity and the traditional goals of unity and harmony. Legal intervention in the interest of both the society and the conflicting parties is necessary.

It has often been maintained that the ethnocentric pride of the Dinka makes them impervious to alien cultures. It should, however, be remembered that Dinka conservatism has been primarily one of assimilation rather than of total rejection of alien ways. The fact that they are among the least touched by modernization may well be due more to the preservative policies of British colonialism than to Dinka conservatism. One may venture to say that because of their intense pride the Dinka could be very receptive to change provided that they see its advantages and that it augments their sense of dignity rather than violates it. The desire to so integrate themselves into the higher strata of the new situation as to justify the carry-over of their indigenous sense of dignity and pride may indeed make them more adaptable than those who are more subserviently disposed to change. We have demonstrated in the foregoing chapters that the Dinka are not only changeable, but that change in their society has already intensified and a modern-interest group has emerged. On the other hand we have also demonstrated that threat to their sense of dignity and pride in the transitional period is having grave repercussions.

Although modernization among the Dinka still needs to be hastened, the bases of traditional value shaping and sharing are giving way to the forces of modernization and novel forms of turmoil. Traditionally, the deprived participants displayed negative attitudes but did not openly oppose their deprivers. The traditional pattern of class distinction which was preserved by *cieng* accommodated two seemingly opposed phenomena, stratification and egalitarianism. The application of identical principles to all value institutions produced identical stratifications throughout the value-institutional structures, with each pyramid supported by the other. Thus, the notion of unity and harmony opposed any self-assertiveness that might destroy the equilibrium. The interdependence of welfare values and deference values had the same effect.

While attempting to remedy stagnation and certain aspects of inequity in the traditional system, modern decision-makers have not manipulated the fundamental principles of tradition to minimize disruption. In some respects they have attempted to utilize traditional practices, but without appreciating their underlying principles. For example, the attitude of the colonial administrators with respect to power was that "We must learn to regard [the chiefs] as members of a natural aristocracy, the traditional rulers of the country, and we must treat them as such. . . . They are the holders of local authority . . . the authority of birth." [1] Yet, there was no understanding, or application of the traditional checks and balances on the chief.[2] The chief in his turn did not know or observe the intricate controls on power in the cultural background of his colonial benefactors. This mutual misapprehension was aggravated by the fact that colonial administration did not impart Western ideas and institutions of democracy as a whole. Thus, totalitarian tendencies were encouraged in a community which, while stratified, was essentially democratic in that the paramount chief reflected tribal conscience. This was what Professor Lucy Mair had in mind when she described the traditional authority of Dinka chiefs in these somewhat normatively ambiguous terms.

> Some of them were regarded with great respect, and they were described in ideal terms as if they were rulers who commanded obedience. But one has to take such descriptions with some skepticism because, in a world as wicked as the one we live in, it is rarely possible to command obedience without commanding force.[3]

The abuse of power against which Professor Mair was warning has already developed. The chief is now both the beneficiary and the victim of such abuses. The institution itself is now threatened by them.

1. Eboue, "Memorandum on Native Administration," 25 *Sudan Notes and Records* 44 (1943).

2. Since his power in traditional society was spiritual, it could not be effective unless legitimately exercised. The exception is where an object of a chief's feared curse suffers from an unnecessary guilt conscience.

3. Mair, *Primitive Government* 48 (1962).

Another example of unbalanced development caused by improper guidance has been in the introduction of alien religions. Their agents did not make allowance for the religion of the Dinka. Traditional beliefs were condemned with little regard to whether they were repugnant to the basic principles of the new religion, and if blatantly contrary to it, they were denounced with vehemence. For instance, a polygynous convert was required to divorce his wives. In a society where family solidarity is so important, this, though not ill-intended, doomed the wives and offspring to much suffering. We have also seen the conflict between a converted schoolboy and his parents, who are normally his model of behavior. It is one thing to learn that one's parents lack scientific knowledge; but it is quite another thing to be taught that they are "sinners." We saw how a parent would pray for his spiritually lost son. Indulgent as the parent may be, can children bring about change persuasively if they are regarded as spiritual outcasts? Furthermore, since in Dinka religious thought people do not face God only as individuals but also as interdependent members of groups, a religion which teaches that on the day of "final judgment" everyone will stand for himself and only for himself is bound to create conflict in the Dinka child. People's names are of immense importance for identification of lineage, clan, environment, personality, etc., among the Dinka. Yet Christian or Muslim names, whose meaning and pronunciation were beyond the ability of most parents, were given to the converts.

Religion is a guide to man in a world he does not understand. It is his interpretation of his life and environment,[4] his protection against the feeling of insecurity involved in the unknown that surrounds him. This feeling of insecurity need not be an apprehension of the Christian or Mohammedan Hell, nor need it be any form of physical pain. It lies in the long chain of events connected with life: where we came from, what we are doing, and where we are going—all the features of the mystery of the unknown that entangles us. What is unknown to a man varies with prevailing circumstances in a given time and space, but in all cases his religion decorates his ignorance and makes it beautiful and peaceful. It is his experience and the experience of those who preceded him—back to those too distant to recall. It is part of his culture. To import new religion in toto is to superimpose a culture—a culture that is necessarily assumed superior because it is God-given, and therefore must prevail should there be a conflict.[5] Such a conflict can have very serious implications.

4. This was the conclusion of the conference on High God in Africa which was held in Ibadan, December 14–18, 1964 and in which the writer participated.

5. This is, for instance, the case with Islamic law in the Sudan. In practice, however, various judicial techniques which are in accordance with Islamic law have

The attitude of the modernizers in the field of religion also illustrates how modern education and the new values that accompanied it overlooked most of the essential values of traditional society.

In most of Africa, national governments still seek to build on tradition, although there is a tendency to identify modernization with Westernization. Some believe that the modernizing process should take time, while others want a sudden change, but most are convinced that the end product will be full Westernization. When the desire to fuse Western values with those of the recipients is expressed, it is often dismissed as wishful thinking.[6] The African who has been introduced to the new value context is often inclined to repudiate traditional values. The desire for culture synthesis of the primordial with the novel occurs among only a small fraction of the educated. Modernizing schemes are often hurriedly executed with little or no consideration of the totality of the social value context.

The dynamics of cultural diffusion show that such proposed transformation is impossible, since selection among values is inevitable. Professor Herskovits explained the inevitability of mutual influence from crosscultural interaction.

> Whenever peoples having different customs come together, they modify their ways by taking something from those with whom they newly meet. They may take over much or little, according to the nature or the intensity of the contact, or the degree to which the two cultures have elements in common, or differ in basic orientations. But they never take over or ignore all; some change is inevitable.[7]

To hold otherwise is to ignore, indeed distort, history and the variety of civilizations. "The quest for modernity," it has been observed, "depends upon and often finds support in the ideological upsurge of traditionalism. In this process, tradition may be changed, stretched, and modified, but a unified and nationalized society makes great use of the traditional

---

been used to modernize it. The Moslems would not consider this a change but a realization of Islamic law. For such changes see, for example, Anderson, "The Modernization of Islamic Law in the Sudan," *Sudan Law Journal and Reports* 292 (1960).

6. In 1960, Professor David McClelland expressed this opinion to a conference on the Social Consequences of Industrialization: "Western and Eastern intellectuals observe that they sincerely hope the East can develop economically without losing the many valuable features of its existing way of life and institutions. . . . Such statements, while admirable in many ways, are simply incompatible with the psychological requirements for a modern society." Quoted in Busia, *The Challenge of Africa* 136 (1962).

7. Herskovits, *The Human Factor in Changing Africa* 6 (1962).

in its search for a consensual base to development." [8] If indiscriminate transformation is attempted, or selection is not articulated, the benefits remain minimal, the society becomes torn between the old and the new, and disintegration results. The conviction that planned cultural synthesis is impossible frustrates hope, blocks initiative, and nourishes fatalism. Even if development of all societies, whether Western or not, were to follow the same path, the expectation of identical outcomes assumes that followers have to experience the hazards and losses the pioneers experienced. It fails to see that the full contribution of a pioneer lies not only in his great achievements, but also in his failures. Through these failures, pioneers provide those who follow with an opportunity to avoid some of their predecessors' difficulties and increase gains.

Also important in today's international scene are the outmoded racial implications of holding that there is but one road to development. Such theories "make Anglo-American . . . forms either inevitable or necessarily superior outcomes of . . . processes in new nations." [9] As Africans become significant participants in the world community, such a hypothesis, even if held by the Africans themselves, can only nurse ill feelings and impair fruitful cooperation. Although Africans have tended to confuse equality with identity, a reaction is occurring which is bound to increase. "African nationalists have been compelled to develop their own counter-attack; to answer the myth of African barbarism and backwardness with the counter-myth of African civilization and achievement." [10] Such embitterment can have serious repercussions on the global scale. Nor is the attempt to rediscover indigenous cultures very fruitful. Often only those who are thoroughly assimilated into new cultural contexts and are therefore the least authentic in traditional terms feel the strains of a lost identity and advocate its rediscovery. These people are prone to misrepresent tradition either out of ignorance or deliberately in order to justify preconceived ideologies to mobilize nationalistic sentiments. Such modern concepts as "primitive communism," "communalism," "one-party system," "African socialism," and the like may be genuine attempts to translate tradition into modern language,[11] but usually the original meaning is lost in the outcome.

Lack of integration in the process of acculturation also affects the merit of adopted Western value-institutional elements. They are often

8. Gusfield, "Tradition and Modernity," 72 *American Journal of Sociology* 351, 358 (1967).

9. Ibid.

10. Quoted in Hodgkin, *Nationalism in Colonial Africa* 173 (1957). See also Senghor, *Nationhood and the African Road to Socialism* 90–96 (1963); Nkrumah, *Consciencism* 62–63 (1964); Broakway, *African Socialism* 30–32 (1963).

11. Hodgkin, op. cit. supra note 10. See also Sigmund, *The Ideologies of the Developing Nations* 170–80, 193–94, 197–202 (1963).

selected out of their value context, with the result that they are divorced
from the checks and balances underlying their forms in Western culture.
This mode of importation, coupled with pretended dismissal of traditional values and institutions—for it is never quite successful—is open
to gross perversions.

It is often popularly asserted that technological progress has outpaced
the development of social conditions and spiritual culture. The threat
of this imbalance is more acute in Africa because of the unique intensity
of change.

Professor Radcliffe-Brown wrote of the disillusionments inherent in
the African social revolution.

> The first changes are inevitably destructive of the existing system
> of obligations. How far the disruption of the existing order will
> go, and in what direction reconstruction will be attempted or pos-
> sible, it is at present impossible to judge. The sanctions provided by
> kinship systems for the control of conduct are being weakened. New
> sanctions, of which the agents are the policemen and the priest or
> minister of the Church, are proving much less effective than those
> of which the agents were kinsmen speaking with the authority of
> the ancestors behind.[12]

The words "inevitably destructive" are appropriate only insofar as some
degree of destruction of the old system must occur in the process of
change. However, the destruction presently experienced is the outcome
of faulty guidance.

In the Sudan, disregard for tradition has been carried even further
by the successors to colonialism. While the sophisticated Northerner is
tending more toward Western civilization,[13] the course of change for the
Negroid South is being diverted to Arab-Islamic civilization before
Western modernization. Southern culture is thus subjected to two stereo-
typed notions of modernization, Arabization and Westernization. Traditional decision-makers are exploited to ensure the dominance of the
national decision-makers and their Arab-Islamic civilization. After a
long and intimate relationship with Africans, Professor Herskovits wrote
of ". . . the frustrations and resentments that result when any people
live under a system where freedom of action, as defined by the values
and ends of their culture, is denied them. These reactions occur whether
the denials are enforced by those among their own people who have
seized power, or are imposed by foreign peoples; but they are especially

12. Radcliffe-Brown, "Introduction to the Analysis of Kinship System," Bell and
Vogel, eds., *A Modern Introduction to the Family* 246–47 (1960).

13. See Trimingham, *The Christian Approach to Islam in the Sudan* 61 (1948).

acute, as the world has found to its costs, when the factor of racial differences enters." [14]

As new and unintegrated indulgences are introduced to an isolated few, a new form of stratification is introduced and participants at all levels of social organization become overtly competitive, with the deprived becoming opposed to the system and the indulged pledged to support it. As there are two sets of indulgences and deprivations due to the existence of modern and traditional value systems, stratifications are complex and so is the battle over values.

Opposition between the deprived and the deprivers, though originating in the family, is severely repressed within it. It is more manifest on the tribal level, and most apparent on the national level. As the deprivers become threatened by opposition, they intensify deprivations, thereby nourishing further opposition.

In these circumstances, it is easy to foresee the paradoxes of emancipation in terms of extremes. Educated Southern and Northern youths whom the writer interviewed not only predicted but preferred a social revolution, if necessary with violence, "to get things going." [15] This attitude is implicit in the ideologies of communism and the Muslim brotherhood, which between them gain the adherence of most of the Northern youth.[16] A feature of this radicalism was revealed in 1964 when long-lasting student opposition to General Ibrahim Abboud's military dictatorship culminated in a successful revolution which was initiated by the university students and supported by a mass uprising. For a time the youth had the upper hand and produced some emancipating trends. The voting age was lowered from twenty-one to eighteen. Women were granted the right to vote. There was (and still is) a cry for the abolition of the institution of chieftaincy. The influence of youth in both the South and the North brought the two groups closer to an understanding, since their identical value positions make them more appreciative of each others' problems. Communism was not only legalized but had a great impact on national and foreign policies; Muslim brotherhood had similar influence on the government. The change was short-lived. With elections, traditional factions resumed control. Communism was outlawed and its representatives from the graduates' constituencies were unseated from Parliament. The graduates' constituencies themselves were abolished as discrimination in favor of the educated. But the struggle is not over; an even fiercer attempt at a take-over is to be expected.

14. Herskovits, op. cit. supra note 7, at viii.

15. This revolutionary disposition was illustrated earlier in songs by schoolchildren against tradition. See Chapter 3, pp. 62–63.

16. The point is made by K. D. D. Henderson in his *Sudan Reminiscences* 17 (1962).

This predicted assumption of power is bound to affect Southern chiefs severely, as the attitude of the educated Southerners who will assume control is bound to differ from that of the educated Northerners who inherited power from the British. The latter were largely from urban communities and were not directly subjected to tribal chiefs as agents of colonial administration. Not only will there be an attempt to deprive chiefs of power, but a more pervasive paradox in the shaping and sharing of power is expected. Though striving to free the people from domination by both the Northerners and chiefs, the educated class is likely to assume that the people are not competent to exercise their freedom adequately and will concentrate power in itself to speed up development, allegedly in the interest of the people.

It may be argued that the gulf between the educated class and the chiefs will narrow as the present generation of older chiefs gives way to its sons who will be most likely to have education of one level or another. There are already a few cases where educated sons or relatives of chiefs have succeeded, and in the North some of them are quite well educated. There are, however, a few points to consider in this prediction. First, one should distinguish the situation in the North from that in the South where the government's policy of chiefs remaining traditional is articulated toward the objective of keeping the demands of the tribes minimal in the modern context. Therefore, examples of highly educated chiefs in the North do not suffice for predicting trends in the South. Even if educated individuals were to succeed as chiefs, as long as the philosophy behind the succession of an educated person is one of stepping into his father's shoes, the effect of education will continue to be minimized. It was said earlier that members of youth warrior sets who succeed their elders suddenly acquire the outlook of their elders. Educated individuals who become chiefs as exceptions and not because of a redefinition of qualifications are likely to do the same. The case of the thirty-one-year-old Sayed Saddig El Mahdi, son of the late Imam of the Ansar sect whose party, the Umma, now rules, shows how conflict with elders over power can frustrate one's role and may destroy one's career. Although the problem has its roots in the succession of Sayed El Hadi to the Imamship as the most senior member of the family instead of Saddig (who, though the eldest son of the late Imam, was, among other reasons, considered too modern), the immediate crises occurred over Saddig's attempt, as president of the Umma party, to separate politics from religion against the will of his uncle, the patron of the party. The conflict led to the fall of Saddig's wing of the party and of Saddig as the prime minister. He even lost his seat in Parliament. There is an even more fundamental reason why the mere succession of educated individuals will not change the system. As long as primogeniture, rather than merit, is the rule, seniority will continue to be a dominant factor. In any case, the fact that the present generation of illiterate chiefs will be succeeded by the educated does not imply a change in the emphasis on age. The young too grow old.[17]

The preceding are examples of what is likely to result from unguided or ill-guided emancipation. It is this situation which calls for the carefully balanced intervention of the law as an instrument of social policy.

TRANSITIONAL INTEGRATION AS AN ALTERNATIVE

The law must integrate competing interests if justice is to be done and modernizing forces are to be mobilized with minimum disruption. The strategy of transitional integration seeks to adjust the bases and therefore the roles of the traditional system without punishing those whom it benefits the most.

With the emergence of policy sciences of development, chances for achieving the goals we have outlined are maximized. As Professor Lasswell put it, "The goals of development are gaining clarity; the historical perspective deepens; the interdependence of conditioning factors is better understood; the probable lines of future growth are more fully projected; and the invention and evaluation of policies designed to maximize or at least to achieve minimum results are forging ahead." [18] As Dr. Busia of Ghana correctly points out, "Planning is based on the assumption that some choice and control is possible." [19] In making this fundamental recommendation, the support of the government is assumed, for without it nothing but the predicted revolution could change the situation.

Since modernization of Dinka society is an objective and since tradition still predominates, special indulgences to the modernizers, actual or potential, are necessary to accelerate the process. However, reversing the situation into a new inequitable structure in which traditionals and their traditions are disregarded would only replace old problems with new ones.

Since modernization involves acculturation, the strategy expounded

17. In a system where forward-lookingness is the guiding principle, this is no problem except insofar as age becomes a factor in the realization of forward-lookingness. See p. 348 infra.

18. Lasswell, "The Policy Sciences of Development," 17 *World Politics* 286 (1965). For an example of guided change, see "the Vico's Case," 8 *American Behavioral Scientist* (1965). In particular, see Lasswell, "The Emerging Policy Sciences of Development," 8 *American Behavioral Scientist* 28 (1965).

19. Busia, *The Challenge of Africa* 138 (1962).

here particularizes the concept of cultural synthesis now espoused in Africa.[20] That cultural synthesis is not merely wishful thinking but a feasible objective has been persuasively argued by Dr. Busia.

> New ways must always be seen in the context of the old. The changes a society accepts at any given time are small relative to its total culture. There is always opportunity for a new cultural pattern borrowed from outside to be molded by the borrowers to make it fit into their own cultural milieu; in that sense, the borrowed cultural pattern becomes their own.
>
> A new musical instrument may be accepted, but it will probably be used to play tunes that fit into the rhythmic and all the other musical traditions of those who have borrowed it; ballroom dancing may be borrowed, but the quick multiple rhythms of "high life" may replace the gainly waltz; . . . For, in the context of culture, we are not dealing with forces that operate independently of human will.[21]

Preference for an idea or practice should not depend on its time sequence or its cultural origin. Instead, selection should be based on what is most conducive to articulated goals. This precludes perspectives and operations which attach merit to novelty, cling to the old merely because "it is that of our fathers," see world cultural diffusion only in terms of Westernization, or resent the process of crosscultural adoption as a threat to the romanticism of diversity. Undoubtedly the time factor may be complementary to the value content. It is evident, for instance, that technological improvement is continually in the limelight. Some cultural environments are richer than others in certain values. Since acculturation is a process of cultural compromises, the interacting cultures cannot be hybridized in their full identities except insofar as those aspects which are adopted should envision the whole cultural context from which they are borrowed. Nor is selection a momentary event. The essence of change means that what is required to suit the particular moment itself keeps changing. Hence the significance of the term "transitional integration." But a broad classification in terms of short-, middle-, and long-range forecasts may be adopted to facilitate planning. Some principles may be rejected immediately as opposed to postulated

20. In the words of Jahnhein Z. Jahn: "African intelligence wants to integrate into modern life only what seems valuable from the past. The goal is neither the traditional African nor the black European but the modern African. This means that a tradition seen rationally, whose values are made explicit and renewed, must assimilate these elements which modern times demand; and in this process the European elements are so transformed and adapted that a modern, viable African culture arises out of the whole." Jahn, *Muntu* 16 (1961).

21. Busia, op. cit. supra note 19, at 136–37.

goals. Others may be tolerable for short-term purposes, although ultimately eliminated. Certain principles may be judged conducive to other goals and should be retained. Alternatives may be invented which are unknown. In this integrating approach, the consequences of each proposed change should be seen in their indulging and depriving terms and in relation to all the value processes. The ultimate reconstruction should then be a choice of maximum advantage and minimum disadvantage. In addition, the prevention of the predicted disadvantages of change should be attempted.

Here, we focus on the Dinka, but postulates concerning their modernization may be applicable to more inclusive situations. Admittedly, it is still a matter of conjecture whether the convergence of various cultures in the world community process will ultimately result in an integrated "world culture" or "world civilization." However, in the light of present interaction not only between nations but also between individuals, it may be speculated that while diversities of one form or another will always continue, a form of world culture is likely to evolve. It was predicted earlier that the more the deprived become indulged in modern values, the more their demands for participation in modern values will be extended. Logically, this must put the global level within future horizons. Through the present and predicted interaction, the world has provided a meeting point between two great extremes—tradition and modernity. More important than the fact of interaction itself is the ultimate aim of fostering the unity of man on the global level. Future civilization will be an amalgam of the interacting individual cultures. The richness of this outcome will come from the variety of its ingredients and the degree to which they have complemented each other. This will be the natural result of human interaction, but it will be best achieved through conscious articulation and planning. Remote as folk cultures like that of the Dinka may seem, it is through such planning that individual cultures should make their contribution to the emergent world community. As a UNESCO committee expressed it, "The problem of international understanding is the problem of relations of cultures. From these relations must emerge a new world community of understanding and mutual respect." [22] In a world where the rate of change is unprecedented, the potentials of such convergence are on the brink of extinction. The challenge lies in how the extremes of our world can now meet, compromise, and create higher values.

There are many who believe that such a compromise is not only impracticable but also undesirable in that it will retard progress. The writer dissents from both views. Although integration is admittedly difficult to expound and practice, there is little doubt about its feasibil-

22. UNESCO, *Interrelations of Culture* (1953).

ity. The obstacle in the way of cooperation between the old and the new is always assumed to rest with the traditionals; it is believed that they do not wish to concede any of their traditional privileges. We have attempted to show that the disposition of the traditionals is more complex than this interpretation reveals. We have seen that the chiefs and elders consider the educated class as "their eyes," with which to see modern issues. Consequently, the educated sometimes represent their traditional elders in modern situations. However, because the legal system discourages such cooperation, the benefits of this disposition are kept minimal. We have seen that an educated family member representing his group to the chief or higher authorities is likely to be labeled as "too proud" or "presumptuous" and is most likely to clash with such authorities. We have also seen how traditional diviners and healers admit that both they and the modern doctors are concerned with the patient's well-being, and advise their patients to make use of modern medicine in addition to divination or traditional medicine. These are only examples showing that tradition and modernity are complementary and have become accepted by the traditionals as such. It is only if they see no compromising attitude among the moderns that the traditionals feel themselves threatened and slam the door.

The allegedly uncompromising attitude of the educated class is also more imagined by the traditionals than it is real. Their obedience and submissiveness to traditional seniors is evidence of their recognition of traditional authority and of a disposition to cooperate. We have seen that when they represent their elders they act as advisers and not as superiors. The growing revolutionary attitude of the educated is largely the result of their misconstruing the fears of the traditionals as indicative of basic incompatibility, thus impeding cooperation. If collaboration were given legal recognition and its workability demonstrated, these mutual suspicions could be reduced, if not removed. The idea of young men working together with elders is not new, since young men sometimes succeed their fathers. The difference is that whereas such young men step into the shoes of their seniors, to work on equal footing with elders, the suggested system would give them positions in their own right. But the difference would not be so fundamental as to be unacceptable to the elders.

The argument that transitional integration between tradition and modernity would retard progress is an extremism which this work seeks to avoid. If time minimizes the price of change and increases the net outcome, then time is a virtue which must not be sacrificed. Modernization is not an end in itself; it is an attempt at value maximization which, together with tradition, should be subordinated to the goal of human dignity. The suggested strategy of transitional integration favors modern traditionalism over traditionalism and modernity as such. Similarly, it favors modern traditionals as better equipped for strategic roles. The decision-maker's personal perspectives and skills should be molded in such a way as to enable him to transcend any one cultural context to appreciate other cultures from which adoption is desired. Transitional integration among the Ngok, while favoring modernization, seeks to balance the various interests of tradition and modernity which interact in participation, overriding goals, and value institutions.

Integration of Participants

In considering the basis of participation, whether in the family, the tribe, or the nation, special and general interests, which coexist in individuals and groups of various dimensions, should be balanced in the common interest. On the family level, this requires considering the interest of society in the family, the interest of family members as a union, and the individual interest of each member. Regard must be paid to the competing interests of those predisposed to modernization and those who seek to perpetuate the status quo. Although these interests are kept separate for the sake of clarity, they are interrelated.

Man is a social being, and the first unit he normally enters is the family. Although societies may disagree about the extent of the powers that should be reserved to the family, they generally agree about its indispensability.[23] In the interest of society, the law may protect the family against the outside world, or it may even restrain the members of the family themselves in order to maintain the family institution.

The family is an institution of mutual interest among its members. Where the consent of the parties is a condition precedent to marriage, the mere fact of marriage is an indication of the solidarity inherent in the family. Solidarity is implicit in the fact that husband and wife are essentially complementary. Children's survival and general well-being depend very largely on the parents, and they are a prolongation of the lives of their parents. Family solidarity is of vital significance in law. Whether an obligation is owed to society at large, to outsiders, or to other family members, solidarity may ease the burden of such an obligation. "If there is little solidarity within the family, the obligation imposed by the group may seem oppressive, but if there is a great deal of solidarity, the obligations may be accepted as natural and not even felt as obligations." [24] The law should be based on what is the normal, that is,

23. Article 16 of the Universal Declaration of Human Rights states that the family is the fundamental unit of society.
24. Bell and Vogel, "Toward a Framework of Functional Analysis of Family Behavior," *Modern Introduction to the Family* 24 (1960).

that the family is an entity which not only integrates, but also unifies its members with all their duties and rights.

Despite their fundamental solidarity, individual members of the family may differ and even conflict in their interests. Differing interests call for separate and individual protection against outsiders, and internally conflicting interests need to be secured as between the parties to the relationship. The tendency of Western law which comprises most of modern African law has been to afford more protection to the independent members by delimiting the interests of the head of the family originally envisioned in purely economic terms.[25] This, in the opinion of the writer, has been carried to an extreme which has tended to disrupt the unity and the harmony of the family. Theories and practices based on this disruptive emancipation have largely failed to put the family into a broad perspective. As Friedmann puts it, "the Western concept of family law contains fundamental tensions and conflicts, which recent social developments have brought to the surface and intensified."[26] Consequently, the main concern "is not in connection with securing interests in the domestic relations against the rest of the world but rather in connection with the conflicting interests of the parties to such relations among themselves."[27] If individual interests of the family are

25. Roscoe Pound summarized the development of the law governing the interests of family members: "In Roman law we find all manner of interests of dependent members of the household so treated as interests of the head of the household as to show that he is standing legally for a group of kindred which is or was the jural unit. Thus, for example, injury to dependent members of the household is legally cognizable as *iniuria* (insult) to the head; the *pater familias* is insulted through the intentional injury to one of his household. Accordingly the first stage in the legal development of this subject treats these interests solely as individual property interests of the head of the household. Before the law, the interest is one of substance— the interest of a freeman in the control of those subject to his power. Wife in *manus,* child in *potestas,* and slave in *mancipium* in the eyes of the law stand as property, to be protected, transferred and dealt with as other objects of ownership. In the second stage, property interests of wives and children begin to be recognized and the identification of the legal unit with the moral unit in the stage of equity and natural law leads to recognition of interests in personality of wife, child and slave and a consequent abrogation of the *ius vitae necisque.* In the case of wife and child, the recognition of these interests leads to restriction of the disciplinary power of the head of the household to correction and restraint of those who from tender years and want of descretion require to be cared for. Presently in a fourth stage individual interests of the wife and of the dependent child are definitely disentangled from group interests and come to be emphasized through recognition of the social interest in the moral and social life of the individual, which calls especially for legal securing of a human life to those who are dependent." Pound, "Individual Interests in Domestic Relations," 14 *Michigan Law Review* 177, 179–80 (1916).

26. Friedmann, *Law in a Changing Society* 207 (1959).

27. Pound, supra note 25, at 177. This tug-of-war conception of the family is remarkably apparent in Pound's enumeration of types of interest in family relations

so opposed as to be lacking in mutuality, it is difficult, at least from the point of view of the individual, to justify the *raison d'être* of the family. Even if it were justified, to protect only the individual in the interest of the society—whether such protection is against the outside world or between the members—is to encourage the disintegration of the family as an institution of social welfare. In fact, although it is sometimes argued that the contraction of the family circle in modern society has intensified its vitality (so that without it, at least during the early years of growth, the individual is seriously handicapped, if not doomed) the development of individual interests at the expense of the common interests of the family as represented by its head has resulted in a progressive breaking down of the institution.[28]

We have shown that the Dinka family is characterized by tensions and conflicts and that the law should be more concerned with the interests of family members inter se than it has been. To remedy the present evil does not justify undermining the institution and endangering all, including society.

Such protection as is here advocated for the dependent members of the family should not lose sight of the social interest in the institution itself and the need for solidarity in the family, both of which may call for sacrifices on the part of the individual. Whatever the economic difficulties of a family, for instance, it cannot be liquidated as if it were a company in bankruptcy. Other means that give consideration to the broader and more complex nature of the relationship must be resorted to. Though elementary, this starting point is fundamental to the more consistent and policy-oriented emancipation of the dependent members. It is also by seeing all sides of the family that the areas in which men and women complement each other by virtue of their differences can be better understood and the problems of confusing equality with identity can be avoided.

In the tribe, as in the family, the strategy of transitional integration calls for the balancing of three interests: interest in the tribe as such,

---

which the law is required to secure: "These are (1) interests of parents, demands which the individual may make growing out of the parental relation; (2) interest of children, demands which the individual may make growing out of filial relation; (3) interest of husbands, demands which the individual husband may make growing out of the marital relation; and (4) interests of wives, demands which the individual wife may make growing out of the marital relation. In each case, as has been said above, claims may be made against the world at large and also against the other party to the relation." Id. at 181.

28. Sir Henry Maine wrote, under a chapter entitled "Disintegration of the Family," "The movement of the progressive societies has . . . been distinguished by the gradual dissolution of family dependency and the growth of individual obligation in its place. The individual is steadily substituted for the Family, as the unit of which civil laws take account." Maine, *Ancient Law* 168 (1963).

the solidarity of tribal participants, and the interest of its individual groups. It seems to be a general trend that "the role of traditional values in the form of segmental loyalties and principles of legitimate authority are of great importance in understanding the possibilities for the occurrence of unified and stable politics at a national level." [29] The modern history of constitutional development in Africa has been characterized by many problems which have "consistently shown that indigenous, or tribal, groups wish to maintain their political identity. Indigenous groups have often refused to exchange European domination for what they fear may be similar control by other indigenous groups." [30] Overlooking the realities of the situation has sometimes caused more problems than it has solved.[31] Needless to say, we do not mean to advocate confining people's outlook to the tribal community, as this would be incompatible with what we have stated again and again—the need for extending loyalties. However, tribal identification is a fact which must be reckoned with, and it is not altogether negative. Since the goal posited here is as harmonious a change as possible, the existence of tribal loyalty requires recognition. Instead of merely being tolerated, it should be effectively utilized toward desired goals. In fact, tribal identification is today an impediment to broader national loyalties partly because it was used for that purpose by colonial powers who thought themselves threatened by change and emergent nationalism. The evils of "tribalism" are not inherent in the institution. Words like "tribe" and "tribalism" have become so loaded with emotions and so prejudicially equated with reaction that few pause to give further thought to the matter.[32]

The recognition of tribal identity may require the protection of the interests of a tribe against other national groups or may lead to the restraint of some disruptive internal forces. Correlative to tribal identity is tribal solidarity. The strength of group ties which is contained in the goals of unity and harmony extends to the tribal level, and as family solidarity entitles its members to mutual rights and imposes on them mutual obligations, so should tribal solidarity. The law may compel participants to work for their community in such areas as collective farming, road construction, and mass education.

The final set of interests on the tribal level are those of individual groups such as chiefs and elders, women, warrior groups, and the educated class. These sets of participants have become definite interest

29. Gusfield, supra note 8, 357.

30. Busia, op. cit. supra note 19, at 71.

31. The Congolese problem is a standard case. The Nigerian Civil War affords another example. The Sudanese is typical but not as well known.

32. See Busia, op. cit. supra note 19, at 71, where Dr. Busia of Ghana makes the same point.

groups, and much of the turmoil now dominating the scene rotates around their differences. With the emergence of articulate opposition, interests become more competitive and the issue turns into one of groups attempting to keep other groups out or to oust those in control. In this struggle each group overemphasizes its special interests, which are in turn endangered by overlooking common interests.

The foregoing sets of participants' interests are also observable on the national level. There is the nation state, a measure of solidarity of its citizens, and the interests of its raciocultural groups. Sudan as a nation exists, and in a world where the goal is the formation of broader entities, this existence has its legitimate claims. Apart from this somewhat externalized evaluation, Sudanese of various identifications have a measure of loyalty to the country. Indeed, when in 1958 Egypt disputed the Northern territory of Halaib with the Sudan, all Sudanese, Northerners and Southerners alike, were ready for its defense, although it lay in a remote area. When Sudanese meet outside their country there is often an affinity that pulls them together, whatever the turmoil between the sections they represent. Despite this, there are undoubtedly group interests which compete. Fundamental among these are the interests of the raciocultural groups. The law, especially constitutional law, should regulate these interests to minimize the deprivations of the disadvantaged while not unduly depriving the privileged.

Integration of Goals

In line with the transitional integration of roles is the need to integrate goals: the postulated goal of human dignity; the traditional myth of permanent identity and influence and the goals of unity and harmony contained in *cieng;* the objectives of freedom from Northern domination and of modernization represented by the educated Dinkas; and the governmental goal of national unity.

Human dignity calls for the establishment of a social order which gives maximum regard to the dignity of man both in society and as an individual; an order in which sharing in production of all values is widespread, and the actual production is high; an order in which there is broad sharing in the consumption of all values; an order in which persuasion rather than coercion is emphasized. In the last section revolutionary trends were predicted which will probably restrict the freedom of the individual. Restriction of freedom has often been justified under the pretext of achieving urgent needs without which there is no human dignity. The advocates of such deprivations are often the first to repudiate colonialism with the argument that freedom is too high a price for security and good government. But freedom, if it is to maximize the realization of human dignity, should not be directed toward purely individual ends. The ideal utilization of freedom is to serve one's own interests in harmony with the interests of one's fellowmen. It is this that optimizes the worth of the individual. But unless this concern for the interests of others is voluntary, unless it is achieved through persuasion and the exercise of free will rather than by coercion, it loses its worth.

While the postulated human dignity is a concept above the various goals competing in Dinka society, we approach it through the combination of these goals. Development is here conceived as a refinement of what exists among the people themselves. If imported goals are to be given a solid foundation, their roots must be explored in the context of adoption. It is by this process that initiative can be induced and development viewed as a task of self-realization and promotion. Our first step in this direction has been to review Dinka ideals of what their society ought to be. The concept of *cieng* was examined with this objective in mind. By emphasizing harmony and deference toward fellow human beings, *cieng* adverts to important facets of human dignity.

Modernization represents a phase of human dignity insofar as it implies the maximization postulate. The Dinka urgently need the benefits of science and technology. They are still victims of nature in most value processes at a time when answers to many of their problems have already been found.

These goals have to be seen within the context of broadened loyalties. In an era in which events within individual nations may threaten world security, this cannot be viewed as remote. The goals postulated for the Dinka envision inclusiveness for the nation as a whole. The urgency of implementing order cannot be overemphasized in view of the indignities caused to human beings, both individuals and groups. Both sides need to realize the importance of ending North-South violence promptly and reestablishing order to facilitate the task of reintegration and development toward the higher goals of human dignity. Persuasion rather than coercion should be adopted as the strategy for fostering national unity. Unity is an obvious virtue, but it should not be achieved at the price of the more important, though often overlooked, virtue of human dignity. Such an approach often defeats its own cause.

Integration of Values and Institutions

Integration of values and institutions is an important requisite to balanced change, to be effected both within each culture and between cultures interacting in the process of modernization. Within Dinka culture, the system should be reviewed as an interfusion of all the values and institutions constituting the culture, for culture is composed of inter-related and interdependent elements. If one important aspect of culture changes, other aspects will undergo concomitant change. Manipulation of one value should give consideration to all the other values. Integration of values and institutions between cultures has already been seen as an aspect of acculturation implicit in the process of modernization. Articulation and manipulation should be in terms of interlacing multi-cultural elements if the decision-maker is to derive maximum benefits from other cultures. Whether within or between cultures, since values are intimately interrelated, their equilibrium should be maintained, for to enhance one out of balance with the rest is to upset the whole system.

APPLICATION OF TRANSITIONAL INTEGRATION

Modernizing Integration of Roles

The application of transitional integration requires that measures be taken to dispose the traditionals toward modernization and to mobilize their action according to their perspectives and operational characteristics. It also requires disposing the educated class toward tradition and mobilizing their action according to their qualifications. To dispose the traditionals and the educated, specific indulgences conducive to, or compatible with, the goals of those concerned may be conferred as bases for their participation. Deprivations may be imposed passively by enhancing the base values of the unprivileged while not interfering directly with the value positions of the privileged. The thread of effects in each of the other values and how they approximate or depart from this goal, seen within the ambit of human dignity, is important for a final selection of policies.

Earlier, we saw that conflict over values is repressed within the family and strikingly expressed on the tribal and the national levels where the dynamics of participation are in confrontation. Since we consider the urgency of the solution to be proportional to the intensity of the problem, and since it is there that fundamental control of the processes lies, it is there that action is most needed. Although the solution of the problem on the national level would contribute to its solution on the tribal level, our direct concern is with the tribe, but cooperation of the national decision-makers is a prerequisite. Since the national problem is explained in terms of tribal processes, solving the problem on the tribal level would in turn have a pacifying effect on the national situation. Adjustment of the roles which familial processes have projected to the broader levels is bound to result in adjustments in familial roles. For example, enhancing the power position of women, the educated class, and the youthful warrior groups on the tribal level would promote their familial positions. A young man who is appointed a chief, a court member, or a councillor cannot be superior on the tribal level while retaining his traditional inferiority on the family level. If subordinated participants become more productive and accumulate wealth on their own rather than through their families, the chances are that their property rights on the family level would be enhanced. But family law should not wait until these changes are crystallized; it should accompany and facilitate the changes. As pacification of the tribal situation can aid pacification of the national situation, corrective measures on the family level could reinforce tribal solutions. For this purpose, changes in family law will be suggested later. Our concern with respect to transitional integration is to lay the foundation and provide guidelines for creative and comprehensive action; we do not intend or attempt to make exhaustive suggestions.

An appropriate starting point is the myth of permanent identity and influence which combines individualism and communalism. It could be turned into an effective agent of modernization, but it needs redefining in order to be forward- rather than backward-looking. The subjective identity, instead of being seen as a prolongation of the past chain of ancestry which must depend for its influence on invoking and identifying with the past achievements of the dead, should emphasize the achievements of the living in terms of modernization, whether such achievements benefit the individual, his family, the tribe, or broader communities. Indulgences and deprivations in all values should be directed toward this reorientation.

A similar process of redefinition is necessary to remold the goals of unity and harmony. Traditionally, they preserved the status quo; in the envisaged society, they should foster a group spirit and a collective effort. Whether it be political action, economic cooperation, or public works like the building of dispensaries, schools, or roads, such effort could be a dynamic force in modernization. The persuasive aspect of unity and harmony, if intensified and expounded in accordance with the overriding goal of human dignity, could diminish the use of coercion to mobilize human resources or to suppress political dissent. If the concepts of unity and harmony are well redefined and applied in terms of modernization, such coercion hardly becomes necessary. The use of traditional notions in this reorientation process is an integral part of the strategy of transitional integration. Such concepts as *cieng* [33] could communicate the message effectively and identify innovation with the pre-existing culture, thus aiding its acceptance.

While the myth of continuity and the goals of unity and harmony are the most obvious because of their overriding significance in traditional

33. Which contains the goals of unity and harmony. See Chapter 2, pp. 24–29.

society, the paramount guideline is the principle of broader shaping and sharing of all values. In order to do justice and mobilize vital human resources in the control and manipulation of values, changes in the traditional hierarchy are necessary.

This poses the initial question of whether the mythicals should be considered as shapers and sharers. Since it is necessary to use the myth of permanent identity and influence, the question is easily resolved in the affirmative. But their bases for continuity are automatically altered. If a person's immortality is conditioned by his innovative achievement, then the dead cannot participate solely because of the fact of their having continued the ancestral line. The continuity of the dead becomes a part and a justification for the forward-looking myth of continuity. As modernizing achievement alters human experience, the essentials, or at least the forms, of the divinities who participate with the dead in the mythical arenas also change.

Among the living, we have seen that the chiefs and the elders represent the mythical participants. Since the chief, as the head and representative of the whole hierarchy, is pivotal, discussing transitional integration in relation to his role implies discussing it in relation to the roles of all chiefs and elders. Action relating to him will come from superior national decision-makers; that relating to his subordinates will come from him.

We have seen how traditional expectations in Ngok society have centered around the chief as the head in all value pyramids and how his position has been reinforced by modern power. We have also seen that traditionally the chief was the innovator who has recently been outpaced by change and made suspicious of it. Nonetheless, the institution and the person occupying it still command great allegiance. So authoritative is the chief that his word is not only law, but is often complied with instantly. Whether it be the collection of funds for private or public purposes, road construction or work in private or public fields, building of private or public houses, mobilization for the vaccination of people or cattle, experimental growing of cotton as a cash crop, or any such functions, an order from the chief directed to individuals or groups usually receives prompt and favorable response. The vestiges of youthful disobedience described earlier are not only rare in relation to the head chief, but, when they occur, they receive serious punishment. The combined deference and awe which the Ngok have for their chief makes both the institution and the person important bases for constructive policies. Conversely, any adverse policies are almost doomed to failure. But a distinction should be drawn between immediate policies and middle- or long-term plans. While the institution and the present chief should go together without any radical changes as to his qualifications, later periods would require such changes. Ideally, since the Ngok expect the chief to be qualified to pioneer change, the person who should head an integrated system should be among the more modernized. But while the present chief is not, his influence is a potential asset for immediate action. Besides, to the Ngok, who view the educated as not sufficiently integrated to be entirely considered part of the local community, the chief is considered relatively modern. The issue then is to make use of his pivotal position and of whatever degree of modernization he has and to modify the conditions that intensify his resistance to change. In this, two levels of action which should run concurrently are necessary. The first concerns the qualification of the chief, the second his action toward the implementation of the policies of integrated modernization. In both, manipulating his position should confer indulgences on him. When deprivations are necessary, they should, as much as possible, be imposed indirectly.

On an abstract level, it is useful to establish the expectation that the chief's continued identity and influence depends largely on his achievement as a modernizing leader, whether such achievements be in politics, law, education, economics, health, or any other field. Because of the special religious and moral connotations of immortality, whatever its expression, certain ritual symbols may provide useful guidance. The reverence the Dinka have for the graves of the dead chiefs is an example. Once a year, or more frequently according to whether or not an urgent need calls for the invocation of the dead chiefs, ceremonies are conducted on shrines specially prepared in their memory. Although a modernizing myth of permanent identity and influence could use comparable but modern symbols to maintain a dead person's image, it should not indulge people only after death for their modernizing achievements. It should indulge a person immediately while also guaranteeing for him within his lifetime continued influence after death. Symbolic indulgences, such as naming a law, a club, a scholarship, a school, a dispensary, a road, a cattle-breeding center, an experimental farm, or any such developmental projects after a chief, could ceremonially be conferred on these bases. The ceremonies should publicize the principle and should be accompanied by such public festivities as dances, sports, and feasts. Such strategies, which already exist in schoolboys' songs praising even an illiterate chief for introducing such modern values as education, modern medicine, or a modern market are significant ways of ensuring him a form of permanence and also increasing his motivation for modernization. The continuation of the process of veneration through ritual ceremonies over shrines or through other methods could maintain the achieving image of the dead and aid the motivation of the living. By conferring these and other indulgences selectively on chiefs at all levels of the power hierarchy, the competitiveness implicit in the pride of the Dinka and the individualist aspect of the myth of permanent identity and influence could combine with its group consciousness to promote achievement for the common good.

Strategies for inducing the chief to preserve the traditional goals of unity and harmony with the view to using them for modernizing purposes could similarly be formulated. The modern chief should be disposed to realize his importance as a unifying and harmonizing leader, who, through his knowledge of the "words of wisdom and truth," is able to resolve conflicts and reconcile adversaries by persuasion. With this as his basis of action, he is likely to arouse collective action without resort to coercion.

In addition to inducing the chief toward integrated modernization by reinterpreting the fundamental myth and goals of traditional society, inducive measures also need to be taken through all value processes. Since their deprivation in modern skills and enlightenment is an important factor in the chiefs' resistance to modernization, a compulsory educational program, on a local or national basis, might be adopted. Apart from disposing him toward modernization in general, this program should concern itself with the guidance of modernization and the role of law in such guidance. The program should place special emphasis on the ideology of transitional integration and the dangers of nonconformity to its principles, especially insofar as the political future of the traditional leaders is concerned. The chiefs could also be enlightened for the purpose of modernization by frequent official visits to the modern sector within the country and abroad. Past trends show that whenever a chief returns from travels to such areas, he not only brings back modern objects which set examples to his people, but spends a considerable period of time conversing with his constantly attentive audience on the general impact of his travels. Usually, such occasions call for songs of praise.

Rectitude is another example of an area where disposition might be effected. A moral commitment to the interest of society in terms of modernization should be encouraged and made part of the educational program suggested above. The use of public funds for public purposes, the unbiased selection of the best-suited persons for public offices, and the importance of justice in the administration of the law are other examples of what should be emphasized and included in the curriculum. A symbol expressing the ideology of integrated modernization might be consecrated to the chief's authority. We have seen how religious symbols of office, such as the sacred spears, are both highly revered and functional. In fact, the Ngok often attribute the general upheavels of disruptive change to the fact that the present chief does not honor the sacred spears of office as frequently as his predecessor. Even relatively new symbols rapidly acquire high honor. For instance, some years ago the present chief was presented with a sword by the late Sayed Abdel Rahman el Mahdi, the son of the original Mahdi and the Patron of the now ruling Umma party. In a short while the sword acquired both a political and a ritual or religious significance. This initiation song is about the protective power of the sword which a wife of the chief held near the singer, a relative of the chief, as he was being initiated.

> We lay down on the ground
> And the mother of Mading came with the Sword
> Acong de Jok, raise the Sacred Sword
> Mother of Mading, raise the Sacred Sword
> Raise the Sword to God in the sky
> The Sword is endowed with the breath of God.

There is, therefore, sufficient reason to believe that a government-given symbol for progress could have considerable effect not only on the chief but also on his followers.

Another example of value indulgence as a conditioning factor and a basis for modernization is respect and the Dinka sense of pride, honor, and dignity. At present, chiefs receive honors which are sometimes expressed in the form of robes of honor. The bases for conferring such an honor are not articulated but they are supposedly administrative ability. On both the local and the national level, forms of honor, whether through robes or gifts of a modern nature, could be annually conferred on the basis of modernizing achievement. Since chiefs of all levels are competitive, this could be done on the basis of competition between fragments of the tribe and nationally between tribes. Also associated with respect, and including affection as well, is the use of such traditional strategies as praise in song in modern national media like the radio. All Dinkas enjoy praise in songs. The customary way of asking a special favor of a chief is to compose songs in his praise, visit him in his home, and entertain him and his council with these songs. To hear oneself praised in a song on the radio gives an even greater pleasure. The content of such praise should be directed toward inducing the chiefs' greater commitment to integrated modernization. Here also the competitive characteristics of the chiefs could be used.[34] Since modernization, as we have postulated it, requires identification with broader arenas, such strategies would also be relevant to national affection. The fact that the content of such songs would prize modernization highly would also be enlightening to the chief and his people.

34. Already Radio Omdurman has broadcast songs in praise and to the delight of some Dinka chiefs and their people.

So far, we have discussed the short-range role of the chief in transitional integration on the understanding that, though traditional, he is a potential agent for modernization. For middle- and long-range purposes, however, a more direct qualification for leading integrated modernization should be demanded. The time of succession to the present chief is a convenient point for implementing this. A vacuum would then be created and no traditional character would be dominant enough to frustrate the requirements of more modern qualifications. Here, too, expectations should be balanced. The first is the strongly held view that a chief should be from the chiefly lineage. The second is the view becoming increasingly established that the educated are "the eyes" of their traditional society in the modern context. An educated chief would therefore ensure more security to his society. The combination of these two factors means that to be effective the chief must be qualified to lead a society in transition while envisaging change in terms of tradition. He should derive legitimacy and symbolic importance from the traditional system but at the same time he should be among the most qualified for modernizing innovation. While primogeniture should be modified in favor of elections, the chiefs should be from the chiefly lineage to moderate the dangers or fears of radicalism that would otherwise ensue. But he should be formally educated. The educated understand the modern processes better, but the sons of the chief have a hereditary advantage in addition to their education. Because of this disposition on the part of the traditionals, and because sons of the chief are among the better educated in society, it would be easy to secure their leadership whether by appointment or by open elections. The latter is preferred as more strategic because it would emphasize individual merit. This would have a greater appeal to the moderns and encourage their cooperation with the elected chief. The need for the restriction to the chiefly lineages would disappear as modernization proceeds and changes the expectations of the people in favor of achievement rather than birth.

To ensure continued motivation, the chief should be reelected or reappointed periodically. His term should be long enough to permit implementation of his policies but short enough to avoid stagnation. In order to satisfy traditional expectations for permanence, the chief could be eligible for reelection throughout his life, except for specific cases of incapacity to be defined by law.

With the chief disposed toward modernization, whether by special program or because of his education, the way is paved for a modernizing disposition in the rest of the participants and for the implementation of the policies of integrated modernization. Indulging reinterpretation and modernizing reorientation of the myth of permanent identity and influence and the goals of unity and harmony, as well as conferring indulgences in all values, could also be applied to the rest of the traditional participants. Since modernizing changes conditioned by broader shaping and sharing of values would promote the value positions of the traditionals, it would not be difficult to win their support. The same principle applies to the educated class who, through cooperation with the traditionals, not only would gain indulgences but would also find such indulgences useful bases for fulfilling their goals of modernization. Except for the few who would prefer a revolution, such recognition is most likely to resolve the present ills. The problem, therefore, would be to formulate a program of action which would utilize the distinctive characteristics of the various participants: chiefs and elders, warrior groups, women, and the educated class.

Transitional integration would require the active participation of all these groups in tribal decision process. Their disposition could further be enhanced by a special training comparable to the one suggested for the chief which would prepare them for cooperation in accordance with the principles of transitional integration. Each age set among the traditionals, from the elders to the newly initiated, could elect members to represent it in each of the decision-making bodies. The educated could similarly elect representatives from each of the four levels of education: elementary, intermediate, secondary, and postsecondary. A minimum age of sixteen might be fixed for voting and eligibility for election. Since elementary and intermediate school students are generally under sixteen, only graduates who have not proceeded to secondary school would qualify. The inclusion of women in courts or assemblies might be too revolutionary; however, women could have an association which would be coordinated with the community decision-makers in women's affairs. This association should reflect the different age groups on the traditional level and the educated women in their various institutional levels. The foundation for this already exists in traditional society, for men's and women's age sets have representatives to voice their views on issues of special relevance to their groups. The fact that women have recently been extended suffrage on the national level is an additional foundation. The various male and female traditional and modern representatives should be reelected or reappointed every few years to ensure continued allegiance to the ideals of the new system.

The degree to which these institutions can modernize the society depends on the degree to which their powers in the maintenance of public order, administration of justice, education, road construction, economic development, health regulation, and other value-institutional fields are adequately enhanced. The fact that the proposed institutions would be more enlightened than the present ones is enough to justify increasing their powers.

As to whether the concept of separation of powers should be introduced, two factors call for consideration. Traditional unification of functions is supported by the expectation that an authority who cannot pass orders, judge on their basis, and execute his judgments is insignificant to the Dinka. This is why the attempt to strip subtribal chiefs of judicial authority has not been effective. On the other hand, separating functions could open channels for more progressive participation. There has already been some speculation about appointing a chief's son or relative as a judge while the chief himself remains the head of the administration. This principle could be extended in a way consistent with transitional integration. The educated and the youthful warrior groups could be made more active in certain functions within the existing decision bodies while leaving the paramount chief as head of the whole complex of power institutions. For instance, specialists, or committees of educated men, might be appointed to perform for the chief's council and court such functions as intelligence, recommendation, and appraisal.[35] In doing so they should be given brief but intensive training in the ideology and practice of transitional modernization with particular reference to the roles they would play. This training should especially emphasize the tact necessary for guiding traditional elders, including the chief, without threatening their positions. The warrior groups could perform such applying functions as that of the police or modern tribal army. There exists today a class of amateur policemen who exemplify the proposed function. Because of the insufficiency of the police force, which was mentioned earlier, the chief appoints some individuals to execute court judgments and serve in other administrative positions without official appointment or salary. Through such functions they are introduced to, and influenced by, modernization. The suggested recruitment would be temporary and should rotate among the group. As with the amateur policemen, their power position would probably be enough to satisfy them, while opening them to modernization. Some material or other consideration for their services might also be given them.

To continue the traditional goals of unity and harmony, the decision-makers should emphasize traditional modes of persuasion and resort to coercion only when persuasion fails. Both criminal and civil procedures should be educational in that they should be aimed at making the wrongdoer appreciate the nature of his wrong in terms of cultural synthesis. The court should aim at mediation and reconciliation between conflicting parties, but it should be backed with a police force to make the law effective where persuasion is impotent. Such emphasis on persuasion in accordance with the norms of unity and harmony could win

35. Such a committee could be a watchdog for a close implementation of the principles of transitional integration.

decision-makers greater deference which might provide bases for modernizing influence.

The implementation of these fundamental principles could result in the establishment of an integrated constitutive process capable of transforming the present negatives into dynamics of modernization in all value processes. These negatives and potential dynamics for development are more striking among the warrior groups, women, and the educated.

Apart from the coercion by the chief, which was introduced by modern government and which can easily be controlled by a change of policies and of the conditions necessitating it, the role of the warrior group is the most coercive and destructive. Earlier, we argued that the alternatives to authoritative power and other acceptable means of influence adopted by these groups are violence, preoccupation with cattle, and unproductive skills primarily directed toward attracting girls. We saw that to have endured the pain of initiation not only qualifies them to socialize with girls but entitles them to the excited attention and affection of their relatives and of society in general. This is in addition to the conferring respect, certain aspects of responsibility, skills, identification with cattle symbolized by personality oxen, and other values. It was seen earlier that when a warrior succeeds to a position of authority, he suddenly abandons his coercive disposition and acquires the persuasive manner of the elders. By incorporating the group on a representational basis, a similar transformation could be expected.

More needs to be done to eliminate coerciveness among young warriors and mobilize their potentialities for innovating creativity in power and the other values. The status of an initiate should be conferred by elaborate but bloodless rituals. Such rituals should substitute disposition for modernization as a basis for participation in the decision process, winning affection, respect, and other values. For instance, a system by which group members would accumulate points toward initiation or demonstrate their qualification by constructive achievement as determined by a team of judges is a possible line of action. The judges could include a number of girls to build on the traditional youth motivation as well as to enhance the status of girls. That period of training prior to and subsequent to initiation could provide occasion for intensive training in the various ways through which their group spirit might be used. These could be in the field of economic development, civil work projects, political action, and other value-institutional activities. After initiation is completed, age-set activities could continue in such areas as sports, more economic breeding of cattle, increased and diversified agricultural production, building of schools, construction of roads, and other areas where physical abilities and competitiveness are desirable. The foundation for this already exists. As we said earlier, age-set competition over such constructive work as cultivating the chief's fields, building his houses, and constructing roads has become established.

A similar process of transformation is required in the role of women. Traditionally, their role has been to serve the interests of men in accordance with the myth of permanent identity and influence. The emphasis on unity and harmony tends to maintain this stratification, but, as we have argued,[36] the negative attributes which the Dinka ascribe to women are rooted in the subordination of women. The hostility and the violence of the warrior groups are in part aimed at winning the respect and affection of girls. Women accompany men in the battlefield to encourage the warriors by their presence, to collect and rearm them with spears, cook for them, and help the injured. In their group songs women sometimes even provoke wars by praising their corresponding subtribal male age sets' fighting ability or by insulting the enemy's age sets. This is quite apart from their reputed image as jealous, disuniting, and practicing loathed magic. The proposed transitional integration aims at promoting the status of women to utilize them for modernization and to eliminate the negatives prompted by their deprivations. Their suggested participation in the power process, though not entirely integrated, is a step in this direction. However, action in all value processes is necessary to make their role a constructive one. Female age sets could continue to motivate male age sets, but in the constructive roles suggested. Whether it be through songs, judging in competitions, providing water and food, or merely keeping men company, they could catalyze the men's achievements. But Dinka women traditionally have less communal spirit than men have. For example, while male group activities continue into middle age and, to a lesser extent, throughout life, women's activities in age sets largely stop after marriage. Each then becomes an individual who, instead of identifying with corresponding male groups, identifies only with her husband except insofar as he represents his group. The reason for this is easily seen in terms of the myth of permanent identity and influence which is aimed at maintaining the male lineage and dominance. Since women's age sets are formed at intervals about twice those of men, because of size and age discrepancy they are less cohesive. This, too, is aimed at benefiting men, who tend to marry women much younger than they are. In order to retain women's group interest, their age setting should be identical to that of men. Also, initiation for women should be introduced with a modernizing program of training and ceremonies similar to that of men's age sets. The status of an initiate, with its accompanying respect enhancement, should be conferred upon fulfillment of such requirements as learning to sew, nursing the sick, mastering modern techniques of hygiene, making traditional handicrafts for

36. This point comes up in the various values illustrated.

marketing, and the like. The fact that they will elect representatives to the suggested women's association and be active in its work would also promote their group identity and influence. While promoting group spirit among Dinka women, it should be realized that their present individualist disposition, as we shall illustrate, has positive aspects to be built upon for the purposes of modernization.

The role of the educated, too, is capable of such transformation. At present their perpetual political opposition to the chief and government is an unproductive alternative to participation in authoritative power. But their role as potential modernizers is particularly important not only because they already possess modern strategic values of skills and enlightenment, but also because modernization is their articulated objective. Since their present lack of effectiveness is primarily caused by their deprivation in power, their active participation in the suggested integrated decision process is likely to have a conspicuous impact both on themselves and on the society. But the initial step to induce them to return to the tribe and to be prepared to appreciate tradition and co-operate with the traditionals will require an intensive nation-wide campaign. The fact that the chief will be disposed toward change will minimize the tensions and conflicts which contributed to the educated's having left the tribe. As an educated chief takes over, according to our middle- and long-range plans, they would be encouraged by the prospects of implementing their objective of modernizing their society. From these will also result indulgences in respect, affection, rectitude, and well-being. While those already educated in the present system would require some orientation in the role of tradition in transitional integration, the products of the future system of education, which we will discuss later, would largely be prepared to cooperate tactfully with the traditionals. We will also suggest a form of association between the warrior groups and the educated which should lead to mutual understanding. While indulgences to all and in all modern values as bases of participation in power and other values is a necessary goal, the role of the educated requires special attention since they represent a cultural force whose potentials by far outweigh their present share of values as bases for modernization. This is related to the importance of recognizing the changes which have already taken place and in which the law is lagging.

Along the lines of the preceding examples, transitional integration could be effected by building on tradition in each of the value processes and by seeing each action as permeating a network of value institutions.

In affection, the cooperation of the decision-making bodies toward one objective would foster a sense of broader and constructive unity. The symbol of the chief as the father of the fictionally extended family could be helpful in this. The security the chief gave to the needy could be a basis for a form of modern welfare system which could safeguard for every individual minimum indulgences in wealth, well-being, enlightenment, skills, and other values. The traditional system of age grading could be used as a method of extending social identifications and fostering solidarity for constructive purposes. We have seen that much of the tribal hostilities carried out by age sets rests on subtribal competitiveness, for age grading is on a subtribal basis. By unifying the system and initiating young men on a tribal basis as one age set with one name and one "father," a wider circle of affection can be created. The same process could be applied to female age sets. By making their age setting identical with that of men, as has been suggested, solidarity among women is extended and coordinated with that of corresponding male groups. Except for representation in decision-making bodies, one could include the educated class in the traditional system of age grading. To a certain extent, it already identifies and is identified with corresponding age sets of traditional society. This would provide bases for modernizing influence within the age set, the effect of which would permeate all value processes. In a manner similar to the traditional age grading but more extensive in scope, the educated consider themselves as "one age set." This would be an important basis for such modernizing projects as social, economic, educational, and sport associations. This should result in a kind of Dinka self-help in which the more indulged in strategic modern values would feel a special social responsibility to the less indulged to share these values. The war spirit of the young could be turned toward a war against poverty, ignorance, and disease. Through adequate educational and social orientation, such possible obstacles as snobbery against the uneducated could be modified. The remnants of such snobbery can have their own usefulness insofar as they might induce motivation for mobility among the uneducated and motivation for teaching among the educated.

While broader identifications need to be fostered in the interest of collective action, the individualist aspect of the myth of permanent identity and influence which traditionally extended into group exclusiveness and encouraged factionalism should be retained and used constructively. In the course of our suggestions we have often referred to the usefulness of traditional competitiveness, which is an offspring of this.

In respect process, the basis for a broader and modernizing shaping and sharing would be laid by such innovations as deference in power and affection. Conditioning respect by modernization could be an effective motivation. The suggested replacement of physical courage in initiation with modernizing achievement is an illustration. Uneconomical preoccupation with cattle could be discouraged by such activities as competition in local fairs. The most productive farmer in agricultural produce or animal husbandry could be honored. This could be extended to all values. Among the educated, honors could be conferred upon young men according to their success in teaching traditionals to read and write, introducing new methods of agriculture and animal husbandry, or promoting trade or other aspects of modern economy.

In the field of wealth, Dinkaland is among the richest in the country's natural resources, especially in livestock, forests, agricultural land, and water, including such riverine resources as fish. Nonetheless, developmental projects are concentrated in the modern sector and, as we saw earlier, the Ngok, far from becoming richer, are becoming poorer and more dependent on local Arab merchants. Reliance on these Arab merchants, which is shared even by the chiefs, goes very far. Almost all salaried Ngok Dinkas assign their income to them to receive goods in advance and, for that reason, at increased prices. The merchants receive the salaries when due and usually when already spent. This has increased their power. But their influence is strongly curtailed by their raciocultural identity, and often there is a strong conflict between their increased economic power and the people's resentment toward them as outsiders.

In the light of the above, alternatives should be adopted which would both benefit the Dinka and reduce the sentiment felt against the Arab merchants and extended to the Northerners as a whole. A program of cooperation which would join the efforts of the Dinka in production, marketing, supply of local needs, reinvestment in developmental projects, and provision of social services is needed. With an integrated system disposed toward economic progress, given the existing natural resources and the dynamics of group spirit combined with individual or group competitiveness, there exist sufficient bases for a considerable and speedy improvement. Such an alternative would be beneficial both for the Dinka and the nation, for it is an established fact that the future of the country depends on such resources as agriculture and livestock in which the traditional sector is the national source. A development centered on the traditionals would not only exploit such resources but would also be conducive to a broader shaping and sharing of wealth, since the overwhelming majority of the people are in this sector.

Earlier, we demonstrated that cooperation in agriculture, animal husbandry, and other economic activities is an important aspect of *cieng*, but that the emphasis of the traditional system was on the deferential aspect of assisting in producing the same amount the individual or the group would have produced without help. We also showed that such cooperation was initiated by the individual through such methods as beer brewing, slaughtering beasts for meat, or any other methods of feasting for the group. These demonstrate the bases for a free, cooperative movement. Such cooperation was not merely economic, for we saw how the people received material help from relatives, friends, or the chief according to their needs in such areas as food, animals for sacrifice, and fees for the services of a curer. Cooperation provides a sound foundation for a constructive use of group spirit for economic development and the establishment of a welfare system which, while ensuring all members a share in community values, allows individual interests sufficient freedom to compete.

Such a cooperative movement was suggested by the British and plans were begun before independence but, as we said earlier, internal conflicts between the educated Dinka officers appointed and the chief, together with discouragement by the postcolonial administration, frustrated the project. Future action is more likely to succeed, since it would be undertaken in the new spirit of suggested integration.

Once established, the cooperative society could be the center of Ngok economic and social life. It could buy Ngok agricultural and other products at reasonable prices, and by guaranteeing minimum prices, it could avoid such discouragements as happened with the successful but discontinued growing of cotton as a cash crop. The cooperative would market the products outside or sell them to local consumers at reasonable prices. The tribe, subtribes, sections, families, other associations, and individuals could be legal persons capable of holding stocks or shares. The cooperative could invest in other areas and diversify the economy by introducing modern scientific and technological techniques and new agricultural products, as well as by establishing dairy farming, encouraging local industry, providing year-round agricultural production through irrigation, providing transportation and communication, and even providing educational, health, and other social services.

The role of the chief, who would represent public interest both as the traditional "father" of the tribe and as a modernizing leader, could contribute effectively to the success of the cooperative. Several times in the past, the chief has innovated economic change. For instance, he introduced a modern market and pioneered the sale of cattle. He once encouraged the growth of cotton as a cash crop but, though tribal production was high, cotton prices were very low that year and the Dinka lost motivation. He requested and was granted a provisional permit by the government for the establishment of a modern agricultural scheme and a fishery along the Kir River after experts had inspected the area and favored the projects, but they were never executed, according to the chief, because of a lack of experts to plan and run them. The chief has also appealed for cattle and money for public purposes several times in the past and has always received a favorable response. These past events show that with the support of the chief, the spirit of cooperation could be aroused in the people. While undue reliance on money for initiating economic progress should be discouraged in favor of labor, a certain amount of capital would be required, and whether paid by cattle or money, the chief could obtain a reasonable sum through taxation to which the Dinka have already become adjusted. Furthermore, by issuing strong proclamations against such tendencies as unwillingness to produce more than is enough for subsistence, overconsumption, and unwillingness to save, he could effectively contribute to economic development. For long-range purposes, the chief should, as part of his training, have some knowledge of the basic principles of economic development, or have access to a qualified adviser or advisers, so that he can not only encourage but actively participate in guiding economic change. This is not necessarily to say that he would direct economic change, but that he would understand it, be able to cooperate with trained administrators, and know what was happening if his people's cooperative work was abused.

The role of the warrior groups in production is of obvious importance. Their manpower is now wasted in such activities as unnecessary far-off herding sometimes aimed at avoiding cultivation, which is left to women and senior members of the family. Many cathartic songs praise women for having offered to exempt men from cultivation. It is this group of young men which is now causing a drainage of manpower into the cities for labor. Ways have already been suggested of fostering more productive occupations and evolving respect for agriculture and other economic activities within the tribe. It has also been suggested that warrior age-set spirit could be utilized in such public works as road construction and cultivation of public fields. These activities, which have already become established, could facilitate economic progress considerably. Since the group would be entitled to the fruits of its own labor, an even greater motivation would be added to its activities. Competition, which already marks public labor, could be encouraged through prizes or other forms of honor.

Women have always been more involved in agriculture and more economical than men. As we said earlier, it is in land that their property rights are most pronounced, for although a wife cannot dispose of her land or its produce without her husband's consent, he cannot deprive her of her land or agricultural produce. Another factor is the responsibility of women for feeding their families and guests. For this reason, and because of their more individualist tendencies, they have a greater tendency to save than men have. Being able to produce food or such simple property as goats and sheep in times of unexpected need is a highly regarded virtue in a woman. Women have also developed an inclination toward trade. Traditionally, Dinkas loathed trade and it is still unpopular. When it first appeared, songs were composed insulting women who adopted it. Women, having had little or no property rights, found trade a source of independent wealth acquisition and continued selling such things as chickens, sesame, groundnuts, okra, tobacco, dairy produce, sugarcane, beer, and locally manufactured household goods. In turn they buy clothes, beads, sheep, goats, and cattle. These characteristics promise a considerable economic contribution by women. The suggested cooperative could encourage them even more in agriculture, trade, and local industry.

By virtue of possessing modern skills, the educated would play an important role in the cooperative movement. Students could also be compelled to do some teaching during their long holiday. Educated women could similarly help train women in those modern skills which are more suited to them. As part of national assistance, as well as of the cooperative society, some educated men could be given scholarships in the various areas where more modern skills would be needed.

In well-being, to eliminate the coerciveness of the traditional warrior groups which threatened personal security, the measures already suggested under other values would give them constructive rather than destructive alternatives. Reliance on magicoreligious cures, which are rooted in the feeling of guilt on the part of those subordinated in confrontation with their superiors, could be reduced by the equalization of their status. A form of modern health insurance could be introduced on the basis of traditional social consciousness. Traditionally, however, medical services were paid for, and only the needy were assisted. We saw earlier that with this expectation, the Dinka now show little confidence in the free medical services rendered under the national health service but insist on paying for it to ensure good care. Despite this inclination, they can not fully afford these services. A more integrated development among the Ngok might charge them a nominal fee, thus deriving some revenue which might help improve the services. Transitional integration in Dinka society requires that, while it is necessary to introduce modern techniques of disease prevention and cure and other scientific technological means of enhancing well-being, the present conditioning of the Dinka necessitates the recognition of the traditional methods of prevention and cure. Transitional integration would therefore advocate the recognition of traditional medicine and its integration with modern medicine. Although there are few qualified modern Dinka professionals, they could work with traditional healers, and modern techniques could be applied in the study and application of traditional medicine. To take one example, bone specialists can work with modern orthopedists. Even in the area of psychiatry, the diviner and his modern counterpart could learn from each other. In any case, their patients in the Dinka context would be cultural hybrids. This is not to underestimate the difficulties, but rather than tear the society apart between disciplines that coexist, the decision-makers would do better to harmonize. Indeed, the suspicions of the Dinka against modern medicine could be reduced if the confidence of traditional medicine men was won and they helped to administer modern medicine complementary to their traditional function.

Skills and enlightenment are areas where transitional integration would be most strategic. We have emphasized the role of the educated to help educate their fellowmen, but in order for integration to be balanced, the subject matter, as well as those who teach it, should reflect both tradition and modernity. Modern teachers who are well versed in tradition could be utilized; but genuine synthesis would come from using articulate traditional elders or even traditional young men specialized in traditional knowledge, be it political, historical, or ethical. One school which accepted only sons of chiefs was run by a system of tribal adminis-tration with chiefs of all hierarchies, elders, and policemen. The chiefs tried cases and inflicted sentences which in serious cases had to be confirmed by the headmaster before they were executed. Such a system, which differs from what traditional Dinka children do in that it was not a game, could be a useful way of introducing schoolchildren to the functioning of tribal institutions in which we have suggested their participation. The system cited was modeled on the tribal administration as established by colonial rule. Chiefs were therefore appointed and they followed adversary proceedings in their adjudication. Changes which would introduce elections and emphasize persuasion would be better oriented toward training for transitional integration.

With respect to rectitude, its two aspects, responsible conduct and religious faith, should be kept separate, though both are revelant to the strategy of transitional integration. Our analysis shows that, tradition-ally, rectitude was largely negated by the youth warrior groups who through excessive use of violence demonstrated a high degree of irre-sponsibility. Although this has largely been minimized by British rule, it still persists. Women play a more negative role; they are reputed to contravene Dinka notions of rectitude by their abhorred jealousies and black magic. Both these roles, we argued, are attributable to the low position they occupy in traditional value pyramids. The educated today are in a somewhat analogous position. Their perpetual opposition to the chiefs and the government is seen as irresponsibility by these power elites. In the case of some Southerners this has reached the point of violence in the form of guerrilla warfare against the North. Again, our analysis has traced these characteristics to the deprivations of the edu-cated, especially those in authoritative power. Rectitude assumes an ad-ditional dimension in the form of competition between Christianity and Islam; the former identified with the South, the latter with the North.

This, seen as one of unequal treatment in favor of Islam, provokes indignation which is also rooted in real or felt deprivation. Various strategies have already been suggested which would indulge these various groups with the view to eliminating the negative implications of their deprivations. Controversy over religious freedom could be minimized by prohibiting the teaching of religion in government schools, though a code of ethics which contains basic moral principles of integrated Dinka society could be formulated and authorized as the basis of ethical instruction. This is not to foreclose the legitimate right of private bodies and families to give instructions in any religion or denomination of their choice.

Since the Ngok situation has much in common with the situation in most, if not all, traditional communities of the Sudan, which constitute well over 80 percent of the population, the foregoing strategies for transitional integration are expected to be generally applicable, though they require adaptation to the particular conditions prevailing within each individual community. Among communities, integration requires measures proportional to the magnitude of the problems. In particular, the Southern Problem requires recognition of the racially and culturally distinct groups and the balance of their exclusive and inclusive interests to eliminate the Southern feeling of domination by the North and to promote Southern appreciation for national independence from the Anglo-Egyptian colonialism. Such equilibrium is compatible with the Northern demand for unity only if there is a genuine and substantial decentralization. While we venture to make these general remarks, our focus remains on the Ngok; therefore, we refrain from formulating further recommendations.

The strategy of transitional integration is an attempt to speed up development in a balanced and harmonious manner at the least human cost. The role of the law in its broadest sense is interwoven into the whole process, and is one of shaping, leading, accompanying, and following. Balancing claims according to the policies of transitional integration would largely be ensured by the integration of the decision process. Change affects people at different rates and has already created cultural diversity. New problems calling for new solutions continually result from the variabilities in response to change. While legislation and administrative orders will be needed, it is here that the function of the judge and the flexibility of the system become vital. But certainty in the law should only be modified and not totally sacrificed. A degree of certainty and universality, in the sense that the same law applies to all, is possible if by this is meant that the law should predict and respect the diversity of the system. But certain principles must be formulated to guide diversified application. In accordance with transitional integration, the guiding theme of these principles should be progressive justice; the law should aim at providing the "have nots" with bases for contributing to the maximization of values.

Such an approach may be illustrated in greater detail with family law, whose principles are quite standardized. We have already warned against the inertia in the laissez-faire policy toward family law and advocated an alternative which would closely adapt family law to the constant changes in value shaping and sharing as a result of the progressively equalizing effects of transitional integration. Here, we do not exhaust areas where family law might be called to mind nor are we forwarding a draft legislation. We are merely illustrating possible action in the law as generally understood and applied by courts, whether it be the outcome of judicial lawmaking itself, by legislation, or otherwise. These suggestions are based on the premise that although modernization is a goal, tradition is still a fact, and in certain respects a desirable one. They also consider the interest of the family as a group, the interest of the husband-father as the head of the family, and his interest as an individual. The primary objective is to enhance the role of the wife and the children in order to enable them to participate more effectively in the shaping and the sharing of all values. Subordination according to wife's or mother's marital order should be discouraged in favor of ability and talent. In the light of these preferences, our suggestions illustrate with marriage, torts, and property rights.

Such institutions as levirate, being extreme implicates of the overemphasis on the myth of permanent male identity and influence, with all its traditional inequities and impediments to change, should be discouraged in accordance with the policy of deemphasis on the procreational expression of the myth. Ghost marriages, being more akin to normal marriages, could be outlawed immediately without much resistance. Levirate is far too established to be eliminated directly, but it should not be imposed on any unwilling party. In highly exceptional circumstances, such as where the interests of children are at stake, such imposition may only be made after careful consideration of all the competing interests. The effects of such changes would promote the status of women and therefore their participation. The recognition of their right of decision enhances their respect position and gives them bases for affection insofar as each may choose the one she wants. By exercising such a right, their power is also enhanced. The change would also minimize the power of the dead, whose role would otherwise be continued by ghost marriage and levirate. This would lessen the awe for them which now provides the bases for rectitude and endangers the psychic well-being of women.

The rules relating to age qualification in marriage also require reinterpretation and modification. At present, women are permitted to marry before puberty, but marriage may only be consummated after it. Such a situation permits a woman's family to commit her to marriage either without her consent or when she is too young for meaningful consent. This means forcing her to marry a man of whom she does not approve, thus denying her affection. This also connotes disrespect and deprives her of power. The effects are pervasive in all values. Corrective measures would have an opposite effect. But in a society where the status of women is seen largely in terms of marriage, early marriage also means security. The proposed change should balance these factors and permit early betrothal after puberty but fix the minimum age for the completion of marriage at majority as seen in relation to initiation (which has been estimated to take place at ages sixteen to nineteen). Since traditional Dinkas do not think of age in terms of years, the minimum limit should be both age sixteen for those who think of age in years, and initiation for those who do not. Because women are not initiated, this should be seen in terms of their age grouping. At present, female age sets correspond to male age sets, but female grading takes place at longer intervals. Corresponding female sets therefore include girls who are much younger than their corresponding males. This we have seen to be a factor in the diagonal trends of ages in marriages. By making the age grading of males and females correspond more accurately, minimum age for marriage could be more accurately calculated. These changes should be seen in conjunction with those relating to consent, for while early betrothal continues to some extent, the increase in the minimum age for marriage would mean giving an adult female opportunity to become more rational and less susceptible to undue influence in exercising her right of consent. This means modifying the Dinka theory that betrothal is a degree of marriage which antedates its consequences and effects. While it need not be considered a trial period, it should be terminable, though the rights and duties of betrothal might necessitate certain punitive or compensational measures, depending on who initiates and for what reason. For instance, a breach initiated by a girl betrothed before majority is more understandable than a breach of betrothal by her father with the view to surrendering her to a wealthier person, or by her fiancé with the intention of redirecting his choice.

Priorities by order of age and mother's marriage should be modified. It is obvious that the present system is part of the stratification based on the myth of permanent identity and influence. With respect to girls, the issue is less problematic. The Dinka realize this and permit a younger sister to marry, although her husband should materially compensate the older sister. Changes here would not make much difference. With respect to males, the present situation discourages motivation. A young man who believes that his marital chances depend on laboring for money and individually acquiring cattle may find such cattle used for the marriages of senior relatives with hardly any consideration for him. This, which is only an example of deprivation resulting from such subordination, makes some men migrate from home, make money, buy cattle, marry, live with their wives for a long time, and then return with a family too well established to be broken by the demands of their seniors. Of course, the unity and cooperation of the family is an important aspect of our postulated development, but initiative should also be induced. While a measure of assistance is to be expected from a brother with self-acquired wealth, the proposed reform should permit him to use such wealth for his own marriage unless his personal acquisition of wealth was part of a family plan. Apart from the economic initiative such reforms would induce, they would make family affection more accessible to younger brothers, enhance their respect in society, and provide them with bases for power not only within the family but in other arenas. The fact that economic opportunities for personal acquisition of wealth would be in modern economic processes is enough to indicate the overall modernizing effects.

Equalitarian measures are also called for in relation to consent in marriage. While the father's consent, provided it is not unreasonably withheld, should remain significant for the sake of family consensus and unity, the consent of the parties should also be required.

Although bars on grounds of exogamy force marriage outside one's circle and today even outside one's tribe, thereby widening affection circles, their extremism unduly hampers unions, especially those that could produce models of progressive families, since most educated men and women come from related backgrounds.

Polygyny, being behind women's notorious jealousies and conflicts which now give rationalization for many injustices against them and their children, should be discouraged. But outlawing it instantly would not be advisable or practical. In such cases as a man's marrying with the understanding that the marriage remains monogamous, a subsequent marriage in violation of this should either be invalid or should provide ground for divorce by the wife. If, for reasons of finance, education, affection, or the like, a second marriage is deemed detrimental in the particular circumstances of the family seen especially from the point of view of modern living, such a marriage should be prevented.

Formalities of marriage as a legal requirement call for simplification to meet the mobile conditions of modern society and to put more focus on the role of individual parties. Registration may be introduced as a way of dispensing with the elaborate time-consuming celebration of traditional society. The occasion should also be utilized for informing the parties of their marital rights and duties under the new law and of ways to improve their family living in modern terms. In the absence of registration, actual handing over of the bride should conclude the marriage. The institution of bride wealth, at the basis of women's inferiority, needs modification in a manner to be elaborated with respect to property.

The present law is adequately discouraging to divorce, but with decline in the importance of bride wealth, the increased role of the immediate parties and especially of the wife as a result of the suggested indulgences in affection and other values, the dominance of group interest which worked against divorce is likely to weaken and demand for divorce is likely to increase. While this would call for the formulation of preventive measures, divorce laws may require adaptation to such demands. As our discussion of divorce law showed, such need has already arisen with respect to unions where differences between the parties have increased with the discrepancies in their rate of change.

The present legitimacy rules are commendable insofar as they integrate the children. However, the problems of confusion between the pater and genitor which are now ignored but which seriously affect the psychological well-being of those concerned, call for attention. Some suggested changes, such as abolishing ghost marriage, discouraging the levirate, fixing the hand-over stage for validity of marriage, and making the parties' consent a condition, may minimize the problem.

With respect to sexual torts, the situation is open to some doubts. On first impression one feels that the law would be creating a loophole in the protection of the family if such wrongs were eliminated. On the other hand, if, as we speculated earlier with respect to the educated class, the effect of equality on the psychology of the litigants is that it is embarrassing to bring such actions, then that fact might justify their elimination. However, even in the Western World where equality is more obviously pursued, people still sue. The situation would be better resolved in the light of concrete evidence as to who sues and why. It is highly doubtful, however, that wholesale abolition of sexual torts, as has been extracted by some modern jurisdictions, would be the right measure. Even in these modern cultural situations, its justification has been doubted. According to Prosser, the "Heart-Balm" acts in the United States "reverse abruptly the entire tendency of the law to give increased protection to family interest and the sanctity of the house, and undoubtedly they deny relief in many cases of serious and genuine wrong." [37] Until further evidence suggests a popular feeling to the contrary, causes of action based on sexual wrongs, tortious or criminal, should be maintained but reformed. It may be argued that the determination of damages is too difficult to be attempted. In answer, we may say that it is no more difficult than in some of the other injuries recognized by modern law, such as nervous shock and injury to reputation.

37. Prosser, *Torts* 910 (3rd ed. 1964).

The more modern the society becomes the better equipped it is with scientific means of assessing injury, so that such a plea is not altogether justifiable. Considering the biological differences in the light of the all-inclusive nature and the objectives of the family, the consequences of sexual torts on women are bound to be different from those on men. The law should take cognizance of that fact in the process of emancipation of women. In certain cases (e.g. where the affection of the husband is alienated and he deserts the house, leaving the wife and children with no support) the consequences are much graver on the wife. In an act of adultery however, confusion over paternity can only arise on the side of the wife.

Defamation as a tort primarily against the descent groups and elders should be broadened to enhance respect for the reputation of women and youth. Such enhancement is not only in accordance with human dignity, but essential to the constructive contribution in the integrated system envisaged.

Vicarious liability in traditional society is largely insured by the solidarities of the lineage and the clan. In this sense, the liability has rested on the individual wrongdoer, and payment by his kinsmen is to lessen the burden on him. In modern society a person may protect himself with an insurance policy, and thereby distribute the burden throughout a larger population. Before that stage is reached in Dinka society, personal responsibility should be encouraged in order to induce individual initiative. Vicarious responsibility nonetheless plays a significant role in today's Dinka society in that it both aids the distribution of burdens throughout a larger population and fosters the group feeling of some responsibility for the wrong of the member, thus motivating them to check him. The happy medium between the discouragement and the utilization of vicarious responsibility is better left to the particular circumstances of a case. Thus, where it would curtail the productive endeavors of a relative to aid and promote the wrong person, it should not be allowed. Where a situation is normally appropriate, it should be permitted.

Intrafamily liability poses a paradox. In principle, members of the family should not be able to sue each other in tort, but unless this was possible, the present inequities would not be checked. A middle approach would be either to establish special family courts to handle such litigation in a manner even more persuasive and reconciling than suggested for the tribe, or to authorize the ordinary courts to approach such matters in that manner. The present traditional courts practice the latter, but the bias is in favor of the status quo. The proposed court should emphasize the other side in order to achieve the desired balance.

With respect to property, we have demonstrated the significance of the individual within the ambit of communalism, and how the patriarch, whether within the family or its fictional extensions, is the dominant individual, how cooperation is practiced, and how individual and social interests are correlated. At common law, unity of the household was given effect through community of property, but that was based on inequality. A somewhat similar situation prevails in Dinka society. Anglo-American law (some American states excepted) [38] has introduced reforms which have brought separation of goods in the family. But it has been observed that "nature, driven with a pitchfork, comes back. Despite the separation of property of husband and wife, the merger of many of their worldly possessions is and remains a fact." [39] There can be only one suggestion for the Dinka: where there is community of goods, development should liberate the wife to the level of equality without disrupting the unity of the spouses. What is required is true partnership in which both have equal though perhaps not identical powers. As Professor Kahn-Freund has argued: "A system of equality between the legal status of married and that of unmarried women and of men is compatible with a matrimonial regime of joint property of the spouses." [40] With respect to the children, the determining factor for capacity to hold property should be age rather than marriage; but before they are separated, adult children should form part of the unity.

Transitional integration is a strategy of checks and balances which can be applied to all fields of the social process, with the law occupying a pivotal position as an instrument of control. By building on the dynamics of tradition but remolding and redirecting them, transitional integration makes it possible to utilize their positives, to minimize their negatives, and to approximate the goals of modernization as a means of enhancing values and therefore conducive to the objectives of human dignity.

Transitional Integration and the Future of Customary Law in the Sudan

The role of customary law in the proposed transitional integration raises pertinent questions as to its future in the context of what Dr. Farran called "cohabitation of laws." [41] The raciocultural and religious diversities which this cohabitation purports to accommodate result in problems of unity and disunity which require solutions. The gravest of these problems is the cleavage between the Muslim Arab North and the

38. California, Texas, Arizona, Louisiana, Nevada, New Mexico, and Idaho. Even in these states the application of community property is largely limited to certain types of property and ownership. Generally see Lay, "A Survey of Community Property," 51 *Iowa Law Review* 625 (1966).

39. Kahn-Freund, "Inconsistencies and Injuries in the Law of Husband and Wife," 15 *Modern Law Review* 136 (1952).

40. Id. at 134.

41. Farran vii.

predominantly pagan Negroid South. This cleavage, though recognized
by the legal system, poses major problems of transition for which no
solutions have so far been attempted. At present, the legal system is a
dualism which is unlike the dualism familiar in other African countries
in that its components are not customary and general, but Islamic and
civil. The latter term is also used in contrast to the local system within
the civil system. There thus exists a complex situation which is both
tripartite in that it comprises Islamic, local, and general legal systems,
and dual in that it embodies two hierarchies, Islamic and civil.

The Islamic division consists of Islamic or Sharia courts, which were
established under the Sudan Mohammedan Law Courts Ordinance of
1902, and which form an independent hierarchy headed by the Grand
Kadi. They are empowered to apply "the authoritative doctrines of the
Hanafia [42] jurists except in matters in which the Grand Kadi otherwise
directs in a judicial circular or memorandum in which case the decision
shall be in accordance with such other doctrines of the Hanafia or other
Mohammedan jurists as are set forth in such circulars or memoranda." [43]
Their jurisdiction covers such personal matters as succession, wills,
legacies, gifts, marriage, divorce, family relations, or the constitution of
wakfs [44] where both parties are Muslims or in the case of mixed or non-
Muslim parties where both parties consent to the jurisdiction.[45] Although the majority of the Sudanese are Muslims, Sharia courts function
within a relatively small community. The greater portion of the Muslims
fall under the jurisdiction of tribal or local courts. Virtually all the
Sharia judges are trained only in Islamic law in Egyptian universities
or in the branch of Khartoum Law Faculty specialized to Sharia. Consequently, these judges administer Islamic law in isolation, though amid
a fabric of legal interaction and conflict. Their jurisprudential vision of
Islamic law is that it is God-given and uncompromisingly correct.[46] This
is not to imply immutability in Sharia. On the contrary, the provision
empowering the Grand Kadi to issue circulars and memorandums can
be, and has been, used to bring Islamic law in accord with the changing
conditions of the modern Muslim world.[47]

42. One of the four orthodox schools of Islamic jurisprudence.

43. Regulation 53 of the Sudan Mohammedan Law Courts Ordinance promulgated
under the Sudan Mohammedan Law Courts Ordinance of 1902, which established the
present system of Islamic courts.

44. Muslim trusts.

45. Their jurisdiction is similar to that of the civil courts under Section 5 of the
Civil Justice Ordinance.

46. Cf. Anderson, "The Adaptation of Muslim Law in Sub-Saharan Africa," in
African Law, Adaptation and Development 149–50 (1965).

47. See, for instance, Anderson, supra note 5 and "Law Reform in the Middle East,"
32 International Affairs 43 (1956).

The local division is composed of native and chiefs' courts. Native courts are constituted under the Native Courts Ordinance of 1932, applicable to the six provinces of the North excepting the Ngok Dinka of Kordofan Province. These courts are empowered to apply "The Native law and custom" prevailing in the area of their jurisdiction, provided it is not repugnant to "justice, morality, or order." [48] Their "native law and custom" is an amalgam of Islamic and customary laws.[49] Some of the customary laws are remnants of their pre-Islamic laws and customs.[50] Others might even have evolved subsequently.[51] In any case, the customary laws of these tribal communities have distinct characteristics and are not typically customary.[52] This is why customary law in the Sudan is more identified with the pagan South.

The chiefs' courts are constituted under the Chiefs' Courts Ordinance of 1931, applicable to the Southern provinces and the Ngok Dinka of Kordofan in accordance with a special order of the governor-general in council 1944.[53] The judges are traditional elders and are mostly illiterate.

48. Section 9(1) (a) of the Native Courts Ordinance. See Abu Rannat (former Chief Justice), "Relationship Between Islamic and Customary Law in the Sudan," 4 *Journal of African Law* 11 (1960).

49. Farran observes about the evolution of an integrated Muslim customary law among these tribes that "Most, if not all, of the tribes involved were converted to Islam long ago. Accordingly, and by a gradual process of change, it may be argued, their pre-Islamic customs have ceased to prevail and the rules of Mohammedan law have taken their place . . . as the custom of the tribe in question. . . . What these courts in fact apply is not *pure* Mohammedan law, but Mohammedan law as modified by Custom." Farran 254. Referring to the same process of amalgamation in other parts of Africa, Professor Anderson says, "Islamic law has never fully ousted the indigenous law, but either co-exists with it as a separate and distinct system, each being applied in suitable circumstances, or else has fused with it into an amalgam that may be termed 'Islamic law' or 'native law and custom' according to taste or local practice." Anderson, "The Adaptation of Muslim Law in Sub-Saharan Africa," Kuper and Kuper, eds., *African Law, Adaptation and Development* 153 (1965).

50. Dr. Farran wrote, "A point which it is easy to overlook is that some tribes of Mohammedan Sudanese, especially in the Western Provinces of Darfur and Kordofan, have customs, obviously dating back to the period before their conversion to Islam." Farran 137.

51. This is made easier by the fact that, unless introduced through formal education, Islam advanced itself through preexisting indigenous lines. Rather than obliterate animistic ideas and institutions, it cloaked them with the concepts and outward, but highly ritualized symbols of traditional mode of life and evolving customs along traditional lines but under the banner of Islam. See Farran 227 and Trimingham, op. cit. supra note 13, at 44.

52. In fact, so fanatically though superficially Muslim are these tribes that they believe their laws to be part of Sharia even when they may in fact be contrary to Sharia. This recalls Professor Anderson's observation that the amalgamated law may be termed "Islamic law" or "native law and custom," according to taste or local practice.

53. The Chiefs' Courts Ordinance Application No. 1 Order.

The ordinance empowers them to try criminal and civil cases involving the natives of the South and according to the customary law prevailing in that territory, provided it is not repugnant to justice, morality, and order.[54]

The civil division consists of civil courts, as opposed to Islamic and local courts. These are the common courts and are the least limited in terms of people and the territory they govern, as well as the laws they apply. In criminal jurisdiction, they apply the Sudan Penal Code and the Code of Criminal Procedure together with other criminal statutes and regulations. In civil jurisdiction, Section 5 of the Civil Justice Ordinance of 1900 as reenacted in 1929 provides:

> Where in any suit or other proceeding in a civil court any question arises regarding succession, wills, legacies, gifts, marriage, divorce, family relations, or the constitution of Wakfs, the rule of decision shall be:—
>
> a) Any custom applicable to the parties concerned which is not contrary to justice, equity or good conscience, and has not been by this or any other enactment altered or abolished and has not been declared void by the decision of any competent court.
>
> b) The Mohammedan law in cases where the parties are Mohammedan, except insofar as that law has been modified by such custom as is above referred to.

Subsection (b) was a device to cover tribal communities in the North who, though Muslims, still retained indigenous laws administered by native courts.[55] The provision gives customary law priority over Islamic law. "Except insofar as that law has been modified by such customs as is above referred to" means either that pure Islamic law will not apply to those people to whom customary law is applicable, or that Islamic law as modified by their customs will apply to them. Virtually all the judges being Muslims, this interpretation is not likely to withstand the postcolonial Muslim nationalism.[56] Indeed, it is generally contended that such repugnancy clauses as are applicable to other laws cannot be applied to Islamic law, since it is God's prescription.

A report on native law in Darfur Province [57] illustrates this unconditional commitment to Islam. A custom provided that a tribal leader

54. Section 7 of the Chiefs' Courts Ordinance.

55. See Farran 137.

56. Ibid.

57. Written by Khartoum law students who had gone on a tour of tribal areas, visiting local courts and acquainting themselves with customary laws. "Native Law in Darfur" (Unpublished manuscript in The Faculty of Law), Khartoum University (1960).

might marry more than four wives,[58] which is the limit imposed by Islam. This custom was recognized in a number of tribes. In criticism of the British judge who had upheld the custom, the reporters wrote that "the conflict was not between state-made legislation and custom, but between faith and custom. . . . It is legitimate to wonder whether it was wise of the British Administrators to uphold and enforce a custom that violated the basic principles of the people's religion." [59] This argument, though religiously understandable, destroys itself on its own terms, for courts do not enforce faith unless it is supportable by law. The critics would have been better off with the argument they discarded, namely, that the dispute was between state-made legislation and custom, for it could be argued in favor of Islam that since Section 5(a) provides for the application of "custom" if among other reasons it "has not been by this or any other enactment altered or abolished" and Subsection (b) provides for the application of Islamic law to Muslims, Subsection (b) could be construed as part of "this enactment" covering succession, wills, marriage, and the like, abolishing customs which are against Islamic law. This is presumably what the chief justice meant when he wrote of the Homr of Kordofan that "many of [their] customs, such as those relating to land, trespassing cattle and so on, fall outside the scope of Sharia. But some of their customs relating to personal status differ from the relevant rules of Sharia." [60] Sharia in its broad sense would have a greater scope, but, in this particular sense, the chief justice must have meant only that part of Sharia recognized by state legislation. Even then, one is still faced with the phrase "except insofar as that law has been modified by such custom as is above referred to." [61] Whether one construes the phrase as an exclusion of Islamic law where there is an applicable customary law, or as applying to situations where Islamic law had been adapted to local conditions (in which case the adapted form applies), it is difficult to see what would legally justify Islamic law to prevail over customary law. The issue is more academic than real because civil courts do not apply Islamic law often, since, as we have seen, according to Section 38 of the Civil Justice Ordinance, "Civil Courts shall not be competent to decide in a suit to which all parties are Mohammedans except with the consent of the parties." [62]

Just as Islamic law is favored, customary law is disfavored. A number of factors account for this. The obvious one is that customary law is

58. A custom which prevails in most parts of Africa.
59. The report cited, op. cit. supra note 57, at 7.
60. Abu Rannat, supra note 48, at 11.
61. Section 5(b) of the Civil Justice Ordinance.
62. See *Nur el Huda Abdel Ghani v. Omar Hassan* (1953) Digest No. 24.

seen in opposition to Islamic law and is, accordingly, resented. Besides, as we said earlier, since customary law in the North has assimilated Islamic principles, customary law as commonly understood is identified with the South and to encourage it would be to impede national integration.[63] Furthermore, modernization in the Sudan focuses on the already relatively modern section, mainly The Three Towns, and such areas as are governed by customary law are too remote to those who govern the country from Khartoum.[64] There is also the general feeling that customary law is inferior and therefore something to be ashamed of, or at least not to be encouraged by any means including the mere knowledge of it.[65] This view seems to be shared by the educated class in the South. Of course, customary law plays an important role in the problems of identity which mark the South-North relations, and this works in its favor among the educated Southerners. On the other hand, they consider it "primitive," and it is sometimes used against them by their traditional opponents who wield tribal power. They therefore do not want to identify with it. When the present writer was conducting an investigation into Ngok Dinka customary law, he was often warned by this class and the more progressive among the traditionals that he should not record such customs as would embarrass the Dinka in front of others. A combination of these and other factors has subordinated customary law to Islamic law. While the latter is taught not only in the Sharia division but also in the general division of the Faculty of Law, customary law is not. An expatriate who shows interest in the study and the teaching of customary law is likely to be suspected of "imperialist" motivation. To the majority of Sudanese its disappearance is only a matter of time, and the shorter the time, the better. Yet, over 80 percent[66] of the populace is still governed by customary law, and through original jurisdiction, revision, and appeals, civil courts are continuously confronted with customary law. The result is often a miscarriage of justice. "One of the many difficulties of the administration of justice in the Sudan today is that the Northern Sudanese magistrates have no knowledge, judicial or private, of the customary law of the pagan."[67] This ignorance is aggravated by the fact that the scanty law reporting that exists does not cover cases decided by local courts.

One judge told the present writer during the latter's field work that

63. See, for example, Farran 29–31, 66–67 and Thompson, "Sources of Law in the New Nations of Africa: A Case Study from the Republic of the Sudan," *Wisconsin Law Review* 1146, 1162 (Fall 1966).

64. Ibid.

65. While this was the case throughout Africa, it has been reversed by postcolonial policies in most countries.

66. Estimates vary from over 80 to over 90 percent.

67. Farran 282 note 11.

he could attend his court of appeal but should not expect to learn from it since he, the appellate authority, knew nothing about Dinka law. Asked how he could decide on appeals in ignorance of the law, the judge replied that as they did not want to embarrass the chiefs, they would usually allow their judgments to prevail. It is true that the influence of the chief depends largely on the extent to which his judgments are respected by higher authorities. On the other hand, the concept of appeal would be meaningless if this concession were carried to an extreme. A happy medium cannot be reached in ignorance of the law. In sharp contrast with the automatic endorsement of chiefs' decisions is the dismantling application of repugnancy clauses to customary law. Whether it is "justice, morality, or order" or "justice, equity, and good conscience," these clauses are potential tools for the development of customary law, but cultural bias coupled with ignorance of the law may render them destructive to the administration of justice. When the writer asked a province judge what standard was used in applying repugnancy clauses he said, "Of course, the standard of a decent and civilized society, not that of a primitive tribe." [68] In one case, a young judge with Khartoum legal training was shocked by the Ngok Dinka custom of compensating the husband of an adulterous wife. He argued that it was an equitable maxim that a wrongdoer could not benefit from his own wrong, and, according to him, the interests of husband and wife were so identical that for the husband to recover for his wife's wrong was to benefit wrongfully. He therefore asked the writer to advise the chief on his behalf to abolish the custom. His argument was evidently based on one side of the case, and an exaggerated one at that. He did not know the point of view of the society in which the custom prevailed.

68. A judge once told the writer of an incident which will illustrate the point. A Ngok Dinka man and woman came to his court. The man complained that the woman was refusing to live with him as his wife and asked the court's order to compel her to do so. The woman, probably sophisticated by town influence, told the judge that she was not the complainant's wife but his brother's widow. On proving the facts, the judge ordered the woman free and held the levirate contrary to Section 7 of the Chiefs' Courts Ordinance. He told the writer that he was going to instruct the chief of the tribe to abolish the custom throughout the tribe. When the writer explained the significance of the levirate in Dinka society and produced a book to illustrate its existence in other Southern tribes, so sympathetic was the judge that he stopped talking about ordering a sudden abolition of the custom and asked his secretary to type the relevant pages of the book.

We do not necessarily question the justice of the particular decision; but the suggestion that the custom be outlawed throughout the tribe was a hazardous step which, as the judge himself admitted, could only be explained by cultural conditioning and ignorance of customary law. Citing this incident, Dr. Farran remarked, "It is by no means easy for anyone—even a judge—to put aside certain fundamental bases of thought: moral standards we may call them." Id. at 16.

The custom is found in almost all African traditional societies and is rooted deep in their cultures. Even in Western law, in which he was trained, it is a tort in some jurisdictions. In any case, one may wonder whether it could be established that the interests of the wife and her husband in violation of sexual rights are joint. The outcome of a case of adultery may be to their common economic advantage, but in Dinka society it is most unlikely that the wife would benefit. Even the husband must abstain from the dairy products of cattle given as adultery compensation, or any food acquired through such cattle. Usually they are disposed of in settling debts or in marriage. But whether there is a common material advantage or not, the wrong cannot be common. How can a husband be a party to a wrong which violates his sexual rights, and why should he be hampered from a remedy simply because one of the parties injuring him incidentally benefits from the compensation due to him? The situation would, of course, be different if the husband traded on his wife or in any way consented to the commission of the wrong. As it was, the writer explained the importance of the custom among the Dinka and the judge was persuaded not to prescribe its abolition.

The problem cannot be approached as a series of isolated facts, nor should we be understood to oppose the application of the repugnancy clauses to reform the law in a desirable manner. In one case, for instance, the judge skillfully induced self-scrutiny among the Dinkas by pointing out to them the negative implications of a custom in a present-day Dinka society.[69] His success illustrates a creative use of the repugnancy clauses to develop customary laws with the least possible disruption and with as much support from public sentiment as possible. What is desirable, therefore, is not a rejection of the qualifying provisions, but their skilled application.

Although civil courts are expressly empowered to apply Islamic law and customary law, the main source of the law they apply is contained in Section 9 of the Civil Justice Ordinance which states that "In cases not provided for by this enactment or any other enactment for the time being in force the court shall act according to justice, equity and good conscience." Theoretically, this provision is a further ground for applying any law, including such principles of Islamic law or customary law as are conducive to "justice, equity, and good conscience." Practically, it has become a tool for the importation and adaptation of Anglo-American law, which provides now the bases for the general law of the country. Since personal matters under Section 5 were left to local law, Section 9 provided for a partial reception of what is often referred to as "lawyers' law," [70] torts, commercial law, evidence, civil and criminal

69. *Matet Ayom v. Deng Majok* and *Nyuong v. Wor*, cited in Chapter 7, pp. 268–69.

70. See, generally, Twining, "Some Aspects of Reception," *Sudan Law Journal and Reports* 229, 232–33 (1957); Thompson, supra note 63, at 1148.

procedure, conflict of laws and public law, as opposed to "people's law" in which tradition is so deep-rooted that it should be left to customary law.[71] This distinction is so blurred that it can mislead. Studies of African customary laws have shown that they cover all aspects of law. Although certain problems covering modern exigencies are not answerable by customary law, general classes of law such as contracts, torts, evidence, property, and criminal law are covered in a form reflecting the conditions they serve. Partial reception brought the modern expression of these categories. In its mode of reception, the Sudan, among all British-administered territories, was unique in that there was no statute expressly providing for the importation of English law and in using such terms as "justice, morality, and good conscience" to modify the legal system of a conquering power.[72] This explains the fact that the delegates at the London Conference of 1959–60 on the Future of Law in Africa smiled when this Sudanese qualification was mentioned.[73]

The adaptation of Anglo-American law to the circumstances of the country points up the importance of customary law or custom. An illustration of local limitation as applied to individual cases is provided in *Sudanese Government v. El Baleila Balla Baleila*,[74] where a nomadic Arab killed an engineer whose train had run over his cattle. Many factors combine to make cattle immensely important to the nomadic Arab, so that to kill them in a manner he must have thought brutal was held to be sufficient provocation to reduce murder to simple culpable homicide. The concept of the "reasonable man" was held not to be uniform throughout the country, but to be varied according to the local conditions of the community of which the accused is a member. Abu Rannat, Chief Justice, in reviewing the decision of the lower court and holding in favor of the accused, said, "The 'reasonable man' referred to in the textbooks is the man who normally leads such life in the locality, and is of the same standards as others . . . The accused in this case is an unsophisticated nomadic Arab who knows little about the world . . . The real test is whether an ordinary Arab of the standard [of the accused] would be provoked or not." [75]

In yet another case,[76] a major court considered as circumstantial evidence, in accordance with the local custom of Kakwa tribe in the South, the fact that for a person to slaughter a sheep and bang his own head against the wall of a house of the deceased's relatives was evidence of having killed that person.

---

71. Ibid.
72. For an example of what existed elsewhere in British Africa see Allott 18.
73. See 4 *Journal of African Law* 77 (1960).
74. *Sudan Law Journal and Reports* 12 (1958).
75. Ibid.
76. *Sudan Government v. Yoele Lowiya. Sudan Law Journal and Reports* 69 (1959).

This is the essence of Section 9 as expressed in the celebrated dictum of Owen, Chief Justice, that we are guided but not bound by English common and statute law. This dictum, as has been observed, "has been repeated often enough to become a judicial cliché." [77]

Actual creativity in the application of Section 9 should not be exaggerated. We have already seen how ignorance of traditional laws impedes such creativity. Since national legal training is in Anglo-American and Islamic law, the sources of law utilized under Section 9 are limited. Even the appreciation and consequently the application of Anglo-American law are usually faulty because of the scarcity of Anglo-American reports and other legal literature, particularly in the more isolated areas. Furthermore, lack of adequate reports and other publications on Sudanese law leaves the judges unaware of their own laws, whether statutory or judge-made.[78] Inconsistent and erroneous application of the law is the consequence. In *Khartoum Municipal Council v. Michael Cotran*,[79] the court rejected the Road Traffic Ordinance of 1945 and applied the English Contributory Negligence Act of 1945, which came about a month after the Sudan legislation providing for apportionment in contributory negligence. The court reasoned that "the English Act of 1945 relating to Contributory Negligence would be applicable in equity, justice and good conscience." In an earlier case,[80] the Court of Appeal recognized the injustice of the English last opportunity rule and yet upheld it under the misconception that the court was bound by prior authorities on the point, though the views of these authorities were merely obiter dicta. Marrogordaba J., as he then was, said, "I concur, though not without regret . . . This rule, though never in my opinion consonant

77. Thompson, supra note 63, at 152. In *Nicola Episcopoulo v. the Superior of the African Catholic Mission*, the plaintiff and defendant were registered owners of adjoining plots of land. In constructing certain buildings on his own land, the defendant mistakenly allowed his buildings to encroach on the plaintiff's land. The plaintiff brought action claiming that the defendant be ordered to remove the buildings on the plaintiff's land, or, in the alternative, that the defendant be ordered to pay the plaintiff compensation for the loss of enjoyment of the land built on. The Court of Appeal held, *inter alia*, that the English law on the point, which allowed a trespasser who has built in good faith on another's land to be turned off by that other, who may keep the buildings without compensating the builder, or even sue the builder for damages if the buildings had damaged the land, had gone too far in its protection of landowners against trespassers, since it might produce great injustice in certain cases. Although the court did not follow Egyptian and Ottoman laws on the point, it considered them and found them also inapplicable. 1 *Sudan Law Reports (Civil)* 31 (1964).

78. Thompson, supra note 63, at 1154–60. See also Guttman, "Law Reporting in the Sudan," 6 *International Comparative Law Quarterly* 685–89 (1957) and Twining, "Law Reporting in the Sudan," 3 *Journal of African Law* 176–78 (1959).

79. *Sudan Law Journal and Reports* 85 (1958).

80. *Abu Gabal v. Sudan Government* Appeal Cases 3/194.

with justice, equity and good conscience . . . was always recognized by this court."

The foregoing has shown the complexities of Sudan legal problems, lack of articulation in policies, and the inadequate equipment of the decision-makers to handle the task of law reform. Customary law still commands the allegiance of the majority and is interwoven into the various sources of Sudanese law, religious and secular. Nonetheless, it receives the least attention. There is much talk about law reform in the Sudan, but the reform envisaged centers around Islamization and Aribization in the sense of making the law reflect Islamic-Arabic culture more than it does now.[81] A significant faction of the legal profession advocates a shift to the civil law system with the view to codification and translation into Arabic, probably after the model of Egyptian law.[82] There is also a call for the abolition of local courts, leaving customary law to be applied by the civil courts. Alternatively, it is sometimes suggested that local courts be constituted of legally trained personnel instead of tribal chiefs. These and others are still the rattlings of empty vessels. Nothing constructive has been suggested and no action is in sight. Informed and responsible men realize that the system cannot dispense with courts which handle a heavy load of litigation in a country which, though better in this respect than most countries in Africa,[83] has an insufficient number of trained lawyers, especially when the trained few are completely ignorant of customary law.

Of course, the system cannot remain forever divided. As Abu Rannat, the former chief justice, said to the London Conference on the Future of Native Law in Africa, "In the future, it is likely that a Sudan Common Law will develop as an integral part of the society now emerging in the Sudan; it will not be based on religious adherence, but upon the social customs and ethics of the Sudan as a whole." [84] At the moment, social ideals should not be confused with social realities. The existence of differences is a fact which perhaps with wisdom can be turned into an asset. To ignore diversity and pretend that there is at present any

81. For practical difficulties associated with the idea generally see Twining, supra note 70.

82. The fact that most of the professional lawyers are trained in Egypt or in the Khartoum branch of Cairo University is a factor in this appeal.

83. Legal education was introduced into the Sudan in the 1930s. For the situation in East Africa see Twining, "Legal Education Within East Africa, East African Law Today 115 (1965). Referring to the important role played by local courts today, the Commission of Inquiry into the Southern Disturbances of 1955 reports, "We find that even if judicial personnel were available, the work of the Local Courts for years to come will still have to be maintained." Sudan Government, Southern Sudan Disturbances 10 (1956).

84. Abu Rannat, supra note 48, at 6.

fundamental unity is to deceive oneself and to act upon this deception is to invite disastrous consequences. In the words of a notable judge, "If we fail to appreciate this fact, we will be in the position of a man . . . closing his eyes, and putting his hands on his ears, neither hearing nor seeing the civic, economic, or social realities of Sudanese life." [85] In the first and only textbook on problems of the Sudan legal system, Dr. Farran gave the same advice in unequivocal terms when he said that "to establish a uniform code of law for the present position is as impossible as it is undesirable. As well might one attempt to replace the lush abundance of a tropical garden with the staid formalities of an English public park." [86] It is the author's suggestion that a process of transitional integration by which the competing and conflicting interests of tradition and modernity and of the various participating ethnic, racial, or religious groups are balanced is the only means of developing the national legal system without shaking each of its component parts.

This will raise issues relating to the unification of the courts and the law they apply, as well as whether this law should or should not be codified. In many African countries, the integration of law has reached the level of codification. The London School of Oriental and African Studies has embarked on a project which aims at codifying the law of torts, and the code is meant to be a restatement in a way which would integrate customary law with received Western law.[87]

In a conference held at Ibadan in 1964, Professor Allott emphasized the importance of building on the preexisting legal system.

> Any new law must, in my submission, therefore try . . . so far as possible . . . to build on what is already there. That means, in the common law African countries, the Western type common and statutory law, as well as the indigenous customary and religious laws. To make a new law of civil wrongs, which replaces but at the same time incorporates and synthesizes, the existing multiple legal system, is much more of a challenge than to bring in a quite different law from outside. To try to do as Ataturk did, and introduce a novel law having no previous connection with the country, would be an exercise doomed to failure in the modern African context.[88]

85. Mr. Justice Mudhawi in *Khartoum Municipal Council v. Cotran. Sudan Law Journal and Reports* 85 (1958).

86. Farran 31.

87. Allott and Cotran, "A Background Paper on Restatement of Laws in Africa," (paper delivered at the Conference on Integration of Customary and Modern Legal Systems, Ibadan, Nigeria, August 1964); and Allott, "The Codification of the Law of Civil Wrongs in Common-Law African Countries," (paper delivered at the above conference).

88. Allott, "The Codification of the Law of Civil Wrongs," supra note 87, at 6.

The Sudan, having been dormant, must begin with the preliminary issues. First, the courts should be unified by creating one hierarchy. Local courts, though subordinate, form part of the national judicial system. Since virtually all judges are Muslims and receive some training in Islamic law, there is even less reason for Islamic law to remain in isolation and in the hands of absolutists. Even though the civil judges may be biased as Muslims, chances of fusion and compromises between the various laws would be greater if Islamic law were administered by the same courts that administer the rest of the law.

We have already argued that the institution of chieftainship is far too deeply rooted to be suddenly eliminated, if at all. On the other hand, it is crucial that chiefs be equipped for their role in contemporary society. One obvious qualification should be a certain amount of education. While allowance should be made for the present generation of illiterate chiefs, some sort of training for them should be introduced. For long-range purposes, education should be a precondition to chieftainship.

Apart from reorienting the chiefs, the membership of their courts, as we have suggested for tribal decision-making bodies in general, should be integrated primarily along the line of traditionals and "moderns." This way, a fusion of tradition and modernity may be expected as an articulated or a natural outcome of tribal judicial process. Such an integrated court would also be more competent to deal with the complex diversities now extending into the tribes. This would justify granting them more substantial powers, and such increase in their powers would in turn make them more effective as instruments for integrated transition.

With respect to the demand for separation of powers, in view of the strong expectations for the concurrence of powers, the disadvantages of change would seem to outweigh the advantages. In any case, the present abuse of power could be adequately checked by stringent supervision by national decision-makers. Such supervision could easily be expected with a reformed national system.

The primary step along the lines of reform on the national level is to remedy ignorance. The maxim should be "Study now, reform later," or at best do both concurrently. Professor Allott outlining reasons for the study of African customary law.

> If the uniform legal system is to evolve in a satisfactory manner, one which expresses the characteristic ethics and way of life of the people, it is essential that immediate attention be paid to the present customary law, which reflects, *par excellence,* the people's own choice of legal system. So far as possible one wants to avoid revolu-

tion in the legal sphere and abrupt discontinuity with the past and present. What one seeks is a smooth evolution of legal institutions, so that the new law is based on and is in harmony with the old. To do this, knowledge of the present law is essential.[89]

Customary law, its sociological framework, and its interaction with other systems should be introduced into the law-school curriculum, to be studied not as a static system, but as a part and an agent of social mobility. A portion of the present law-report system should be devoted to customary law in transition. Those whose profession concerns itself with the administration of the law—judges, advocates, and administrators—should receive additional training in these problems. If the judges are well equipped to meet the challenge and guide modernization through customary law, the fact that they are outsiders can be an asset, because conformity to archaic customs is more often expected from an insider than from an outsider.

While the role of an outside judge is important, judges should also be appointed among the local population both because they would have a deeper insight and concern and because this would satisfy the demand of their groups for a greater share in power. The problems of their cooperation with the traditionals would be minimized by the integration of tribal decision-making bodies.

Once the court is integrated and the judges well trained in handling the complex problems of legal synthesis, evolutionary integration should lay stress on case law rather than on legislation. Although legislation is vital in defining goals and laying standards, the courts are continually confronted with the particular problems of social change, and it is necessary that the law be left flexible.[90] This stands against the idea of adopting the doctrine of *stare decisis* [91] at present [92] even if the law reporting should be improved. Similarly, in the interest of unity in

89. Allott, "The Study of African Law," *Sudan Law Journal and Reports* 258 (1958).
90. See Twining, supra note 70.
91. The inadequacy of reports is sufficient argument against the doctrine. See Guttman, "Survey of Sudan Legal System," *Sudan Law Journal and Reports* 7–10 (1956). Cliff Thompson suggests that the balance of confidence in the Court of Appeal and certainty of the law, on the one hand, and conformity to changing conditions, on the other, might be achieved by "the ability and willingness of the legislative power to act quickly to remedy weaknesses in the law, for this would mitigate the political danger of the Court of Appeal being bound by unwanted rules." Thompson, supra note 63, at 1109. This by implication favors the doctrine of *stare decisis*. But, as we have argued, the individualization of judicial problems could not be adequately substituted for by legislative power.
92. Authorities are in conflict on the matter. For example, in *Abu Gabal v. Sudan Government* cited supra (note 81) the court considered itself bound by its previous decision. Generally, the matter is not even raised.

diversity, as well as of flexibility, it is desirable that the law not be codified during such a transitional period.[93] Adoption and adaptation necessitate fluidity to allow progress to take its harmonious though perhaps long way toward a genuine fusion. While codification is not advisable, recording should be encouraged as part of the study of customary law. It would be useful to group customs into those which are uniform, that is, those found in all the tribes, and local customs, those existing in some tribes only.

Where sufficient material has been gathered, a form of restatement comparable to the one undertaken by the Restatement of African Law Project of the London School of Oriental and African Studies should be prepared to guide the administration. Each of the systems interacting could be restated, focusing on itself but also integrating suitable principles from the other systems. The problem of multiplicity of tribes could be minimized by their division into such major subcultural groups as the Nilotic and the Sudanic peoples.[94] These restatements would then need to be revised as often as possible, incorporating much of the development the courts will have made and the degree to which their innovations are universally effected, thereby aiding ultimate fusion.[95]

The Sudan legal system as it now stands has the foundation of an ingenious architect who carefully designed it for the amicable cohabitation of Islamic law, customary law, and the imported general law. This structure provides the principal elements required for development toward a harmonious fusion. How well the system achieves these goals depends on the people who run it. "The major legal systems of the world mainly gain their character, not from the content of their specific legal rules or doctrines, but from the men who did and do dominate the legal system and the administration of justice in their society." [96] The future of customary law in the Sudan thus far depends on the quality of the decision-makers, their articulation of the equitable policies of transitional integration, their proper understanding of the whole context and its diversities, their prediction of what various alternative trends might be, their objective evaluation of such predicted trends, and their selection of alternatives conducive to balanced and harmonious integration and development.

93. See Farran 31.
94. As this might foster a spirit of wider factionalism, it should be carefully conducted.
95. An advisory body might be set up to inform the decision-makers of the progress and assess new measures at the various stages of development toward this fusion.
96. Max Weber, quoted in Twining, supra note 70, at 234.

Conclusion

The Dinka live in a world in which the dignity and survival of a people depend largely on their effective participation in the shaping and sharing of values as defined by global standards. Modernization is crucial to such participation. The challenge for the Dinka is not the initial step toward modernization, for that step has already been taken. Whether modernization is fast or slow, pleasant or painful, it is unremitting. With the effects of science and technology permeating the value-institutional web and giving man the power to mold nature toward his ends, modernization is presumed a betterment of man's conditions. In addition to being an incoming phenomenon, it should be a pursued objective. This is not to underestimate its odds and cons. Indeed, modernization can be hazardous, especially when its hurricanes get a grip on the weak material foundations of tradition. It is, however, our premise that modernization can be shaped and directed to minimize its hazards while accelerating material progress as well as maximizing values toward the overriding goal of human dignity. Using law as a starting point into the complex network of values and institutions, we have attempted to provide basic guidelines in this direction. The processes of value shaping and sharing involve human interactions in which the law as a controlling weapon is pivotal. Through a policy-oriented allocation of values, law can be a dynamic instrument of justice by broadening the sharing of values, and of modernization by indulging actual or potential shapers of modern values. This is likely to lead to a pacification of destructively competitive forces and their mobilization for constructive purposes. The guiding principle should be maximum achievement with minimum human cost.

At present, disruption prevails over Dinkaland and there is every indication that the hurricane causing it is not over. While this is conspicuous on the national level, its foundation is in the family and in the overriding myth of permanent male identity and influence which stratifies people according to sex, generation, and descent, with racial and cultural implications. By accident of history, modernizing impact has built a wide gulf between elders who traditionally headed the value pyramids and the educated youth whose indulgences in modern values have disposed them to demand more than the situation presently allows. But in partial conformity to the traditional rules of familial piety, and in proportion to the magnitude of their demands, their opposition and rebellion is directed against the national constitutive setup which is racially and culturally Arab-oriented and is therefore seen as "alien." The violent confrontation between the South and the North is evidence of this demand for a greater share in national values. But the disruptive implications of the stratifications underlying the myth of permanent identity and influence are not confined to the role of the educated. On the conscious level, women and youth in traditional society do not articulate opposition to subservience; but their protest, though not conceived as such, is expressed in various ways which tend to negate the objectives of their dominant seniors and therefore of society. Whether it be by tribal wars, civil disobedience, or other "wrongful" endeavors as defined by the system, these groups of well over half the total population are the major contributors to destruction.

While, traditionally, the youthful groups and the women were nonconformists in indirect opposition to the system, direct objection has begun to emerge with the introduction of modernity and new notions of equality of sex, age, race, and culture. The more they become modernized, the more their objection, and the more intense its expression on the higher levels where the traditional repressions are less marked. Some of the more articulate not only predict change but desire a revolutionary one and, as revolutions generally do, put the problem in reverse.

The challenge then is to divert this trend and turn the destruction which is already prevalent, and which is predicted to worsen, into modernizing construction. In doing so, it must be borne in mind that not only is tradition still dominant, but it has positive aspects which could facilitate the approximation of human dignity. It is, therefore, prudent to work with tradition and traditionals.

We have suggested and expounded a strategy of transitional integration as an alternative toward the desired balance between tradition and traditionals on the one hand, and modernity and the moderns on the other. While favoritism for the latter is a necessary condition for a significant change, the strategy calls for building on tradition as the basis. We begin with interpreting the myth of permanent identity and influence as a basis for looking forward rather than backward. We stress the traditional goals of unity and harmony expressed in *cieng* as a basis for a modernizing cooperative endeavor and for persuasive policies. But transitional integration calls for more than merely reinterpreting tradition to facilitate modernization; it requires that traditionals and tradition be continually coordinated to maintain the desired balance of change. For this reason we propose that the traditionals and the moderns work together in all value processes. In power, for instance, it is proposed that chiefs, elders, the educated, and the warrior groups should work together in all decision-making bodies. Skills and enlightenment would provide a most strategic integration. In well-being, the recognition of traditional medicine and traditional medicine men and their integration with modern medicine and modern medical professionals is advocated. The same principles are applicable to wealth, affection, and respect. These broad principles will naturally necessitate a detailed creative use of the law in its widest sense.

Although our suggestions have centered on the Ngok tribal level, changes in the fundamental law of the country or at least in the administrative disposition of the national decision-makers are prerequisites to the application of transitional integration. Once successfully applied on the tribal level, transitional integration would have a two-way effect on the family and the national levels. Because it would require the adjustment of familial roles from which tribal roles are projected, a close coordination of family law to the policies of transitional integration is commended. This would in turn facilitate the application of transitional integration on the tribal level. Special measures are needed on the national level to combat such crises as the Southern problem, but since the traditional sector forms the overwhelming majority of the Sudan, and assuming that the Dinka situation has parallels on the traditional sector in general, integrating the national counterelite into the traditional sector could have a pacifying effect and could lay solid foundation for continued progress. Thus, transitional integration aims at establishing a system of public order capable of promoting social justice while mobilizing constructive forces for a modernization conducive to, and conditioned by, the overriding goal of human dignity.

Glossary

As a prelude to the glossary of Dinka terms used in this book a few guiding principles of orthography and pronunciation are included below.

1. All vowels have Latin (new pronunciation) values.

2. The letter *c* is always pronounced as *ch* in "change," not as in "care."

3. The nearest English letter to the Dinka letter *dh* is *th*, but in the Dinka letter the tongue is drawn farther back than in the English *th*.

4. The letters ŋ and ɣ were added to the Roman alphabet by Christian missionaries who developed written Dinka. ŋ equals the English *ng* when they occur at the end of an English word. ɣ has no equivalent in English, but approximates the English *h* with the middle of the tongue pressing the middle of the upper jaw, leaving a much smaller space for air than is the case in the sound of the letter *h*. Here, *ng* and *gh* are used to represent ŋ and ɣ.

5. The letters *ny* are pronounced as in the Italian *gn*, never as in the English "many," as in Latin.

6. When a vowel is doubled, the sound is an elongation of the vowel: *oo* is pronounced something like the *oa* in "goal" and not as in "pool"; *ee* is pronounced like the *a* in "scale"; *ii* is pronounced like the *ee* in "geese"; *aa* is pronounced as in "car"; *uu* is pronounced as in "pool."

7. The letter *g* is always pronounced as in "gain," not as in "George."

8. The single vowel *a* is pronounced as in "car"; *e* approximates the *e*'s in every; *i* is pronounced as in "kill"; *o* is pronounced as in "poll"; *u* is pronounced as in "bull."

abathook	The public, usually assembled, as in court or for any public purpose.
abur	A poor man. The term applies to cattle wealth, and, to a lesser extent, to sheep and goat wealth, but not to money or any other property.
acien	A curse, whether intentionally inflicted by a wronged person or automatically resulting from a wrongdoing. Although the curse may be effective in the lifetime of the wronged person, *acien* usually implies punishment by the spirit of a dead person.
acien pioth (sing. *acien piou*)	Literally "[they] have no hearts." Used to describe a person who is not only inconsiderate but also reckless and irresponsible. It concerns the functions of both the heart and the mind.

adheng	As applied to a man, noble, handsome, elegant, charming, graceful, gentle, hospitable, generous, well mannered, kind, or of marked aesthetic attributes. Also used to mean a gentleman and an initiated man as opposed to a "boy." See *dheeng* below for the noun forms of *adheng*.
agamlong	Literally, "the acceptor of speech." A man who repeats in a high-pitched voice the whole or part of each sentence said in court, prayer, or any public speech. No one can speak without the *agamlong*'s acceptance.
agat wal	Literally, "those who write." Used by the Ngok Dinka to designate the educated.
agoor	Food given by a woman to her husband, son, or any other male relative in private as opposed to the food normally served in the presence of visitors or other companions. The practice is publicly denounced but every wife observes it and every husband expects it.
agorot	A bull sacrificed on or after the marriage of a girl who had been betrothed before the age of puberty, though she has been given in marriage after puberty. (Marriage can only be completed after the parties reach puberty.)
ajiliu	A woman who is generally careless and poor at housekeeping.
akeeth	Incest. Also a skin disease which affects pigmentation and is associated with incest or stepping on the grave of a maternal uncle.
akor	Adultery. Derived from the verb *kor,* to seek.
alaraan	Kin group.
aleeng	Conversation or joking.
alei	Stranger.
alony (pl. *aloony*)	Slave.
amec	Cattle in the custody of a person other than the owner.
anyaal	The descendants of a female agnate.
arueth	Reverse payment of cattle made by the bride's kin to the bridegroom's kin. It approximates one third of the bride wealth paid by the bridegroom's kin.
atheek	Generally, respect. But respect among the Dinka has two meanings: the first is the same as in English; the other consists of avoiding the respected. The term is also applied to the observance of taboos and other rules governing the relationship of humans and their totemic animals or objects.
athiol	A sacrifice made to bless a wound inflicted by a relative or a nonrelative who must provide the sacrificial beast. The ritual signifies the wrongdoer's lack of intention to injure or his repentance. Its performance may mitigate liability for the wrong.

awec	Payment made to a wronged person, not so much to indemnify him materially as to appease and reconcile him.
awil	Solo. The leader of a group in choral singing.
baai (pl. *bai*)	Family, home, village, tribe, country, or people, according to the context of usage.
bany	Chief. Also applied to any person of aristocratic descent.
bany de ring	Literally, "chief of the flesh." The term used by some Dinkas for their chiefs, indicating the inherent nature of divine chieftainship.
bany de wut	Chief of the cattle camp, usually a descendant of a chiefly lineage or the richest man in the camp.
Banydit	Literally, "big chief." Paramount chief or head chief.
biok (spelled *biork* by P. P. Howell)	An institutionalized fight between the last initiated age set and that immediately senior to it, usually in competition for the age set of females corresponding to the youngest male age set.
cieng	As a verb, to look after, to order, to rule, to inhabit, to treat (e.g. a person), to live together, to live in peace and harmony, and to relate to a person. As a noun, human relations, conduct, behavior, habit, personality, custom, law, rule, way of life, culture, essence, and nature. For its significance as a concept of ideal human relations, see pp. 24–29.
cuet	Applied to the punitive action by which a wrongdoer's age set attacks and skewers to death his personality ox to disgrace him for the wrong. Derived from the verb *cuet,* to eat meat.
dejook	A woman's sloppiness or inability to cook, take good care of herself, or to keep the house properly.
dheeng	Nobility, beauty, handsomeness, elegance, charm, gracefulness, gentleness, hospitality, generosity, good manners, kindness, singing and dancing, initiation ceremonies, marriage celebrations, or any demonstration of an aesthetic value. For the significance of *dheeng* as a concept of human dignity, see p. 209.
dhiel	To reclaim a gift (Ngok dialect).
dhien	Literally, "cattle hearth." Used to mean a lineage or a clan.
dhieth	Birth.
dil	To exchange an ox for a cow.
duot yic	Literally, "to tie the belly." Gift made to assist a person who has suffered a loss of a wife, livestock, or any other damage to property.
gam	Acceptance, usually of a proposed bridegroom by the bride.
gar	Initiation.
geem nya	Literally, "the giving of the girl." Signifies the final stage

	of marriage ceremonies when the bride is delivered to the bridegroom's home.
ghoc	Sale and purchase.
ghot thok	Literally, "the doorway of the house." Used to mean a subdivision of the family consisting of a wife and her children or of a senior wife, her junior cowife or cowives, and their children.
gok	An area which is higher and less swampy than the *toc* and is therefore used for wet-season cattle camps.
gol	See *dhien* above.
goor	A war dance in which people run about singly or in line, jumping up and down, bearing themselves as though throwing and dodging spears.
guem	Extortion. Applied to the consummation of a proposed marriage forcibly against an unwilling girl. If her family is against the marriage totally or conditionally, then forced consummation is a grave wrong with serious consequences, but if the bride refuses the consummation of an otherwise valid marriage, then the use of force by the bridegroom with the help of relatives and age mates is lawful.
jak rac (sing. *jong rac*	Literally, "bad spirits." Coined by the Christian missionaries to mean the devil and his spirit agents. Also applied to the divinities of the traditional Dinka religion.
jiliiu	The quality of being an *ajiliu* (see above).
jon nya	Elopement with a girl who is either uncommitted or is betrothed to the person with whom she elopes.
jon tik	Elopement with a "wife," that is, a girl already engaged to another man.
jur (pl. *juur*)	A foreigner other than a Nuer or a Shilluk. Further distinguished by skin color as black (for Negroids), red or brown (for Arabs), and pink (for Europeans).
kany	A debt. Any claim of material value whether based on a loan or not. As a verb, to make a claim of material value.
kec	Literally, "bitter," the quality of being effective at cursing wrongdoers.
kic	Commoners.
kooc e nom	Literally, "standing the head." Immortality through procreation.
kuen thiek	Literally, "counting the marriage." The occasion in marriage celebrations when the relatives of the parties, with the mediation of the public, settle the amount of bride wealth.
kun	The youngest child of a man or a woman.
kwot yeth	The degree of relationship with the descendants of a

	female agnate with five or more intervening ancestresses. At this degree, marriage is permissible according to the rules of exogamy.
la ghot	Literally, "entering the hut." Levirate by which a man cohabits with the widow of his relative to produce children in the name of the dead man.
leer amec	Taking the cattle first paid for betrothal.
leer atooc	Taking the message by which the desire to marry a girl is first expressed.
long	A statement usually connoting a formal delivery in court, an assembly, or prayer.
luk	Lawsuit. Also means persuasion or an appeal to anyone for any purpose.
lum (or *lom*)	Gossip.
luny	Literally, "release." Applied to the final stage of initiation in which the newly initiated are ritually freed as full fledged adults.
mac thok	Literally, "the fireplace," where women cook or sit. Used to mean family or segment of a lineage.
makam	Court members as now appointed in accordance with the Chiefs' Courts Ordinance. Derived from the Arabic word for court, *mahkama*.
masheikh	Junior chiefs, that is, chiefs of sections. Derived from the Arabic word *sheikh*.
mek	To choose, usually a wife.
mioc	A short poetic utterance about one's ox or a significant incident in one's life. Used in dance, in war or hunting when one has hit, or to express an emotion, usually of anger.
mith k'Abun	Literally, "children of the missionaries." The term for the educated class.
naar	Maternal kin. Derived from the word for maternal uncle.
neen	A witness to whom a statement defamatory of another is made.
Nhialic	God. Occasionally applied to lesser divinities but understood to be one.
nhiar	To love or like.
nom gol	Clan head.
Omda	Ngok title for chief of a subtribe. Derived from Arabic.
paan	Possessive form of *baai* (see above), that is, as belonging to a named person.
peek	To reconcile after a feud or lesser conflict.
peeth	Evil eye.
raan bany	Rich man.
riak maath	Termination of friendship.
ric	Age set.
riem	Blood.

ring	Normally meat or flesh, but also the deity Ring (Flesh), the source of the divine power of chiefly clans.
tiel	Jealousy.
thai	The others. Used by the Ngok to signify non-Ngok Dinkas.
thel	To move an animal by rope. Used for the seizure of cattle by the relatives of a girl who has eloped with a man, whether they are engaged or not.
thuot	Courtship.
tik k'alony	The saying "Woman is a slave."
ting nya	Seeing a girl (for marriage).
toc	Literally, "lying down." A custom by which young men go to distant cattle camps for two or three months, gorge themselves with milk and meat, move as little as possible, get fat, and compose songs about matters of serious concern to them. *Toc,* pronounced differently, also means swampy savannah land used for dry-season cattle camps.
turuk	Turk, applied to the British who took over the administration of the Sudan from the Turks and the Egyptians.
waak	Literally, "bathing." Applied to songs composed during the period of lying, *toc* (See above).
waar	Agnatic stepkin.
wakil	The Ngok term for the deputy to the head chief. Derived from Arabic.
wak thok	Literally, "washing the mouth." A custom by which a bridegroom, who must abstain from the food of his relatives-in-law as a gesture of self-respect and deference for them, is paid one or more cows by them as a token to persuade him to break his abstinence.
walen	Uncle.
Wali	The guardian of either party in a Muslim marriage.
wei	Literally, "breath." Used to mean life or health.
wendit	The eldest son of a man or a woman.
wut	Cattle camp. Also the term applied to any territorial unit, such as a section or a subtribe. Even the tribe may also be called *wut,* but usually it is called *baai* (see above).
yieth	Clan divinities.

Index